THE

|||||||||||||||||||||||||||||||
D1290476

ISLAND

■ POST-

CONTEMPORARY

INTERVENTIONS

Series Editors: Stanley Fish

and Fredric Jameson

▪ THE

REPEATING

ISLAND

▪ *The Caribbean*

and the Postmodern

Perspective

▪ ANTONIO BENÍTEZ-ROJO

Translated by James Maraniss

▪ *Duke University Press   Durham and London 1992*

Second printing, 1995

© 1992 Duke University Press

All rights reserved

Printed in the United States of

America on acid-free paper ∞

Permissions to reprint appear on page 303

Library of Congress Cataloging-in-Publication

Data appear on the last

printed page of this book.

To Fernando Ortiz,

the distant master, on

the half-century of his

CONTRAPUNTEO

Contents

■ *Acknowledgments*

I would like to thank the John Carter Brown Library and the Amherst College Faculty Research Program for their support in the writing and translation of this book.

I could not have written this book without the encouragement, help, and advice of many friends and colleagues. I would like to thank especially Hilda O. Benítez, Mavis C. Campbell, Rosalina de la Carrera, Julia Cuervo-Hewitt, Ginny Ducharme, Vera M. Kutzinski, Sydney Lea, William Luis, René Prieto, Enrico M. Santí, and Doris Sommer.

This book was originally published in Spanish, which uses the convention of the masculine pronoun when referring to readers. Considering that its argument is nonsexist, I have decided to maintain the stylistic practice of the original. I would like to show my appreciation to the following reviewers of the Spanish edition: Luis Aguilar León, Wilfrido Corral, Juan Duchesne Winter, Ricardo Gutiérrez-Mouat, Juan Malpartida, Julio Matas, Adrián G. Montoro, Ineke Phaf, Rubén Ríos Avila, Edgardo Rodríguez Juliá, Soren Triff and Alan West. Some of their remarks were very useful in the process of revising the English edition.

Finally, I would like to thank James Maraniss, Gustavo Pérez Firmat, and Reynolds Smith, for they made possible the present edition. They all have my heartfelt gratitude.

■ THE

REPEATING

ISLAND

■ Introduction: the repeating island

In recent decades we have begun to see a clearer outline to the profile of a group of American nations whose colonial experiences and languages have been different, but which share certain undeniable features. I mean the countries usually called "Caribbean" or "of the Caribbean basin." This designation might serve a foreign purpose—the great powers' need to re-codify the world's territory better to know, to dominate it—as well as a local one, self-referential, directed toward fixing the furtive image of collective Being. Whatever its motive, this urge to systematize the region's political, economic, social, and anthropological dynamics is a very recent thing. For it is certain that the Caribbean basin, although it includes the first American lands to be explored, conquered, and colonized by Europe, is still, especially in the discourse of the social sciences, one of the least known regions of the modern world.

The main obstacles to any global study of the Caribbean's societies, in-sular or continental, are exactly those things that scholars usually adduce to define the area: its fragmentation; its instability; its reciprocal isolation; its uprootedness; its cultural heterogeneity; its lack of historiography and historical continuity; its contingency and impermanence; its syncretism, etc. This unexpected mix of obstacles and properties is not, of course, mere happenstance. What happens is that postindustrial society—to use a newfangled term—navigates the Caribbean with judgments and inten-tions that are like those of Columbus; that is, it lands scientists, investors, and technologists—the new (dis)coverers—who come to apply the dogmas and methods that had served them well where they came from, and who can't see that these refer only to realities back home. So they get into the habit of defining the Caribbean in terms of its resistance to the different methodologies summoned to investigate it. This is not to say that the definitions we read here and there of pan-Caribbean society are false or useless. I would say, to the contrary, that they are potentially as productive as the first reading of a book, in which, as Barthes said, the reader inevitably reads himself. I think, nevertheless, that the time has come for postindustrial society to start rereading the Caribbean, that is, to do the kind of reading in which every text begins to reveal its own textuality.

This second reading is not going to be easy at all. The Caribbean space, remember, is saturated with messages—"language games," Lyotard would call them—sent out in five European languages (Spanish, English, French, Dutch, and Portuguese), not counting aboriginal languages which, together with the different local dialects (Surinamtongo, Papiamento, *Créole,* etc.), complicate enormously any communication from one extreme of the ambit to another. Further, the spectrum of Caribbean codes is so varied and dense that it holds the region suspended in a soup of signs. It has been said many times that the Caribbean is the union of the diverse, and maybe that is true. In any case, my own rereading has taken me along different paths, and I can no longer arrive at such admirably precise reductions.

In this (today's) rereading, I propose, for example, to start with something concrete and easily demonstrated, a geographical fact: that the Antilles are an island bridge connecting, in "another way," North and South America. This geographical accident gives the entire area, including its continental foci, the character of an archipelago, that is, a discontinuous conjunction (of what?): unstable condensations, turbulences, whirlpools, clumps of bubbles, frayed seaweed, sunken galleons, crashing breakers, flying fish, seagull squawks, downpours, nighttime phosphorescences, eddies and pools, uncertain voyages of signification; in short, a field of observation quite in tune with the objectives of Chaos. I have capitalized this word to indicate that I'm not referring to chaos as conventionally defined, but rather to the new scientific perspective, so called, that has now begun to revolutionize the world of scientific research, that is, *Chaos* to mean that, within the (dis)order that swarms around what we already know of as Nature, it is possible to observe dynamic states or regularities that repeat themselves globally. I think that this recent interest of the scientific disciplines, which owes a lot to mathematical speculation and to holography, brings along with it a philosophical attitude (a new way of reading the concepts of chance and necessity, of particularity and universality) which little by little is sure to permeate other fields of knowledge.

Quite recently, for example, economics and certain branches of the humanities have begun to be examined under this brand-new paradigm, constituting perhaps the most inquisitive and encompassing step that postmodernity has taken up until now. In truth, the field in which Chaos may be observed is extremely vast, for it includes all phenomena that depend on the passage of time; Chaos looks toward everything that repeats, reproduces, grows, decays, unfolds, flows, spins, vibrates, seethes; it is as interested in the evolution of the solar system as in the stock market's crashes, as involved in cardiac arrhythmia as in the novel or in myth. Thus Chaos provides a space in which the pure sciences connect with the social sciences, and both of them connect with art and the cultural tradition. Of course, any such diagrammatic connections must suppose very different languages and a communication that is hardly ever direct, but for the reader who is attuned to Chaos, there will be an opening upon unexpected corridors allowing passage from one point to another in the labyrinth. In this book I have tried to analyze certain aspects of the Caribbean while under the influence of this attitude, whose end is not to find results, but processes, dynamics, and rhythms that show themselves within the marginal, the regional, the incoherent, the heterogeneous, or, if you like, the unpredictable that coexists with us in our everyday world.

To experience this exploration has been instructive as well as surprising to me, since within the sociocultural fluidity that the Caribbean archipelago presents, within its historiographic turbulence and its ethnological and linguistic clamor, within its generalized instability of vertigo and hurricane, one can sense the features of an island that "repeats" itself, unfolding and bifurcating until it reaches all the seas and lands of the earth, while at the same time it inspires multidisciplinary maps of unexpected designs. I have emphasized the word *repeats* because I want to give the term the almost paradoxical sense with which it appears in the discourse of Chaos, where every repetition is a practice that necessarily entails a difference and a step toward nothingness (according to the principle of entropy proposed by thermodynamics in the last century); however, in the midst of this irreversible change, Nature can produce a figure as complex, as highly organized, and as intense as the one that the human eye catches when it sees a quivering hummingbird drinking from a flower.

Which one, then, would be the repeating island, Jamaica, Aruba, Puerto Rico, Miami, Haiti, Recife? Certainly none of the ones that we know. That original, that island at the center, is as impossible to reach as the hypothetical Antillas that reappeared time and again, always fleetingly, in the cosmographers' charts. This is again because the Caribbean is not a common archipelago, but a meta-archipelago (an exalted quality that Hellas possessed, and the great Malay archipelago as well), and as a meta-archipelago it has the virtue of having neither a boundary nor a center. Thus the Caribbean flows outward past the limits of its own sea with a vengeance, and its *ultima Thule* may be found on the outskirts of Bombay, near the low and murmuring shores of Gambia, in a Cantonese tavern of circa 1850, at a Balinese temple, in an old Bristol pub, in a commercial warehouse in Bordeaux at the time of Colbert, in a windmill beside the Zuider Zee, at a cafe in a barrio of Manhattan, in the existential *saudade* of an old Portuguese lyric. But what is it that repeats? Tropisms, in series; movements in approximate direction. Let's say the unforeseen relation between a dance movement and the baroque spiral of a colonial railing. But this theme will be discussed later, although the Caribbean really is that and much more; it is the last of the great meta-archipelagoes. If someone needed a visual explanation, a graphic picture of what the Caribbean is, I would refer him to the spiral chaos of the Milky Way, the unpredictable flux of transformative plasma that spins calmly in our globe's firmament, that sketches in an "other" shape that keeps changing, with some objects born to light while others disappear into the womb of darkness; change, transit, return, fluxes of sidereal matter.

There is nothing marvelous in this, or even enviable, as will be seen. A few paragraphs back, when I proposed a rereading of the Caribbean, I suggested as a point of departure the unargued fact that the Antilles are an island bridge connecting, "in a certain way," South and North America, that is, a machine of spume that links the narrative of the search for El Dorado with the narrative of the finding of El Dorado; or if you like, the discourse of myth with the discourse of history; or even, the discourse of resistance with the language of power. I made a point of the phrase "in a certain way" because if we were to take the Central American ligament as our connection between continents, the result would be much less fruitful and would not suit the purposes of this book. That connection gains objective importance only on maps concerned with our current situation seen as geography, geopolitics, military strategy, and finance. These are maps of the pragmatic type which we all know and carry within us, and which therefore give us a first reading of the world. The words "a certain way" are the signs of my intention to give meaning to this text as an object of rereading, of a "certain kind of" reading. In my reading, the link that really counts is the one made by the Caribbean machine, whose flux, whose noise, whose presence covers the map of world history's contingencies, through the great changes in economic discourse to the vast collisions of races and cultures that humankind has seen.

From Columbus's machine to the sugar-making machine

Let's be realistic: the Atlantic is the Atlantic (with all its port cities) because it was once engendered by the copulation of Europe—that insatiable solar bull—with the Caribbean archipelago; the Atlantic is today the Atlantic (the navel of capitalism) because Europe, in its mercantilist laboratory, conceived the project of inseminating the Caribbean womb with the blood of Africa; the Atlantic is today the Atlantic (NATO, World Bank, New York Stock Exchange, European Economic Community, etc.) because it was the painfully delivered child of the Caribbean, whose vagina was stretched between continental clamps, between the *encomienda* of Indians and the slaveholding plantation, between the servitude of the coolie and the discrimination toward the *criollo,* between commercial monopoly and piracy, between the runaway slave settlement and the governor's palace; all Europe pulling on the forceps to help at the birth of the Atlantic: Columbus, Cabral, Cortés, de Soto, Hawkins, Drake, Hein, Rodney, Surcouf . . . After the blood and salt water spurts, quickly sew up torn flesh and apply the antiseptic tinctures, the gauze and surgical plaster; then the febrile wait through the forming of a scar: suppurating, always suppurating.

Its having given birth, however, to an ocean of such universal prestige is not the only reason that the Caribbean is a meta-archipelago. There are other reasons of equal weight. For example, it is possible to defend successfully the hypothesis that without deliveries from the Caribbean womb Western capital accumulation would not have been sufficient to effect a move, within a little more than two centuries, from the so-called Mercantilist Revolution to the Industrial Revolution. In fact, the history of the Caribbean is one of the main strands in the history of capitalism, and vice versa. This conclusion may be called polemical, and perhaps it is. This is surely not the place to argue the issue, but there's always room for some observations.

The machine that Christopher Columbus hammered into shape in Hispaniola was a kind of *bricolage,* something like a medieval vacuum cleaner. The flow of Nature in the island was interrupted by the suction of an iron mouth, taken thence through a transatlantic tube to be deposited and redistributed in Spain. When I speak of Nature in the island, I do so in integral terms: Indians and their handicrafts, nuggets of gold and samples of other minerals, native species of plants and animals, and also some words like *tabaco, canoa, hamaca,* etc. All this struck the Spanish court as meager and tepid (especially the words), so that nobody—except Columbus—had any illusions about the New World. A machine of the same model (think of a forge with its sparkling clangor and combustion), with an extra bolt here and a bellows over there, was installed in Puerto Rico, in Jamaica, in Cuba, and in a few miserable settlements on terra firma. At the time of the great conquests—the fall of the upland civilizations of the Aztecs, the Incas, and the Chibchas—Columbus's machine was quickly remodeled and, carried on Indians' backs over the sierras, set into motion in a half dozen new places. It is possible to fix the date when this machine began working. It happened in the spring of 1523, when Cortés, manipulating the levers and pedals, smelted down a part of the treasure of Tenochtitlán and selected a smattering of deluxe objects to be sent through the transatlantic tube. But this prototype was so defective that the transporting machine—the tubing—got irreparably broken some ten leagues from Cape San Vicente, in Portugal. French privateers captured two of the three inadequate caravels that carried the treasure to Spain, and the Emperor Charles V lost his whole share (20 percent) of that year's Mexican revenue. This couldn't be allowed to happen again. The machine had to be perfected.

I think I ought to clarify at this point that when I speak of a machine I am starting from Deleuze and Guattari's concept. I am talking about the machine of machines, the machine machine machine machine; which is to say that every machine is a conjunction of machines coupled together, and each one of these interrupts the flow of the previous one; it will be said rightly that one can picture any machine alternatively in terms of flow and interruption. Such a notion, as we will see, is fundamental to our re-reading of the Caribbean, for it will permit us to pass on to an even more important one.

In any case, in the years that followed the Cape San Vicente disaster the Spaniards introduced major technological changes and surprising elaborations in their American machine. This was so much the case that, by around 1565, Columbus's small and rudimentary machine had evolved into the Grandest Machine on Earth. This is absolutely certain. It's proven by statistics: in the first century of Spanish colonization this machine yielded more than one-third of all the gold produced in the whole world during those years. The machine produced not only gold but also silver, emeralds, diamonds, topaze, pearls, and more. The quantity of molten silver that fell in droplets from that enormous shelf was such that the haughtiest families of Potosí, after dining, tossed their silver service out the window along with the leftover food. These fabulous deliveries of precious metals were the result of various innovations, for example: guaranteeing the availability of the necessary cheap manpower in the mines through a system known as the *mita;* using wind energy and marine currents to speed up the flow of oceanic transportation; implanting a costly system of security and control from the River Plate estuary to the Guadalquivir. But, above all, establishing the system called *la flota,* the fleet. Without the fleet system the Spaniards would not have been able to hoard within the walls of Seville any more gold or silver than they could fit into their pockets.

We know who thought up this extraordinary machine: Pedro Menéndez de Avilés, a cruel Asturian of genius. If this man, or someone else, had not invented the fleet system, the Caribbean would still be there, but it might not be a meta-archipelago.

Menéndez de Avilés's machine was complex in the extreme and quite beyond the reach of any nation but Spain. It was a machine made up of a naval machine, a military machine, a bureaucratic machine, a commercial machine, an extractive machine, a political machine, a legal machine, a religious machine, that is, an entire huge assemblage of machines which there is no point in continuing to name. The only thing that matters here is that it was a Caribbean machine; a machine installed in the Caribbean Sea and coupled to the Atlantic and the Pacific. The perfected model of this machine was set in motion in 1565, although it had been tested in a trial run a bit earlier. In 1562 Pedro Menéndez de Avilés, commanding forty-nine sailing ships, set off from Spain with the dream of stanching the leaks of gold and silver caused by shipwrecks and pirate or privateer attacks. His plan was this: all navigation between the West Indies and Seville (the only port that allowed transatlantic trade) would be undertaken in convoys consisting of cargo ships, warships, and light craft for reconnaissance and dispatch; the cargoes of gold and silver were to be boarded only on given dates and in only a few Caribbean ports (Cartagena, Nombre de Dios, San Juan de Ulúa, and some other secondary ones); forts would be built and garrisons stationed not only at these ports but also at those defending the entrances to the Caribbean (San Juan de Puerto Rico, Santo Domingo, Santiago de Cuba, the eastern coast of Florida, and, especially, Havana); all of these ports would be bases for squadrons of coast guard and patrol ships, whose mission would be to sweep the waters and coastal keys clean of pirates, privateers, and smugglers, while at the same time providing rescue service to convoys in trouble. (The plan was approved. Its lineaments were so solid that 375 years later, during the Second World War, the Allies adopted it to defend against attack from German submarines, cruisers, and planes.)

Generally the name *flota* (fleet) is given to the convoys that twice a year entered the Caribbean to come back to Seville with the great riches of America. But this is not entirely correct. The fleet system was itself a machine of ports, anchorages, sea walls, lookouts, fortresses, garrisons, militias, shipyards, storehouses, depots, offices, workshops, hospitals, inns, taverns, plazas, churches, palaces, streets, and roads that led to the mining ports of the Pacific along a sleeve of mule trains laid out over the Isthmus of Panama. It was a powerful machine of machines knowingly articulated to suit the Caribbean's geography, and its machines were geared to be able to take greatest advantage of the energy of the Gulf Stream and the region's trade winds. The fleet system created all of the cities of the Spanish Caribbean and it made them, for better or for worse, what they are today, Havana in particular. It was there that both fleets (those of Cartagena and Veracruz) joined to form an imposing convoy of more than a hundred ships to begin the return voyage together. In 1565 Pedro Menéndez de Avilés, after slaughtering, with indifferent calm, nearly five hundred Huguenots who had settled in Florida, finished his network of fortified cities with the founding of St. Augustine, today the oldest city in the United States.

As we speak in our astonishment of the inexhaustible richness of the Mexican and Peruvian mines, we should think of them as machines joined to other machines; we should see them in terms of production (flow and interruption). Such mining machines, by themselves, would not have been much help in accumulating European capital. Without the Caribbean machine (from Columbus's prototype to the working model of Menéndez de Avilés), Europeans would have been in the absurd position of the gambler who hits the jackpot at the slot machine but who has no hat in which to catch his winnings.

We can speak, nevertheless, of a Caribbean machine as important or more so than the fleet machine. This machine, this extraordinary machine, exists today, that is, it repeats itself continuously. It's called: the plantation. Its prototypes were born in the Near East, just after the time of the Crusades, and moved toward the West. In the fifteenth century the Portuguese installed their own model in the Cape Verde Islands and on Madeira, with astonishing success. There were certain entrepreneurs—like the Jew Cristóbal de Ponte and the *Sharif* of Berbery—who tried to construct machines of this family in the Canaries and on the Moroccan coast, but the venture was too big for any single man. It turned out that an entire kingdom, a mercantilist monarchy, would be needed to get the big machine going with its gears, its wheels, and its mills. I want to insist that Europeans finally controlled the construction, maintenance, technology, and proliferation of the plantation machines, especially those that produced sugar. (This family of machines almost always makes cane sugar, coffee, cacao, cotton, indigo, tea, bananas, pineapples, fibers, and other goods whose cultivation is impossible or too expensive in the temperate zones; furthermore, it usually produces the Plantation, capitalized to indicate not just the presence of plantations but also the type of society that results from their use and abuse.)

So much has already been written about all of this that it is not worth the effort even to sketch out the incredible and dolorous history of this machine. Still, something must be said, just a few things. For one: the singular feature of this machine is that it produced no fewer than ten million African slaves and thousands of coolies (from India, China, and Malaysia). All this, however, is not all: the plantation machines turned out mercantile capitalism, industrial capitalism (see Eric Williams, *Capitalism and Slavery*), African underdevelopment (see Walter Rodney, *How Europe Underdeveloped Africa*), Caribbean population (see Ramiro Guerra, *Sugar and Society in the Caribbean*); they produced imperialism, wars, colonial blocs, rebellions, repressions, sugar islands, runaway slave settlements, air and naval bases, revolutions of all sorts, and even a "free associated state" next to an unfree socialist state.

You will say that this catalog is unnecessary, that the whole subject is already too well known. (The theme of the plantation will be treated in some of the subsequent chapters as well.) But how is one to establish finally that the Caribbean is not just a multiethnic sea or a group of islands divided by different languages and by the categories Greater and Lesser Antilles, Windward Islands, and Leeward Islands? In short, how do we establish that the Caribbean is an important historico-economic sea and, further, a cultural meta-archipelago without center and without limits, a chaos within which there is an island that proliferates endlessly, each copy a different one, founding and refounding ethnological materials like a cloud will do with its vapor? If this is now understood, then there is no need to keep on depending on the old history books. Let's talk then of the Caribbean that we can see, touch, smell, hear, taste; the Caribbean of the senses, the Caribbean of sentiment and pre-sentiment.

From the apocalypse to chaos

I can isolate with frightening exactitude—like the hero of Sartre's novel— the moment at which I reached the age of reason. It was a stunning October afternoon, years ago, when the atomization of the meta-archipelago under the dread umbrella of nuclear catastrophe seemed imminent. The children of Havana, at least in my neighborhood, had been evacuated; a grave silence fell over the streets and the sea. While the state bureaucracy searched for news off the shortwave or hid behind official speeches and communiqués, two old black women passed "in a certain kind of way" beneath my balcony. I cannot describe this "certain kind of way"; I will say only that there was a kind of ancient and golden powder between their gnarled legs, a scent of basil and mint in their dress, a symbolic, ritual wisdom in their gesture and their gay chatter. I knew then at once that there would be no apocalypse. The swords and the archangels and the beasts and the trumpets and the breaking of the last seal were not going to come, for the simple reason that the Caribbean is not an apocalyptic world; it is not a phallic world in pursuit of the vertical desires of ejaculation and castration. The notion of the apocalypse is not important within the culture of the Caribbean. The choices of all or nothing, for or against, honor or blood have little to do with the culture of the Caribbean. These are ideological propositions articulated in Europe which the Caribbean shares only in declamatory terms, or, better, in terms of a first reading. In Chicago a beaten soul says: "I can't take it any more," and gives himself up to drugs or to the most desperate violence. In Havana, he would say: "The thing to do is not die," or perhaps: "Here I am, fucked but happy."

The so-called October crisis or missile crisis was not won by J.F.K. or by N.K. or much less by F.C. (statesmen always wind up abbreviated in these great events that they themselves created); it was won by the culture of the Caribbean, together with the loss that any win implies. If this had happened, let's say, in Berlin, children there would now be discovering hand tools and learning to make fire with sticks. The plantation of atomic projectiles sown in Cuba was a Russian machine, a machine of the steppes, historically terrestrial. It was a machine that carried the culture of the horse and of yogurt, the cossack and the mouzhik, the birch and the rye, the ancient caravans and the Siberian railroad; a culture where the land

is everything and the sea a forgotten memory. But the culture of the Caribbean, at least in its most distinctive aspect, is not terrestrial but aquatic, a
sinuous culture where time unfolds irregularly and resists being captured
by the cycles of clock and calendar. The Caribbean is the natural and indispensable realm of marine currents, of waves, of folds and double-folds,
of fluidity and sinuosity. It is, in the final analysis, a culture of the meta-
archipelago: a chaos that returns, a detour without a purpose, a continual
flow of paradoxes; it is a feed-back machine with asymmetrical workings,
like the sea, the wind, the clouds, the uncanny novel, the food chain, the
music of Malaya, Gödel's theorem and fractal mathematics. It will be said
that in that case Hellas does not meet our canon for meta-archipelagoes.
But yes, it meets it. What's happened is that Western thought has kept on
thinking of itself as the diachronic repetition on an ancient polemic. I am
referring to the repressive and fallacious machine made up of the binary
opposition Aristotle *versus* Plato. Greek thought has been subjected to such
sleight of hand that Plato's version of Socrates has been accepted as the
limit of the tolerable, while the glowing constellation of ideas that made up
the Greek heaven by way of the Pre-Socratics, the Sophists, and the Gnos-
tics has been ignored or distorted. This magnificent firmament has been
reduced almost as if we were to erase every star in the sky but Castor and
Pollux. Certainly, Greek thought was much more than this philosophical
duel between Plato and Aristotle. It's just that certain not entirely symmet-
rical ideas scandalized the faith of the Middle Ages, modern rationalism,
and the functionalist positivism of our time, and it's not necessary to pursue this matter, because we're speaking here of the Caribbean. Let's say
good-bye to Hellas, applauding the idea of a forgotten sage, Thales of
Miletus: water is the beginning of all things.

Then how can we describe the culture of the Caribbean in any way other
than by calling it a feedback machine? Nobody has to rack his brains to
come up with an answer; it's in the public domain. If I were to have to
put it in one word I would say: performance. But performance not only in
terms of scenic interpretation but also in terms of the execution of a ritual,
that is, that "certain way" in which the two Negro women who conjured
away the apocalypse were walking. In this "certain kind of way" there is
expressed the mystic or magical (if you like) loam of the civilizations that
contributed to the formation of Caribbean culture. Of course there have
been some things written about this too, although I think that there's a
lot of cloth left to be cut. For example, when we speak of the genesis of
Caribbean culture we are given two alternatives: either we are told that

the complex syncretism of Caribbean cultural expressions—what I shall call here *supersyncretism* to distinguish it from similar forms—arose out of the collision of European, African, and Asian components within the Plantation, or that this syncretism flows along working with ethnological machines that are quite distant in space and remote in time, that is, machines "of a certain kind" that one would have to look for in the subsoils of all of the continents. But, I ask, why not take both alternatives as valid, and not just those but others as well? Why pursue a Euclidian coherence that the world—and the Caribbean above all—is very far from having?

Certainly, in order to reread the Caribbean we have to visit the sources from which the widely various elements that contributed to the formation of its culture flowed. This unforeseen journey tempts us because as soon as we succeed in establishing and identifying as separate any of the signifiers that make up the supersyncretic manifestation that we're studying, there comes a moment of erratic displacement of its signifiers toward other spatio-temporal points, be they in Europe, Africa, Asia, or America, or in all these continents at once. When these points of departure are nonetheless reached, a new chaotic flight of signifiers will occur, and so on ad infinitum.

Let's take as an example a syncretic object that has been well studied, let's say, the cult of the Virgen de la Caridad del Cobre (still followed by many Cubans). If we were to analyze this cult—presuming that it hasn't been done before—we would necessarily come upon a date (1605) and a place (el Cobre, near Santiago de Cuba); that is, within the spatio-temporal frame where the cult was first articulated upon three sources of meaning: one of aboriginal origin (the Taino deity Atabey or Atabex), another native to Europe (the Virgin of *Illescas*), and finally, another from Africa (the Yoruba *orisha* Oshun). For many anthropologists the history of this cult would begin or end here, and of course they would give reasons to explain this arbitrary break in the chain of signifiers. They would say, perhaps, that the people who today inhabit the Antilles are "new," and therefore their earlier situation, their tradition of being "a certain kind of way," should not count; they would say that with the disappearance of the Antillean aborigine during the first century of colonization these islands were left unconnected to the Indoamerican mechanisms, thus providing a "new" space for "new" men to create a "new" society and, with it, a "new" culture that can no longer be taken as an extension of those that brought the "new" inhabitants. Thus the Virgen de la Caridad del Cobre would turn out to be exclusively Cuban, and as the patron saint of Cuba she would appear in a kind of panoply along with the flag, the coat of arms, the statues of the founders, the map of the island, the royal palms, and the national anthem; she would be, in short, an attribute of Cuba's civic religion and nothing more.

Fine; I share this systemic focus, although only within the perspective offered by a first reading in which—as we know—the reader reads himself. But it happens to be the case that after several close readings of the Virgen and her cult it is possible for a Cuban reader to be seduced by the materials that he has been reading, and he should feel a reduced dose of the nationalism that he has projected on to the Virgen. This will happen only if his ego abandons for an instant his desire to feel Cuban only, a feeling that has offered him the mirage of a safe place under the cover of a nationality that connects him to the land and to the fathers of the country. If this momentary wavering should occur, the reader would cease to inscribe himself within the space of the Cuban and would set out venturing along the roads of limitless chaos that any advanced rereading offers. This being so, he would have to leap outside of the statist, statistical Cuba after searching for the wandering signifiers that inform the cult of the Virgen de la Caridad del Cobre. For a moment, just for a moment, the Virgen and the reader will cease to be Cuban.

The first surprise or perplexity that the triptych Atabey-Nuestra Señora-Oshun presents us is that it is not "original" but rather "originating." In fact, Atabey, the Taino deity, is a syncretic object in itself, one whose signifiers deliver to us another signifier that is somewhat unforeseen: Orehu, mother of waters to the Arawaks of the Guianas. This voyage of signification is a heady one for more than one reason. In the first place it involves the grand epic of the Arawaks; the departure from the Amazon basin, the ascension of the Orinoco, the arrival at the Caribbean coast, the meticulous settlement of each island until arriving at Cuba, the still obscure encounter with the Mayans of Yucatan, the ritual game of the ball of resin, the "other" connection between both subcontinental masses (such was the forgotten feat of these people). In the second place, it involves also the no less grand epic of the Caribs: the Arawak islands as objects of Carib desire; construction of large canoes, preparations for war, raids on the coastal islands, Trinidad, Tobago, Margarita, ravishing the women, victory feasts. Then the invasion stage, Grenada, St. Vincent, St. Lucia, Martinique, Dominica, Guadeloupe, the killing of the Arawaks, the glorious cannibalism of men and of words, *carib, calib, cannibal,* and *Caliban;* finally, the Sea of the Caribs, from Guyana to the Virgin Islands, the sea that isolated the Arawaks (*Tainos*) from the Greater Antilles, that cut the connection with the South American coast but not the continuity of cultural flow: Atabey-Orehu, the flux of signifiers that crossed the spatio-temporal barrier of the Caribbean to continue linking Cuba with the Orinoco and Amazon basins; Atabey-Orehu, progenitor of the supreme being of the Tainos, mother of the Taino lakes and rivers, protector of feminine ebbs and flows, of the great mysteries of the blood that women experience, and there, at the other end of the Antillean arc, the Great Mother of Waters, the immediacy of the matriarchy, the beginning of the cultivation of the yucca, the ritual orgy, incest, the sacrifice of the virgin male, blood and earth.

There is something enormously old and powerful in this, I know; a contradictory vertigo which there is no reason to interrupt, and so we reach the point at which the image of Our Lady venerated in el Cobre is, also, a syncretic object, produced by two quite distinct images of the Virgin Mary, which were to wind up in the hands of the chiefs of Cueiba and Macaca, and which were adored simultaneously as Atabey and as Nuestra Señora (this last in the form of an amulet). Imagine for a moment these chiefs' perplexity when they saw, for the first time, what no Taino had seen before: the image, in color, of the Mother of the Supreme Being, the lone progenitor of Yucahu Bagua Maorocoti, who now turned out to be, in addition, the mother of the god of those bearded, yucca-colored men; she who, according to them, protected them from death and injury in war. *Ave Maria,* these Indians would learn to say as they worshipped their Atabey, who at one time had been Orehu, and before that the Great Arawak Mother. *Ave Maria,* Francisco Sánchez de Moya, a sixteenth-century Spanish captain, would surely say when he received the commission and the order to make the crossing to Cuba to start copper foundries in the mines of El Prado. *Ave Maria,* he would say once again when he wrapped the image of Nuestra Señora de Illescas, of whom he was a devotee, among his shirts to protect him from the dangerous storms and shipwrecks of the hazardous passage to the Indies. *Ave Maria,* he would repeat on the day he placed it upon the humble altar in the solitary hermitage of Santiago del Prado, the merest hut for the poor Indians and Negroes who worked the copper mines.

But the image, that of Nuestra Señora de Illescas, brought to Cuba by the good captain, had a long history behind it. It is itself another syncretic object. The chain of signifiers now takes us across the Renaissance to the Middle Ages. It leads us to Byzantium, the unique, the magnificent, where among all kinds of heresies and pagan practices the cult of the Virgin Mary was born (a cult unforeseen by the Doctors of the Church).

There in Byzantium, among the splendors of its icons and mosaics, a likeness of the Virgin Mary and her Child may have been plundered by some crusading and voracious knight, or acquired by a seller of relics, or copied on the retina of some pious pilgrim. At any rate the suspicious cult of the Virgin Mary filtered surreptitiously into Europe. Surely it would not have gone very far on its own, but this happened at the beginning of the twelfth century, the legendary epoch of the troubadours and of *fin amour,* when Woman ceased to be Eve, the dirty and damned seducer of Adam and ally of the Serpent. She was washed, perfumed, and sumptuously dressed to suit the scope of her new image: the Lady. Then, the cult of Our Lady spread like fire through gunpowder, and one fine day it arrived at Illescas, a few miles away from Toledo.

Ave Maria, the slaves at the El Prado mines repeated aloud, and quickly, in an undertone that the priest could not hear, they added: *Oshun Yeye.* For that miraculous altar image was for them one of the most conspicuous *orishas* of the Yoruba pantheon: Oshun Yeye Moro, the perfumed whore; Oshun Kayode, the gay dancer; Oshun Aña, the lover of the drum; Oshun Akuara, she who mixes love potions; Oshun Ede, the *grande dame;* Oshun Fumike, she who gives children to sterile women; Oshun Funke, the wise one; Oshun Kole-Kole, the wicked sorceress.

Oshun, as a syncretic object, is as dizzying as her honeyed dance and yellow bandanas. She is traditionally the Lady of the Rivers, but some of her avatars relate her to the bays and the seashores. Her most prized objects are amber, coral, and yellow metals; her favorite foods are honey, squash, and sweets that contain eggs. Sometimes she shows herself to be gentle and ministering, above all in women's matters and those of love; at other times she shows herself to be insensitive, capricious, and voluble, and she can even become nasty and treacherous; in these darker apparitions we also see her as an old carrion-eating witch and as the *orisha* of death.

This multiple aspect of Oshun makes us think at once of the contradictions of Aphrodite. Both goddesses, one as much as the other, are at once "luminous" and "dark"; they reign over a place where men find both pleasure and death, love and hate, voluptuousity and betrayal. Both goddesses came from the sea and inhabit the marine, fluvial, and vaginal tides; both seduce gods and men, and both protect cosmetics and prostitution.

The correspondences between the Greek and Yoruba pantheons have been noted, but they have not been explained. How to explain, to give another example, the unusual parallel of Hermes and Elegua? Both are "the travelers," the "messengers of the gods," the "keepers of the gates," "lords of the thresholds"; both were adored in the form of phallic stone figures, both protect crossroads, highways, and commerce, and both can show themselves in the figure of a man with a cane who rests his body's weight on one foot alone. Both sponsor the start of any activity, make transactions smooth, and are the only ones to pass through the terrible spaces that mediate the Supreme Being and the gods, the gods and the dead, the living and the dead. Both, finally, appear as naughty, mendacious children, or as tricky and lascivious old men; both are the "givers of discourse" and they preside over the word, over mysteries, transformations, processes, and changes; they are the alpha and omega of things. For this reason, certain Yoruba ceremonies begin and end with Elegua's dance.

In the same way, Africa and Aphrodite have more in common than the Greek root that unites their names; there is a flow of marine foam that connects two civilizations "in another way," from within the turbulence of chaos, two civilizations doubly separated by geography and history. The cult of the Virgen de la Caridad del Cobre can be read as a Cuban cult, but it can also be reread—one reading does not negate the other—as a meta-archipelagic text, a meeting or confluence of marine flowings that connects the Niger with the Mississippi, the China Sea with the Orinoco, the Parthenon with a fried food stand in an alley in Paramaribo.

The peoples of the sea, or better, the Peoples of the Sea proliferate incessantly while differentiating themselves from one another, traveling together toward the infinite. Certain dynamics of their culture also repeat and sail through the seas of time without reaching anywhere. If I were to put this in two words, they would be: performance and rhythm. And nonetheless, I would have to add something more: the notion that we have called "in a certain kind of way," something remote that reproduces itself and that carries the desire to sublimate apocalypse and violence; something obscure that comes from the performance and that one makes his own in a very special way; concretely, it takes away the space that separates the onlooker from the participant.

From rhythm to polyrhythm

Nature is the flux of an unknowable feedback machine that society interrupts constantly with the most varied and noisy rhythms. Each rhythm is itself a flux cut through by other rhythms, and we can pursue fluxes upon rhythms endlessly. Well then, the culture of the Peoples of the Sea is a flux interrupted by rhythms which attempt to silence the noises with which

their own social formation interrupts the discourse of Nature. If this definition should seem abstruse, we could simplify it by saying that the cultural
discourse of the Peoples of the Sea attempts, through real or symbolic sacrifice, to neutralize violence and to refer society to the transhistorical codes
of Nature. Of course, as the codes of Nature are neither limited nor fixed,
nor even intelligible, the culture of the Peoples of the Sea expresses the
desire to sublimate social violence through referring itself to a space that
can only be intuited through the poetic, since it always puts forth an area
of chaos. In this paradoxical space, in which one has the illusion of experiencing a totality, there appear to be no repressions or contradictions; there
is no desire other than that of maintaining oneself within the limits of this
zone for the longest possible time, in free orbit, beyond imprisonment or
liberty.

All machines have their master codes, and the codebook to the cultural
machine of the Peoples of the Sea is made up of a network of subcodes
holding together cosmogonies, mythic bestiaries, remote pharmacopoeias,
oracles, profound ceremonies, and the mysteries and alchemies of antiquity.
One of these subcodes may lead us into the labyrinth of Minos, another to
the Tower of Babel, another to the Arawak version of the Flood, another
to the secrets of Eleusis, another to the garden of the unicorn, others to
the sacred books of India and China and to the divining *cauris* of West
Africa. The keys to this vast hermetic labyrinth refer us to "another" wisdom that lies forgotten in the foundation of the postindustrial world, since
at one time it was the only form of knowledge there. Clearly, I don't have
an interest at this point in saying that all peoples are or at one time were
Peoples of the Sea. What I do care to establish is that the people of the
Caribbean still are this in part, and everything seems to indicate that they
will continue to be so for some time, even within the interplay of dynamics that carry models of knowledge proper to modernity and postmodernity. In the Caribbean, epistemological transparency has not displaced the
dregs and sediments of the cosmological arcana, the spatterings of sacrificial blood—as we shall see in the chapter on the work of Fernando
Ortiz—but rather, unlike what happens in the West, scientific knowledge
and traditional knowledge coexist as differences within the same system.

Then what kind of performance is observed before or beyond the chaos
of Caribbean culture? The ritual of supersyncretic beliefs? Dance? Music?
By themselves, none of these in particular. The regularities that the culture
of the Caribbean shows begin from its intention to reread (rewrite) the
march of Nature in terms of rhythms "of a certain kind." I'll give an ex-

ample right away: Let's suppose that we beat upon a drum with a single blow and set its skin to vibrating. Let's suppose that this sound stretches until it forms something like a salami. Well, here comes the interruptive action of the Caribbean machine; it starts slicing pieces of sound in an unforeseen, improbable, and finally impossible way.

To anyone interested in the way machines function, I ought to say that the Caribbean machine is not a Deleuze and Guattari model of the kind we saw some pages back (the machine machine machine). The specifications of that model are clear and final: here is a flow machine; we hook up an interrupting machine, to which another interrupting machine is then connected, making the previous interruptor appear to be in motion. We're dealing with a system of relative machines, given that, according to how it's seen, the same machine may be one of flow or of interruption. The Caribbean machine, on the other hand, is something more: it is a technological-poetic machine, or, if you like, a metamachine of differences whose poetic mechanism cannot be diagrammed in conventional dimensions, and whose user's manual is found dispersed in a state of plasma within the chaos of its own network of codes and subcodes. It is a machine very different from those we've been discussing up to now. In any event, the notion of poly-rhythm (rhythms cut through by other rhythms, which are cut by still other rhythms)—if it takes us to the point at which the central rhythm is displaced by other rhythms in such a way as to make it fix a center no longer, then to transcend into a state of flux—may fairly define the type of performance that characterizes the Caribbean cultural machine. A moment will be reached in which it will no longer be clear whether the salami of sound is cut by the rhythms or these are cut by the salami or it is cut in its slices or these are cut by slices of rhythm. This is by way of saying that rhythm, in the codes of the Caribbean, precedes music, including percussion itself. It is something that was *already there,* amid the noise; something very ancient and dark to which the drummer's hand and the drumhead connect on a given moment; a kind of scapegoat, offered in sacrifice, which can be glimpsed in the air when one lets himself be carried away by a battery of *batá* drums (secret drums to whose beats the *orishas,* the living and the dead, all dance).

It would, however, be a mistake to think that the Caribbean rhythm connects only to percussion. The Caribbean rhythm is in fact a metarhythm which can be arrived at through any system of signs, whether it be dance, music, language, text, or body language, etc. Let's say that one begins to walk and all of a sudden he realizes that he is walking "well," that is, not just with his feet, but also with other parts of his body, which nonetheless adjusts admirably to the rhythm of his steps. It is quite possible that the walker in this circumstance might experience a mild and happy sensation of well-being. All right, there's nothing particularly special about this yet, nothing that we could call "Caribbean"; we've simply taken up the conventional notion of polyrhythm, which presupposed a central rhythm (the rhythm of footsteps). It's possible, though, that a person might feel that he wants to walk not with his feet alone, and to this end he imbues the muscles of his neck, back, abdomen, arms, in short all his muscles, with their own rhythm, different from the rhythm of his footsteps, which no longer dominate. If this should come to pass—which finally would be only a transitory performance—he would be walking like the anti-apocalyptic old women. What has happened is that the center of the rhythmic ensemble formed by the footsteps has been displaced, and now it runs from muscle to muscle, stopping here and there and illuminating in intermittent succession, like a firefly, each rhythmic focus of the body.

Of course the process that I just described is no more than a didactic example, and therefore somewhat mediocre. I haven't even mentioned one of the most important dynamics working toward the decentering of the polyrhythmic system. I'm talking about the very complex phenomenon usually called improvisation. Without it one could never arrive at the optimal rhythm for each particular muscle; one has to give them their freedom to look around at their own risk. Thus, before a person can walk "in a certain kind of way," his entire body must pass through an improvisational stage.

This theme is nowhere near exhausted, but we have to keep moving. I know that there must be doubts and questions at this point, and I'll try to anticipate a few. Someone might ask, for example, what the use is of walking "in a certain kind of way." In fact, there's not much use in it; not even dancing "in a certain kind of way" is of much use if the scale of values that we use corresponds only with a technological machine coupled to an industrial machine coupled to a commercial machine. A jazz improvisation (jazz being a kind of music that dwells within the Caribbean orbit), which achieves a decentering of the canon by which a piece has been interpreted previously, is hardly useful either. The improvisation can be taped by a record company, but the product is a recording, not the improvisation, which is linked indissolubly with a space and time that cannot be reproduced. Of course the company in question will try to persuade us that it is not selling us a phantom. And this company or another will try to convince us that if we acquire certain audio components we'll be able to hear the phantom improvisation better than the improvisation itself. Which is not necessarily false, of course. The deception lies in giving out that "listening" is the only sense touched by improvisation. In fact, improvisation, if it has reached a level that I've been calling "a certain kind of way," has penetrated all of the percipient spaces of those present, and it is precisely this shifting "totality" that leads them to perceive the impossible unity, the absent locus, the center that has taken off and yet is still there, dominating and dominated by the soloist's performance. It is this "totality" that leads those present to another "totality": that of rhythm-flux, but not that of rhythms and fluxes that belong to industrial production, to computers, to psychoanalysis, to synchronicity and diachronicity. The only useful thing about dancing or playing an instrument "in a certain kind of way" lies in the attempt to move an audience into a realm where the tensions that lead to confrontation are inoperative.

The case here is that we are speaking about traditional culture and its impact on Caribbean beings, not about technological knowledge or capitalist consuming practices, and in cultural terms to do something "in a certain kind of way" is always an important matter, since it is an attempt to sublimate violence. Further, it seems that it will keep on being important independently of the power relations of a political, economic, and even cultural nature that exist between the Caribbean and the West. Contrary to the opinions of many, I see no solid reasons to think that the culture of the Peoples of the Sea is negatively affected by the cultural "consumerism" of the industrial societies. When a people's culture conserves ancient dynamics that play "in a certain kind of way," these resist being displaced by external territorializing forms and they propose to coexist with them through syncretic processes. But aren't such processes perhaps a denaturing phenomenon? False. They are enriching, since they contribute to the widening of the play of differences. To begin with, there is no pure cultural form, not even the religious ones. Culture is a discourse, a language, and as such it has no beginning or end and is always in transformation, since it is always looking for the way to signify what it cannot manage to signify. It is true that in comparison with other important discourses—political, economic, social—cultural discourse is the one that most resists change. Its intrinsic desire, one might say, is one of conservation, as it is linked to the ancestral desire of human groups to differentiate themselves as much as possible from one another. Thus we may speak of cultural forms that are more or less regional, national, subcontinental, and even continental. But this in no way denies the heterogeneity of such forms.

A syncretic artifact is not a synthesis, but rather a signifier made of differences. What happens is that, in the melting pot of societies that the world provides, syncretic processes realize themselves through an economy in whose modality of exchange the signifier of *there*—of the Other—is consumed ("read") according to local codes that are already in existence; that is, codes from *here*. Therefore we can agree on the well-known phrase that China did not become Buddhist but rather Buddhism became Chinese. In the case of the Caribbean, it is easy to see that what we call traditional culture refers to an interplay of supersyncretic signifiers whose principal "centers" are localized in preindustrial Europe, in the sub-Saharan regions of Africa, and in certain island and coastal zones of southern Asia. What happens when there arrives, or there is imposed commercially, a "foreign" signifier, let's say the big band music of the forties or the rock music of the past thirty years? Well, among other things, the mambo, the cha-cha-cha, the bossa nova, the bolero, salsa, and reggae happen; that is to say, Caribbean music did not become Anglo-Saxon but rather the latter became Caribbean within a play of differences. Certainly there were changes (different musical instruments, different tunes, different arrangements), but the rhythm and the way of expressing oneself "in a certain kind of way" kept on being Caribbean. In reality, it could be said that, in the Caribbean, the "foreign" interacts with the "traditional" like a ray of light with a prism; that is, they produce phenomena of reflection, refraction, and decomposition. But the light keeps on being light; furthermore, the eye's camera comes out the winner, since spectacular optical performances unfold which almost always induce pleasure, or at least curiosity.

Thus the only thing that walking, dancing, playing an instrument, singing, or writing "in a certain kind of way" are good for is to displace the participants toward a poetic territory marked by an aesthetic of pleasure, or better, an aesthetic whose desire is nonviolence. This voyage "in a certain kind of way," from which one always returns—as in dreams—with the uncertainty of not having lived the past but an immemorial present, can be embarked upon by any kind of performer; it's enough that he should connect to the traditional rhythm that floats within him and without him, within and without those present. The easiest vehicle to take is improvisation, doing something all of a sudden, without thinking about it, without giving reason the chance to resist being abducted through more self-reflexive forms of aesthetic experience, irony for example. Yes, I know, it will be said that a poetic voyage is within reach of any of the earth's inhabitants. But of course, achieving the poetic is not exclusive to any human group; what *is* characteristic of the Caribbean peoples is that, in fundamental aspect, their aesthetic experience occurs within the framework of rituals and representations of a collective, ahistorical, and improvisatory nature. Later on, in the chapter devoted to Alejo Carpentier and Wilson Harris, we shall see the differences that there can be between those voyages in pursuit of the furtive *locus* of "Caribbeanness."

In any event, we can say that the Caribbean performance, including the ordinary act of walking, does not reflect back on the performer alone but rather it also directs itself toward a public in search of a carnivalesque catharsis that proposes to divert excesses of violence and that in the final analysis was *already there*. Perhaps that is why the most natural forms of Caribbean cultural expression are dance and popular music; that is why Caribbean people excel more in the spectator sports (boxing, baseball, basketball, cricket, gymnastics, track and field, etc.) than in the more subdued, austere sports where space for the performer is less visible (swimming), or is constrained by the nature of the rules of the sport itself, or perhaps the silence required of the audience (shooting, fencing, riding, diving, tennis, etc.).

Although boxing is a sport that many people detest, think for a moment about the capacity to symbolize ritual action that boxing offers: the contenders dancing on the mat, their bouncing off the ropes, the elegant jab and sidestep, the flourish of the bolo punch and the uppercut, the implicit rhythm in all weaving, the boxers' improvised theatrical gestures (faces, challenges, disdainful smiles), the choosing to be villain in one round and gentleman in the next, the performances of the supporting players (the referee who breaks up a clinch, the cornermen with their sponges and towels, the cut man, the doctor who scrutinizes the wounds, the announcer with his fantastic tuxedo, the judges attentively looking on, the bell man), and all of that on an elevated and perfectly illumined space, filled with silks and colors, blood spattering, the flash of the cameras, the shouts and whistles, the drama of the knockdown (will he get up or won't he?), the crowd on its feet, the cheering, the winner's upraised arm. It's no surprise that the people of the Caribbean should be good boxers and also, of course, good musicians, good singers, good dancers, and good writers.

From literature to carnival

One might think that literature is a solitary art as private and quiet as prayer. Not true. Literature is one of the most exhibitionistic expressions in the world. This is because it is a stream of texts and there are few things as exhibitionist as a text. It should be remembered that what a performer writes—the word *author* has justifiably fallen into disuse—is not a text, but something previous and qualitatively different: a pre-text. For a pre-text to transform itself into a text, certain stages, certain requisites, which I won't list for reasons of space and argument, must be gone through. I'll content myself by saying that the text is born when it is read by the Other: the reader. From this moment on text and reader connect with each other like a machine of reciprocal seductions. With each reading the reader seduces the text, transforms it, makes it his own; with each reading the text seduces the reader, transforms him, makes him its own. If this double seduction reaches the intensity of "a certain kind of way," both the text and the reader will transcend their statistical limits and will drift toward the decentered center of the paradoxical. This possible impossibility has been studied philosophically, epistemologically, through the discourse of poststructuralism. But poststructuralist discourse corresponds to postindustrial discourse, both discourses of so-called postmodernity. Caribbean discourse is in many respects prestructuralist and preindustrial, and to make matters worse, a contrapuntal discourse that when seen à la Caribbean would look like a *rumba,* and when seen à la Europe like a perpetually moving baroque fugue, in which the voices meet once never to meet again. I mean by this that the space of "a certain kind of way" is explained by poststructuralist thought as episteme—for example, Derrida's notion of *différance*—while Caribbean discourse, as well as being capable of occupying it in theoretical terms, floods it with a poetic and vital stream navigated by Eros and Dionysus, by Oshun and Elegua, by the Great Mother of the Arawaks and the Virgen de la Caridad del Cobre, all of them defusing violence, the blind violence with which the Caribbean social dynamics collide, the violence organized by slavery, despotic colonialism, and the Plantation.

And so the Caribbean text is excessive, dense, uncanny, asymmetrical, entropic, hermetic, all this because, in the fashion of a zoo or bestiary, it opens its doors to two great orders of reading: one of a secondary type, epistemological, profane, diurnal, and linked to the West—the world outside—where the text uncoils itself and quivers like a fantastic beast to be the object of knowledge and desire; another the principal order, teleological, ritual, nocturnal, and referring to the Caribbean itself, where the text unfolds its bisexual sphinxlike monstrosity toward the void of its impossible origin, and dreams that it incorporates this, or is incorporated by it.

A pertinent question would be: how can we begin to talk of Caribbean literature when its very existence is questionable? The question, of course, would allude more than anything to the polylingualism that seems to divide irreparably the letters of the Caribbean. But I would respond to this question with another: is it any more prudent to consider *One Hundred Years of Solitude* as a representative example of the Spanish novel, or the work of Césaire as an achievement of French poetry, or Machado de Assis as a Portuguese writer, or Wilson Harris as an English writer who left his homeland (Guyana) to live as an exile in England? Certainly not. Clearly, one could quickly argue that what I've just said doesn't prove the existence of a Caribbean literature, and that what in fact exist are local literatures, written from within the Caribbean's different linguistic blocs. I agree with this proposition, but only in terms of a first reading. Beneath the turbulence of *árbol, arbre*, tree, etc., there is an island that repeats itself until transforming into a meta-archipelago and reaching the most widely separated transhistorical frontiers of the globe. There's no center or circumference, but there are common dynamics that express themselves in a more or less regular way within the chaos and then, gradually, begin assimilating into African, European, Indoamerican, and Asian contexts up to the vanishing point. What's a good example of this trip to the source? The field of literature is always conflictive (narrow nationalism, resentments, rivalries); my example will not be a literary but a political performer: Martin Luther King. This man was able to be a Caribbean person without ceasing to be a North American, and vice versa. His African ancestry, the texture of his humanism, the ancient wisdom embodied in his pronouncements and strategies, his improvisatory vocation, his ability to seduce and be seduced, and, above all, his vehement condition as a dreamer (*I have a dream* . . .) and as an authentic performer make up the Caribbean side of a man unquestionably idiosyncratic in North America. Martin Luther King occupies and fills the space in which the Caribbean connects to the North American, a space of which jazz is also a sign.

To persevere in the attempt to refer the culture of the Caribbean to geography—other than to call it a meta-archipelago—is a debilitating and scarcely productive project. There are performers who were born in the Caribbean and who are not Caribbean by their performance; there are others who were born near or far away and nevertheless *are*. This doesn't excuse the fact, which I pointed out earlier, that there are common tropisms, and that these are seen with greater frequency within the marine flows that extend from the mouth of the Amazon to the Mississippi delta, that bathe the north coasts of South and Central America, the old Arawak-

Carib island bridge, and parts of the United States that are not completely integrated into its technological marrow; furthermore, we would perhaps have to count New York, a city where the density of Caribbean population is noticeable, but, as I said, these geographical speculations leave a lot to be desired. Antilleans, for example, tend to roam the entire world in search of the centers of their Caribbeanness, constituting one of our century's most notable migratory flows. The Antilleans' insularity does not impel them toward isolation, but on the contrary, toward travel, toward exploration, toward the search for fluvial and marine routes. One needn't forget that it was men from the Antilles who constructed the Panama Canal.

Well then, it is necessary to mention at least some of the common regularities which, in a state of flight, the Caribbean's multilinguistic literature presents. In this respect I think that the most perceptible movement that the Caribbean text carries out is, paradoxically, the one that tends to project it outside its generic ambit: a metonymic displacement toward scenic, ritual, and mythological forms, that is, toward machines that specialize in producing bifurcations and paradoxes. This attempt to evade the nets of strictly literary intertextuality always results, naturally, in a resounding failure. In the last analysis, a text is and will be a text ad infinitum, no matter how much it tries to hide itself as something else. Nonetheless, this failed project leaves its mark on the text's surface, and leaves it not so much as the trace of a frustrated act but rather as a will to persevere in flight. It can be said that Caribbean texts are fugitive by nature, constituting a marginal catalog that involves a desire for nonviolence. Thus we have it that the Caribbean *Bildungsroman* does not usually conclude with the hero's saying good-bye to the stage of apprenticeship in terms of a clean slate, nor does the dramatic structure of the Caribbean text ordinarily conclude with the phallic orgasm of climax, but rather with a kind of coda which, for example, would be interpreted in the Cuban popular theater by a rumba danced by the entire cast. If we look at the Caribbean's most representative novels we see that their narrative discourse is constantly disrupted, and at times almost annulled, by heteroclitic, fractal, baroque, or arboreal forms, which propose themselves as vehicles to drive the reader and the text to the marginal and ritually initiating territory of the absence of violence.

All of this refers, nevertheless, to a first reading of the Caribbean text. A rereading would require of us a stop to look at the rhythms proper to Caribbean literature. Here we will soon notice the presence of several rhythmic sources: Indoamerica, Africa, Asia, and Europe. Well, as we know, the polyrhythmic play that makes up the copper, black, yellow, and white rhythms (a conventional way of differentiating them) that issue from these sources has been described and analyzed in the most diverse ways and through the most varied disciplines. Clearly, nothing like that will be done here. In this book there will be discussion only of some regularities that break off from the interplay of those rhythms. For example, white rhythms, basically, articulate themselves in a binary fashion; here is the rhythm of steps marching or running, of territorializing; it is the narrative of conquest and colonization, of the assembly line, of technological knowledge, of computers and positivist ideologies; in general these rhythms are indifferent to their social impact; they are narcissistic rhythms, obsessed with their own legitimation, carrying guilt, alienation, and signs of death which they hide by proposing themselves as the best rhythms existing now or ever. The copper, black, and yellow rhythms, if quite different from one another, have something in common: they belong to the Peoples of the Sea. These rhythms, when compared to the ones mentioned earlier, appear as turbulent and erratic, or, if you like, as eruptions of gases and lava that issue from an elemental stratum, still in formation; in this respect they are rhythms without a past, or better, rhythms whose past is in the present, and they legitimize themselves by themselves. (This theme will be touched on again in Chapter 4.) One might think that there is an irremediable contradiction between the two kinds of rhythms, and in fact there is, but only within the confines of a first reading. The dialectic of this contradiction would take us to the moment of synthesis: *mestizo* rhythm, *mulato* rhythm. But a rereading would make it apparent that *mestizaje* is not a synthesis, but rather the opposite. It can't be such a thing because nothing that is ostensibly syncretic constitutes a stable point. The high regard for *mestizaje,* the *mestizaje* solution, did not originate in Africa or Indoamerica or with any People of the Sea. It involves a positivistic and logocentric argument, an argument that sees in the biological, economic, and cultural whitening of Caribbean society a series of successive steps toward "progress." And as such it refers to conquest, to slavery, neocolonialism, and dependence. Within the realities of a rereading, *mestizaje* is nothing more than a concentration of differences, a tangle of dynamics obtained by means of a greater density of the Caribbean object, as we saw in the case of the Virgen del Cobre, who, by the way, is known as "la Virgen mulata." Then, at a given moment in our rereading, the binary oppositions Europe/Indoamerica, Europe/Africa, and Europe/Asia do not resolve themselves into the synthesis of *mestizaje,* but rather they resolve into insoluble differential equations, which repeat their unknowns through the ages of the meta-archipelago. The literature of the

Caribbean can be read as a *mestizo* text, but also as a stream of texts in flight, in intense differentiation among themselves and within whose complex coexistence there are vague regularities, usually paradoxical. The Caribbean poem and novel are not only projects for ironizing a set of values taken as universal; they are, also, projects that communicate their own turbulence, their own clash, and their own void, the swirling black hole of social violence produced by the *encomienda* and the plantation, that is, their otherness, their peripheral asymmetry with regard to the West.

Thus Caribbean literature cannot free itself totally of the multiethnic society upon which it floats, and it tells us of its fragmentation and instability: that of the Negro who studied in London or in Paris, that of the white who believes in voodoo, that of the Negro who wants to find his identity in Africa, that of the mulatto who wants to be white, that of the white man who loves a black woman and vice versa, that of the rich black man and poor white man, that of the mulatto woman who passes for white and has a black child, that of the mulatto who says that the races do not exist. Add to these differences those that resulted—and still result in certain regions—from the encounter of the Indoamerican with the European and of the latter with the Asian. Finally, add to all of this the unstable system of relations which, amid uncompromising alliances and conflicts, brings together and separates the Native American and the African, the Native American and the Asian, the Asian and the African, but why go on with this? What model of the human sciences can predict what will happen in the Caribbean next year, next month, next week? We are dealing obviously with an unpredictable society that originated in the most violent currents and eddies of modern history where sexual and class differences are overlaid with differences of an ethnographic nature. (This theme is continued in Chapter 6.) Nevertheless, to reduce the Caribbean to the single factor of its instability would also be an error; the Caribbean is that and much more, including much more than what will be dealt with in this book.

In any case, the impossibility of being able to assume a stable identity, even the color that one wears in his skin, can only be made right through the possibility of existing "in a certain kind of way" in the midst of the sound and fury of chaos. To this end, the most viable route to take, it's clear, is that of the meta-archipelago itself, above all the paths that lead to the semipagan hagiography of the Middle Ages and to African beliefs. It is in this space that the majority of the Caribbean cults are articulated, cults that by their nature unleash multiple popular expressions: myth, music, dance, song, theater. This is why the Caribbean text, to transcend its own cloister, must avail itself of these models in search of routes that might lead, at least symbolically, to an extratextual point of social nonviolence and psychic reconstitution of the Self. The routes, iridescent and transitory as a rainbow, cross at all points the network of binary dynamics extended by the West. The result is a text that speaks of a critical coexistence of rhythms, a polyrhythmic ensemble whose central binary rhythm is decentered when the performer (writer/reader) and the text try to escape "in a certain kind of way."

It will be said that this coexistence is false, that finally it ends up as a system formed by the opposition Peoples of the Sea / Europe and its historical derivations. A rereading of this point, nevertheless, would have more imaginative consequences. Relations between Peoples of the Sea and the West, like all power relations, are not simply antagonistic. For example, at bottom, all the Peoples of the Sea want to occupy the place that they occupy geographically, but they would also like to occupy the place of the West, and vice versa. Put differently, any Person of the Sea, without ceasing to be such, would like at bottom to have an industrial machine, one of flow and interruption, to be perhaps in the world of theory, science, and technology. In a parallel fashion, the world made by the Industrial Revolution, without ceasing to be such, would like at times to be in the place of the Peoples of the Sea, where it once was; it would like to live immersed in Nature and in the poetic, that is, it would like once more to own a machine that flows and interrupts at the same time. The signs of the existence of this double paradox of desire are wherever you look—the New Age movement and the environmental movement in the United States and Europe, the industrializing plans and taste for the artificial in the Third World— and I'll return to this contradictory theme in the last chapter. With matters in this state, the opposition of theoretical machine versus poetic machine, epistemological machine versus teleological machine, power machine versus resistance machine, and others of the like will be quite other than fixed poles that always face each other as enemies. In reality, the supposed fixity of these poles would be undermined by an entire gamut of relations that are not necessarily antagonistic, to open up a complex and unstable kind of existing that points to the void, to the lack of something, to repetitive and rhythmic insufficiency which, finally, is the most visible determinism to be drawn in the Caribbean.

And finally I want to make it clear that to undertake a rereading of the Caribbean gives one no license to fall into idealizations. In the first place, as Freud would see, the popular tradition is also in the last analysis a machine that is not free from repression. Certainly it is no technologico-positivist machine that is indifferent to the conserving of certain social linkages, but in its ahistoricity it perpetuates myths and fables that attempt to legitimate the law of patriarchy and hide the violence inherent in every sociological origin. Further—following René Girard's reasoning—we can agree that the ritual sacrifice practiced in the symbolic societies implied a desire to sublimate public violence, but this desire was emitted from the sphere of power and pursued objectives of social control.

In the second place, the critical coexistence that I have spoken of tends to unfold in the most unpredictable and diverse forms. An island can, at a given moment, bring closer together or move farther apart cultural components of diverse origins with the worst of possible results—which, luckily, is not the rule—while on a contiguous island the seething and constant interplay of transcontinental spume generates a fortunate product. This chance circumstance makes it possible that, for example, the degree of Africanization in each local culture will vary from island to island, and that the Plantation's acculturating impact will make itself known asymmetrically.

As to the rest, the Caribbean text shows the specific features of the supersyncretic culture from which it emerges. It is, without a doubt, a consummate performer, with recourse to the most daring improvisations to keep from being trapped within its own textuality. (I refer the reader to Chapter 7.) In its most spontaneous form it can be seen in terms of the *carnaval*, the great Caribbean celebration that spreads out through the most varied systems of signs: music, song, dance, myth, language, food, dress, body expression. There is something strongly feminine in this extraordinary *fiesta:* its flux, its diffuse sensuality, its generative force, its capacity to nourish and conserve (juices, spring, pollen, rain, seed, shoot, ritual sacrifice—these are words that come to stay). Think of the dancing flourishes, the rhythms of the conga, the samba, the masks, the hoods, the men dressed and painted as women, the bottles of rum, the sweets, the confetti and colored streamers, the hubbub, the carousal, the flutes, the drums, the cornet and the trombone, the teasing, the jealousy, the whistles and the faces, the razor that draws blood, death, life, reality in forward and reverse, torrents of people who flood the streets, the night lit up like an endless dream, the figure of a centipede that comes together and then breaks up, that winds and stretches beneath the ritual's rhythm, that flees the rhythm without escaping it, putting off its defeat, stealing off and hiding itself, imbedding itself finally in the rhythm, always in the rhythm, the beat of the chaos of the islands.

■ *PART I*

SOCIETY

From the

plantation

to the

Plantation

In the town of El Caney, near Santiago de Cuba, there is a formation of ruins crowning the place's most important height. It is the old fortress of El Vizo, torn apart by artillery in the final days of the Spanish-American War. There, below those grapeshot-creased walls, one sees a bronze buckler set out to honor the valor of General Vara del Rey, who, rather than accept the easy terms of an honorable surrender, defended his position stubbornly until falling dead among the handful of men to which his garrison had been reduced. The buckler and its words of commemoration, as well as the restorative work that enables access to the very tower of the redoubt, are signs of the Cubans' admiration for his conduct.[1] Nothing more natural, if he had died fighting against Spain. But it wasn't like that. Vara del Rey was a severe and hardened military man who fought to the end in order to prolong, if only for a couple of hours, a Spanish dominion over that fortified ridge in the Sierra Maestra, harassed by Cuban and American troops.

The world does not swarm with gestures of this type, even less in the non-Caribbean Latin American countries, where there still remains, ever since the era of the wars of independence, a certain resentment toward everything Spanish. In the Caribbean, though, the citizenry has kept as its very own the stone walls that its colonial past inspired, even the most questionable ones, as happened with the El Vizo fortress. One can actually say that there is no city in the Spanish Caribbean that does not hold a kind of cult worship of its castles and fortresses, its walls and cannons, and by extension the "old" sections of the city, as with Old San Juan and

Old Havana. Colonial buildings are regarded there with a rare mixture of familiarity and respect. They have an almost occult prestige, which comes from what lies behind them, something like what's aroused in children by grandmother's huge wardrobe.

One can't help noticing this, no matter how little the Spanish colonization of America could ever be seen as better than anyone else's. Indeed, if one looks into the pages of any local history, he will be struck head-on by its having been authoritarian in civic matters, monopolist in commerce, intolerant in religion, slaveholding in production, actively hostile to reforming currents, and discriminatory toward Indians, mestizos, blacks, mulattos, and even toward creoles born of European parents.

Nonetheless, as we shall see, the Spanish colonial picture in the Caribbean differed substantially from the scheme that predominated in the continental territories, above all in the great viceroyalties of New Spain and Peru. These differences arose during colonization from within the process of adapting the power of the mother country to geographical, demographic, economic, social, and cultural conditions that acted in a specific way in the island area of the Caribbean and, to a lesser extent, along the mainland coast. I mean by this that the Spanish Caribbean is part of Latin America, but also part of a considerably more complex region, characterized by its military and commercial importance, its linguistic and ethnological pluralism, and by the proliferating character of the Plantation.

It also holds true that although the characteristics just mentioned might serve an attempt at definition, the fact that England, France, and Holland—plus Sweden and Denmark on a smaller scale—should have arrived there much later than Spain and Portugal, and above all that they (unlike the Iberian nations) should have steered their economies along the most radical capitalist paths, helped to lend a heterogeneous aspect to the colonial Caribbean. So if it's clear that there are certain regular and common features, held in place by experiences more or less shared—European conquest, the native peoples' disappearance or retreat, African slavery, plantation economies, Asian immigration, rigid and prolonged colonial domination—there are other obvious factors that would keep the area from being coherent.

Testimony written by the many travelers to the Caribbean generally provides valuable information toward any attempt at positing differences between the various blocs of colonial territory. At the end of the last century, the historian James Anthony Froude commented:

Kingston is the best of our West Indian towns and Kingston has not one fine building in it. Havana is a city of palaces, a city of streets and plazas, of colonnades and towers, and churches and monasteries. We English have built in those islands as if we were but passing visitors, wanting only tenements to be occupied for a time. The Spaniards built as they built in Castile, built with the same material, the white lime-stone which they found in the New World as in the Old. The palaces of the nobles in Havana, the residence of the governor, the convents, the cathedral, are a reproduction of Burgos or Valladolid . . . And they carried along with them their laws, their habits, their institutions and their creed, their religious orders, their bishops and their Inquisition.[2]

Without beginning for the moment to put forth the causes behind this visible difference—economic, social, and cultural—between the principal city of a Spanish Caribbean colony and that of any neighboring colony administered by England, I am now going to present a contrary judgment, to the effect that one may draw an impression of important features held in common by the different colonial blocs. Père Jean-Baptiste Labat writes:

I have travelled everywhere in your sea of the Caribbean . . . from Haiti to Barbados, to Martinique and Guadaloupe, and I know what I am speaking about . . . You are all together, in the same boat, sailing on the same uncertain sea . . . citizenship and race unimportant, feeble little labels compared to the message that my spirit brings to me: that of the position and predicament which History has imposed upon you . . . I saw it first with the dance . . . the merengue in Haiti, the beguine in Martinique and today I hear, *de mon oreille morte,* the echo of calypsoes from Trinidad, Jamaica, St. Lucia, Antigua, Dominica and the legendary Guiana . . . It is no accident that the sea which separates your lands makes no difference to the rhythms of your body.[3]

Apart from the intimate nuances of this text, it is interesting to see how Labat, an astute observer, sets out, at the end of the seventeenth century, the hypothesis of a common Caribbean culture—expressed through music, song, dance, and rhythm—unbounded by the linguistic and political frontiers imposed by the various colonial powers. That is, while Froude directs himself to the differences, Labat lets himself be overtaken by the similarities.

It is precisely the unequal reading of these differences and similarities, or if you like these centrifugal and centripetal forces at work in the Caribbean, that has led investigators of the region to take positions around the axis of unity/diversity, especially in the field of culture. We have to recognize, though, that—in addition to the constricting violence that any binary focus imposes—the scarcity of comparative studies that transcend a single linguistic zone, and also of investigations that could be termed interdisciplinary or encompassing, renders any more or less objective judgment of this matter difficult to make. Further, the presence in the past of strong plantation economies in the Brazilian northeast and the southern United States does not make it any easier to delimit the area clearly. Nor should we skip lightly over the difficulty presented by the staggered exploitation of the region, an obstacle that has suggested a comparative method that relies on a nonsynchronic comparison of socioeconomic data.[4] In this way one could compare Cuban society of the nineteenth century, by then dominated by a plantation economy, with that of Saint-Domingue in the eighteenth century, and either one of the two with that of Barbados at the end of the seventeenth century, when the expulsion of the Dutch from Brazil spread to that region the era's most advanced sugar production technology. The fact that this method has been proposed and confirmed in the heart of the community of specialists who study the region is very significant. They propose the Plantation as the parameter for analyzing the Caribbean, while at the same time speaking of the contradictory effects (or voids) that its proliferation has imposed upon the whole area. Thus, if we may venture a leap of the imagination, the Caribbean could be seen as well as a loosely bounded figure combining straight lines and curves, let's say, a spiral galaxy tending outward—to the universe—that bends and folds over its own history, its own inwardness.

In any case one has to conclude that, in spite of the array of difficulties facing any study of the region, one can always resort to one of the three general types of reading that the Caribbean now offers, that is, Labat's unified and unifying, Froude's entirely severalized, and one we call here the reading of Chaos, of the Milky Way,[5] where we detect dynamic regularities—not results—within the (dis)order that exists beyond the world of predictable pathways. I think that each of the three points of view is valid, and that each one constitutes the most viable course for examining one or another aspect of the Caribbean discourse. Here, in this book, the underlined attitude is that of the reader typed as Chaos, but without any desire to deny or to repress the validity of other readings. If I should be reproached for taking a too-eclectic position in this matter, I will answer that this is probably the case, but I am not the only one to hold to this position, and I would refer the critic to Chapter 4, where there is a discussion of Fernando Ortiz and his typically Caribbean position in the face of modern scientific thought.

The complexity that the multiplication of the Plantation—each case a different one—brought to the Caribbean was such that the Caribbean peoples themselves, in referring to the ethnological processes that derived from the extraordinary collision of races and cultures thus produced, speak of syncretism, acculturation, transculturation, assimilation, deculturation, indigenization, creolization, cultural *mestizaje,* cultural *cimarronaje,* cultural miscegenation, cultural resistance, etc. Which illustrates not just that these processes occurred again and again, but also, and above all, that there are different positions or readings from which they may be examined.

Here, in this chapter, I do not propose a model kit for constructing the Caribbean. My only aim is to undertake a kind of voyage of revisitation, or better yet, of scrutinization, toward points which, because they lie within the Caribbean discourse, tend to be of interest to those who enjoy reading the region's cultural codes. One of those points is the argument between those who argue that centripetal forces are stronger than centrifugal ones in the Caribbean and those who think the opposite; that is, the old unity/diversity debate. Among the latter we find the historian Frank Moya Pons, who says the following about particularity:

> For the majority of the population of the area, to speak of the Caribbean has meaning only as a convenience in geography classes; for most of its people the Caribbean as a living community, with common interests and aspirations, just does not exist. Practically, it seems more sensible to think of several Caribbeans coexisting alongside one another. Although it is frequently said that the local economies follow a similar pattern, in fact the cultures and social structures of the region vary considerably, and consequently, lifestyles and political behavior vary as well.[6]

I think that there is a good deal of truth in what Moya Pons says. A Haitian or a Martinican feels closer to France than to Jamaica, and a Puerto Rican identifies better with the United States than with Surinam. Further, it is evident to me that the cultural panorama of the Caribbean is supremely heterogeneous. How then can one be sure that a Caribbean culture even exists?

Although it may seem contradictory, I think that the quickest route toward defining a substantial form of Caribbeanness is not the cultural one.

Perhaps it would be more productive to take first, for example, the way that Sidney W. Mintz proposes:

> To begin with, it is inaccurate to refer to the Caribbean as a "cultural area," if by "culture" is meant a common body of historical tradition. The very diverse origins of Caribbean populations; the complicated history of European cultural impositions; and the absence in most societies of any firm continuity of the culture of the colonial power have resulted in a very heterogeneous cultural picture. And yet the *societies* of the Caribbean—taking the word "society" to refer here to forms of social structure and social organization—exhibit similarities that cannot possibly be attributed to mere coincidence. It probably would be more accurate (though stylistically unwieldy) to refer to the Caribbean as a "societal area," since its component societies probably share many more social-structural features than they do cultural features.[7]

Following this, Mintz presents an essay that has come to be a classic text in the historiography of the Caribbean, not so much for its innovation as for its articulation. After considering the differences that he sees within the area, Mintz reaches the conclusion that the great majority of Caribbean nations present parallel socioeconomic structures, which were determined by the same concurrent phenomenon: the plantation. Which is to say, apart from the fact that the plantation economy existed in other zones of the American continent, it is only in the Caribbean region that its dynamics produce a kind of socioeconomic instability whose morphology is repeated, becoming more or less ascendant from colonial times until the present. Hence the Caribbean, by virtue of this judgment, may be defined as a *societal area*.

Without beginning here to argue the details of this way of seeing the Caribbean, I think that one must agree with Mintz that the plantation seems indispensable to studying the societies of the area. In my opinion, nonetheless, the plantation could turn out to be an even more useful parameter; it could serve as a telescope for observing the changes and the continuities of the Caribbean galaxy through the lenses of multifold disciplines, namely, economics, history, sociology, political science, anthropology, ethnology, demography, as well as through innumerable practices, which range from the commercial to the military, from the religious to the literary. I think that the arrival and proliferation of the plantations is the most important historical phenomenon to have come about in the Caribbean, to the extent that if it had not occurred the islands of the region might today perhaps be miniature replicas—at least in demographic and ethnological terms—of the European nations that colonized them.

I believe, in fact, that one of the most reasonable ways to explain the regular differences that we notice in the area is to begin with the plantation; still more, I think that its multiplied presence may be used in establishing differences not just within the Caribbean itself but also in its relation to Europe, Africa, Asia, North and South America. I believe that beyond their nature—sugar, coffee, etc.—, beyond the colonizing power that set them up, beyond the epoch in which the dominant economy in one or another colony was founded, the plantation turns out to be one of the principal instruments for studying the area, if not indeed the most important. This is so because the Caribbean, in substantial measure, was shaped by Europe for the plantation, and the generalized historical convergences shown by the different territories in the region are always related to that purpose. For these reasons, it would seem premature to venture an opinion about whether or not a Caribbean culture exists before reviewing the circumstances surrounding the development of the plantation economy and its impact on the sociocultural surfaces of the area, that is, until organizing the discourse of the Plantation.[8]

Hispaniola: the first plantations

It is curious that a man like Froude, a historian on a trip devoted to making political observations in the Caribbean, and a representative of the conservative interests of the British Empire, should have censured his countrymen for not having acted in the West Indies in a "civilizing" way, as the Spaniards had done in Cuba. He seems not to have realized that the ostensible differences that he perceived between Kingston and Havana did not come about just because of civic or administrative factors, but also owed their existence to economic and social phenomena that had had asymmetrical repercussions in the two cities. The most important of these, in my view, was the Plantation, and the asymmetry that I speak of derives from the stretch of time—about a century—that lay between its advent in Jamaica and its tardy formation in Cuba. But I'll take this matter up later; let's move on now to a rehearsal of the context within which the earliest American plantations sprang up.

The first plantations were started up in Hispaniola around the second decade of the sixteenth century. Both Bartolomé de Las Casas and Fernández de Oviedo tell in their histories of the sprouting up of sugar mills, and they offer at the same time some curious data about the industry's beginnings. Unlike other economic initiatives, the plantations of Hispaniola sprouted up rather by chance in the right place. They did so at a moment of crisis, when, the island having run out of Indians and gold, it was abandoned en masse by its settlers, who had caught the fever of the newest discoveries and the call to enrichment that was coming from Mexico. Those who, for one reason or another, decided not to leave the colony began to think up enterprises that would allow them to subsist there. The first projects move us nowadays to laughter—using the shells of the big turtles to make and export shields, or sowing groves of *cañafístola* to flood Spain with its purgative sap—but someone remembered the sugarcane that Columbus had brought to the island, and he began to get molasses and brown sugar using rudimentary machines. The details of this genesis and its extraordinary literary implications are offered in the next chapter. Here it is enough to say that the crown very soon sponsored the development of sugar plantations with loans, debt moratoria, tax exemptions, machinery, technical advice, and above all, authorization for an increased African slave importation to guarantee their functioning. It should be added, though, that if these plantations grew out of Hispaniola's colonists' initiative, the first prototypes had arisen in the Near East, some three centuries back, moving westward at the rate of their being perfected and adjusted to Iberian mercantile practices. It can even be said that the last gold from Hispaniola was produced through a model of exploitation and division of labor rather like that found on the Spanish-run plantations.[9]

The plantations' development having been boosted and protected by the crown—which saw in them a means of settling the colonists on the land—they extended themselves relatively quickly. The sugarcane was milled in two types of machines: the *trapiche* (moved by animal power) and the *ingenio poderoso* (moved hydraulically). The exports of sugar to Seville began in 1517 with a modest *caxeta* (nougat). Nevertheless, five years later a ship arrived from Hispaniola loaded with 2,000 *arrobas* (25 tons) and in 1525 they were already talking in Seville of "three ships freighted with loaves of sugar." In 1542 the exports from the island reached the figure of 1,200 tons, a large total for the time.[10] Soon the number of mills on Hispaniola grew in such a way that the famous Alcázar of Toledo was built with the money collected through a tax on sugar coming from the island to Seville.

Regarding the other colonies in the Caribbean that had followed Hispaniola's example, thirty mills are spoken of in Jamaica in 1523, and ten in

Puerto Rico, which—doubtless all of them *trapiches*—produced some 170 tons. It is also known that toward the second half of the sixteenth century the exports from Cuba reached an annual average of 460 tons.[11]

But the sugar plantation couldn't go much further at that time. The cost of a mill was always very high. The historians of the Indies speak of hydraulic *ingenios* costing even forty and fifty thousand ducats. It's enough to say that with the sale of one of them the founding of the second university in Santo Domingo was financed. Add to this the fact that the price of a slave then was one hundred ducats, more or less, and that no fewer than 120 slaves were needed to operate a hydraulic mill. Moreover, the European demand for sugar in the sixteenth century was considerably reduced and the supply in the market kept growing. In addition to the sugars produced in Spain and in other non-American colonies, Spanish as well as Portuguese, one must bear in mind that the mill crossed over very early from the Antilles to the mainland. In 1531 Hernán Cortés had three significant mills in Mexico, and in 1560 Peru began exporting sugar to Seville. In Brazil, the manufacture of sugar, begun in 1533, had grown so that in 1584 there were more than sixty large plantations, with a total production of 2,000 tons, requiring the services of forty ships in exporting the product to Lisbon. Mercantile competition became so acute that the Canary Islands, even with much cheaper shipping costs than those of the Americas, had to convert a large part of their cane fields to the production of wines. So that as the seventeenth century approached, sugar manufacturing was no longer the business that it had been, and much less so in the Antilles. It is concerning approximately this time that one can start to talk about a first and prolonged sugar recession, with a consequent loss of interest on the part of the crown in continuing to protect its manufacture. Of course, in this regard, we must appreciate that the mining in Mexico and Peru, to Spanish eyes, was coming to be something like an industry for producing coins, in which capital investment was minimal and whose operating costs were practically nil when Indian labor could be counted on. It seemed logical to Spanish thinking of the time to stop investing resources in sugar production, given ever more competitive market conditions. We should also keep in mind the crown's attachment to feudal institutions, and its politics of keeping in line any incipient capitalist ventures by traders and manufacturers, especially overseas. These were the reasons, among others, that the Antillean plantations languished. Insofar as the Spanish islands are concerned, one can't speak of a sugar bonanza until the second half of the eighteenth century, when a cluster of factors favored the introduction of the modern plantation, along the lines of models already set in motion by Holland, England, and France in their Caribbean possessions.

Nevertheless, the brief and modest sugar boom in the Spanish Antilles in the sixteenth century left an indelible mark on the islands' society. According to Las Casas, the first *trapiche* appears on Hispaniola in 1516, and immediately slaves are in demand. Thus in 1518 Spain began to deal in African slaves on a large scale when a license was issued for the distribution of 4,000 Negroes in four years, 2,000 of them destined for Hispaniola. The contract was renewed in 1523, and again in 1528. In 1540, with the plantation practice now generalized, Las Casas estimated the number of slaves at 30,000, and gave the figure of 70,000 for the rest of the colonies. Even if we take Las Casas's figures as exaggerated, it is certain that in the second half of the century the Negro's demographic presence in the Antilles was substantially greater than that of the white colonists. It is interesting to see how Las Casas observes so acutely that, unlike the first Negroes brought to Hispaniola, those who were working there then on the sugar plantations died quickly of the hard work. The system's repressive character rapidly carried over to the sphere of colonial administration, which explains Diego Colón's cruelty in punishing his slaves after their revolt of 1522. It is a curious thing to notice, during the short period of the sugar bonanza in Hispaniola, the appearance of certain constants which reached their critical point later, when the plantation system achieved a transformation of colonial society in the Caribbean in a more or less generalized fashion, in what we call the plantation society, or simply the Plantation. For example, the series that has as its subject the slave, pertaining to: demand, purchase, work, depreciation, flight, *palenque* (runaway settlement), revolt, repression, replacement. This gives an idea of the rapid dynamic and the intense measure of exploitation intrinsic to the plantation machine. One also observes, as a common characteristic of the early New World plantations, that the sugar mills, almost without exception, belong to officials of the crown. Who owned the powerful sugar mills of Hispaniola? Diego Colón, viceroy; Cristóbal de Tapia, inspector; Esteban de Pasamonte, treasurer; Diego Caballero de la Rosa, *regidor* of Santo Domingo; Juan de Ampieza, agent of Ferdinand and Isabella; Antonio Serrano, *regidor* of Santo Domingo; Alonso de Avila, royal accountant; Alonso de Peralta, precentor of the cathedral; Francisco de Tapia, commander of the fortress of Santo Domingo, etc. Oviedo, in his *Historia general*, gives enough details to enable us to affirm that those great mills passed from fathers to sons, thus building up an incipient sugar oligarchy that combined and united the political, economic, and social power. On the mainland the same thing happened; we've already noted that Cortés owned three mills in Mexico, and it must be noted that in Brazil the sugar manufacturing began with the mill belonging to the governor of the *Capitanía* of San Vicente.

The concentration of the power of sugar manufacturing in the hands of the colony's royal functionaries can be explained by the latter's being the only ones to have capital and influence enough to undertake the venture, which required not only a huge monetary investment but also connections with the court for the obtaining of loans, moratoria, machinery, land, technicians, and above all, slaves. And so the New World's first plantations lay down the basis for the building of a colonial society of an oligarchic type, depending on the crown's commercial monopolies, which included the slave trade. This, as will be seen shortly, was to have a decisive bearing on which geographic zones and localities, which types of economies, and which social strata would act as the principal generative contexts of creole culture.

The emergence of creole culture

Near the end of the sixteenth century, when sugar entered into its period of recession—which stopped the accelerating march toward the Plantation— a new economy was presenting itself as a way out for the colonists of Hispaniola. This new trade was in leather, whose military, naval, domestic, and aesthetic importance kept growing from year to year, to the extent that we could say that it was as useful a product as plastic is in our time. Hispaniola, like the rest of the Greater Antilles, found itself particularly well set up for the export of hides to the European market. The various types of cattle that Christopher Columbus brought with him had proliferated at a geometric rate and, protected by the scant demand for meat among the island's small population, they reverted to a wild state in the great stretches of virgin lands. Further, one would have to say that these animals' hides were of the very best quality. The island's natural pasture had nutritional levels much higher than those of the European countries, since the lands had never been exhausted through agricultural exploitation. Better food and a more benign climate had contributed to the improvement of the varieties of cattle which had been brought over a century earlier, and which produced bigger, thicker, shinier hides than any that had been seen on the European markets. Thus, at the dawn of the seventeenth century, the Antillean hides were as attractive or more so than sugar, which was still consumed by only a privileged layer of society, and even there more as something from the pharmacopoeia.

Now, the production of hides had characteristics quite different from those of sugar. In the first place there was scarcely any need to own land, since the cattle roamed in areas which in many cases hadn't yet been touched by the royal concessions; in the second place, only a very small capital was needed, since the cattle, in abundant herds, were found well within the reach of the lasso and the lance; finally, and obviously, there was no need for great numbers of slaves, since a mere handful were enough for one family in the hunting and skinning work that the industry required. Unlike sugar manufacturing, the production of hides was an almost spontaneous enterprise, which any inland colonist could tackle; it was a domestic industry that required no costly machinery or equipment, nor did it demand technicians from Madeira or the Canaries, nor did it require influence at court or on the colonial government; it was, in short, a small but stable industry, belonging to the people, but still rich, and as I will soon demonstrate, destined to become a subversive business. The fact that the cattle were concentrated far from the capital and the major cities of Hispaniola benefited the population that lived in the so-called *banda norte*, which also included the land at the far west of the island. In spite of this advantage, their isolation must have seemed an insuperable obstacle to these colonists. This can be better understood if we remember that the royal monopoly of the *Casa de Contratación* authorized only the port of Santo Domingo, situated at the island's southeast, for trading with Seville. This being the situation, the colonists of the *banda norte* had to carry their bundles of hides across rivers, forests, and mountains before reaching the capital. This situation, naturally, not only made it difficult to transport the merchandise, but also increased its cost and lowered the profit margin. As could be expected, the people of the *banda norte* asked the crown time and again to authorize their region's ports. But these requests went unheard, which fostered a trade in contraband, called *rescate* (ransom) at that time, with merchants who came from the powers rivaling Spain.

As far as we can know for certain, the first of these merchants was the celebrated John Hawkins, among the high points of whose biography stands the effrontery of having started, in 1561, the clandestine English smuggling of slaves into the Caribbean. Nevertheless, it is quite possible that Portuguese traders came earlier. In spite of the crown's doing all it could to dismantle the illicit export of hides—which in importance very quickly surpassed the legal traffic—its achievements in this matter were abundantly surpassed by its failures. The people of the *banda norte* showed so much initiative that they even organized trade fairs that were attended by merchants from England, France, Holland, Italy, Portugal, and other nations. It is known that the fair at Gonaives, for example, was a preferred event for those daring traders, who occasionally behaved as privateers as well.

In any case, it can be said that the abundance of cattle, the high demand for leather, the mercantile expansion of the rival powers, and the crown's refusal to concede commercial freedoms rapidly contributed toward the making of a certain kind of society in the northern and western regions of Hispaniola. It was a matter of enterprising people, *mestizos* and *mulatos* in large measure who, because they lived far from the cities, stayed outside of the orbit of the colonial bureaucracy, the military garrisons, and the Church's watchful eye. They formed a social group of the *nouveaux riches,* within the commercial orbit of capitalist Europe, unforeseen in the arrangements fostered by the Council of the Indies or in the royal decrees; they subsisted in a self-sufficient manner, with their backs turned to the mother country and the island's capital; they ate from English plates, they used French knives, and they dressed in fine Holland shirts; they imported wines, furniture, tools, arms, fashions, and many other objects, and they read "heretical" books, including Bibles that were translated into Spanish by expert Flemish Jews. It is true that they also imported slaves, but they did not constitute a slave society in the economic sense of the word, that is, in the sense conferred by the Plantation. Here the black slave did not live in confinement, nor was the work rule extreme. Further, there is proof that many of them also worked in the smuggling business. Moreover, even in the cases in which the *banda norte*'s inhabitants did not possess land legally, the open cattle grazing in the coastal savannas, forests, and valleys must have imparted a natural feeling of belonging, a particular form of de facto property owning that linked the person with the place.

In this socioeconomic matrix human relations would tend to be more individualist, more dynamic if you like; families were brought together through ties of marriage and godfathering, and blacks and women could express themselves more freely than in the capital. It was something of an ambulatory society, defined by its mounted nature, mobilized on horseback or in wagons to greet any contraband ship announced by a cannon shot. Days of real festivity would follow, in which commercial deals were realized to the sound of the European lute and the African drum, of the Spanish ballad and the tavern songs of Plymouth, la Rochelle, Antwerp, Genoa, and Lisbon; days of dancing and drinking, where fried steak alternated with lobster, where there was smoking and gambling and lovemaking, and not a few times there was fighting even to the death. When this latter happened, the governor would get reports of "Lutheran corsairs" captured and hanged, or of some village that was sacked and burned by "heretical pirates." In this society with its free habits, under the common interest of its contraband trading and separated from the centers of colonial power by distance and by mountain ranges, the people properly called creoles (*criollos*) and also, significantly, people of the land (*gente de la tierra*) started to emerge.

Within the framework of this early creole society, localized in the isolated areas of the Antilles and on the shoreline that ringed the Caribbean, the African slave played an active role in the process of forming the local cultures. Unlike the Negro at the sugar mill, the slave inscribed within the leather economy did not find himself subject to a regime of imprisonment and forced labor, and so he had the possibility of becoming a cultural agent. If we take into account that the populations of these marginal localities carried a fair amount of Taino blood and still nurtured some of the native customs that had helped the first settlers to identify with the physical environment, it's easy to see that we're seeing a cultural phenomenon much more complex than the one resulting from the collision of races within the straitened and cruel orbit of the plantations. Certainly, these marginal creole societies—which were also present in other places in the Caribbean—did not constitute some kind of colonial Arcadia, above all for the slaves, who had after all been pulled away from what was their own. But the interplay of ethnologic pluralism, within a more open social panorama than that prevailing in the capital or plantations, allowed the springing up of a generalized racial type with Taino, European, and African origins, which both received and spread a supersyncretic culture characterized by its complexity, its individualism, and its instability, that is to say, creole culture,[12] whose seeds had come scattered from the richest stores of three continents.

Naturally these early non-sugaring creole societies entered quite soon into conflicts with the colonial bureaucracy. Not only were they depriving the Sevillan monopoly of the earnings that came out of the clandestine trade, but they also dealt freely with Spain's politico-religious enemies who were getting ever more familiar with the Caribbean's coasts, ports, and defenses. This situation of open rebellion against the crown's dispositions provoked the issuance of menacing royal directives ordering the colonial functionaries to take the most drastic measures against the illicit trade. Given that the latter was carried out with "heretic" merchants, the measures also involved religious sanctions. And so the villages involved in contraband were threatened with hanging and excommunication, and the threats soon became actions. The events in which such repressions unfolded turn out to be so interesting within the history of the Caribbean in those years that they have inspired poems, novels, essays, and many studies. Here we shall be able to consider briefly only three cases, having to do with the creoles of Hispaniola, Venezuela, and Cuba. What happened in these places was of such magnitude that it may be linked to the appearance of a second Caribbean age, in which the area became internationalized, ceasing to be a maritime region administered only by the Iberian powers.

Contraband, repression, and consequences

In 1603, Philip III's final answer to the contraband issue reached Santo Domingo. The royal decree called for the destruction and depopulation of three villages in the *banda norte:* Puerto Plata, La Yaguana, and Bayaja. After a period of waiting during which the question was argued between the neighbors of these villages—Santo Domingo as well—and the colonial administration, the governor, Osorio, decided to march at the front of a corps of harquebusiers to carry out the crown's instructions. For reasons that have remained obscure, Osorio's destructive appetite was beyond what the king had called for. In addition to the three villages already noted, Monte Cristy, San Juan de la Maguana, Neiba, Santiago de los Caballeros, Azua, Ocoa, and Las Salinas were destroyed as well. The round of summary judgments and burnings commenced in March of 1605 and ended in October 1606. In this period the members of eighty-two families, including women, were hanged, and thousands of people were removed to the environs of Santo Domingo with almost no baggage but the clothing they wore and the few cattle they could round up. A document from the time relates complainingly:

> The comfort, enticement, and security given to them for leaving their towns and coming to the new places was to force them to leave with their livestock within twenty-four hours; and when these had passed, the houses, belongings, farms, and mills were burned, the yucca was pulled up, and the rest of the crops devastated, leaving them, with their women, little children, and newborns in the midst of a wasteland,

at the mercy of the rainstorms . . . having to cross over many large
and furious rivers and roads and rough, difficult, and dangerous paths,
with the belongings they could pull together in twenty-four hours.[13]

In this extreme repression, known in the local history as *las devastaciones,*
100,000 head of cattle, 15,000 horses, and one mill were lost. But, above all,
almost half of the territory of Hispaniola was lost, and stayed deserted and
at the disposition of whoever wished to land there. This situation made it
possible for many fugitive slaves and groups of international adventurers
to settle in the zone, to pick up again on their own the leather business. It
was the well-known buccaneers who very quickly built forts in the island of
Tortuga, facing the northwestern coast of Hispaniola, thus beginning the
saga of Caribbean piracy. In later times, these territories were controlled
by France, having been ceded to this nation by Spain according to the provisions of the Treaty of Ryswick (1697). It was there that there emerged
the famous Saint-Domingue, which very soon came to be the richest plantation colony in the world, until its liberation in 1804 under the name
of Haiti.

The destruction and the depopulation of the villages of the *banda norte*
is not only the harshest collective repression undertaken by Spain against
its own colonists in any part of America, but also the most unjust. It's true
that on seeing their houses and haciendas burned a large group of creoles—including slaves—put up resistance to the governor's soldiers in the
Guaba valley, but at the same time chance gave the latter the opportunity
to show their loyalty to Spain. It happened that an entire Dutch squadron
that was marauding the coast offered the help of their men and their guns,
on the condition that they declare themselves to be subjects of Maurice of
Nassau. The creoles' answer, in spite of their military weakness, was a firm
negative. As a coda to this episode of the devastations, one would have to
add that the colony took centuries to recover from the adverse economic
and social consequences that the incident produced.

Parallel to the contraband in hides, there had grown up an illicit traffic
in tobacco in Venezuela. In a manner similar to that used on Hispaniola,
though not as radical, the crown prescribed the most severe proceedings.
The measure was open and direct: the burning of the tobacco fields and
the total prohibition of the crop, in spite of the commercial loss that this
entailed. With this measure enforced the crown hoped to drive the foreign merchants from the colony's coasts, and in fact that is what happened.
Except that the "tobacco fever" thereupon unleashed itself on the neigh-

boring island of Trinidad, which had been excluded from the royal directive. We know that toward 1607 no fewer than twenty ships loaded illicit tobacco in Trinidad, and that one year later the number increased to thirty. We also know that toward 1611 some 200,000 pounds of illegal tobacco were consumed in England, France, Holland, and Germany, it being taken for granted that the demand would increase endlessly. Nonetheless, at this time, only 6,000 pounds reached Seville through legal trading.

When the situation in Trinidad became unsustainable because of the recurring repressive measures, the foreign traders decided to install themselves on their own account and at their own risk on certain spots along the coast with the intention of growing the coveted plant. Thus it can be said that the first non-Iberian establishments in the Caribbean arose in the stretched-out deltas of the Orinoco and the Amazon, although they clearly could not constitute anything permanent and they scarcely held on for the time needed to bring one crop to harvest. One of these merchants, an Englishman named Thomas Warner, concluded that the coast of South America was too dangerous and set out to explore the Lesser Antilles. These islands—discovered and baptized by Columbus on his second voyage—had not been colonized for two reasons: in the first place they lacked precious metals and pearl shoals; in the second place they were inhabited by the Caribs, perhaps the fiercest and most warlike aborigines in all America. The Spaniards used to call them the useless islands, and they were visited only occasionally by the ships of the fleet to pick up water or firewood. Warner, as far as he was concerned, was interested only in planting tobacco, and he thought that he could take on the Caribs on one of the smaller islands. In the middle of his explorations, he disembarked one day on the island of San Cristóbal—now St. Kitts—and he verified the presence of fertile land and many springs. This happened in 1622, and after two years of organizing work in London, during which he founded a colonizing company, he returned to St. Kitts with a group of enterprising people. A few months later a French privateer, whose ship was at the point of shipwreck, arrived and also resolved to settle there. The little territory of St. Kitts was amicably divided between Englishmen and Frenchmen and, when the problem of the Caribs had been solved, it became the region's first non-Iberian colony. Naturally, Warner's initiative was emulated very soon. By around 1630 the Brazilian northeast and the entire bridge of islands a thousand miles long connecting Venezuela with Puerto Rico was in the hands of England, France, and Holland. That was the price that Spain—and Portugal to a lesser degree—paid for maintaining an obsolete commercial monopoly, for not knowing how to appreciate the commercial value of these territories, and for wanting to separate the creoles from any capitalist initiatives. Seville and Lisbon, which in the sixteenth century had been active centers of the expansion of the European world system,[14] passed very rapidly into the condition of intermediate cities directly and indirectly controlled by the mercantile capital of other nations. The great riches of America that arrived at the Iberian piers were forwarded at once to German, Italian, Flemish, French, and English lenders and merchants. The Peninsular epoch had passed, and from then onward its overseas territories, on which the sun never set, were to be exploited, without the inhabitants knowing it, by foreign capital which left only crumbs to the Iberian world.[15]

Concerning the creole culture that I have spoken of, it is easy to see that with the dismembering and repression of the social groups from which it emerged, its transformation became slower and its changes less radical. This happened, for example, in Hispaniola. There the devastations halted the colony's rhythm of socioeconomic transformation while at the same time suppressing the cultural influence of the foreign traders. But, above all, when the number of slaves was reduced by their massive flight from the devastated regions, the African components of the cultural interplay became weaker and lost prestige, to the extent that they began to cease being perceived as real. Later on, the Haitian annexation of Santo Domingo (1822–1844) also contributed to the rejection of the Negro, and in time the eastern part of the island—today the Dominican Republic—began to explain its more or less brown color by means of an imaginary foundational *mestizaje* with the Indian.[16] It is only very recently that this deeply rooted "whitening" myth has begun to be dismantled. Nevertheless, things did not happen this way in Cuba. There, the crown's repressions of the smuggling trade, if no less drastic in their intent, did not have the same practical effects, because of some curious events toward which we shall now turn briefly.

One would have to say first that Cuba's own creole culture was born on the eastern part of the island, in intimate connection with the *banda norte*. In a way very like that occurring on Hispaniola, Havana was the only authorized commercial port, a fact that would also mark the visible differences between this colony's western and eastern regions. Havana, because of its proximity to the Gulf Stream and its being situated facing the Florida Straight—then the best route to the Atlantic—entered into the fleet system, with the gathering there of the galleons coming from Mexico,

Portobelo, and Cartagena that were to undertake a return trip to Spain. Its rapid commercial growth would lead to its becoming the most visited city in the Caribbean. The eastern regions of Cuba, however, presented a different picture. Excluded from the great commerce's benefits and separated from Havana by hundreds of miles of dense forests, they began a contraband cattle-raising economy parallel to Hispaniola's. Thus the inhabitants of Bayamo and Puerto Príncipe—the seats of the illegal trade—felt themselves much more closely linked to those of Bayaja and La Yaguana, in Hispaniola, than to the Spaniards and creoles residing in Cuba's western region. We may establish this relationship as well with the creoles who lived on Jamaica's north coast, who were equally involved in contraband. In fact it may be said that all of the island people found to the west, east, and south of the Windward Passage constituted the first creole population, culturally speaking.[17]

In the case of Cuba, the natives of the eastern districts were branded by the colonial bureaucracy as heretical, excitable, vague, lazy, smugglers, etc. The certain thing is that in 1604, upon learning of the harsh measures taken by the crown to wipe out smuggling, the creoles of Bayamo chose rebellion as a form of protest. The official response was rapid and conclusive: hangings, excommunications, and the sending of soldiers and magistrates to the region by sea. With the object of avoiding bloodshed, the bishop Cabezas Altamirano decided to go to Bayamo as well. He did not manage to reach the city. He was captured by a Huguenot privateer who was blockading the mouth of the Cauto River, who kept him as a hostage until an Italian merchant, whose ship was anchored nearby, had the grace to put up the money for his ransom. With the bishop now free, the creoles saw the chance to ingratiate themselves with the Church and, announcing their decision to avenge the insult, they organized a multicolored troop of Indians, whites, and Negroes which succeeded in killing the privateer. As might be supposed, the bishop interceded with Philip III to arrange a pardon for the creoles, and his gesture had the greatest success. This circumstance had as its result that the villages engaged in contraband in eastern Cuba did not suffer a punishment like that inflicted by Osorio on the *banda norte* of Hispaniola. The region's inhabitants continued to smuggle more than ever, and the type of society generated by the leather economy lasted until the beginning of the nineteenth century. Its complex cultural forms also endured and, sometimes withdrawing into themselves while at other times extending outward, they made up a long-lasting creole culture.

As we know, the bishop's kidnapping and the battle against the French privateer's men underlay the composition by Silvestre de Balboa—a Canarian by birth, notary of Puerto Príncipe, and married to the daughter of a Taino chief—of the poem *Espejo de paciencia*. It is there the word *criollo* appears in writing for the first time in Cuba, applied to the hero of the piece, a Negro slave named Salvador.[18] The conditions of racial equality in which the local ranks fight against the French and, above all, the fact that Salvador is rewarded with his freedom for having personally beaten the privateer make this text the first within Caribbean literature to express a desire for racial, social, and cultural equality, a sentiment which was probably already being articulated through the whole area that bordered on the Windward Passage. We ought also to remember that accompanying the text of the *Espejo de paciencia* there were in the manuscript six sonnets of other poets of the region, which say such things as "this creole sonnet of the land"; "come to Christian Puerto Príncipe / and you will enjoy a new paradise"; "fortunate beautiful isles"; "the beloved homeland"; "Gilded isle of Cuba or Fernandina / from whose high eminent peaks / descend streams, rivers and brooks / refined gold and the finest silver." This indicates that Silvestre de Balboa's poem should not be taken as an isolated case, but rather as an example of a kind of literature that was cultivated in the eastern zone. In the *Espejo de paciencia* as well as in the accompanying sonnets, there is a passion for the island's natural world. There is no mention of Spain, but rather of Cuba, Puerto Príncipe, Bayamo, Yara, and Manzanillo, of the creole, of the mountain ranges and rivers of the region, of the local fauna and flora. Around this time the supersyncretic cult of the Virgen de la Caridad del Cobre appears, which, as we have seen, proposes a fusion of the cults of Atabey (Taino), Oshun (Yoruba), and Our Lady, constituting also an early appearance of the creoles' integrationist desire.[19] According to the oral tradition, the Virgen appeared to three humble men whose boat was about to founder in the midst of a storm in the bay of Nipe, miraculously saving their lives. The supposed names of this trio were: Juan Criollo, Juan Indio, and Juan Esclavo. In this way the Virgen de la Caridad represented a magical or transcendental space to which the European, African, and American Indian origins of the region's people were connected. The fact that the three men carried the name Juan—they are known as the Three Juans—that they were together in the same boat, and that all were saved by the Virgen conveys mythologically the desire to reach a sphere of effective equality where the racial, social, and cultural differences that conquest, colonization, and slavery created would coexist without violence. This space—which can be seen at the same time as a utopia to be reached or as a lost paradise to be recovered poetically—is repeated time and again in the diverse expressions that refer to the Virgen, such as images, medallions, prints, lithographs, printed prayers, songs, popular poetry, and even tattoos.

One should add to this that—beyond literature and religious beliefs—the popular cuisine also expresses this same desire for integration. The oldest and most prestigious dish in Cuba, called *ajiaco,* is achieved by filling a thick, flavorful broth with native (maize, potato, *malanga,* boniato, yucca, *ají,* tomato), European (squash, dried beef, fresh beef, pork, and chicken), and African (plantains and yams) ingredients.[20] But creole culture's most important signs can be found in popular music and dance. These emerge near the end of the sixteenth century, out of the interplay of European and African components, and they travel quickly from east to west, together with the occupation of professional musician.[21] Exported to Seville through the port of Havana, they quite probably were the immediate antecedents—if not the dances themselves—of what became known there as the sarabande and the chaconne. But we shall come back to this later. The important thing now is to point out that, after the devastations in Hispaniola and the taking of Jamaica by the English in 1655, the eastern zone of Cuba remained in practice as the only active seat of culture of the Windward Passage type. There, linked to the illegal leather economy, it produced notable happenings in religion, literature, music, dance, and cooking. Recognizing itself as "creole"—in literature at least—it extended itself throughout the island while at the same time enriching its interplay with components characteristic of other locales, above all of Havana (for example, the cult of the Virgen de Regla, which is an attempt to reconcile the *orisha* Yemaya with Our Lady).

Notwithstanding the individual importance of these supersyncretic manifestations in everything that touches on the points of generation of various cultural discourses, I think that their greatest contribution resides in their carrying the wish to reach the state of racial, social, and cultural nonviolence that we have been observing. This wish kept reiterating itself in Cuba during the period of creole dominance and it must have contributed greatly to the formation of a desire for nationhood, since it bespoke a just homeland for all and carried a utopian project of coexistence that made up for the fragmentary, unstable, and conflictual Antillean existence. It must have been particularly useful during the wars of independence, since it would not just help in getting whites and Negroes to fight against a common enemy, but would also enable men of color to reach high commands and positions in the Liberating Army and the Republic of Arms. It is very significant that, among all Cuban institutions, it was in fact the Asociación de Veteranos—the great majority of those who fought against Spain were people of color—that proposed and finally succeeded in getting the Virgen de la Caridad recognized by the Vatican and by the state as Cuba's patron saint. For the old soldiers, the Virgen, in her role as the *Gran Madre mulata,* was a much more concrete and direct representation of the *patria blanquinegra* than were the abstractions on the new republic's flag and seal. It is also very significant that previously, within the realm of political ideas, this idea of ethno-patriotic assimilation should have been taken up by José Martí. As we know, Martí did not limit himself to repeating it only among Cubans, but rather he projected it out toward all of Hispanoamerica, proposing the idea of a *mestizo* continental homeland. Moreover, now in our own epoch, it is easy to recognize a previous reading of the powerful matriarchal myth of the *Virgen* in the works of Fernando Ortiz, Lydia Cabrera, Amadeo Roldán, Wilfredo Lam, Alejo Carpentier, Nicolás Guillén and many other Cuban intellectuals and artists who discovered the enormous cultural possibilities that lay within the Afro-European interplay.

Among the texts that the many travelers to Cuba have written, I have found one that succeeds in describing, in sufficient detail, the sociocultural field over which the old families of the interior moved at the beginning of the nineteenth century, that is, before the plantation system incorporated them or threw them out. The text refers to the island's eastern region, which three centuries earlier had been the enclave of the contraband leather economy, and it was written by the French traveler Julien Mellet, who was called *El Americano:*

> The majority of the inhabitants are mulattos or quadroons and have irregular customs . . . Bayamo is a city built on an enchanting plain, fertile with cotton, sugarcane, coffee, and tobacco. This plain, furthermore, produces much maize, vegetables, plantains, and a bit of rice. There is also a large crop of *yarey* . . . The women are very pretty and they dress very well and with as much or more elegance as in the capital, of which I will speak more later; but they have the defect of drinking and smoking very often . . . Their table is, in truth, very clean and many dishes are served; but one looks in vain for more agreeable things, that is, bread and wine. The first is replaced by the *casabe* and others of the country's roots, fried or broiled, and by rice cooked with

a great quantity of ground pepper . . . After this another dish is served
the mere sight of which is enough to disgust anyone not in the habit
of eating it. This big dish consists of potato roots and plantains, with
a few bits of salted meat, all cooked together . . . Wine is replaced
by water, which is served in beautiful English pitchers . . . After the
meal the slaves bring cigars and then, everyone smoking, they continue drinking until time for the siesta . . . After two or three hours
they awaken and smoke more cigars. Moments later coffee is served,
which one must drink in order to avoid being ridiculed, and immediately the girls of the house begin to play the guitar and to sing rather
indecent songs. That is how most of the inhabitants pass their lives.[22]

Later on, Mellet speaks of the creoles' liking for games of chance and
he gives an extended and critical description of the festive pilgrimages to
the shrine of the Virgen de la Caridad. The reproaches that the traveler
makes of the locals' customs are to their greatest credit, as far as their creole
nature is concerned. Mellet judges the creole culture from the viewpoint
of his own European values and he does not understand the mysteries of
the *ajiaco* nor does he know how to appreciate the glorious combination of
coffee and tobacco, which soon would spread throughout the world. But,
above all, he does not understand a freer way of living, more natural, further from the moralizing conventions of European-style Christianity, from
codes regarding good manners, and from the deep tensions that in Europe
separated the members of a single family according to their age, their sex,
and their degree of kinship with the chief. That is why he censures the
social behavior of the "girls" and the creole woman, without noting that
this came essentially out of a quality of resistance to the patriarchal discourse of the West, because everything creole, in Cuba, had flowed since
the beginning from the source that was a Virgin who held everyone in
her lap.

The island creole and the mainland creole

The creole in the Spanish Antilles was not the same as the one on *tierra
firme*. In the Antilles it was not necessary to deculturate the Indian, because he disappeared with servitude on the *encomienda*, and with massa-
cres, famines, mass suicides, and contagious diseases that the conquistadors
brought and against which his organism had no defense. Of the aboriginal
peoples' rapid depopulation, Eric Williams, basing himself on Las Casas

and Oviedo, says: "The results are to be seen in the best estimates that have been prepared of the trend of population in Hispaniola. These place the population in 1492 at between 200,000 and 300,000. By 1508 the number was reduced to 60,000; in 1510 it was 46,000; in 1512, 20,000; in 1514, 14,000. In 1548 Oviedo doubted whether five hundred Indians of pure stock remained."[23]

Of course this ethnic calamity was not limited to Hispaniola. The Bahamas' native population disappeared completely within a very few years, victim of slave-capturing expeditions; Cuba also suffered these expeditions, as did other islands and mainland coasts, and it had to endure further the special phenomenon of induced famine when the natives were prohibited from tending their crops. The demographic catastrophe that Las Casas would observe in Cuba caused him to renounce his *encomienda* and make himself the defender of the Indians, whose race he saw disappearing day by day.

The quick annihilation of the Antillean Indian resulted in the islands' remaining empty, that is, as islands where the only testimony of ancient habitation was to be looked for in the first chronicles of the conquest and in certain aboriginal words used to name the toponymy, flora, fauna, and objects unknown in Europe. In a matter of half a century, the Greater Antilles were definitively populated by people from Europe and Africa, from different cultures, whose economic relations under the aegis of the mother country were to give shape to a colonial society lacking the Indian's living presence.

The situation on the mainland of America was otherwise. Especially on the huge plateaus of Mesoamerica and South America, where there existed densely settled civilizations based on irrigation (*civilizaciones de regadío*), with notable urban development and much more hierarchy than the indigenous Antillean societies. Although the impact of the conquest and the first decades of colonization would cause millions of deaths, the territories were not depopulated as a result. The Indian survived, and he did so carrying within him many of his various peoples' oldest traditions. It was precisely the Indian's tenacious cultural resistance that motivated the Spanish crown to undertake a vast and intense campaign of Christianization, which was unlike the mass baptisms that the Antillean Indians had uncomprehendingly received. In Mexico and Peru, above all, the deculturation of the native was undertaken to enable him to participate as a docile worker in the colonization's socioeconomic project. Thus the Aztec temples and palaces were demolished, the Mayans' painted books were burned, the

Incas' agrarian structure was dismantled, and the *encomienda* was conceded on a hereditary basis for one, two, and even three generations. The tribunes of the Inquisition's Holy Office, practically unknown in the Caribbean, acted severely there against those suspected of practicing old "idolatries" or new "heresies." The religious orders, charged with the deculturating work, took possession of the fields and towns, enriching themselves to such a degree that they aroused the envy of the Spanish kings.

Certainly, there was African slavery in the great continental viceroyalties, but the Negro was gradually assimilated by the mass of ladinos.[24] More-over, the plantation had a rather limited effect in these great colonies, in which "civilizing" the existing settlements was of greater importance than exploiting the land.[25] The gaudy viceregal city—think of Bernardo de Bal-buena's description in his *Grandeza mexicana*—was, in the first place, a center of political, religious, and economic power that radiated its adminis-trative functioning outward over subjects whose numbers exceeded those of many European nations. Its economic direction was not tilted toward the export of plantation products, as was the case in the Caribbean, but toward extracting the greatest possible quantity of precious metals from the abundant mining resources that existed there. The mines were not worked by slaves who had to be bought; they were worked by ladinos who had been enrolled through the *mita,* an indigenous form of conscription that the Spaniards transformed into a rotating system of forced labor from which there was no release. Moreover, the economic situation of a Mexi-can or Peruvian landowner was not related to any kind of monoproductive agriculture meant for export and dependent on the slave trade, but rather to an agriculture that was scarcely exportable and based on the lending of personal services and on small payments from the villagers who took care of the fields. It is to be supposed that the landowners of the great viceroyalties did not feel themselves bound tightly to the mother coun-try, as surely was the case with the slaveholding planters of the Caribbean. It was a question of the former's being landed barons, for the most part descendants of conquistadors, who disdained the royal functionaries and were at the same time disdained by them. They were the first to disobey the laws passed to protect the Indians' human rights, and the first to rebel against any royal decree that affected their interests as landlords and *en-comenderos.* They were always suspicious in the crown's eyes, which was the reason that they were discriminated against and denied a chance to hold high administrative, military, and religious posts.

The Caribbean planter's problematic economy, on the other hand, was directly tied to the interests of the Spanish state. With mining resources completely exhausted at the beginning of the sixteenth century along with all Indian labor, the only possible Antillean export—as we have already seen—was agricultural products, which accounts for the region's early sugar, leather, and tobacco economies. So from the time of the first plantation on Hispaniola, continuing the slave trade was an interest common to the planter and the crown. This dependence became much tighter at the end of the seventeenth century—by about the time the European world system had generated millions of new consumers of plantation products, and demand for sugar, tobacco, coffee, cacao, cotton, dyes, etc. created the need to furnish the Caribbean plantations with large Negro contingents. The most representative colony of this time is Saint-Domingue (the former *banda norte*), which had completed the transition from the plantation to the Plantation in the few decades that it had been under French administration. According to the available statistics, the colony had 792 mills, 197 million coffee trees, 24 million cotton plants, almost 3 million cacao trees, and 2,587 indigo factories. These represented a capital investment of about 1,500 million francs, and their production was of such volume that France used 63 percent of its ships to carry the merchandise to its ports.[26] The census of 1789 gives the following round numbers: white population, 40,000 (owning 8,512 plantations); mulattos and free Negroes, 28,000 (with 2,500 plantations), and slave population 452,000 (representing 90 percent of the total population).[27] The sugar production that year was more than 141 million pounds.

In 1791, when Boukman's uprising initiated the colony's revolutionary process, Saint-Domingue's plantations began to disintegrate under the rebels' incendiary torch. A year later, the plantation interests of Havana's creoles, represented by Francisco de Arango y Parreño, convinced Spain of the need to take advantage of the market's scarcity of sugar caused by the events in Saint-Domingue, and Cuba began its transition toward the Plantation. Immediately the slave traffic to the island increased markedly, mills multiplied around Havana, and within a few years they invaded the western region. In its implacable march, burning entire forests in its boilers, the sugar-milling machine began to shape another Cuba ("*Cuba grande*"), which did not correspond to the creole interests of the non-sugaring regions ("*Cuba chiquita*"). This is easily seen if one bears in mind that the sugar plantation, even within the conditions of the time, was an extensive cultivation that demanded great stretches of good land, massive slave importations, and Spain's commercial, military, and administrative protection. Furthermore, the creole existing outside the sugar plantation held or had the use of the most productive land, was not essentially a slave owner, and lacked political influence because he was far from Havana, even tending toward a desire for independence. In any case the common interests of both the planters and the crown—which also owned mills—made things such that, in spite of the existence of serious contradictions between the colony and the mother country, the creole sugarocracy, as it was called, would teeter for years between the extremes of independentist sentiment and fear of the ruin that must accompany the slaves' emancipation, since the thousands of Negroes who worked the plantations would surely be needed to defeat the Spaniards. This helps to explain that it was only the creoles living in the eastern and central provinces who would participate in the struggles for independence.[28]

Thus we can see that relations between the creole and the mother country in Hispanoamerica entailed different degrees of compromise; this was lesser in the cases of the mainland colonies, and greater in the island ones, where the desire for racial, political, social, and cultural integration with independentist force was expressed only in a type of society marginal to the Plantation's power discourse. It is significant that Simón Bolívar, at the beginning of his liberation campaigns, did not have slavery's abolition among his plans. Doubtless his origin among the Venezuelan aristocratic planters was weighing on him. He changed his opinion only when, having been beaten by the Spanish troops, he sought help from Haiti. There, President Pétion made him see that it was not feasible to free the Americas from Spain if the liberty to be gained was not for everyone.

In the viceroyalties of Nueva España, Nueva Granada, and Río de la Plata, and even in Peru, the most slaveholding of all, the colonial socioeconomic structure was less an obstacle to the landowners' independentist feelings. The many royal functionaries kept coming and going, the viceregal courts followed one upon the other, the parish priests were promoted and left for other towns, the military garrisons kept getting moved around and their ranks renewed; but the creole on the hacienda and the ladino always stayed put, held to the land. Hence Thomas Gage, as early as 1630, made the following observation:

> The condition of the Indians of this country of Guatemala is as sad and as much to be pitied as of any Indians in America . . . They suffer great oppression from the Spaniards, live in great bitterness and are under hard bondage . . . They are not allowed the use of any weapons

or arms not even the bows and arrows which their ancestors formerly used. So whereas the Spaniards are secured from any hurt or annoyance from them because they are unarmed, so any other nation that shall be encouraged to invade that land will also be secure from the Indians. Consequently, the Spaniards' own policy against the Indians may be their greatest ruin and destruction, for the abundance of their Indians would be of no help to them . . . Lastly, the Creoles, who are also sore oppressed by them, would rejoice in such a day, and would yield, preferring to live with freedom and liberty under a foreign people rather than be oppressed any longer by those of their own blood.[29]

If Gage was quite right in seeing the unbridgeable chasm that undermined colonial society, he was deceiving himself to presume that the creoles would consent willingly to a life under French, Dutch, or English domination. History demonstrated the exact opposite. The creole landowner, especially in the great viceroyalties, was in many cases a direct descendant of the conquistadors and first colonizers; he felt the land to be his own, but at the same time he could not forget his Iberian descent, the customs of the old country, his Catholic faith. The clumsy discrimination of which he was the object and the economic stagnation from which he suffered separated him from the crown but not from Spanish traditions; his aspirations were of a *caudillista* type, and when independence was achieved he was to be seen among the conservative ranks, along with such men as Iturbide and Rosas.

In short, we can say that in the islands the creole sugar power resided in its links to the mother country within an economic relationship connected to the European world system, which tended to heighten the degree of dependency. In the viceroyalties, though, creole agriculture was not dominated by the plantation; the scarce profits were achieved through the ladino's servitude and tributes as he worked the land with a mixture of medieval and indigenous techniques, and sold the products—all but the hides—in local markets. To this one must add the limitations imposed by the trade monopoly, which banned wheat and wine production to prevent competition with Spanish imports. It is easy to see that the mainland creole was considerably closer to independence than was the Antillean plantation creole, upon whom titles of nobility and other sinecures kept raining.

There was also, as Gage observes, the matter of the Indian. Contrary to what occurred in the Antilles, the native people in the viceroyalties survived and gradually their demographic importance began to grow and compensate for the losses of the early years of colonization. The Indian of Central and South America, deculturated or not, managed to subsist, and he could always verify the conquest's violent impact by comparing his miserable state with the portentous ruins of his past, which gave clear testimony of the civilized achievements that men and women of his own blood had realized. The enslaved Indians to whom Gage refers had before them the architectonic remains of the great Mayan cities in which their ancestors would have lived. How could they be made to feel no rancor toward the race that now held sway over them? I think that this explains in part why everything Spanish often rouses a certain resentment in the continental nations that were once Spanish colonies, unlike what happens in the Dominican Republic, Cuba, and Puerto Rico.

The Plantation and the Africanization of culture

The history of the non-Hispanic possessions in the Caribbean is complex in the extreme. In any event, this book does not hope to cover the history of the different colonial blocs. It is of interest nonetheless that the presence of Spain's rival powers in the area coincided, almost from the first years, with the sustained and dizzying increase in the demand for sugar and other tropical agricultural products, thanks to the increase in consumer demand that capitalism aroused. With rapid enrichment as their incentive, the Caribbean colonies belonging to England, France, and Holland began to exploit the land with total abandon according to the model of the slave plantation. In fact, after a brief period characterized by the presence of the small landholder and the European artisan, attended by servants of the same race and creed whose services were contracted for a fixed number of years, the plantation economy, with its continuous slave importations, burst upon the Caribbean scene.

Spain, in a state of total economic, political, and social decadence during the last years of the Hapsburg rulers and embroiled in successive wars with the nations that had the most influence upon the European world system, did not participate actively in this stage of commercial expansion and capital accumulation. Moreover, its Caribbean colonies were the objects of uninterrupted attack from privateers and pirates, as likewise was the traffic in riches transported from the Indies to Seville. We must bear in mind that the first of these attacks materialized in 1523, and that the so-called age of piracy ended at about 1720; that is to say after two centuries of constant boardings, combats, burnings, and sackings. All of that without even counting the many official wars in which the Caribbean found itself involved, from Valois's to Teddy Roosevelt's. This is why the efforts of the colonial governments were to be centered, especially from the sixteenth to the eighteenth century, on the construction of forts and the adoption of defensive measures to protect not just the port cities but also the galleons that circled the Caribbean picking up loads of gold and silver in Cartagena, Portobelo, and San Juan de Ulúa.[30] Thus the Greater Antilles—what remained of them after the French and English occupations—if they in fact did keep on producing some sugar within a system of trading posts, stayed apart from a true plantation economy and therefore apart from the massive introduction of slaves. At the start of the eighteenth century, when the machinery of the plantations had been installed firmly in the English, French, and Dutch colonies, the Spanish islands presented demographic, economic, and social panoramas that were very different from those that predominated in the rest of the Caribbean.

The fact that Spain was not to undertake to build a politics of the plantation in its Antillean colonies until the end of the eighteenth century had consequences of such importance as to differentiate historically the Hispanic from the non-Hispanic islands. If we compare the demographic figures corresponding to the different colonial blocs, it will be seen that the percentage of slaves relative to the rest of the population was much lower in the Spanish Antilles than in the rival powers' colonies; at the same time it will be observed that the free Negro and mulatto population is much more important in the former than in the latter, as can be seen in the table.

The demographic and social structure of Spain's colonies in the Caribbean, with a smaller proportion of slaves and a greater number of whites and freedmen, is a reflection of its late exposure to the transformative dynamics of the plantation economy. The possibilities for analysis that figures of this kind offer are of incalculable value to the full appreciation of the differences that come into play in the Caribbean region. The difference that Froude noticed between Havana and Kingston can be explained in large part by the fact that at the beginning of the eighteenth century the island of Cuba was more a colony of settlement than of exploitation, and that its economic activity was limited by a monopolist, restrictive mercantile regime that had yet to implant the plantation structure firmly. The situation in Jamaica, however, was becoming very different. After a period characterized by the protection of privateers and pirates who raided the Spanish colonies, a period dominated by the interests of the Brotherhood of the Coast and by Henry Morgan's presence in Port Royal, the colonial administration broke away from the buccaneers and set its eye on perfecting the plantation system. By 1800, as the table shows, 88.2 percent of its population consisted of slaves, and "white power," made up of planters, employees, traders, functionaries, and military men, counted for a mere 4.4 percent of the total number of inhabitants. I mean by this that while Havana grew like a city similar to those in Spain—as Froude would observe —Kingston grew like a city of the Plantation; that is, scarcely more than an urban precinct dominated by sugar warehouses, commercial offices, the governor's house, the fort, the docks, and the slave shacks. When the creoles of Havana in those years were to feel like setting the stages for an expansion of the sugar industry, it was a matter of people who were born there, people who came from the oldest families, who had lived there for years in relation to civic institutions like the Church and the school, the book industry and the press, the patriotic society and the university, the consulate and the department of public works, the botanical garden and the theater, etc. Consequently, Havana was transformed into a city of plazas, esplanades, towers, walls, palaces, and theaters, all this before it was to turn out to be the capital of the Plantation. When the latter started to materialize, it had to adapt itself to the model of settlement that we have just described.

The differences that existed among the Caribbean colonies, and even the differences that we now perceive, were created in large part by the epoch in which the Plantation took over within each. Thus, in Froude's time, one could observe in the British colonies, in relation to the Spanish ones, a lesser degree of economic diversification, a smaller number of smallholders and artisans, a more restricted internal market, a poorer system of transportation and communications, a more reduced middle class, a weaker institutional life, a more deficient system of education, a greater conflict with the language of the mother country, and a tardier appearance of arts and letters.

Hence the differences that Froude saw between the cities in the Spanish colonies and those of the English ones was owing mainly to the epochs in which they had set themselves as capitals of the Plantation. Some had sprung up in a more or less normal fashion and others were marked, almost from their founding, by slaveholding despotism, impermanence, absentee ownership, and price instability on the international sugar market. Froude did not realize that cities such as Kingston, Bridgetown, Georgetown, Cayenne, Fort-de-France, Paramaribo, etc. had been built in fact as Planta-

Caribbean Population by Castes, Early 19th Century

				Slave population	
Colony	Year	Total population	Slave population	As % of colony's total	As of n wh
British Antilles					
Anguilla		?			
Antigua	1832	35,412	29,537	83.4	89
Bahamas	1810	16,718	11,146	66.7	87
Barbados	1834	100,000	80,861	80.6	92
Barbuda		?			
Berbice	1811	25,959	25,169	97.0	99
Bermuda	1812	9,900	4,794	48.4	91
Demerara	1811	57,386	53,655	93.5	96
Dominica	1811	26,041	21,728	83.4	87
Essequibo	1811	19,645	18,125	92.3	96
Grenada & Carriacou	1811	31,362	29,381	93.6	96
[Br.] Honduras	1790	2,656	2,024	76.2	84
Jamaica	1800	340,000	300,000	88.2	89
Montserrat	1812	7,383	6,537	88.5	94
Nevis	1812	10,430	9,326	89.4	93
St. Christopher	1812	23,491	19,885	84.6	90
St. Lucia	1810	17,485	14,397	82.3	88
St. Vincent	1812	24,253	22,020	90.8	94
Tobago	1811	17,830	16,897	94.8	98
Tortola		?			
Trinidad	1811	32,664	21,143	64.7	73
Virgin Islands					
Danish Antilles					
St. Croix	1841	—	20,000		
St. John		?			
St. Thomas	1841	7,000	5,000	71.4	76
Dutch Antilles					
Saba		?			
St. Eustatia	1850	2,500	2,000	80.0	95
St. Martin	1850	3,600	3,000	83.3	
Curaçao	1833	15,027	5,894	39.2	47
Surinam	1830	56,325	48,784	86.6	90
Spanish Antilles					
Cuba	1827	704,487	286,942	40.7	32
Puerto Rico	1860	583,181	41,738	7.1	14
Santo Domingo	1791	125,000	15,000	12.0	
Swedish Antilles					
St. Bartholomew	1840	7,000	?		
French Antilles					
Guadaloupe	1836	107,810	81,642	75.7	
Martinique	1789	96,158	83,414	86.7	94
Saint-Domingue	1791	520,000	452,000	86.9	94
Guiana					
St. Martin (part)	1836	3,869	2,925	75.6	
Marie Galante	1836	13,188	10,116	76.7	
Saintes	1836	1,139	569	49.9	
Desirada	1836	1,568	1,070	68.2	

Source: Franklin W. Knight, The Caribbean The Genesis of a Fragmented Nationalism (New York: Oxford Universi
Press, 1978).

	Free non-white population			White population		
Number	As % of total	As % of all non-whites	As % free	Number	As % of colony's totals	As % free
3,531	10.0	10.7	64.0	1,980	5.6	36.0
1,600	9.6	12.6	29.2	3,872	23.0	70.8
6,584	6.5	7.5	33.9	12,797	12.7	66.1
240	1.0	1.0	30.3	550	2.0	69.7
451	4.6	8.6	8.7	4,755	48.0	91.3
2,223	3.9	4.0	51.3	2,108	3.6	48.7
2,988	11.4	12.1	69.3	1,325	5.2	30.7
757	3.9	4.0	50.0	763	3.9	50.0
1,210	3.9	4.0	61.0	771	2.5	39.0
371	14.0	15.5	58.7	261	9.8	41.3
35,000	10.2	10.5	70.0	15,000	4.4	25.0
402	5.4	5.8	47.5	444	6.1	52.5
603	5.8	6.1	54.6	501	4.8	45.4
1,996	8.5	9.1	55.4	1,610	6.9	44.6
1,878	10.7	11.5	60.8	1,210	7.0	39.2
1,406	5.7	6.0	62.9	827	3.4	37.1
350	2.0	2.0	37.5	583	3.2	62.5
7,493	22.9	26.2	63.3	4,353	13.3	36.7
?				3,200		
?				?		
1,500	21.4	23.0	75.0	500	7.2	25.0
?				?		
100	4.0	4.8	20.0	400	16.0	80.0
?	—	—	—	600	16.6	—
6,531	43.5	52.6	71.4	2,602	17.3	28.6
5,041	8.9	9.4	66.8	2,500	4.4	33.2
106,494	15.1	27.1	25.5	311,051	44.1	74.5
241,037	41.3	85.2	44.5	300,406	51.5	55.5
?						
?						
5,235	5.4	6.0	33.3	10,636	11.0	66.7
28,000	5.3	6.0	41.0	40,000	7.6	59.0

tion ports; they answered the requirements of societies where, on average, nine out of every ten inhabitants had been slaves at one time, and this fact made it superfluous to think about adopting measures that would contribute to raising, to a degree greater than that which was strictly necessary, levels of urbanization, institutionalization, education, public services, and recreation. Although slavery had already disappeared when Froude visited the Caribbean, the Plantation continued to exist, and the region's cities still showed the marks of their recent slaveholding past. One should also consider that, for many years, the ethnocentric and colonialist thinking of the European mother countries refused to admit that the Caribbean population of African origin had any need of living standards as dignified as those prevailing in their own societies. From this viewpoint and the reactionary opinions that it engendered, of which Froude was one of the best known purveyors, the Afro-Caribbean was a lazy being, unenterprising, irresponsible, and likely to acquire all sorts of social defects; a collective being incapable of governing himself and of properly constituting a state; in sum, a second-class citizen who had to be kept at a distance and who would have to be content with very little.

One ought to ask whether the differences that Froude saw extended analogously into the cultural sphere. I think that they did. But I also think that these differences are closely related to the processes that transformed the plantation into the Plantation. To show this we may begin with an accepted premise, let's say, the fact that if it's quite easy to find African cultural features within each of the Caribbean nations, it is no less certain that those features present themselves in each case with a unique extension and depth. For example, it is generally agreed that Haiti, Cuba, and Jamaica are, in this order, the islands whose cultures show a greater degree of Africanization. Moreover, among the Antillean islands with the least African culture, Barbados is usually presented as the first example.

Our demonstration's second step would be, naturally, to elaborate a satisfactory explanation of this phenomenon using the plantation/Plantation conversion, or better, to offer a hypothesis applicable not just to these four islands but to all the Antilles. Let's start with Haiti.

In 1804, when the Haitian nation was formally constituted under the government of Dessalines, about 90 percent of the adult population had been slaves. If one takes into account that in the latest years of colonization the Plantation was absorbing 40,000 new slaves,[31] and that the life expectancy of a slave under the conditions of intense exploitation did not reach ten years, one has to conclude that the great majority of this population had been born in Africa. That is to say that when Haiti emerged as a free nation the African components of its culture not only dominated over the European ones, but were more active, or if you like, on the offensive, as they had been exalted during the revolutionary process in the struggle against the slaveholding power of the whites. Even more, the revolts led by Boukman, Jean François, and other leaders—which we shall consider in Chapter 4—were organized under the influence of the *loas* of voodoo, a belief whose supersyncretism is dominated by African elements. Later on, after Dessalines—a former slave—was assassinated, the country stayed divided with Christophe in the north and Pétion in the south, reunifying in 1818 under Boyer's government. The fact that both Pétion and Boyer represented the group of rich, Catholic, and enlightened mulattos made it turn out that hundreds of thousands of Negroes fell under the control of the new "mulatto power," not as slaves, certainly, but surely in a position of servitude that kept them from leaving the plantations on which they worked. Thus the Plantation reorganized itself anew in Haiti, although under other work and power relations. It is easy to suppose that this vast population of hundreds of thousands of men and women of African origin maintained many of their customs, among them the cults that the Church prohibited. These old slaves—like Ti Noel of *El reino de este mundo*—were the ones who kept alive the cults devoted to Damballah, to Papa Legba, to Ogun, the voodoo and petro cults, with their ritual sacrifices, to whose sacred drums the greater part of the Haitian population, especially in the countryside, still responds.[32]

If the former slaves had known a more complete liberty in Boyer's time, the Africanness of the culture would surely be even greater now. In any case, I think that it is possible to sustain the argument that the rapid and intense expansion of the plantation system in French Saint-Domingue, perhaps the most accelerated model of the Plantation that the world has ever seen, brought as its consequence an unusual density of African population. As it was liberated within the span of a single generation, its members had scarcely become acculturated toward European ways—voodoo shows this clearly—and the cultural components that they brought with them prevailed in the interplay over those that came from Europe via the mulattos. It is rather significant that the new republic rejected the name Saint-Domingue to adopt that of Haiti, which was the Taino name for Hispaniola when Columbus arrived; and also that Haitian *Créole* should take a considerable number of words from the aboriginal language. To my mind, this indicates that as far as the past was concerned there was a popular preference for what was aboriginal over what had come from Europe.

But how do we explain Cuba's having now a more Africanized culture than those of Barbados or Jamaica? If we look at the statistical table, we shall see that its slave population was less than 41 percent, while Jamaica's, in 1800, was more than 88 percent. Moreover, if we compare the cultural life on the two islands throughout our century, we see that Cuban religious beliefs, music, dance, painting, literature, and folklore show an African influence unequaled in any other Antillean nation except Haiti. What happened in Cuba that didn't happen in Jamaica or in Barbados? I think that many factors come in to play here to differentiate one island from another, but I believe that one of the most important is the late date at which the Plantation was first set up in Cuba. The number of Negroes introduced upon the island between 1512 and 1761 is estimated at 60,000, which puts the annual average at some 250 slaves. The majority of them did not work on sugar plantations—Cuba exported the product in very limited amounts at that time—but were distributed within the leather economy, produce cultivation, public works, and domestic service. We already know that in the eastern provinces the Negro participated actively in the formation of the early Antillean culture that we have called creole culture; from there, at least in its magical-religious beliefs, its music and its dances, it moved on to Havana, where it would adapt itself to the specificities of the local culture.

There is proof that there existed, in the seventeenth century, what we would call a creole culture in Havana and in other important localities, each of them different from the others. This would have been nurtured by feasts to various patron saints or Virgins—sequences of days in which people made music, danced, ate certain dishes, and entertained themselves with all kinds of games and pastimes. In 1714, for example, the Virgen de Regla (Yemaya in the syncretic cult) was consecrated as Havana's patron, setting off festivals that lasted for eight days and in which whites, slaves, and free Negroes participated.[33] But this also happened with the patrons of any other place, not even counting dates such as the one dedicated to the Virgen de la Caridad, whose prolonged festivals were celebrated throughout Cuba in different ways.[34] On these dates, the so-called *cabildos,* which were associations of slaves and free Negroes grouped together according to their African nations of origin, played an important role. I mean to say by all this that, before the formation of what we could call a Cuban national culture—a phenomenon that occurred later under the Plantation—it is possible to imagine a type of creole culture characterized by the variety of its local manifestations but also, above all, by the participation of the Negro, slave or not, in conditions advantageous to him as an acculturating agent. It should be noted how high the percentage of free Negroes was in Cuba; in 1774, for example, they made up 20.3 percent of the entire population, a figure that tells of their mobility and their being in position to exert cultural influence in the process of Africanization. At the end of the eighteenth century, when the machinery of the plantation began to extend itself into the environs of Havana, there already existed a kind of creole culture, considerably Africanized, in many places on the island.[35]

In Jamaica's case, the most interesting comparison is with Barbados, which is taken today—as I've said—as one of the least Africanized islands in the Caribbean. Let's take a brief look at each island's plantation history. The English landed on Barbados in 1625. The island's early labor force was made up of colonists, Carib Indians, white slaves, criminals, deported political prisoners, and indentured servants. In 1645 there were 18,300 whites, of which 11,200 were landowners, and 5,680 Negro slaves—three whites for every Negro—in an economy based on small-holding cultivation of tobacco. In 1667, though, there were 745 owners and 82,023 slaves.[36] What had happened? The sugar Plantation had arrived and, displacing the tobacco small holdings, took up nearly all the land on the island. In 1698, a mere thirty years later, there was a ratio of nearly eighteen slaves for each white man.

Concerning Jamaica, the first thing to take into account is that it was colonized by Spain at the beginning of the sixteenth century, and it fell into England's hands in 1655; that is, it lay for 150 years within the Spanish colonial system and its northern zone was a depository of creole culture of the Windward Passage type. When the Spaniards left the island, many slaves ran off and stayed for years in the country's inland mountains. As we know, during the earliest years of English rule the city of Port Royal replaced Tortuga as home of the buccaneers of the Brotherhood of the Coast. England, and France and Holland as well, used their services in making war on Spain. Their best-known leader was Henry Morgan, who was without a doubt the most popular man in Jamaica during the decade of the 1660s. Morgan sacked cities in Cuba, Nicaragua, Mexico, Venezuela, and Panama, leaving behind an entire cycle of legends, whose literary implications will be taken up in Chapter 6. The sack of Portobelo yielded 100,000 pounds sterling, and in the capture of Maracaibo 260,000 doubloons were taken.[37] It is no exaggeration to say that in the Jamaica of those years there was an economy based on privateering, in which the Negro participated. But Charles II's restoration brought peace with Spain, and in the last decades of the century the investors' interest turned to the already existing plantation business. During the eighteenth century Jamaica completed its transition to the Plantation and surpassed Barbados as a sugar exporter. It is calculated that more than 600,000 slaves entered the colony between 1700 and 1786.[38]

Now having both islands' history sketched out before us, we can observe the phenomenon that the greater or lesser Africanness of the islands' present-day cultures does not necessarily correspond to the Negro population's demographic importance, but may be explained rather by the epoch at which the Plantation machinery was set up. The later it was implanted, as happened in Jamaica when compared to Barbados, the Africans already living there, slaves or not, would have had occasion actively to bring their cultural influence to bear on European things for a more prolonged period of time. In Plantation conditions, in spite of the enormous percentages reached by the numbers of slaves in relation to the total population, the African was reduced to living under an incarcerating regimen of forced labor, which stood in the way of his being able to exert a cultural influence upon the European and creole population. Still more, he was living under a deculturating regimen that took direct action against his language, his religion, and his customs, as African practices were looked upon with suspicion and many of them were controlled or prohibited. Furthermore, the plantation owners would spread out their slave contingents according to place of origin so that communication between them would be more difficult in case of revolt. One should add to all this the fact that slave children born on the plantation were very soon separated from their mothers, thus impeding the transmission of cultural components through a maternal tie. Finally, we must remember that one of every three slaves died during his first three years of intense exploitation. In more general working conditions, half of Barbados's slave population had to be renewed every eight years, and of Jamaica it has been observed that 40 percent of the slaves died in a period of three years.[39] In my opinion, one has to conclude that the Negro slave who arrived at a Caribbean colony before the Plantation was organized contributed much more toward Africanizing the creole culture than did the one who came within the great shipments typical of the Plantation in its heyday.

In reality, the key to Africanization lay, to my way of thinking, in the degree of mobility that the African possessed when he came to the Caribbean. A state of rebellion allowed the freest cultural expression, as was the case with the Haitian slave. He is followed in order by the *cimarrón* (runaway slave)—an important factor in Jamaica—since in the *palenques* (settlements of runaways) a kind of life was lived that was characterized by the interplay of African components exchanged among men and women coming from different regions of Africa; these components were carried throughout their lives by the *palenques*'s members, and they could be communicated to the outer world in various ways, as will be seen in Chapter 8. After the cimarron, there came in successive order the freedman, the urban slave, the smallholder's slave, the slave who worked on non-sugar-growing plantations, and finally, the so-called *esclavo de ingenio* (mill slave). In spite of the natural differences of opinions held by different investigators of the Caribbean, the judgment that the slave on the sugar plantation was the most intensely exploited and repressed seems to be 100 percent unanimous. In my opinion, consequently, this slave would have been the least active African agent in the process of communicating his culture to the creole social milieu.

We also observe, in each Caribbean nation, cultural differences with respect to Asian components. There were colonies, such as Santo Domingo and Puerto Rico, that had no Asian immigration in the last century, owing to their relative abundance of local labor in relation to their plantations' requirements. Nevertheless, in the majority of the area's island and mainland territories, the scarcity of African manpower—or its high price—made the planters turn their eyes toward southern Asia in search of new sources of cheap labor. Thus there arrived in the Caribbean vast contingents of workers contracted under an arrangement similar to that of the previous *engagés* or indentured servants. These immigrations, nevertheless, did not issue from a single cultural womb, but rather from the most diverse Asian territories, such as India, China, and Java. Furthermore, they were not distributed evenly among the region's different colonial blocs. For example, the great majority of the Indians went to the English colonies, while the Chinese and the Malays were concentrated, respectively, in Cuba and Surinam. So that the notable Asian cultural influences in the Caribbean, in line with their diverse origins, show themselves through very different codes. One should not forget, however, that it was the Plantation that demanded their incorporation into the area.

The Plantation: Sociocultural regularities

As we have seen, the Plantation proliferated in the Caribbean basin in a way that presented different features in each island, each stretch of coastline, each colonial bloc. Nevertheless—as Mintz would see—these differences, far from negating the existence of a pan-Caribbean society, make it possible in the way that a system of fractal equations or a galaxy is possible. The different sugar-producing machines, installed here and there through the centuries, can be seen also as a huge machine of machines in a state of continuous technological transformation. Its inexorable territory-claiming nature made it—makes it still—advance in length and depth through the natural lands, demolishing forests, sucking up rivers, displacing other crops, and exterminating the native plants and animals. At the same time, ever since it was put into play, this powerful machine has attempted systematically to shape, to suit to its own convenience, the political, economic, social, and cultural spheres of the country that nourishes it until that country is changed into a *sugar island*. Of this subject, Gilberto Freyre and Darcy Ribeiro, respectively, referring to the case of the plantation of the Brazilian northeast (which, insofar as it shows these and other effects, might be taken simply as another Caribbean island), say:

> The *Casa Grande* [planter's residence], together with the slave cabins, represents in itself an economic, social, and political system: a system of production (*latifundio,* monoculture); a system of labor (slavery); a transportation system (oxcart, sedan chair, palanquin, horse); a religious system (familial Catholicism, with a cult of the dead, etc.); a system of family and sexual life (patriarchal polygamy); a system of domestic and personal hygiene (urinal, banana grove, bath in the river or standing with a washbasin); a political system (bossism, cronyism). The *Casa Grande* was at once a fortress, a bank, a hospital, a cemetery, a school, an asylum for widows, orphans, and the elderly . . . [40] It was the sincere expression of the needs, interests, and the broad rhythms of patriarchal life, made possible by the sugar revenues and the slaves' productive work.[41]

The *fazenda* [hacienda] constitutes the basic structuring model for Brazilian society. Around it the social system is organized as a body of auxiliary institutions, norms, customs, and beliefs whose purpose is to safeguard its being and persistence. So also do the family, the people, and the nation spring out of and develop from the *fazenda*'s effects and as such are defined by it.[42]

The extraordinary effects of the sugar-making machine's dynamics in colonial societies—to the point where these latter seem almost an enlarged reflection of the former—do not end with the abolition of slavery. Certainly there are changes and adjustments to go with this new situation, but the plantation machine in its essential features keeps on operating as oppressively as before. For example, the sugar expansion that the Antilles experienced in the first decades of the twentieth century unleashed dynamics similar to those seen a century or two earlier. The best lands were appropriated or controlled by the planting companies, and the peasants and smallholders were displaced violently to the marginal zones, unserved by the improved methods of transport and communication that the planting interests introduced. On this subject, Mintz writes: "During the transformation of the plantation sectors into modern factories in the field, particularly after 1900, the peasant sectors fell farther behind, as modern roads, communications systems, and company stores developed in the coastal zones. Thus the contrast between peasants and plantations has to some extent become even sharper in this century."[43]

In a way similar to what occurred in Barbados in the seventeenth century, sugarcane became the *primera agricultura,* in opposition to other forms of agricultural business. This peculiarity, combined with the practice of monoculture, determines the contradictory fact that an essentially agricultural country finds itself having to import food. In generalized conditions of low productivity and relative scarcity of manpower, this factor has disastrous consequences, since the great plantation machine—its sectors involving agriculture, industry, transport, communications, administration, and commerce—needs enormous masses of material and labor resources, snatching them cyclically from the country's other economic activities. In critical situations of this kind, it is not uncommon to resort to the rationing of food products. In 1970, when the Cuban government tried to produce ten million tons of sugar, the country was virtually paralyzed, or, if you like, changed into an enormous state-run plantation on which the cane harvest lay down the law.

The sugar-milling complex—the plantation's heart—created to hold perpetual dominion, would tend to subsist in the most adverse external market conditions, competing there with prices lower than the cost of production if need be. This situation fits the type of social structure that we observe in the statistical table. Clearly, this hierarchized structure will always seem ideal to the small group that holds the economic power by force, and thus its rigidity and disproportion will essentially persist under more modern work relations, and will continue to exert a similar influence in all of the different spheres of the national life.

If we bear in mind that the Plantation was a proliferating regularity in the Caribbean sphere, it becomes difficult to sustain the idea that the region's social structures cannot be grouped under a single typology. It is true that the Plantation's model differs from one island to another, and that sugar's hegemony begins in Barbados, passes to Saint-Domingue, and ends in Cuba, spreading itself out in time and space over three centuries. But it is precisely these differences that confer upon the Plantation its ability to survive and to keep transforming itself, whether facing the challenge of slavery's abolition, or the arrival of independence, or the adoption of a socialist mode of production.

Nonetheless, our agreeing with Mintz that the Caribbean may be defined in terms of a *societal area* is far from affirming, necessarily, the existence of a common pan-Caribbean culture. It is true that I have spoken here about the presence of an early creole culture around the Windward Passage, of a variegated creole culture in the different locales, and even of a national culture. But in all this I have in no way meant to suggest that these cultures are *unities*, in the sense that they admit a stable and coherent reading. In my opinion, any expression of culture—a myth, a song, a dance, a painting, a poem—is a kind of impersonal message, at once vague and truncated; an obscure and previous desire that was already moving around here and there and that can never be interpreted entirely by a performer or read completely by a reader; every effort by the one or the other to fill this essential gap will fail to lead him toward a goal, but will issue into lateral movements, spiralings, steps that go forward but also backward—let's say, different styles of dancing the rumba. And so, nothing and nobody can provide us with the absolute truth about what a local culture is, much less a national culture. How then can we presume that it's possible to define with any precision what lies within or without the culture of our extremely complicated archipelago?

In any case, for the present-day observer it is more or less evident that in the expressions that manifest themselves in the diffuse Caribbean zone there are components that come from many places around the globe, and that these, it seems, are not constant, stable, homogeneous, or even parallel among the nations, regions, and localities that claim the title of being Caribbean. It was precisely this state of chaos that moved Mintz to look for a form of Caribbeanness not within the cultural sphere but rather in the economic and social patterns. I think also that there is considerable truth in Moya Pons's opinion with respect to a lack of any pan-Caribbean consciousness, and in his alternative of taking the Caribbean as a series of Caribbeans situated next to each other, which offers a certain analogy with Froude's observations. But Labat's testimony is also self-evident: "It is no accident that the sea separating your lands establishes no differences in the rhythms of your bodies." And we must pay attention to that statement, above all because it refers directly to the question of culture, which is what concerns us. What does Labat point to as a regular feature common to the entire Caribbean? One element: rhythm. It is rhythm that, in his words, puts all the Caribbean peoples in "the same boat," over and above separations imposed on them by "nationality and race"; it is rhythm—not a specific cultural expression—that confers Caribbeanness. So that if Mintz defines the region in terms of a "societal area," one must conclude that Labat would have defined it in terms of a "rhythmical area."

How does Labat demonstrate this special rhythmic quality? He looks at performances. It's true that his opinions concerning the creoles' dances are not those of a specialist—although they have been credited by Fernando Ortiz, Janheinz Jahn, and others—but it happens that they, even though empirical and hastily written down, are largely confirmed in the eighteenth century by Moreau de Saint-Méry, one of the most serious and enlightened authorities on everything Caribbean of his time. For example, Labat speaks of the existence of a dance (or rhythm) called the *calenda* which enjoys the greatest popularity in the entire area, and which is danced as much by the Negro slaves and the free Negroes as by the white creoles, even the nuns, in the Spanish colonies. Labat offers the following description of this dance:

> What pleases them the most and is their most common diversion is the *calenda,* which comes from the Guinea coast and, judging by all its antecedents, from the kingdom of Ardá . . . The dancers array themselves in two lines, facing each other, the men on one side, the women on the other. The spectators form a circle around the dancers and drummers. The most gifted sings a *tonadilla,* improvised to deal with some current matter, and the tune's refrain is repeated by all the dancers and spectators, and accompanied by clapping hands. The

dancers raise their arms, as if they were playing castanets, they jump, turn, and spin, they approach to within three feet of each other and then they move backward following the beat, until the sound of the drum tells them to join together, with the thighs of some beating against those of others, that is, the men's with the women's. On seeing them, it seems that their bellies are beating together, when in truth their thighs alone are joined. They soon back away, pirouetting, to repeat the movement with supremely lascivious flourishes . . . They dance the *calenda* in their churches and Catholic processions, and the nuns do not stop dancing it even on Christmas eve upon a raised theater in the choir, facing the railings, which are open so that the populace may have the aid of these good souls in celebrating the Savior's birth. It is true that no men are let in with them . . . And I would like to think even that they dance it with a very pure intent, but how many spectators would judge them as charitably as I do? [44]

A century later, Moreau de Saint-Méry writes of the same dance, calling it the *kalenda,* [45] which has not changed much since Labat's time. It is still an extremely popular and widespread dance, and it continues with its same format of two lines divided by sex that come together in the center and then separate, while the chorus claps and repeats the singer's improvisations. In Moreau de Saint-Méry's opinion the dance takes the name *kalenda* from one of the drums—the largest and most deep-sounding—that enter the rhythm, although it is very probably the other way around, since Fernando Ortiz, in his *Nuevo catauro de cubanismos,* has listed this dance under the name *caringa* or *calinda,* deriving the word from that of an ancient region and river in the Congo. In any case, this dance's rhythm and its circular and antiphonal style were spread out through the entire region in the seventeenth and eighteenth centuries, and the dance was a permanence from which a variety of folk dances may have sprung, such as the *chica,* the *yuka,* the *zarabanda,* etc.[46] But here we are not interested in trips to the origins of things, for no matter how pleasant they may be they usually lead to the vertigo that comes with a desire to explain what can't be explained. We are interested, nevertheless, in establishing that, at least since the seventeenth century, there are rhythms common to the entire Caribbean, rhythms that follow a kind of polyrhythmic and polymetric percussion very different from European percussive forms, and which are impossible to write down using conventional notation. Of this mysterious property of Caribbean music, Ortiz informs us:

The usual tools of "white" musicology are insufficient. "The famous violinist Bohrer has confessed to me that he tried vainly to decipher a contrabass part performed every night in 'La Habanera' by a black man who couldn't read a single note" (N. B. Rosemond de Beauvallon, *L'ille de Cuba*, Paris, 1844). Emilio Grenet thinks correctly that, "properly speaking a *habanera* . . . has never been written down . . . It could be said that its creative principle is its rhythmic structure, but if the musician is not imbued with 'Cuban feeling' the musical product will never be a *habanera* in the strictest sense of the word" (*Popular Cuban Music*, Havana, 1939). Torroella, the popular composer and pianist, told us: "Music that is most characteristically Cuban can not be written down or put inside a musical staff. And it is natural that this should be the case, because much of it comes to us from the Negroes, and they, when they came to Cuba, did not know how to write, either." "But many Negroes now can write," we argued. And he answered us: "Yes, but don't you know that among the blacks there is always a secret being kept?" At the end of the last century, the great musician "of color" Raimundo Valenzuela also taught this when, asked how to read and perform the extraordinary figure called the *cinquillo*, so intriguing to students of Afro-Cuban music, he said that he would never explain it because the *cinquillo* was "a secret" . . . When the maestro Amadeo Roldán conducted the Orquesta Filarmónica in performing his *Rebambaramba*, upon reaching a certain moment in the piece he left the drummers free of his baton so that they could execute certain complicated rhythms in their own fashion . . . Today we hardly balk at accepting the impossibility of placing Negro music within the staff. "I doubt that it's possible with the present method of notation to set down an absolutely faithful transcription of all of the peculiarities of African music, for its true nature is to resist all setting down." (W. D. Hambly, *Tribal Dancing and Social Development*, London, 1926) [47]

But to think that Afro-Caribbean rhythms apply only to percussion would be to simplify enormously their importance as a common cultural element. Regarding the rhythms that come into play in the dance, and even in song, Ortiz continues to inform us:

> With regard to the transcription of the dances and their steps and figures, we find ourselves facing the same obstacles . . . To the classical ballet's way of thinking there is a choreographic vocabulary in which each step has its name . . . But it is as yet impossible to put

to music paper the rapid and extremely complex movements of the
African dance, in which feet, legs, hips, torsos, arms, hands, head,
face, eyes, tongue, and finally all human organs take part in mimetic
expressions that form steps, gestures, visages, and uncountable dance
figures . . . Furthermore (with regard to song), "it is essential to recognize that transcriptions and analyses of phonograph records, no matter how carefully done, can never tell the whole story of the relation
between the musical styles of the New World and of Africa, nor can
it establish the differences between the musics of different regions of
the New World, since, as Hornbostel observes, the problem also includes a consideration of the intangible aspects of singing technique
and the habitual practices behind the accompaniments and the key
changes. (Melville J. Herskovits, "El estudio de la música negra en el
Hemisferio Occidental," *Boletín Latinoamericano de Música*, V, 1941)[48]

But even to restrict the Caribbean's rhythms to the dance and to song is
to be flagrantly reductive. Consider a paragraph written by E. Duvergier
de Hauranne on the occasion of his visit to Santiago de Cuba in the last
century:

The alley that runs behind the market presents a lively spectacle every
morning: carts drawn by oxen or mules, grotesquely loaded donkey
trains, horsemen wearing huge straw hats who, on nervous, rear-
ing horses, open a difficult passage through crowds of Negroes and
people of color. Vigorous men come and go carrying barrels and baskets; others carry bundles of goatskins, cages filled with chickens. The
Negresses, dressed in light cotton and scandalous kerchiefs, let themselves be seen for an instant before the tumult, balancing, on their
heads, the basket of fruits or vegetables that they steady at times with
their arm rounded like a pitcher's handle; some, beneath their bal-
anced loads, parade through the crowd with the flexible movements
of untamed cats; others, their hands on their hips, advance with little
steps, swaying in humorous insouciance. On the market's patio and
along the length of the porch roofs that surround it, squatting vendors
peddle their wares laid out on tables or on the ground itself: fruits,
flowers, plants, pottery, brilliant swatches of silk, red and yellow silken
handkerchiefs, fish, shellfish, casks of salt fish and meat; there are piles
of oranges, pineapples, watermelons, crested cabbages, hams, golden
cheeses, layers of plantains and onions, of mangoes and yams, lemons
and potatoes spread out confusedly beside bunches of flowers. The

walkway is so elevated that it almost reaches the level of the displays, so that with any misstep an old Negress could be spilled upon on a basket of eggs crushed. The buyers buzz about like a swarm of flies; they haggle, they gesticulate, they laugh, they babble in the harmonious colonial *patois*.[49]

Notice that the center of this picture is held by the Negresses of Santiago who open paths, with their bundles and baskets, through the marketplace. What are the words that the writer uses to characterize their movement? No others, certainly, than ones that attempt a representation of inner rhythms: "balancing, on their heads, baskets of fruits . . . they parade through the crowd with the flexible movements of untamed cats . . . they advance in little steps, swaying in humorous insouciance." It's clear that Hauranne, a foreigner, saw that these Negresses walked in a "certain kind of way," that they moved in a way entirely different from that of European women. And it is not only movement that differentiates them, but also plastic immobilities—silences—such as "carrying their hands on their hips," or balancing baskets on their heads "with their arm rounded like a pitcher's handle." But Hauranne goes even further in his description. It is easy to see that he makes an effort to communicate an overall rhythm that can be broken down into separate, more or less autonomous rhythmic planes—polyrhythm: the rhythm of the oxcarts, together with the donkeys and horses; the rhythm of the Negresses, which we have just seen, together with the rhythm of the men who come and go carrying bundles and burdens and chicken cages; finally the heteroclitic, variegated, and seething plane of colors, odors, tastes, tactile sensations, and sounds where Hauranne inscribes fruits, fish, cheeses and hams, silk swatches and pottery, eggs and flowers, flies swarming and buzzing, laughter and gesticulation and babbling in an undecipherable but lilting language. These are rhythms that can be "seen" and even "heard" in the manner of Afro-Caribbean percussion.

What Hauranne tried to represent with his pen, his compatriot Mialhe and the Spaniard Landaluze tried to communicate through painting and lithography, also in the past century. Their respective compositions *Día de Reyes (La Habana)* and *Día de Reyes en La Habana* work to capture the rhythms of the drums, of the dances, of the songs, of the fantastic dress and colors that this annual holiday, where the slaves were freed for one day, set out upon Havana's streets in an enormous carnivalesque spectacle. It is precisely this rhythmic complexity, rooted in the forms of the ritual sacrifice and directed toward all of the senses, that gives pan-Caribbean cultures a way of being, a style that is repeated through time and space in all its differences and variants. This polyrhythm of planes and meters can be seen not just in music, dance, song, and the plastic arts, but also in the cuisine—the *ajiaco*—, in architecture, in poetry, in the novel, in the theater, in bodily expression, in religious beliefs, in idiosyncrasies, that is, in all the texts that circulate high and low throughout the Caribbean region.

Let's hear Carpentier as he speaks of colonial window gratings:

> We would have to make an immense inventory of gratings, an endless catalog of ironwork, to define fully the baroque features that are always implicit and present in the Cuban town. There is, in the houses of the *Vedado*, of Cienfuegos, of Santiago, of Remedios, the white and intricate grating, almost plantlike in its abundance and in the tangles of its metal ribbons, with pictures of lyres, flowers, vaguely Roman vases, amid infinite spirals that form, in general, the letters of the woman's name that was also given to the villa over which she ruled, or a date, a succession of historically significant numbers . . . The grating also is home to rosettas, peacock tails, interwoven arabesques . . . enormously luxuriant in this displaying of bolted, crossed, and interwoven pieces of metal . . . And there is also the austere grating, barely ornamented . . . or the one that presumes to make itself unique with a gothic figuration, a florid pattern never seen before, or a style derived surprisingly from that of St. Sulpice.[50]

And there is not just the polyrhythmic chaos of window gratings, but also of columns, balconies, panes of glass that crown doors and windows with their fabulous semicircles. That deafening conjunction of architectonic rhythms, Carpentier says, was giving Havana "that style without a style that over the long term, through a process of symbiosis, of amalgamation, establishes itself as a peculiar baroqueness that stands in for a style, inscribing itself within the history of urban behaviors."

Rhythms, rhythmic planes that mix together like the sacred *batá* drums. And nevertheless within this forest of sounds and turbulences there are meaningless regularities that act as vehicles for the drummers and dancers to unleash their violence and reach the trance, or better, the transition, to a world without violence. I haven't found a definition of rhythm better than the one given by the African poet Léopold Senghor:

> Rhythm is the architecture of being, the inner dynamic that gives it form, the pure expression of the life force. Rhythm is the vibratory

shock, the force which, through our senses, grips us at the root of our being. It is expressed through corporeal and sensual means; through lines, surfaces, colors, and volumes in architecture, sculpture, or painting; through accents in poetry and music, through movements in the dance. But, doing this, rhythm turns all these concrete things toward the light of the spirit. In the degree to which rhythm is sensuously embodied, it illuminates the spirit . . . Only rhythm gives the word its effective fullness; it is the word of God, that is, the rhythmic word, that created the world.[51]

In commenting on the polymeters and polyrhythms in African cultures, Janheinz Jahn says:

Common to both basic forms is the principle of *crossed rhythms;* that is, the main accents of the basic forms employed do not agree, but are overlaid in criss-cross fashion over one another, so that, in polymetry for example, the particular basic meters begin not simultaneously but at different times.[52]

It is precisely this crossed or chaotic rhythm that makes Hauranne's description of the marketplace attractive. Does this mean that the Caribbean rhythm is African? If I had to answer this question, I would say not entirely. I would say that the crossed rhythm that shows up in Caribbean cultural forms can be seen as the expression of countless performers who tried to represent what was already here, or there, at times drawing closer and at times farther away from Africa. The marketplace that Hauranne describes is a coming together of rhythms in which there is much of the African, but also the European; it is not a "mulatto" mixture, if that term is meant to convey a kind of "unity"; it is a polyrhythmic space that is Cuban, Caribbean, African, and European at once, and even Asian and Indoamerican, where there has been a contrapuntal and intermingled meeting of the biblical Creator's *logos,* of tobacco smoke, the dance of the *orishas* and *loas,* the Chinese bugle, Lezama Lima's *Paradiso,* and the *Virgen de la Caridad de Cobre* and the boat of the Three Juans. Within this chaos of differences and repetitions, of combinations and permutations, there are regular dynamics that coexist, and which, once broached within an aesthetic experience, lead the performer to re-create a world without violence, or—as Senghor would say—to reach the Effective Word, the elusive goal where all possible rhythms converge.

■ *PART 2*

THE

WRITER

2

Bartolomé de Las Casas:

between fiction

and the

inferno

In 1875, three and a half centuries after their writing, the first volumes of the *Historia de las Indias*, by Bartolomé de Las Casas, were published in Madrid.[1] The appearance of this notable work, which in George Ticknor's judgment was a "veritable treasure of information,"[2] was owing to the indefatigable efforts of the Cuban historian José Antonio Saco. It is easy to see why Saco resolved to set himself up as champion of Las Casas's voluminous manuscript. In the first place there is the fact that the *Historia de las Indias* was in reality a history of the Caribbean,[3] and Saco was the first Caribbean social scientist to study the Plantation's problematics from a nationalist perspective.[4] Second, Saco had been working since 1841 on his *Historia de la esclavitud*,[5] and Las Casas's text, because it spoke of how, when, and why African slavery had emerged in the Antilles, was an "origin" to which his own *Historia*, in search of legitimation, could refer. Las Casas had been precisely among those who had advised the crown to introduce black slaves in the New World's first plantations, and was, at the same time, one of the first to lament the consequences of the slave traffic. Saco, then, was to see Las Casas as something of a founder of the contradictions that he himself felt in being both a Cuban and a historian.

Saco's "filial" feelings toward Las Casas are expressed clearly in his inclusion, in the appendix of his own *Historia de la Esclavitud* of 1879, of his article written fourteen years earlier, "La *Historia de las Indias* por Bartolomé de las Casas y la Real Academia de Madrid," in which he argued furiously for the publication of Las Casas's manuscript and reproached the

Academy for having dismissed the work for political reasons.[6] In so doing, Saco not only underlined his own role as Las Casas's champion and vindicator, but he also proved that his own *Historia de la Esclavitud* had a place within the orbit of Las Casas's thinking, in the rupture that it brought to a discursive practice that justified the conquest, the *encomienda*, and the slave trade, and in the foundation that it could provide in conceiving a socioeconomic Utopia for the New World, that is, a providential space in which Europeans, aboriginal peoples, and Africans might live industriously according to religious and civic principles, and where violence toward the Indian and the Negro would be condemned equally by the earthly power of the crown and the Church's spiritual judgment.

Las Casas's having been himself an *encomendero* and a promoter of African slavery gave his *Historia* a charge of guilt and a capacity to set things right that is lacking in other texts usually studied now under the rubric of chronicles of the Indies. Also—and in this it does admit comparison with other chronicles, for example, *El primer nueva corónica y buen gobierno*, by Felipe Guamán Poma de Ayala—Las Casas's text could be taken as the historical basis for a nationalist argument aimed at questioning the legitimacy of the Spanish colonial rule in America, to which Cuba was still subject. That is why Saco, who would reach his paradoxical Cuban consciousness after beginning with wishfulness, racism, guilt, historical responsibility, and fear of the island's being totally Africanized, and who, at the same time, would be one of the builders of the country's nationalist thought, was to recognize himself more in Las Casas's ideas than in those of any other chronicler or historian of the Indies. Thus, in his eyes, his *Historia* could have no more useful antecedent than Las Casas's *Historia*, which had been prohibited up until that time.

Why had the publication of the *Historia de las Indias* been held up for so many years? We must remember that in his time Las Casas was public enemy number one to conquistadors, royal functionaries, colonizers, and even to chroniclers and historians of the Indies. His decisive role in the enactment of the so-called *Leyes Nuevas* (New Laws), which protected the Indian from the *encomienda*'s excesses and, above all, the publication in 1552 of the caustic *Brevísima relación de la destrucción de las Indias* stirred up protests in Spain and America that were so loud as to be undiminished even after his death. These strong and continuous attacks—as Lewis Hanke says—could have contributed to Las Casas's decision to postpone for forty years, until after his death, the publication of the manuscript.[7] But when those years passed, the *Brevísima relación* had turned into the generative text par excellence of the black legend concerning the Spanish colonial undertaking, to the extent that it was republished continuously by Spain's rival powers. This situation moved the Inquisition, in 1660, to issue a condemnation of Las Casas's pamphlet and to effect its withdrawal from publication, for having "defamed the celebrated conquerors of the new world"[8] and for being "a book pernicious to the deserved national reputation."[9] As we know, Las Casas's ideas took on particular importance in the first decades of the nineteenth century when the great majority of Spain's American colonies fought to gain their independence. New editions of the *Brevísima relación* appeared in Bogota, Puebla, Paris, London, and Philadelphia, and it is logical to suppose that in that revolutionary climate the *Historia de las Indias*, the text of which at times differs little in intention from his famous pamphlet, would not be published.

In any case, when the Real Academia de la Historia decided to sponsor the publication of one of the great still-unpublished manuscript histories of the Indies, it showed itself favorable only to Oviedo's work, which was printed in a deluxe edition in 1851, with extensive notes and a laudatory introduction.[10] The Academy's public reasons for not printing Las Casas's manuscript were based on the contention that the most worthwhile information it contained had already been included in Herrera's *Décadas*,[11] and the rest, according to Fernández de Navarrete, consisted of "prolix and importunate digressions which make heavy and tiresome reading, always challenging the Spaniards' right to conquest and always incriminating their behavior."[12]

At this point, I think I ought to make it clear that my intention in this chapter is precisely to analyze and argue one of the many "digressions" that made publication of the *Historia de las Indias* so undesirable to the Academy in those years. But the act of rereading what for centuries had been depreciated and held worthy of only a single and partial kind of reading calls perhaps for some reflection. When Fernández de Navarrete, the Academy's spokesman, said that Las Casas's "digressions" went against Spain's "right" to conquest, he acted as a censor in two ways. Certainly he was editing the discourse of the conquest to communicate only the Spaniards' "right" and not that of the Indoamericans, but also, at the same time, he was censoring the text on its own expressive plane, as its "digressions" conspired against a rhetorical unity that was itself taken as "right," as law. So one has to conclude that the Real Academia de la Historia, in those years at least, was not inclined to tolerate obvious differences of form and content in the texts that it published. To Fernández de Navarrete, the "digressions" that Las Casas's text exhibited were synonymous with chaos; they were subversive nodules that eroded the truth and rhetorical unity of the discourse of the conquest, a discourse that had much of the theological about it. Analogously, when Saco argued for the publication of the *Historia de las Indias*, he did so from a frankly modern standpoint. Saco, as a modern social scientist, wished for the discursive presence of a reading that would be disobedient and oppose itself to the supposed truth and supposed unity of the Academy's single-voiced reading. This latter was a truth from "over there," but what was needed was a truth from "over here," that is, a text that was something more than a pamphlet, a full-fledged history that would provide the opposing version of the conquest and would decry African enslavement, thus founding a properly constituted Latin American and—above all—Caribbean historical discourse. Exiled, banned, called a bigamist, a polemicist, a hustler, attacked continually from one side and the other, José Antonio Saco would have known from personal experience that there were disregarded "truths" (readings) that were no less true than those that had been already established, and that history, if it was to survive as a modern discipline, needed both. In this way, Saco, in defending Las Casas's version and in inscribing himself as a historian within Las Casas's discourse, very probably assured that his name and his texts would spring up time and again in Cuba whenever there was a political or socioeconomic debate of a nationalist kind.

It might be said that the chronicles, as objects for reading, have followed this decentering direction, especially whenever they point to doubtful origins, differences, and intertextualities. One line of the most recent Hispanoamericanist criticism—certainly not the least prestigious one—has begun to pay particular attention, for example, to the many digressions or nodes of chaos that appear in the texts of that vast and inconsistent protocol covering America's discovery, exploration, conquest, and colonization which we call the chronicles. This is so much the case that it is hardly plausible now to analyze any of these texts individually without devoting some space to such "digressions," especially when they try to sidestep the main thematic discourse and take on forms resembling those of the short story, of dramatic works, of the novel, that is, of fiction.[13] It's easy to see that the term *digression* has a logocentric root and, therefore, is unwelcome in the most recent literary criticism, which sees no compelling reason to subordinate literary to historical discourse, especially when the latter organizes itself in terms of a plot like one that could be found in a fictional narrative.[14] Enrique Pupo-Walker, the critic to have studied these brief texts most acutely and extensively, replaces "digression" with "intercalated fiction," "intercalated tale," "intercalated story," "imaginative or anecdotal interpolations" and other terms.[15] I think that they are all valid and the use of one or another of them depends on the nature of the "interpolated" or "intercalated" text being analyzed. In any case, to wind up this necessary preamble, I hereby transcribe Enrique Pupo-Walker's ideas concerning the function of these texts within the chronicles:

> It should be understood first that, in a historical narration, any imaginative creation or anecdotal record is not the text's main substance. Within the history's informative statement the intercalated story can be—and often is—an act of fabulizing, but in general it constitutes a complementary form of historical testimony . . . In practice, the functions that a story intercalated in the historical discourse fulfills can be quite diverse, and frequently call for quite distinct treatment in establishing their connection to the text as a whole. This being so, an extended look at these connections seems indispensable to me in reaching an integral appreciation of the chosen text. I think, in this regard, that a historical analysis that sees the interpolated material as merely the rhetorical froth or insignificant residue of human activity must lead us, without wishing to, toward an impoverished reading. I state it in these terms because with history—and especially in the chronicles of the Indies—using anecdotal material or fabulizing itself serve a subtle understanding that more than once grows out of creative capacities or acute anthropological intuitions . . . In the rich layers that these books contain we will notice, looking from another direction, that the imaginative insertions are not always fortuitous spaces in the tale, but rather appear—sometimes together—as a significant and integral component of the discourse.[16]

Las Casas: Historian or fabulist?

The intercalated tale that I am about to present can be found in chapter CXXVIII of book 3 of the *Historia de las Indias*.[17] The historical scenario from which it emerges involves Hispaniola's society at around the second decade of the sixteenth century. It is a moment important to the island's economy and society. In fact, it's a critical moment, for, as Las Casas tells us, a plague of smallpox took hold and sent a great number of Indians to their graves, sparing only a very few. The ensuing manpower shortage—

Las Casas writes—led the *encomenderos,* now without enough Indians to work the mining business, to set about looking for "farming profits and other means of making money, one of which was to plant *cañafístolos,* of which so many were planted that it seemed the earth had been made to support no other trees" (p. 271). The *cañafístola,* as is well known, was widely used in the Renaissance pharmacopoeia as a cathartic or purgative, and it was certainly an interesting product for export. In any case, Las Casas continues, "the inhabitants of this island, Spaniards, I mean, because one can't speak of Indians any more, were more than a little pleased, because riches were promised to them, with all of their hopes put into *cañafístola* . . . but when they had begun to enjoy the fruits of their labor and their hopes were being fulfilled, God sent a plague to this island and also to the island of San Juan . . . This was the infinite number of ants that there were on these islands, which there was no human manner, of all that were tried, of reducing" (p. 271).

And it is precisely at this point that Las Casas's chaotic fable begins; that is, the interpolated text emerges from a void of Indians and precious metals that he tries to fill up with another void: hope. Of course I can't quote the entire text of the story here. Nevertheless, I will transcribe what I consider to be its skeleton:

> The ants that grew on this island had a greater ability to do damage to the trees and destroy them than did those on San Juan, while the latter were more rabid, for they bit and caused greater pain than if it were wasps that bit and hurt, and there is no defense against them at night in bed, nor could one even live if the bed were not placed over bowls filled with water. The ones on this island commenced eating trees from the roots, which, as though fire had fallen from the sky and burned them, became black and dried out; they struck the orange and pomegranate trees, of which there were many fine groves on this island; . . . they hit the *cañafístolos,* and, as they found them the sweeter, they soon destroyed and wasted them . . . It was, certainly, a great shame to see so many holdings, and such rich ones, annihilated by such a plague, without any recourse; . . . the *cañafístola* plantings on the Vega alone could doubtless supply the needs of Europe and Asia, even if they ate it like bread, for it is such a fertile place . . . Some took action against the plague of ants by digging around the trees as deeply as they could and drowning them in water; at other times they burned them with fire. They found, three or more palm-lengths underground, their seed

and eggs, white as snow, and managed to burn up a bushel or two every day, and when the next day came they found a greater number of ants alive. The monks of San Francisco de la Vega put out a *piedra solimán,* which must have weighed three or four pounds, on the edge of a tile roof; all the ants in the house flocked to it, and as soon as they ate of it they fell dead; and as if they had sent messengers to all within half a league to a league around, calling them to a banquet of *solimán,* there were none, I think, that did not come, and the roads could be seen filled with those coming to the monastery, and at the end they climbed up to the roof and ate the *solimán,* and then they fell dead, so that the surface of the roof was as black as if it had been spread with coal dust; and this lasted as long as did the piece of *solimán,* which was as big as two large fists and like a ball; I saw it as large as it was when they put it out and then again after a few days when it had gone down to the size of a hen's egg or a little bigger. After the monks saw that the *solimán* was doing them no good, merely bringing filth to their house, they got rid of it . . . The Spaniards of this island seeing then the great affliction of this growing plague, which was doing them such harm, without there being any human way of stopping it, those who lived in the city of Santo Domingo agreed to ask the Highest Tribunal for a remedy; they formed great processions imploring Our Lord to free them through His mercy from that noxious plague over their worldly goods; and to receive the Divine favor more quickly, they thought to take a saint as their advocate, the one that our Lord might name; and thus, . . . the bishop and the clergy and the entire city drew lots over which of the Holy Saints would be given them by Divine Providence as their advocate; and the lot fell to San Saturnino, and . . . they cele-brated the feast with great solemnity . . . It was seen from that day onward that the plague began to diminish, and if it did not disappear altogether, that was because of the sins . . . The original cause of this ant infestation, said some, was the importation and planting of plan-tains. Petrarch tells in his *Triumphs* that in the land of Pisa a certain city was depopulated by a plague of ants that came over it . . . and thus, when God wishes to afflict a land or the men in it, He does not lack the wherewithal to afflict them for their sins and He does it with tiny creatures, as in the plagues of Egypt. (pp. 271–73)

Certainly the fictional elements that I see in the text do not lie in the smallpox epidemic or the plague of ants—both events are documented by

Oviedo—[18] nor in the religious services that won San Saturnino's intercession and along with it, the plague's subsiding—this is not the place for doubting miracles. What I perceive clearly as fiction is the thing that makes up the nub of the narration, that is, the corrosive sublimate called *piedra solimán* (bichlorate of mercury) attracting all the ants from a league and a half around and, above all, this *piedra solimán* (a character) opening up its futile battle against the ants, killing them by the thousands, but at the cost of having its volume shrunk more and more every day, losing its substance imperceptibly beneath the minuscule and tenacious mutilations that the insects inflict.

A rereading shows us that Las Casas led everyone in pointing out that he had just stretched the widest limits of credibility, and before he went on to conclude his tale, he wrote:

> [The religious men of the monastery] marveled at two things, and they were worthy of wonder; the force of natural instinct given to creatures sensible and insensible, as seen in these ants, which felt, if it can be said that way, from such a distance, it drawing them toward the *solimán;* and the second, that the *solimán,* as a stone, before it is milled, being as hard as alum, if not more so, and is almost like a stone, that a little tiny animal (such as these ants, which were very tiny) should have the power to bite the *solimán,* and finally to diminish it and reduce it to nothing. (p. 272)

But all of these prolix explanations that Las Casas provides—together with his "I myself saw it" (*yo lo vide*)—do no more than to accentuate the impossibility of the event. There is no doubt that we are in the presence of fiction. What type of fiction? I think that we are dealing here with the *uncanny,* perhaps the most interesting form of chaos to be seen in literature.

Before proceeding, I want to make it clear that I do not intend to take part in the polemic over the chronicles' tendency to mutate into fiction, or the inclination of Renaissance fiction to dress itself up as if it were an account or a memoir or some other civil rhetorical form.[19] The text that I have quoted from Las Casas interests me because it is built on a dramatic structure whose nub, whose bundle of conflicts, permits a reading of the literary uncanny that follows Freud's way of reading such things.[20] But I am interested even beyond this, because this nub or conflictive "center" has displaced, within the text, an unavoidable historical presence, and has usurped its place in the tale. Notice that the tale tells of Indians and Spaniards, but not of Negroes; of the sweetness of the orange, pomegranate, and *cañafístola* trees, but not of sugarcane's sweetness; of plains, gardens, estates, convents, houses, and cities, but not of *trapiches* and sugar mills. The antagonism between the ants and the *piedra solimán* has replaced, within the place of signification, the first existing model of the slave plantation in America.

One might think that the plague of ants took place before sugar manufacturing emerged on Hispaniola. But such is not the case. Las Casas places it in 1519 (p. 270), and Oviedo corroborates this, adding that it lasted until 1521.[21] Moreover, a succinct chronology of the first years of the plantation in the Caribbean yields the following information:

1493 Introduction and first planting of sugarcane on Hispaniola. By Christopher Columbus.

1501 First cane harvest achieved on Hispaniola. By Pedro de Atienza.

1506 First sugar produced on Hispaniola, using a rustic apparatus called a *cunyaya*. By Miguel Ballester and a certain Aguiló or Aguilón.

1515 Sugar first made with an animal-powered *trapiche* on Hispaniola. By Gonzalo de Velosa.

1516 First hydraulically powered mill installed on Hispaniola. By Gonzalo de Velosa and the brothers Francisco and Cristóbal de Tapia.

1517 First sugar nougat ("caxeta") from Hispaniola arrives in Seville on the ships of Juan Ginovés and Jerónimo Rodríguez.

1518 Royal decree from Charles V licensing the importation of 4,000 slaves from Africa to the Antilles. Of these, 2,000 to Hispaniola.

1522 Slave rebellion in the mills belonging to Cristóbal Lebrón, the licentiate Suazo, and Diego Colón. The slaves unite to take the town of Azua, near Santo Domingo, but they are defeated and hanged. A ship under Alonso de Algaba loads 2,000 *arrobas* (25 tons) of sugar destined for Seville.

1523 New royal decree to introduce another 4,000 African slaves into the Caribbean. Of these, 1,500 are for Hispaniola. There are thirty *trapiches* and hydraulic mills in Jamaica. Three mills are constructed in Puerto Rico. In a royal decree, it is assumed that sugar manufacturing is already taking place in Cuba.[22]

So in 1523 the sugar plantation, if still a rudimentary socioeconomic machine, was a reality in all the Antilles, especially on Hispaniola. In the period in which the plague of ants occurred, that is from 1519 to 1521, there are already powerful mills in operation and there have been massive importations of slaves and sugar exports to Seville. Why then does Las Casas keep the plantation's presence out of his account?

This is one of the questions that we will have to answer. But there are others as well. Why is this omission achieved by moving into the uncanny? or rather, what is the purpose of this singular fiction intercalated within the framework of the *Historia de las Indias*, and even, what role does it play in the formation of Caribbean literature and historiography?

Las Casas and slavery

The plague of ants (the event) has been accurately reported by both Las Casas and by Oviedo in their *Historias*; it has settled in those texts as a public reality, socially experienced, an "external" reality; we're dealing here, doubtless, with a *historic* plague. But while Oviedo's text limits itself to an account of this memorable plague—the ants' size and color, the harm that they did, how long the scourge lasted—Las Casas's scholastic rhetoric soon destabilizes his account, and there intrudes within it, to violate it, the uncanny passage. This passage's transformative capacity is such that, in its placement as a conflict between the beginning and the end of the chronicle's narrative, it immediately reorganizes this narrative and renders it in terms of a dramatic tale (presentation, crisis, denouement). Our conclusion is that just one uncanny "effect"[23]—as Poe would see in his theory of the short story—makes for an entirely uncanny tale; that is, the uncanny effect of the *piedra*'s being devoured by the ants transforms the chronicle and turns it into fiction, to the extent that we even doubt that the plague really occurred. This productive effect that the uncanny has must be taken into account in studying the chronicles, since one uncanny touch alone is enough, within our diegesis, to turn a historical account into a piece of literature.

In any event, whenever an uncanny fiction erupts within a chronicle intended to inform us, it should be seen as surrounded by violence. We're dealing here with materials that are not only very different from one another, but also of very different origins. The uncanny comes from "within"; it has much in common with certain dreams—hence its asymmetry, its inscription within the catalog of the extraordinary—, since in Freud's experience it precedes the repression of a castration complex that appears in disguise. So Las Casas's uncanny passage (a dream) stands out markedly from the historical framework in which it is embedded, or rather from which it has erupted, since it comes from "behind" or "within" (the subconscious) like an abscess or a suppurating tumor. Its violent irruption, then, in tearing the fabric of the account, had to leave its trace, just as a dream will include scraps of the realities around it. I mean by this that no matter what underlies the fact of the story of the slaveholding plantation's having been taken over by the uncanny—as will be seen—the territorialization that the uncanny achieves must necessarily have left behind some remnants of the pretextual script that organized the historical plot concerning the plague of ants. In fact, at the very beginning and end of the dramatic tangle (really a phantasmal tangle) that the uncanny gives shape to, we find the scraps of the chronicle that Las Casas never managed to write with his pen. The first of those to appear lies interpolated within a sentence that I did not include in my earlier quote. Las Casas says: "The garden of San Francisco that I spoke of, that was in the Vega, I saw filled with orange trees, that gave fruits sweet, dry, and bitter, and beautiful pomegranates, and *cañafistolos, great trees of cane, of cañafistola,* almost four palms in length, and in a little while I saw it all ruined" (pp. 271–72).

Take a careful look at the words that I've italicized. Las Casas, after enumerating the trees (orange trees, pomegranate trees, and *cañafistolos*), writes "great trees of canes, of *cañafistola.*" In the first place, his explanation that the *cañafistolo* is the tree that bears the *cañafistola* is totally unnecessary and, even if it were needed, the matter has already been clarified in the text itself. In the second place, our attention is drawn to the inexplicable presence of the word *canes,* since there are no cane trees, and Las Casas himself, in speaking earlier of the *cañafistola,* employs the term *canuto* (p. 271), which implies a pod. Moreover, the information that we have concerning Hispaniola in those days, to which Las Casas's and Oviedo's histories have made major contributions, indicates that it was precisely in the Vega—the island's most fertile region—that the first sugar was obtained. So that the "canes" that Las Casas chose to expel from the Vega and hide, by sleight of hand, from the ants, substituting "*cañafistolas*" henceforth as if this were just a matter of repeating two synonyms, can be taken as a vestige of the chronicle that the uncanny has displaced. It is to be noted that when Oviedo tells of the plague of ants and alludes to the damage that they caused, he says: "destroying and burning the *cañafistolos* and orange trees . . . the *sugars* and other goods" (vol. 2, pp. 77–78). In my reading of the Las Casas passage, *canes,* of all the words that Las Casas wrote, is the indispensable one; it is the trace that hints at the presence of an absence: the slaveholding plantation.

The second trace that the plantation's displacement left in the text is what C. S. Peirce calls an "index," that is, a sign that connects phenomeno-logically with what it tries to signify (another sign). This track or clue can be found at the end of the tale: "The cause from which this invasion of ants originated, according to what some said and believed, was the bringing in and planting of the plantains" (p. 273). The phrase stands out immediately, since Las Casas has been telling us—and he will keep on telling us until the very end of the chapter—that the plague began as a punishment from God visited on the Spaniards for the sins that they committed. But it's not this inconsistency that interests me here; rather it's the fact that the plantains indicate the presence of the plantation or, at least, of African slaves. This we can tell with almost absolute certainty because the Spaniards of this epoch did not eat plantains, a fact that Oviedo documents completely. Let's see what he says in this regard:

> This strain of plant was brought from the island of Gran Canaria, in the year fifteen hundred and sixteen, by the reverend father friar Tomás de Berlanga, of the Predicant Order, to this city of Santo Domingo; and from here they have spread to the other towns on this island and all the other islands where Christians live . . . and I saw them there in the city itself within the monastery of San Francisco in the year fif-teen hundred and twenty . . . And also I have heard it said that they are in the city of Almería in the kingdom of Granada . . . and that they came to Almería from the Levant and from Alexandria and from India. (vol. 1, p. 248) [24]

We can conclude from this that in 1520—when he put in at Santo Do-mingo before going on to Darién—Oviedo saw the plantain for the first time. The report of its existence in Almería is a vague "I have heard." But even if it were accurate, this would be the only Spanish city in which the plantain was known. What then would have moved Tomás de Berlanga to bring the plant from the Canaries to Hispaniola? My answer would be: the knowledge that the plantain was an essential element of the African diet, so much so that in many places in the Caribbean it is still called *guineo,* that is, native to Guinea. In 1516, before the first massive importing of slaves had yet occurred, their presence in Hispaniola was already of no small importance, as the first accounts of the island's colonization prove. Furthermore—see the chronology already provided—sugar had been produced there since 1506, and in 1515 and 1516, respectively, *trapiches* and hydraulic mills were installed. If this were not enough, it is in these years that the residents of Hispaniola start clamoring for authorization to begin a large-scale traffic in Negroes. So the plantain, like certain tubers and plants with edible leaves, was brought to the Caribbean to be a food inexpensive to produce, nutritious, and preferred by Africans. It is interesting to observe that, even today, mashed plantain has kept the names that the Africans gave it— *mangú* (Dominican Republic), *mofongo* (Puerto Rico), and *fufú* (Cuba)— which shows that its use was generalized through an Afro-Antillean experience.[25] So the plantain, as one of the "origins" of the plague of ants, now reveals itself to us as a consequence of a greater cause: the transatlantic crossing of the sugar plantation, which, coming from the Near East, had reached the Cape Verde Islands, the Madeiras, the Canaries, and finally Hispaniola.

All this should bring us to the conclusion that the slaveholding plantation was erased by the uncanny in Las Casas's chronicle. Why? What do African slaves, sugarcane, and *trapiches* and mills have to do with the castration complex or the repression of something that returns from banishment via the phantasmal and "other" form of the uncanny?

Here I must mention the next chapter of Las Casas's tale, chapter 129 of book 3 of his *Historia de las Indias*. A more or less objective editing of this chapter would yield the following information:

> The inhabitants of this island entered on another cultivation, and this was to look for a means of making sugar, seeing that the sweet canes grew abundantly in this land . . . Before the mills were invented [1516], some residents, who had something of what they had obtained with the sweat and blood of the Indians, wished for a license to go and buy from Castile some Negro slaves, as they saw that the Indians were dying off, and there were even some . . . who promised the cleric Bartolomé de Las Casas that if he were to bring or get a license to bring a dozen Negroes to this island, they would leave the Indians that they had in freedom; understanding this said cleric, who was in favor with the new king . . . and the repair of these lands being in his hands, he received the king's consent to allow, in order to give the Indians their freedom, that the Spaniards of these islands bring in 4,000 Negroes, at that time, to the four islands . . . Of this notice that the cleric gave he was soon after repentant, judging himself culpable for being inadvertent, because as afterwards he saw and confirmed, as will be seen, that the captivity of Negroes was as unjust as that of Indians, although he had supposed that they were justly in captivity, *although he was not certain that his ignorance and good will in this would excuse him before the*

bar of Divine Judgment . . . But when he was given this license and
it was over, many others kept following, so that more than 30,000
Negroes have been brought to this island, and in all the Indies more
than 100,000, I believe . . . and as the sugar mills grew every day so
grew the need to put Negroes to work in them. [The Portuguese],
seeing that we had such a need and that we paid well for them, went
and still go out every day to capture them, through any vile and in-
iquitous means that they can capture them with; for example, as they
themselves see that they are looked for and desired, they make unjust
wars upon each other, and in other illicit ways they steal one another
to be sold to the Portuguese, so that we ourselves are the cause of
all the sins that one and another commits, as well as those that we
ourselves commit in buying them . . . Formerly, when there were no
sugar mills, our opinion on these islands was that if the Negro did
not happen to be hanged he would never die, because we had never
seen a Negro dead from disease . . . but after they were put into the
sugar mills . . . they found their death and their sickness, and thus
many of them die every day, and for that reason bands of them run
away whenever they can, and they rise up and inflict death and cruelty
upon the Spaniards, in order to get out of their captivity, as often as
opportunity permits, and so the little towns on this island do not live
very securely, for another plague has come over them. (pp. 273–76)

Reading this text is productive in the extreme. Its generative capacity
surpasses even the limits of this chapter. In the first place—this jumps out
at us—we have a proper confession from Las Casas. We're not faced with
a rhetorical stratagem for sidestepping the issues. His confession, coming
from and directed to his history, coming from and directed to his religion,
is a double document that establishes itself at once in Caribbean historiography and in the ethical and social context of the Catholic Church. Clearly
the problem here is the toleration of African slavery, deemed justified by
the state and by Christianity alike, and which even Las Casas had for many
years thought to be just. But his confession is not limited to making public
his repentance for what he has come to see as a sin and a practice disastrous
to political, economic, and social order; neither does it crystallize into a
"denunciation"—a word that seems to fulfill an end in itself within certain narrow interpretations of history—of those who were at one time his
accomplices in the slaveholding business. Las Casas, with an involuntary
flourish of postmodernity that dismantles scholasticism's Thomist hier-

archy, manipulates the binary opposition master/slave in the conditions of the Caribbean plantation, while following a theoretical canon of surprising contemporaneity. Let's take a look at this canon by describing its shape in terms of a *mea culpa,* repeated breast-beatings:

First: I am guilty of not having understood that enslaving the Negro was as unjust as enslaving the Indian.

Second: I am guilty of having requested of the king that more Negroes should be brought to the Indies.

Third: I am guilty of having looked kindly upon the first license to bring 4,000 slaves from Africa.

Fourth: I am guilty of having agreed to the further issuance of these licenses, since I, who enjoyed the king's favor, could have stood in the way of this practice, which has resulted in the enslavement of 100,000 Negroes throughout the Indies.

Fifth: I am guilty of not having warned of the evils that would come with the building of sugar mills on these islands, since as their number grew also would the demand for Negroes increase.

Sixth: I am guilty of not having foreseen that the demand for Negroes would bring with it the organization, by the Portuguese, of a commercial system, based on violence and greed, between Lisbon, Guinea, and the Indies, with enormous contingents of Negroes as its merchandise.

Seventh: I am guilty of not having foreseen that the African Negroes, when they learned what prices their bodies would fetch, would make war on each other to sell one another to the European traders.

Eighth: I am guilty of the early deaths that the slaves suffer in the sugar mills, where they are killed by the hard work and the diseases that arise from their confinement.

Ninth: I am guilty for the Negroes' continuous flight and for their desire for vengeance, which leads them to organize in bands of runaways and to kill and despoil those who had held them as slaves.

Tenth: I am guilty, finally, for the insecurity and anxiety of life on Hispaniola, caused by the uprisings and attacks by groups of runaway Negroes, "which is another plague that has been visited upon it."

And so, in exhibiting his guilt in a kind of decalogue, Las Casas describes a circular figure which, in closing in upon itself, has turned the slave/master opposition completely around. At the end of his act of contrition it turns out to be the "blacks" who unleash their passion upon the "whites." Slavery, then, is no longer structured on the founding principle of hierarchical subordination, but instead the conferral of meaning on the thing called "slave" presupposes also a "free man," and a "dominator"; in reality, "slave" doesn't mean anything, since nobody can be a certain "slave" of anyone else; that is, the word is now exposed and, above all, stripped of its Eurocentric and logocentric charge, which Las Casas himself had assumed to be there at the outset of his confession.[26] In short, the men and women who make up the work force of a sugar mill could be "slaves" and also the members of a republic of runaway Negroes. Let's say Haiti in its formative state: a historical reality.

As we have seen, the description of this canon's circular figure, now so fashionable, has been achieved by starting with a geometrical first cause: guilt. In fact, it has been guilt that led Las Casas to think deeply about African slavery in the Antilles—for which he feels responsible—to the extent that his examination of conscience has taken the form of a "critical analysis," at the end of which the word *slave* does not just mean the *azotado* (whipped), but the *azote* (lash) or "plague" as well. But it's clear that guilt does not constitute a stable place of origin, since it moves immediately toward transgression, which leads to fear. But, in Las Casas's specific case, fear of what? Fear of "Divine Judgment"; that is, fear of the Divine Father, of Divine Law, fear of the absolute punishment of Hell; the eschatological objectification of Oedipus. This, as might be supposed, leads us once more to the Freudian notion of the uncanny and the story of the *piedra solimán* and the plague of ants.

The plague of ants and the uncanny

Freud, as we know, took the uncanny to be that which once was familiar to us but which now appears as something overwhelming. But how do we explain it that something that has been familiar, quotidian, even homely should return to disturb us? In his search for the possible meanings of *Unheimlich*, Freud came upon two orders of distinct ideas concerning its opposite, the *Heimlich*. One of these orders pointed toward the familiar, the other toward the occult, toward what's hidden from view. Moreover, he also came upon an interesting definition that Schelling gave for the *Unheimlich*, and this turned out to be the key to his investigation: *something that should have stayed hidden and secret, but which nevertheless comes to light.* So that the uncanny implies a return of a "reading" that should have remained forgotten; it involves, then, a déjà-vu that is not only unforeseen but also revelatory of something that should not have come back. According to Freud, that something is a repressed complex, a castration complex, a fear of punishment by the Father under the statutes of the Law of the Father.

And so, in all of this, I find a line of thought through which I may explain Las Casas's uncanny narrative. Before coming out with it clearly, however, I would like to return to the brief chronology that I introduced a few pages back. I ask the reader to look there for the information on the year 1522. It deals with a bloody and costly slave revolt. In reporting on it, Oviedo says:

> Therefore I shall give the substance of this turmoil and disturbance of the Negroes working at the mill belonging to the admiral Diego Colom; for it was his slaves who began the uprising . . . Up to twenty of the admiral's Negroes . . . left the sugar mill and went to group together, along with some others who were allied to them, at a certain place. And after forty of them had joined together, they killed some Christians who were unprotected in the countryside and they continued onward along their route toward the town of Azua . . . and there it was learned that the Negroes had reached a cattle ranch, where they killed a Christian stonemason who was working there, and they took a Negro and twelve slaves from that ranch . . . and when they had done all the harm they could they moved on . . . After they had killed nine Christians in the course of their journey, they made their camp at a place one league from Ocoa, which is the site of the powerful sugar mill belonging to the licentiate Zuazo, judge at this circuit, resulting that on the following day . . . the rebellious Negroes thought that they would come up against that mill and kill another eight or ten Christians who were there, and renew their numbers with more Negroes. And they succeeded in doing so, because they found another hundred and twenty Negroes in that mill. (vol. 1, pp. 98–99)

The many Negroes in revolt, who were planning to put the town of Azua to the knife, were defeated in several battles by a detachment of "caballeros" under the viceroy Diego Colón, at whose mill the rebellion had begun. The repression was extreme; the captured Negroes were "spread out hanged at intervals along the road" (vol. 1, p. 100).

Well then, Las Casas could not give a precise account of this event in his *Historia* since it had happened in 1522, that is, two years after the time frame that he had given to his work. Nevertheless, it is easy to see that he refers to these happenings when he says: "They flee in groups when they can and they visit deaths and cruelties upon the Spaniards to escape from their captivity" (p. 176) He quickly adds: "Thus the small towns on this island do not live with much security, for this is another plague that has over-come it." So the slave rebellion is seen by Las Casas as "*another* plague"; then what could have been the earlier plague? The answer is obvious: the plague of ants, which started in 1519 and ended in 1521, one year before the rebellion—in fact two months, since the latter broke out in January of 1522.

Clearly, one must keep in mind here that to Las Casas the plague of ants was a punishment from God; thus the consecutive plagues of slaves and of ants imply a transgression of Divine Law. Exactly what transgression? Well, the first plague recognized in the chapter is the plague of smallpox; this comes on, Las Casas says, in order to put an end to the Indians' torment and, at the same time, to deprive the Spaniards of their use of slave man-power. The third plague, as we have seen already, is of rebellious slaves, and this represents a divine punishment for the many sins that African slavery presupposes. The second plague, that of the ants, is not related to any specific transgression, but it must necessarily be related to slavery. This is evident because the smallpox plague is the punishment for having enslaved the Indian, and the plague of rebellious Negroes is the price that must be paid for Negro slavery. Thus plagues in Hispaniola are the consequence of one transgression: slavery.

At this point it is clear to me that the plague of ants does not refer to the enslavement of the Indian, since there is no metaphorical relationship between the crime and the punishment. I mean by this that, for example, I see a close symbolic relationship between the smallpox plague and the slavery suffered in practice by the Indian on the *encomienda*. Notice that the plague (the punishment) comes in a fashion that is *passive,* parodical if you like; that is, if slavery finished the Indian off slowly and painfully, the appropriate punishment is to free the Indians from their pain and put an end to them once and for all, which would ruin the landowner himself as well. The punishment of the plague of ants, however, comes on in an *active* way; the ants destroy physically whatever they meet in their path, and in so doing they ruin the Spaniards. The astonishing thing about the plague of ants is their ever-growing numbers; their habit is to achieve de-struction through *increase,* while the smallpox plague achieves it through *diminution*. In reality, it turns out to be obvious that the plague of ants is a metaphor for the plague of Negroes, given that the latter's presence *increases* unceasingly, owing to the demands of the sugar plantation, while the Indians' *diminishes* in a parallel fashion with the decreasing importance of the mining economy.

In Las Casas's uncanny narrative, then, the ants (black as "coal dust") are the runaway Negroes who knock down everything in their path and forcibly impose death and ruin upon their masters. We may suppose that Las Casas, who wrote the uncanny chapter almost a half century after the plague, saw, in describing it, a return of familiar things (the African presence on Hispaniola and the 1522 revolt) that had remained hidden, repressed, because they signified a transgression for which he felt guilty and, therefore, fearful of God's punishment: hell, eschatological castration.

But, as I said, this is no more than a suspicion, although—I hasten to add—a well founded suspicion. I'll explain myself better. Las Casas's chapter containing the *mea culpas* is not the only one in which he broaches the subject of African slavery in America; there is another one that precedes it, number 102 of book 3. Here is what Las Casas says about it:

> Because some of the Spaniards on this island said to the cleric Casas, seeing what he intended and that the religious orders of Santo Domingo did not want to absolve those who had Indians if they did not free them, that if he would bring them a license from the king allowing them to bring from Castile a dozen Negro slaves, they would set the Indians free. Remembering this the cleric said in his petition that the Spaniards might be permitted to bring in a dozen Negro slaves, more or less, because with them they could subsist on the land and could set the Indians free . . . The cleric was asked what number of Negro slaves seemed right to bring to these islands; he answered that he did not know, after which a royal decree was sent to the officials of the Sevillian Board of Trade that they get together and ship the number that seemed right to those four islands, Hispaniola, San Juan, Cuba, and Jamaica; it seemed to them that at present 4,000 Negro slaves were enough. (p. 177)

Las Casas gives us the details of how the Flems and the Genoese enriched themselves with this license, and in concluding the matter he adds: "And for the Indians no benefit came from this, it having been ordered for their good and their liberty, for in the end they stayed in their captivity until there were no more left to kill" (p. 178).

Where here are the Negro revolts and the confession of guilt and fear of divine punishment for having contributed to the founding of African slavery in America? Not anywhere. Las Casas shows compassion only for the Indians, following the politics of the Dominicans, his religious order. But when I said "not anywhere" I was referring exclusively to the principal text of the *Historia de las Indias*. In fact the original copy of the work does contain a *mea culpa,* but appearing in the form of a note in the margin. When and why did Las Casas write it? Nobody knows. In any case, on the folio's margin we read: "This advice to give permission for bringing Negro slaves to these islands was given first by the cleric Casas, not seeing the injustice with which the Portuguese take them and make slaves of them; he who, after he realized it, would not have done so for anything in the world, because he then took their being caught and enslaved as unjust, for they have as much power to reason as have the Indians" (p. 177).[27] I ask: why not think that Las Casas wrote this marginal note after the writing of his account of the plague of ants had brought out in him the guilt and the fear that the repressive mechanism of his preconscious had made him forget?

There are reasons that support this hypothesis. In the first place there is the repetition of information about his own role in the slave traffic. Why does this happen? After all both chapters were in the same book 3, fairly near to one another. Further, what is said in chapter 129 doesn't add much to what had already been put forth in chapter 102, if we except the lines about the plague of Negroes and the *mea culpas.* Then why do these appear following the uncanny chapter and not in chapter 102? And of course there is the matter of the marginal note. Why didn't Las Casas show his repentance in the principal text? If he thought the matter so important, why did he express it *a posteriori* and in the form of a marginal clarification? In my opinion, what happened was that when Las Casas wrote chapter 102 his interest was directed fundamentally toward the Indians' sufferings. Later, when he read his own uncanny narration, something made him decodify the metaphor plague of ants / plague of Negroes that his guilt and his fear of divine punishment had kept him from seeing until then. Thereafter he reflected upon his responsibility for the slave traffic and, finally, he repented and he confirmed it; that is, he examined his conscience, found himself guilty, and confessed of that which, beyond the Church's judgment of approval, he knew himself to be a sin deserving of eternal damnation.

The piedra solimán: *Sugar, genitalia, writing*

Let's go back to the uncanny tale. We have the ants and we have the *piedra solimán*. But, what was the *solimán?* Mercuric bichlorate, a corrosive sublimate. Its discovery was owing to alchemy, although in Las Casas's time—and even much later—it was used as a strong disinfectant and a deadly poison. Certainly being attractive to ants does not figure among its properties. Its odor, acrid and caustic, would make it more likely to repel them. It's possible that the function of "attracting" that Las Casas attributes to it derives from its ending in *-imán* (magnet), which has nothing at all to do with its etymology.[28] In any case, we have the ants, in large numbers; a full-fledged plague of black ants, running free in the roads and fields, leveling everything before them. Let's suppose that Las Casas's psyche produces, subliminally, a metaphor: plague of ants / plague of Negroes. Of course this metaphor is instantaneously repressed, for it carries with it a return of the castration complex. The result of this interdiction is that Las Casas cannot, in this passage of his chronicle, give an account of anything having to do with slavery and with sugar. On the other hand, his charge of anxiety produces a "dream," or, to put it less suggestively, a brief piece of uncanny literature, where sugar is represented iconically by the *solimán*. Let's take a closer look at this iconic relationship.

In Las Casas's epoch, sugar is more a pharmacopoeic product than a sweetener. It was consumed most often in the form that we call "sugar *cande*" (from Candia, now Cyprus); that is, rocks made of sugar crystals obtained through a process of slow evaporation. These rocks, coming from the Near East, were what medieval Europe knew as sugar. Their appearance, before being broken up into particles suitable for selling in small amounts, was of a snow-white crystalline mass. That is precisely what *solimán* looks like. Furthermore, there are other interesting relationships between sugar and *solimán*. The latter is a product of alchemy's crucibles, fires, and manipulations; sugar was produced by analogous physical and chemical procedures, though of an industrial kind. Moreover, in Las Casas's mind, each product means *life* and, at the same time, *death*. So that the whitish rock in Las Casas's tale is, clearly, a rock made of sugar and as such it offers itself as nourishment (life) to the ants while killing them at the same time. But let's leave this rock, or this concentration of meanings, to one side to be taken up again later. Let's go now to the ants.

The plague is a punishment from God, and, as a punishment, it should refer directly to transgression, or, better, to transgressors. We've already seen that sugar manufacture presupposed the arrival of more and more slaves, to the extent that the latter, when Las Casas wrote, greatly outnumbered the Spaniards in the Caribbean. So every sugar mill, together with its cane field and its plantain grove, can be taken as an "anthill," that is, as one of the plague's "origins." But, clearly, the plague would begin in a specific anthill (belonging to the viceroy Diego Colón) and from there the ants would go out—escaping the spurious law that had kept them on the plantation—in order to stir up those living in the adjacent anthills. With this achieved, it is now possible to speak of a real plague: many ants, free, black, vigorous, accustomed to working more than any other insect of their size and, therefore, a menace when they get together and move along the roads, sating their implacable, ancient, secret hunger. But these ants, which are God's punishment, also pursue an unearthly objective. The same thing happened with the smallpox plague, which speeded up the salvation of the Indians' souls and gave the Spaniards a chance to repent of having enslaved them. So these ants threatened not just the body but the soul as well. Whose soul? The transgressors' souls, surely, the Portuguese slave traders' souls, the Genoese bankers' souls, the Flemish courtiers' souls, the souls of the ministers of the Council of the Indies and the magistrates of the *Casa de Contratación*, of the landowners in Hispaniola, Puerto Rico, Jamaica, and Cuba and, above all, Las Casas's own tormented soul.

After all this we can agree that the *piedra solimán* is also expressive of the bodies and souls of those who have violated the Law. Notice that it has a double genealogy. On the one hand, alchemy and technology (matter transformed by fire); on the other hand, we must remember that Las Casas's "dream" overtakes him at the very moment when a monk (a consecrated one) places the *piedra* on a flat roof of a monastery (a house of religion). So the *piedra* is a product of human industry, but also of religion; it is profane and sacred matter at the same time; it is an essence that relates to body and soul both. What does the *piedra* look like? It is the size of *dos puños* (two fists)—Las Casas says—although at the end, after being partially devoured, it has been reduced to the size of *un huevo* (an egg, a testicle). Then the *piedra* is the very genitalia of Las Casas's masculine soul, Las Casas the obedient son sworn to serve the Divine Father, and the plague involves a supra-personal and eschatological punishment: Hell.

It may interest us to see how the battle against the ants also suggested their origin, as there was an attempt to burn, in the depths of the earth, "their seed and eggs." But to no avail: "when the next day came, they found a greater number of ants alive." As the *piedra* diminishes, the ants increase. We're dealing with a ferocious battle between origins, although in reality the battle must be won by the ants at the end of time (the Final Judgment), for they are an irremediable plague sent by God. That is why San Saturnino's intercession does not wholly appease God's fury; rather the plague keeps cropping up for as long as sin exists ("and if it did not disappear altogether, that was because of the sins").

I don't feel the need to argue, in this day and age, that Las Casas's guilt about the African slave trade in America has an uncertain and political aspect to it, and not only because we cannot doubt his good faith and the sincerity of his repentance. Negro slavery was already a historical reality in the Indies when Las Casas made his case to the king, and there is no doubt that as an institution it would have kept on growing, as indeed it did even after he intervened to oppose it. In fact the die was already cast for the African slave. West Africa was then the only place in the world that offered Europe a vast reserve of cheap and easily obtainable manpower, in the face of a growing scarcity of indigenous labor in the entire area, including Brazil. Not to mention that the slave trade, from the beginning, was a royal monopoly that enriched not just the Spanish crown but also the traffickers and every kind of intermediary who took part in the sinister business. Las Casas's guilt is limited, and nobody knew this better than he, since he was "not certain" that his ignorance in this matter and his good will would excuse him before divine judgment. So that the ruling given by "Divine Judgment" would be, in his tale, a limited punishment. His castration is not total; the *piedra* is "saved" by the good friars (religion) before it can be completely devoured. There is a mutilation, a partial castration, but Las Casas's soul—though reduced to an egg or testicle—has not lost completely the generative capacity that renders it immortal at the right hand of God.

But the *piedra* is, before it is anything else, *writing*. The tale's first reader was Las Casas himself. We know that he felt the uncanny effect of his own fiction or "dream," since he quickly jumped outside of his plot in order to try to legitimate it as true while at the same time underlining its improbability. Perhaps it was then, at that moment of critical lucidity, when he read the metaphor plague of ants / plague of Negroes, the necessary preamble to his examination of conscience and subsequent repentance. Once contrite, following this intensive self-reading, it was now possible for him to write about sugar and the plague of slaves in the public confession of the following chapter; later, wanting his judgments in this matter to be coherent, he wrote the marginal note beside the text of chapter 102. With his self-analysis he so arranged it that his fear of being punished by the Father would float within the threshold that communicates the uncanny along with the sociological, the literary with the historical.

Derivations from the "Las Casas case"

The only thing left for us here is to comment on some of the implications of the event or "case" that we have just seen. In the first place, we should agree with Pupo-Walker that, in the chronicles, "the imaginative insertions are not always fortuitous spaces in the tale," and that these "acts of fabulizing" constitute, in general, forms that are complementary to historical testimony. To Pupo-Walker's words I would add that there are cases, like that of Las Casas's uncanny tale, that can be taken as proto-historical, since they come out of the historiographic material itself, and even precede the moment at which historiographic discourse properly establishes itself. The same holds true, of course, with regard to fictional discourse, as the fable of the ants and the *piedra solimán* cannot be completely separated—as we've seen—from the historico-social trauma that it wishes to forget, to leave in darkness, but which serves as the vehicle of the latter's returning like a piece of a puzzle that must take its place in the space left empty by the chronicle.

In fact, Las Casas's tale, in the tenacious ambiguity that places it between fiction and history, between transgression and the law, is a very good example of writing as "*pharmacon,*" whose ability to mean anything—everything and nothing—Derrida observes in his analysis of the *Phaedrus*.[29] This irreducible ambivalence, however, does not say much; the uncanny passage, in its double manifestation as proto-historiographic and proto-literary, does not give us a stable signifying procedure, nor may it be taken as setting in motion the effects that legitimate, individually, either of those two discourses. Exactly the opposite: it is no more than a paradoxical signifier within whose limits a mineral from the pharmacopoeia is simultaneously reality and fiction, acrid and sweet, curative and poisonous, body and soul, technology and metaphysic, life and death, monument and mutilation. Certainly its deconstruction has left us with a residue of certain unforeseen regularities that come out from hiding again and again, but these hidden patterns cannot be taken as historiographic or literary results; they merely amount to phantasmal forms of transgression, of guilt and fear before the Father's wrath that speak of a prediscursive violence that both history and literature would like to erase from their accounts. That's all that there is on the other side of Las Casas's uncanny tale, or, if you like, before and beyond the soft, sticky chaos of the writing that organized it.

So, having the "Las Casas case" before us, we can conclude that, in the *Historia de las Indias*, fiction complements the historic testimony, as Pupo-

Walker says, but we can argue equally that the historical text complements the fiction. Curiously, this paradox leaves Las Casas himself in the lurch when, on looking for a center on which to legitimize his tale, he avails himself of one literary and one historical source, with neither looming larger than the other: "Petrarch tells in his *Triumphs* that in the Seignory of Pisa there was a certain city that was depopulated by a plague of these ants that came over it." And then he adds: "Nicolao Leoncio, book 2, chapter 71 of *Varia Historia*, refers solemnly to two cities that were depopulated by crowds of mosquitoes" (p. 273). In this way the uncanny text refers to two tales that are no more legitimate than it, since one may easily conclude that Petrarch's ants and Leoncio's mosquitoes hang from the very dream of violence that his own narrations wished to forget.

To end this chapter, let's look at another direction in which Las Casas's uncanny text expresses itself as a currently important signifier. Keep in mind, before anything else, that the *Historia de las Indias*, in being precisely one of the first texts to refer to the Caribbean, elevates Las Casas into what Foucault would call a "founder of Discourse." [30] This in the sense that Las Casas had the option of publishing, before all the other chroniclers and historians of the Indies, the flow of papers of all kinds that told of the discovery, conquest, and colonization of the Caribbean—not to mention his own observations. But I ought to make it clear at once that what makes Las Casas a founding father of the Caribbean is not his publication of Columbus's diary nor of Pane's notes on Taino culture, nor even his descriptions of nature on the islands or his lexicographic and anthropological information concerning the aborigines. Las Casas can be understood as a founder of the Caribbean on the basis of the chapters of his *Historia de las Indias* that we have looked at here; that is, those that speak of the factors that began the sugar plantation and African slavery in the New World, for it is precisely these troubled institutions that best define the Caribbean and that inform its richest substratum.

Las Casas discovered the plantation's vicious circle: the more sugar, the more Negroes; the more Negroes, the more violence; the more violence, the more sugar; the more sugar, the more Negroes. Not even the king escaped his denunciations: "The moneys from these licenses and permits given to the king in order to obtain them was assigned by the emperor toward the building of the Alcázar that he made in Madrid and in Toledo, and with those moneys they both have been made" (p. 275). Moreover, we have seen that it was no accident that it was none other than Saco who insisted on the publication of the *Historia de las Indias*. As we know, he had been exiled from Cuba for having publicly attacked the slave trade. His reasoning was parallel to Las Casas's, and his conclusions were more or less the same ones that the latter had reached: the slaveholding plantation generated rebellions, that is, "plagues of Negroes" that could annihilate the *"piedra solimán"* that Europe had founded. This had not been said by any other chronicler of the Spanish colonial world. That is why Saco would have recognized himself in Las Casas and would have tried to present himself as a continuer of his work, as fear and guilt toward and for the Negro were very important components of liberal Cuban and Hispano-Caribbean thinking at that time.[31]

But let's take a last look at the uncanny tale. Can we say that we're dealing with an early example of proto-Caribbean writing? I think we can, though only insofar as it touches on the Eurocentric dynamics that seethe within the Caribbean's dense and complex signifiers. We must take it into account that the psychoanalytic performance of Las Casas's text is set in motion because of his responsibility for the enslavement of the Negro and for the plantation, that is, in seeing himself before the Law as having been guilty of "desiring" and putting his hands violently upon what was the Creator's private patrimony. In my opinion this complex allows us to think of Las Casas's psyche as proto-Caribbean—and also his uncanny tale—since this process of transgression, guilt, and fear of punishment for unnaturally "possessing" the African slave within the Plantation's degrading regimen established a modality alien to the medieval European experience, even to the Aristotelian concept of slavery which Las Casas understood very well. Not only this, but because his uncanny text emerged at the Caribbean historical archive's formative moment, its conflictive concerns made up a kind of leitmotiv or leading rhythm to which, necessarily, modern Caribbean historiography would have to connect, as in the case of José Antonio Saco. This is the accepted rule governing the genealogy of all discourse.

Moreover, if we review the best-known and most highly praised—most Eurocentric—of the area's literary works, disregarding the languages in which they are written, we find that they too refer in one way or another to Las Casas's uncanny and guilty tale.[32] So it can be said that the Caribbean literature most highly regarded in the West, and the historiography as well, repeats again and again, within its polyrhythmic variations, the mythological combat between the ants and the *piedra solimán* as an absent presence; an endless combat that must necessarily remain undecided within the problematic interplay of confrontations, truces, alliances, derelictions, offensive and defensive strategies, advances and retreats, forms of domination, resistance and coexistence that the Plantation's founding inscribed in the Caribbean.

3

Nicolás Guillén:

sugar mill

and

poetry

In 1857 the lithography studio of Luis Marquier in Havana completed the printing of the most beautiful and sumptuous book ever published in Cuba. Its title was *Los ingenios* (The sugar mills). The texts were by the landowner Justo G. Cantero and the plates had been drawn from life by Eduard Laplante, a French painter and engraver with an interest in sugar. The work, printed in a large format during the course of two years, was dedicated to the Junta de Fomento (Council on Development) and sold to subscribers.[1]

Laplante's twenty-eight lithographic views have been described and annotated by many art critics. Right now, though, I'm interested in quoting from two sugar historians. In this matter, Manuel Moreno Fraginals says: "The work offers an extremely valuable store of information about the biggest Cuban sugar mills in the 1850s. The plates, extraordinarily beautiful, offer quite naturally an idyllic panorama of the sugar mills, since the owners financed the edition. But from a technical point of view they are unassailable, because of the thoroughness with which the machinery has been reproduced."[2] And here is the judgment of Leví Marrero: "The external beauty captured by the plates of *Los ingenios*, a work that is almost inaccessible today because few copies have been conserved, is in painful contrast to the dark features that it reveals. Laplante meticulously reproduces the implacable reality of slavery, with admirable realism."[3]

The two scholars coincide in pointing out the exceptional beauty of the plates, but beyond that they direct their attention toward different points of reference: Moreno Fraginals sees the machinery, while Leví Marrero notices the slave. In reality, one reading connects with the other, thus enriching the plates' meanings while yet proposing a new reading to the reader. I, for example, in my last rereading, have been able to distinguish an intermediate space between the machinery and the slaves, which I had passed over on previous occasions. This space can be occupied by something vague and contradictory, which attracts and repels at the same time, and which I can reduce to a single word: power.

In fact, I think that those plates and texts constitute a kind of poetic panoply or myth that I can take as a monument to power. Each engraving, each descriptive text, each sugar mill, presents itself as a detail in a greater composition, which we might call an extremely vast lithograph that represents an ensemble of machines joined together, each with its names and its technical specifications: how much land served, type of machinery, how many slaves, production . . . This portentous view, which exists only in my mind, shows a close-up of the interiors of the boiler rooms of certain sugar mills—El Progreso, Armonía, Victoria, Asunción are their simple, optimistic names—juxtaposed to each other so that with a little imagination they can be seen together as the boiler room of one huge sugar mill. There, surprisingly modern machines, apparatuses, and frameworks unfold. They could easily correspond to the factory complexes that Jules Verne designed, since their newfangled forms, in contrast to the barefooted and shirtless Negroes who are occupied in the hustle and bustle of the milling, acquire the virtue of projecting themselves toward the future. This impression grows stronger upon reading Justo G. Cantero's technical descriptions: steam engines made in Glasgow, Liverpool, New York; centrifuges manufactured by Benson and Day; machines perfected by Derosne and Cail; new technologies put in action by Monsieur Duprey and Mr. Dodd. One can see from a mile away that this sophisticated sugar-producing machinery makes up a form of knowledge inaccessible not only to the slaves and coolies who work beneath the nave's huge metal roof, but also to the white-skinned overseers who watch over and control the work. In fact, all human presence seems superfluous here, a mere question of insignificant and perishable organisms that will not survive the institution of the sugar mill, whose machinery is represented as the only legitimate knowledge, as the only enduring truth that exists or will ever exist in Cuba.

On a second focal plane, above the transverse line under which we have been allowed to see, as in a park, the machines and apparatuses up close, there stretch out the beautiful and seignorial structures of about twenty mills. There can be no doubt that this imposing cluster of buildings, roads, rail lines, and soaring chimneys with their tufts of smoke invigorates the countryside's green and peaceable landscape, activates its bucolic inertia by throwing itself over it like a virile allegory of progress, or better, like an irresistible technical drawing coupled to the earth to give it a new purpose. Cantero takes pains to emphasize the sugar mill's patriarchal and generative nature: "The many factories, in their regularity and symmetry, show the traveler from a certain distance an aspect like that of one of Europe's lovely manufacturing towns, and it is even more agreeably surprising next to one's idea about this kind of establishment in the tropics, where one is far from finding the life, order, and industry that so distinguish the old world."[4]

Thus, for Laplante and Cantero both, the sugar mill was, above all, a civilizing agent, a center of "life, order, and industry" which had awakened the creole countryside's languid precapitalist sleep with its song of technology. One guesses immediately that it was under this motto of "life, order, and industry," or others like it, that the past century's sugar expansion in Cuba was carried out.

As I reread the plates and texts of Los ingenios I notice a strong will within the discourse to set itself up in terms of myth, of origin, of truth, of power, legitimate power, inexhaustible power which is the very foundation of law and nationhood, a will to power that has already been articulated in the writings of Francisco de Arango y Parreño, and that has kept on expressing itself—repeating itself—in vast successions of texts throughout the past two centuries. Hence in Cuba, from that time until now, anything that threatens the sugar-producing order, whatever the political and ideological nature of the group managing the power of the sugar mill, is always called anti-Cuban. In reality, ever since the Plantation was first set up, sugar has been carrying out a national security policy that first saw itself as anti-abolitionist, later as anti-independence, then it called itself "democratic" and now "revolutionary." At bottom this national security policy has not changed substantially, it has repeated itself while adjusting to Cuba's historical realities. Its propaganda apparatus has elaborated, through time, such slogans as "without slaves there is no sugar," "without sugar there is no country," and "the Cuban's word: the ten million are coming!" Thus sugar is the same as fatherland, and to produce sugar is to be Cuban. Years ago, when someone sought to change the sugar world's status quo he was identified as an enemy and called a "revolutionary"; now he's called a "counterrevolutionary," although he is the same individual. The extremes bend to form a circle and they don't mean anything. What really matters, what really has national and patriotic significance in the secular religion, is sugar; the only thing that constitutes tradition, the thing that must be preserved and protected is the myth of the sugar mill, which offers itself in perpetuity as the center or genealogical origin of Cuban society.

Of course any subject invested with power relates in many and varied ways to the individual who acts as its object, and vice versa. Thus the power relations that sugar establishes in Cuba flow through many channels, which make up a vast and intricate network of connections upon the sociocultural surface and at the same time establish forms of dependence, domination, subjugation, punishment, control, vigilance, retribution, education, exploitation, defiance, resistance, compliance, coexistence, rebellion, etc. Right now, nonetheless, I am not interested in taking a quick look at the whole range of relationships between the sugar-producing machine and the worker revealed to me in my rereading of *Los ingenios*. I am interested, rather, in postponing, for a moment, a consideration of the unstable status quo or coexistence of differences that these relationships shape, and in starting from the premise that, as far as power is concerned, the economic and social complex of the sugar mill needs and inspires commentaries, among them that of literature. As we know, the Plantation's dynamics and tensions, in proposing themselves as the principal referents of national interest, are perhaps those that contributed most to the founding of Cuban ideas and letters in the first three decades of the nineteenth century. I ought to make it clear at any rate that here I shall observe only the Cuban literary discourse of our century and, principally, that having to do with poetry dealing with the sugar power. It is in this limited context that I propose to focus, above all, on the work of Nicolás Guillén.

From Los ingenios *to* La zafra

Anyone who reads the poem *La zafra* (The Cane Harvest), written in 1926 by Agustín Acosta[5] just after having read Cantero and Laplante's *Los ingenios* will notice astonishing concurrences in the two works. He will observe, for example, that corresponding to Laplante's twenty-eight engravings there are twenty-eight drawings, equally wide-cut, drawn by Acosta's hand, and that the poem's twenty-eight cantos find a referent in Cantero's twenty-eight texts. Both books, likewise, have two introductory sections and a kind of final appendix or coda, which open and close the descriptive texts and plates. But there are other parallels that lead one to conclude that such correspondences are not the work of chance.

In his "Words to the Reader," Acosta declares: "This is not the first time I have put my art at my country's service, but it is the first time I've put it at the service of what constitutes the source of the country's life . . . This book is dedicated to the Cuban government . . . To this entity that orders our destinies, that represents and channels us; to that abstract and indefinable—at times all-powerful—thing that is called government I dedicate this book" (pp. 5–6). That is, in a manner similar to that of Cantero and Laplante, Acosta relates his book to the sugar industry as the "homeland's fountain of life," and he dedicates his verses not to any particular person or social group, but rather to the institution of power which "legitimately" manipulates the stream of life that generates the sugar harvest. It is this abstract institution—called the Junta de Fomento (Council on Development) in the colonial era and the government in republican times—that serves as the administrative or ministerial edifice of the sugar-making homeland.

On reading Acosta's poem, we notice quickly that its title does not refer us to a concrete sugar harvest, but rather to the sugar harvest as a historical process, as a discourse that takes upon itself the representation of what is Cuban. Hence canto 7 treats "Los ingenios antiguos" (the ancient mills), and the next one "Los negros esclavos." The focus on the sugar mill is identical to that of Cantero and Laplante.

Nevertheless, if it is easy to see a strict paradigmatic relationship between *La zafra* and *Los ingenios*, such a relationship, far from establishing a sameness, is meant to establish a binary opposition. In fact, if *Los ingenios* inscribes itself within sugar's totalizing discourse, *La zafra* does so within a discourse of resistance to sugar. This discourse, as far as texts are concerned, is nothing new in Cuba. We see it organizing itself at around the end of the eighteenth century, outside of Havana for the most part, with the appearance of writings of a juridico-economic nature that seek to limit or weaken the dense concentration of power held by the Havana sugarocracy. Their wish is not to erase the sugar mill from the island, but rather to keep its voracious appetite for lands, forests, slaves, and privileges under control in order to preserve the existence of other sources of competing power, such as the tobacco, cattle, fishing, mining, and lumber industries. In any case, while Cantero and Laplante in their book sing of the mill's patriarchal domination and mythify its generative potential as a metaphoric figure that alludes to progress, Acosta's book sings a Sisyphean lament, the bitter and monotonous tune of those condemned ad infinitum to complete the vicious circle of "*zafra*" (harvest) and "*tiempo muerto*" (dead time) that regulates the endlessly reproducing year of sugar production.[6] *Los ingenios* glorifies the monoproductive machine; *La zafra* pities those who depend on it. Both books are directed at the abstract power that connects the sugar machine to society, transforming it into Plantation.

Acosta, in his verses, wishes to erase the difference between slave and free labor; for him, agricultural and industrial laboring on behalf of sugar brutalize both kinds of workers, subjugating them and reducing them equally to an oxlike passivity: "Half naked, sad, in slavish meekness / oxen in the strength of their virility" (p. 70). He also wishes to erase the differences between colonial and republican Cuba. The island was once bound to Spain; now it is chained to the United States. To Acosta, Cuban reality has not moved toward progress, it has remained trapped by the *zafra*'s centripetal force, and it keeps spinning around it. Yankee power has succeeded Spanish power, one founded upon conquest and colonization, the other on military intervention, battleship squadrons, the Platt Amendment,[7] and above all, capital investments in the sugar industry. Thus Acosta uses the word *battleship* to describe the modern, powerful North American sugar mill then anchored on the island:

> Gigantesco acorazado
> que va extendiendo su imperio
> y edifica un cementerio
> con las ruinas del pasado . . . !
> Lazo extranjero apretado
> con lucro alevoso y cierto;
> lazo de verdugo experto
> en torno al cuello nativo . . .
> Mano que tumba el olivo
> y se apodera del huerto . . . !
> (p. 12)

> (Gigantic battleship
> that widens its domain
> and builds a cemetery
> with the ruins of the past. . . !
> Foreign knot tightened
> with profit treacherous and sure;
> rope of an expert hangman
> around the native throat . . .
> Hand that fells the olive tree
> and overwhelms the orchard. . . !)

To better interpret the content and the radical tone of the discourse of resistance at the date in which *La zafra* comes into it, we must remember that, between 1911 and 1927, investments of North American capital in the sugar industry went up from 50 to 600 million dollars; in 1925, the year before *La zafra* was published, North American sugar mills produced 62.5 percent of Cuba's sugar and they owned the biggest *latifundios*. This alienation of the "homeland's fount of life," together with the fact that the Platt Amendment was still in force, explains the strong anti-imperialist tone that was adopted in those years—and in succeeding ones—within the discourse of resistance to the sugar mill's power. Furthermore, the sharp fall in the price of sugar in 1920 had dramatically ended the period known as "*la danza de los millones*," throwing local capital into bankruptcy. The government of Cuba, the seat of power to which Acosta directs himself, represented, in those years more than at any other time, North American interests on the island. In 1927, when *La zafra*'s verses were read, investments from the United States in Cuba, according to the most conservative calculations, climbed to 1,014 million dollars.[8]

In the midst of this situation of diminished sovereignty and economic disaster there emerges the tyranny of Gerardo Machado, one of whose first repressive moves is to shut down the recently founded National Confederation of Cuban Workers (CNOC). So *La zafra* appears at a moment of political, economic, and social crisis, in which the discourse of resistance gets more insistent and calls attention to the vulnerable paradox that the myth of sugar encloses: "grain of our good fortune . . . key to all our ills . . . !" says Agustín Acosta ironically (p. 103).

But Acosta's voice is not the only one to denounce sugar in verse.[9] In the same year there comes "El poema de los cañaverales" (The poem of the cane fields), by Felipe Pichardo Moya. We read in one of its stanzas:

> Máquinas. Trapiches que vienen del Norte.
> Los nombres antiguos sepulta el olvido.
> Rubios ingenieros de atlético porte
> y raras palabras dañando el oído . . . [10]

> (Machines. *Trapiches* coming from the North.
> Oblivion buries the ancient names.
> Blond engineers of athletic bearing
> and outlandish words that wound the ears . . .)

Or if you like:

El fiero machete que brilló en la guerra
en farsas políticas su acero corroe.
y en tanto, acechando la inexperta tierra
afila sus garras de acero Monroe.

(The fierce machete that shone in battle
in political farce its steel corrodes,
and meanwhile, stalking the unskilled land,
there sharpens his claws of steel Monroe.)

Published a few months before *La zafra*, Pichardo Moya's poem touches upon certain referents to which Acosta feels himself compelled to return. The most interesting intertextual relationship is produced in regard to Pichardo's doggerel rhyme of *acero corroe* (steel corrodes) with *acero Monroe* (steel Monroe). In this respect Acosta's rewriting constitutes a critique of the despairing pessimism of "El poema de los cañaverales":

El millonario suelo hoy está pobre;
pero en las manos de los campesinos
el acero no se corroe.
(p. 88)

(The millionaire land is poor today;
but held within the workers' hands
the steel does not corrode.)

That is to say that the generals of the War of Independence may have lent themselves to the political farce that pretends to shape Cubans' destinies, but a second revolution may be reborn in the island's impoverished fields, since the blade of the machete belonging to the worker, the old independence-seeking *mambí*, "does not corrode."

Such allusions to the possible reoccurrence of a revolutionary process are repeated as warnings throughout *La zafra*—"There's a violent smell of sugar in the air"—and even establish themselves in the words that Acosta directs to the reader, to the government, actually, at the beginning of the book: "My verse is an incendiary breeze that carries the seed of I don't know what future fires" (p. 5). In any case, the great majority of the texts upon which *La zafra* is constructed are not of a literary but rather a journalistic sort. Acosta himself acknowledges this debt: "This book aspires to being in Cuban literature something that will leave a lasting record of an era. You will tell me that the truth is in the newspapers as well. They who say this are right. But a work of art influences some spirits in a way quite different from the way that a newspaper does" (p. 7). In fact, the economic and social formulations that one reads in *La zafra*—especially those that oppose the *latifundio,* monoculture, the sugar worker's condition, and the expansion of North American investments—refer in large part to the articles on economics written by Ramiro Guerra y Sánchez, which, first published in the *Diario de la Marina,* were to appear in book form in 1927. I am referring, clearly, to *Azúcar y población en las Antillas.*[11]

It is interesting to observe the subversion of *modernista* poetic language that Acosta undertakes in *La zafra,* without actually going outside the realm of *modernista* poetry. To do this he takes advantage of the multiplicity of meters and rhythms characteristic of this current, and adds to them a prosiness and a will to experiment that foreshadow the vanguardists. Let's look, for example, at a parody of Rubén Darío's "Marcha triunfal":

> Por las guardarrayas y las serventías
> forman las carretas largas teorías . . .
>
> Vadean arroyos . . . cruzan las montañas
> llevando la suerte de Cuba en las cañas . . .
>
> Van hacia el coloso de tierra cercano:
> van hacia el ingenio norteamericano.
>
> y como quejándose cuando a él se avecinan,
> cargadas, pesadas, repletas,
> ¡con cuántas cubanas razones rechinan
> las viejas carretas . . . !
> (pp. 59–60)

> (Along the fences and the roadways
> the carts form long theories
>
> They ford the streams . . . they cross the mountains
> carrying Cuba's fate in sugarcane
>
> They go toward the nearby colossus of iron:
> they move toward the North American engine,
>
> and as though lamenting their approach,
> loaded, heavy, replete,
> they squeak out so many Cuban arguments,
> these old wagons . . . !)

And so, by means of the irony that parody implies, Acosta transforms the dazzling entourage of the armor and the paladins that Darío would leave with us into the dark and rancorous march of the sugar wagons which, with the steps of the oxen, carry "the homeland's fountain of life" to the foreign sugar mill.

From the libido to the superego

Agustín Acosta's far-ranging national antiepic of the sugar industry was followed by the brief but intense poems of Nicolás Guillén. As has been said more than once, there is a striking difference between these two poets' work, Acosta's being of a refined sort that is out of the reach of a general public, while Guillén's stems from an unquestionable desire to capture and deliver a folk essence.[12] In the case that we are dealing with, this difference is extremely important, since it is precisely the discourse of power that confers a legitimate right to speak for the subjugated. So, with Guillén, a voice bursts into Cuban poetry which, though already present in the discourse of resistance, now fills a new, decisive space that contributes to the radicalization of that discourse. This revolutionary voice, as we know, belongs to the descendants of the Africans who were uprooted from their native soil to serve as slaves on Cuba's plantations.

I think it is unnecessary to argue the strict relationship that existed between the sugar economy, as the subject of power, and the slave, as its object. One has to conclude that the most critical social tension that there was in the Cuba of *Los ingenios* took its shape from the opposition between the slaveholding groups—be they sugar producers or slave traffickers—and the slaves. It's clear that the latter's voice, a voice subjected to the most extreme conditions of subjugation, represented the most radical position within the discourse of resistance from within the colonial Plantation. And I think we should not limit this voice's wide resonance by narrowing it to encompass only the range of the socioeconomic discourse. In fact, the slave's voice establishes a complicated alignment of differences that has implications for many discourses. I am not referring only to discourses of an ethnological or anthropological cut, which have already been studied more or less, but rather also to others which have only recently become the object of analysis. I am speaking, for example, of the discourse of desire in its manifestations as sexual pleasure and as knowledge-power. In any case, it is plain enough that the profound differences that the Negro's violent arrival established were reconstructed through the discourse of racism. Starting from the sugar boom at the end of the eighteenth century, this discourse includes the slaves and the freedmen within the rubric of "Negroes" or "people of color." Thus colonial society, now fully vested thanks to sugar, began to see itself as a conflict of races, growing out of the presence of a "white" pole, the dominant minority, and a "black" pole, the subjected majority. The planter/slave contradiction was transcended by the white/black one, helped by the fact that the free Negroes in Cuba made up one-fifth of the total population. This high proportion—greater than in the other so-called sugar islands—was important not just in numerical but also in qualitative terms, since it referred largely to Negroes and mulattos who practiced trades and lived in cities. It has been said that the thing that kept the Cubans from seeking their independence at an earlier time was their fear of freeing the slaves, but something more should be added: the suspicion that the freedmen would unite with them, and then the "Negroes" would represent 60 percent of the population. This fear of the *"peligro negro"* (black peril)—a complex fear that implies guilt, as we saw in Las Casas's narrative—comes out into the open in nationalist reform proposed by Saco, Delmonte, and Luz y Caballero, which advocated a gradual abolition of slavery, and appears in a more or less problematized way in the first Cuban novels, including the texts that are usually grouped under the rubric of "antislavery" or "abolitionist."

As could be expected, this fear of the *"peligro negro"* did not disappear from the Plantation's "white" levels with the abolition of slavery. This explains the long period of transition imposed on the former slave, under the regimen known as *patronato* (trusteeship), before he could attain the position of a free and salaried worker. The year 1880 is given to mark the date of slavery's end in Cuba, but in fact it remained in force, for certain practical purposes, until 1886. In any event, the length of this transition contributed decisively to the former slaves' remaining anchored to the sugar plantation, above all if we take several factors into account which worked against their being a mobile work force. One of those was the scarcity of available land because of systematic and voracious expansion of the sugar industry, which kept the Negro, now liberated, from becoming a rural smallholder, as was the case in Jamaica. Another decisive factor, perhaps the most important one, was the chronic scarcity of cheap manpower that hampered, above all, the work of harvesting the sugarcane. This circumstance moved the sugar power to avail itself of every means within its reach to keep the Negro beside the cane field.[13] This is behind Guillén's well-known poem entitled "Caña" (1930):

El negro
junto al cañaveral

El yanqui
sobre el cañaveral

La tierra
bajo el cañaveral

¡Sangre
que se nos va!
(vol. I, p. 129) [14]

(The Negro
beside the cane field.

The yankee
above the cane field.

The land
beneath the cane field.

Blood
that we lose!)

But, as I said, I don't think that Guillen's anti-imperialism is the most salient feature of his first books. In that sense, Acosta's poem is a much earlier and at the same time much more extensive and direct protest than the one we read in "Caña." For me the truly crucial thing about the poems of *Motivos de son* (1930) and *Sóngoro cosongo* (1931) is the voice of the Negro, which directs itself toward all strata of the Plantation with the intention of investing them with its *desire* and its *resistance*. I mean that Guillén not only reveals the Negro's imprisonment within the plantation, but he also wishes to impregnate society with the Negro's libido—his own libido—transgressing the mechanisms of sexual censorship that the Plantation imposed on his race. Thus, in these poems, we can see the setting up of a representation of neo-African beauty that defies and desacralizes the canons of classical beauty, which were being exalted even then by the *modernista* poets, including Acosta. Suddenly, next to the statues of Apollo and Aphrodite, there appear, carved in dark wood, the figures of Shango and Oshun; next to the swan's neck, the alabaster skin, the emerald eyes, the strawberry mouth, and the porcelain fingernails (poetical materials that turn out to be foreign to Caribbean contexts), there come bursting forth the vital metaphors that attempt to represent a new woman of "strong loins," "flesh the color of a tree that's been burnt," fingernails of "purple grape," and "the tireless foot for the drum's deep dance." This everyday black woman, who suddenly comes to the surface in Caribbean poetry, carries with her the transcontinental mysteries of the African forest, but also the Antillean mystery of Cuba: "that dark crocodile / swimming in the Zambezi of your eyes." And, above all, the mystery of Havana, the mystery of the narrow streets with their old lamps, of the inns and taverns, of the *carnaval,* of the rumba, of the docks, of the whorehouses and the good times. It is the woman of "Búcate plata," of "Mi chiquita," "Secuestro de la mujer de Antonio," of "Sóngoro cosongo," of "Sigue . . ." and of "Rumba." It is the woman of "Mujer nueva":

> Con el círculo ecuatorial
> ceñido a la cintura como a un pequeño mundo
> la negra, mujer nueva,
> avanza en su ligera bata de serpiente.
>
> Coronada de palmas
> como una diosa recién llegada
> ella trae la palabra inédita,
> el anca fuerte,
> la voz, el diente, la mañana y el salto.
>
> Chorro de sangre joven
> bajo un pedazo de piel fresca,
> y el pie incansable
> para la pista profunda del tambor.
> (vol. I, pp. 120–21)

(With the equatorial circle
tied around her waist like a little world,
the Negress, the new woman,
advances wearing her light serpent's dress.

Crowned with palms
like a goddess just arrived
she carries the unwritten word,
the strong loin,
the voice, the tooth, the morning and her spring.

A spurt of young blood
beneath a piece of fresh skin,
and a tireless foot
for the drum's deep dance.)

Much has been said, of course, about these poems' sensuality. I think, nonetheless, that the revolutionary character of this sensuality has been insufficiently emphasized, particularly in the way in which it transforms, changing it into a free and vital desire, the death instinct and the symbols of subjugation [15] that the repressive sugar discourse brought to Cuban society, especially regarding the Negro.[16] Further, we should also point out the presence of other Caribbean values in these poems. Remember that the expression of that which is Caribbean tends to project itself outward, splitting in two and attempting a return to its elusive sources. The literature that recognizes itself as most Caribbean aspires to fold itself toward that impossible sociocultural unity, in an attempt at annuling the whetted violence inherent in the society from which it emerges; therefore it seeks a general, massive public, for behind its performance lies the sacrifice that will save the group from violence. Thus Guillén's desire, the inclusive desire of the Caribbean Negro within a reality restricted by racism, is disseminated along with the rhythm of popular song, and becomes, through the political economy of ritual, the desire of all, the desire of a nationality without racial conflict, of a great homeland where the flowing of the rivers of the world outlines the figure of a telluric saurian that represents the island. And it's the hard realities of the Negro on the Plantation that are covered up in these verses. Here there are, for example, "Hay que tené boluntá," "Caña," "Pequeña oda a un negro boxeador cubano"; except that the message of these texts does not reside in the Negro's lament, but is transcended by a decided song of nationalist affirmation. Far from showing Afro-Cubanness as a negative derivation of the middle passage and of slavery, Guillén's poetry speaks of black men and women who established a firm American presence in "Llegada," and proclaim their laborious cultural victory in "La canción del bongo."

The theme of *Los ingenios* exalted the sugar mill as a myth of national foundation that provided "life, order, and industry" to the homeland; it was destined for the sugar-producing power, and its intent was to affirm the latter's ego by offering it a reading that would speak of its legitimacy and its perpetuity. *La zafra*'s theme was the demythification of the sugar mill;

this poem too was directed to the sugar-producing power, though with an admonitory intention: if there is no alleviation of the socioeconomic problems that grew from the *latifundio,* from monoculture and monoproduction, from unjust labor relations and the loss of sovereignty over "the source of the homeland's life," there would be a violent revolution with unforeseeable consequences. The theme of *Motivos de son* and *Sóngoro cosongo* was not directed toward the sugar power but rather toward all of Cuban society in the context of the Plantation; its message of protest and sensuality connected with the old creole desire that had been carried by the Three Juans of the Virgen del Cobre; that is, with the integrationist myth which we have already looked at and whose aspiration was to construct—if symbolically—a space for racial, social, and cultural coexistence. With this, Guillén offered a way of deflating the Plantation's aggressiveness by way of reinterpreting the nation's origins, that is to say, a not entirely mythological, but rather social search, that involved his own desire for legitimation as a Cuban, being also a "person of color." Of course this voyage of desire in search of its primeval origins was always implicit in the libido of the folk music, the *son,* an ethnologically promiscuous libido which in the final analysis, insofar as it was a supersyncretic musical product that mixed the African drum with the European string, carried the "white" desire for "blackness" and vice versa. But the desire for mixing (*mestizaje*) that Guillén offered in these poems through the metaphor of the *son* went no further than the dialectical and positivist discourse of modernity. Guillén desired a Cuba that was "*mulata*"; that is, a form of nationality that would resolve the deep racial and cultural conflicts by means of a reduction or synthesis that flowed from the proposal of a creole myth; that is, the *mestizo* reality understood as "unity," not as a sheaf of different and coexistent dynamics. This desire is expressed most clearly in his next book, *West Indies, Ltd.* (1934), above all in his well-known poem "Balada de los dos abuelos" (Ballad of the two grandfathers), whose last verses are:

> Sombras que sólo yo veo,
> me escoltan mis dos abuelos.
>
> Don Federico me grita
> y Taita Facundo calla;
> los dos en la noche sueñan
> y andan, andan.
> Yo los junto.
>   —¡Federico!

¡Facundo! Los dos se abrazan.
Los dos suspiran. Los dos
las fuertes cabezas alzan;
los dos del mismo tamaño,
bajo las estrellas altas;
los dos del mismo tamaño,
ansia negra y ansia blanca,
los dos del mismo tamaño,
gritan, sueñan, lloran, cantan.
Sueñan, lloran, cantan.
Lloran, cantan.
¡Cantan!
(vol. 1, p. 139)

(Shadows that only I see,
my two grandfathers watch over me.

Don Federico shouts at me
and Taita Fernando is silent;
they both dream in the nights
and they walk, they walk.
I bring them together.
                                        Federico!
Facundo! The two embrace.
They sigh.
The two
strong heads rise up;
both the same size,
beneath the high stars;
both the same size,
black longing and white longing,
both the same size,
shouting, weeping, dreaming, singing.
They dream, they weep, they sing.
They weep, they sing.
They sing!)

And so, to sum it up, that which is Cuban to Guillén in those years is
that which is *mestizo* seen as a synthesis, a formula with which he tries to
transcend the racial conflict inherent in the Plantation and, in passing, to

offer his mulatto ego a way out. In reality, as we know, this construction's antecedents appear in the thought of José Martí—who was also a Caribbean, and who also directed himself outward—though only in a thin and abstract fashion; it is Guillén who, after reading Spengler and Fernando Ortiz,[17] postulates it concretely and popularly with the example of the *son*. In the poem entitled "Palabras en el trópico," in the same book, there is a clear allusion—"y Cuba ya sabe que es mulata" (vol. 1, p. 136) ("and Cuba now knows that it is mulatto")—to Martí's desire for all of the peoples of "Nuestra America" to recognize themselves as children of a great *mestizo* homeland.

In "West Indies, Ltd.," a long poem that gives the book its title, we see that his verse also goes beyond the strictly Cuban and connects with the discourse of resistance that flows within the pan-Caribbean Plantation. He has pointed out that the sugar-milling machine subjugates historically not the Cuban Negro alone, and now his poetry navigates through all the Antilles. We're dealing here with a memorable moment in Cuban letters; Cuba, for the first time, is linked by a poem to the sugar-producing order that has subjected the whole archipelago, and this not just in social and economic terms, but also in racial ones:

> Aquí hay blancos y negros y chinos y mulatos.
> Desde luego, se trata de colores baratos,
> pues a traves de tratos y contratos
> se han corrido los tintes y no hay un tono estable.
> (El que piense otra cosa que avance un paso y hable.)
> (vol. 1, p. 159)

> (Here there are whites and blacks and Chinese and mulattos.
> Of course, we're talking about cheap colors,
> since through deals and contracts
> the shades have run together and there is no stable tone.
> He who thinks anything else, let him take one step forward
>   and speak.)

Notice the attempt to eliminate the racial violence from the Plantation and to draw an equivalency between the colors of the "whites" and the "blacks, Chinese, and mulattos," by saying that in the end "we're talking about cheap colors." But "West Indies, Ltd.," in spite of representing a formal achievement, as much for its technical complexity as for its length, also represents a step backward in terms of the representation of the libido of the Negro. One might say that Guillén's ego has lost some African resonances in favor of an Antillean and *mestizo* nationalism. Apart from certain distances, the poem can be situated very easily next to *La zafra*; one could even say that it is a rereading of it.[18] Here, unlike in the poems of *Motivos de son* and *Sóngoro cosongo*, one does not feel the vital presence of the Negro's desire, but rather, on the contrary, the superego's repressive manipulation is affirmed. In fact, it is easy to perceive that the poem's voice has stopped being rhythm, music, sexual urgency, dance step, or elemental laughter, to turn toward bitter, moralizing reproaches directed to that "dark smiling folk" that smiles without any reason to:

> Cabarets donde el tedio se engaña
> con el ilusorio cordial
> de una botella de champaña,
> en cuya eficacia la gente confía
> como un neosalvarsán de alegría
> para la "sífilis sentimental"
> (vol. 1, pp. 163–64)

> (Cabarets where tedium tricks itself
> with the illusory cordial
> of a bottle of champaigne
> in whose efficacy the people trust
> as in an arsenate of happiness
> for "sentimental syphilis")

I think that these verses, which display the superego's recriminations, have little to do with the sensuality, say, of "Secuestro de la mujer de Antonio":

> Te voy a beber de un trago,
> como una copa de ron;
> te voy a echar en la copa
> de un son,
> prieta, quemada en ti misma,
> cintura de mi canción.
> (vol. 1, p. 129)

> (I'm going to drink you in one swallow,
> like a glass of rum;

I'm going to put you in the cup
of a *son,*
black girl, burnt within yourself
waistband of my song.)

In any case, "West Indies, Ltd.," with its message of "cutting off heads like cane stalks / zas, zas, zas!" (vol. 1, p. 162), expresses in a way much more radical than *La zafra*'s the prisoners of the cane field in their desire for revenge.[19]

In spite of the fact that his next books—*Cantos para soldados y sones para turistas* and *España*—center on the world antifascist movement, particularly in the context of the war in Ethiopia and the Spanish Civil War, Guillén finds the space to brush against the sugar theme in "La voz esperanzada" in the collection entitled *España*. Here we have a kind of summary where the poet legitimates himself as a son of Martí's "America *mestiza*"—"Yo, / hijo de América, / hijo de ti y de Africa" (vol. 1, p. 216: I, / son of America, / your [Spain's] son and Africa's)—while at the same time recognizing himself as subjugated historically by the sugar-producing power, as seen in the antecedent works of Pichardo Moya and Acosta: "esclavo ayer de mayorales blancos dueños de látigos coléricos; / hoy esclavo de rojos yanquis azucareros y voraces" (vol. 1, p. 215: yesterday a slave of white overseers, the owners of angry whips / today a slave of ruddy yankees, sugaring and voracious). In reality, with the exception of the well-realized verses of "Soldado así no he de ser," in *Canciones para soldados y sones para turistas*, Guillén will not again make himself felt in his poetry of resistance to sugar until the *Elegía a Jesús Menéndez* (1951), where the partisan rhetoric is surpassed by the rich eloquence of the expressive means, and the terse and deeply felt *Elegía cubana* (1952): "Cuba, palmar vendido, / sueño descuartizado, / duro mapa de azúcar y de olvido . . ." (vol. 1, p. 389: Cuba, auctioned palm grove, / dismembered dream, / cruel map of sugar and oblivion . . .). Both elegies reappear in print in *La paloma de vuelo popular. Elegías* (1958), two collections published in a single volume, in Buenos Aires just before the triumph of the Cuban Revolution.

The Communist poet

In the *Elegía a Jesús Menéndez* there is a stanza, the last one, that reads:

Entonces llegará,
General de las Cañas, con su sable,

hecho de un gran relámpago bruñido;
entonces llegará,
jinete en un caballo de agua y humo,
lenta sonrisa en el saludo lento;
entonces llegará para decir,
Jesús, para decir:
—Mirad, he aquí el azúcar ya sin lágrimas.
(vol. 1, p. 436)

(Then he will come,
General of the Canefields, with his saber
made of a huge burnished thunderbolt;
then he will come,
riding a steed of water and smoke,
slow smile and slow greeting;
then he will come to say,
Jesus, to say:
"Look, here is sugar without tears.")

The stanza is interesting because it expresses Guillén's hope for a proletarian revolution which, directed by the sugar workers' unionizing movement, would free the working class from the capitalist class that owns the means of producing sugar. It is what we could call a "communist" stanza, and this in the strictest sense of the word.[20] It has always seemed strange to me, nonetheless, that Guillén, with his profound understanding of the Plantation, should have fallen for the ingenuous pattern of thinking that the mechanical transposition of a European doctrine—as Marxism-Leninism is—to a Caribbean island could be successful as a socioeconomic project; I mean, concretely, that an island-plantation, Cuba for example, could ever produce sugar "without tears." Unfortunately, sugar has been, is, and will be produced with tears, independent of the mode of production in which it is inserted as the product, as long as its character as plantation merchandise is maintained. The phenomena unleashed by the plantation economy are so deep, so complex, and so tenacious—and even more so in the case of sugarcane—that they ordinarily survive the most drastic political changes, the greatest natural and economic catastrophes, and processes of recognized social violence such as wars, foreign occupations, dictatorships, and revolutions. The machinery of the sugar mill, once installed and set in motion, soon becomes almost indestructible, since even when it is partially dismantled, its transformative impact will survive it for many years, and its track will be inscribed within Nature itself, in the climate, in the demographic, political, social, economic, and cultural structures of the society to which it once was joined. This is the sad case of Haiti and of other islands in the Caribbean.

Although we have already looked at the sugar economy's effects, it seems now to me to be an opportune moment to underline the idea that, within the Plantation, power is distributed socially in a very unequal fashion, in its extension as well as its density.[21] Not only is it territorialized by a small minority, but the latter also tends to perpetuate itself in that privileged space, putting itself forth as the only group imbued with sufficient understanding, morality, and prestige to inherit and increase the sugaring patrimony that gives "life, order, and industry" to the nation. Thus a great number of individuals live trapped indefinitely inside the sugar-making network under the groups that successively take hold of the power. In the case of Cuba, as its economy passed from dependent capitalism to dependent socialism, while maintaining as a constant the sugar-making nature of its production, the worker found out in a few years that his surplus value had not ceased to exist at bottom; it was simply that, now, outside of capitalist relationships, it expressed itself in terms of the appropriation of power. Hence, as far as the social distribution of power was concerned, Cuban structures experienced no democratization. Moreover, given that the new controlling group proposed to produce more sugar than ever under an authoritarian and militarist model of direction by the state, itself antidemocratic, the final result has been that the concentration of power in the apparatus of government has reached a density never before seen in Cuba.

In any case, with the triumph of the revolution in 1959, Guillén's poetry enters a new period; that is, he abandons the discourse of resistance to which he had been connected earlier and places himself within the discourse of power. The poems most representative of this period are collected in *Tengo* (1964), where Guillén experiences the mirage that now, within the revolution, all of Cuba is "his," sugar included. Just after this come *Poemas de amor* (1964). In these, running against the official current, the theme shifts from an apology for state power to a defense of the erotic, though no longer with the force and spontaneity of his first books. I think that these poems represent a desire to retrace the course of sensuality in order to find other paths within it by way of which a new perspective might be found. And Guillén certainly finds one. His next book, *El gran zoo* (1967), marks the beginning of a new period. Starting with this collection of zoological epigrams, Guillén's poetry will be characterized by an ambiguity that perhaps responds to his own personal situation: the conflict of being "national poet,"[22] president of the Cuban Writers' and Artists' Union, deputy in the National Assembly, and member of the Central Committee of the Cuban Communist Party, and, on the other hand, feeling the emptiness of these titles, their masklike concavity, their ephemeral position faced with the power, on the island, of the sugar mill (now electrified), the cane field (now mechanized), in short, faced with the unyielding power of the state in its capacity as sugar-producing institution, which has set itself up as the highest truth, as the most valid, permanent, and legitimate entity that has ever existed or ever will exist in Cuba.

The controversial poet

Of the poems in *El gran zoo*, the one entitled "Los ríos" is perhaps the most ambivalent. It's not a question of the poem's being about sugar production in a direct fashion, but rather of an intense reflection in which Guillén questions much of his earlier work, and therefore it is of crucial importance to an understanding of his poetry's latest transformation, above all in its touching upon the problems of culture, history, nationality, and the plantation in the Caribbean. His analysis, then, has here become indispensable. This is the entire text:

> He aquí la jaula de las culebras.
> Enroscados en sí mismos,
> duermen los ríos, los sagrados ríos.
> El Mississippi, con sus negros,
> El Amazonas con sus indios.
> Son como los zunchos poderosos
> de unos camiones gigantescos.
>
> Riendo, los niños les arrojan
> verdes islotes vivos,
> selvas pintadas de papagayos,
> canoas tripuladas
> y otros ríos.
> Los grandes ríos despiertan,
> se desenroscan lentamente,
> engullen todo, se hinchan, a poco más revientan
> y vuelven a quedar dormidos.
> (vol. 2, pp. 229–30)

(This is the snake cage.
Coiled up on themselves,
the rivers sleep, the sacred rivers.
The Mississippi with its Negroes,
The Amazon with its Indians.
They are like the powerful springs
on some gigantic trucks.

Laughing, the children throw
live green islands,
jungles painted with parrots, manned canoes
and other rivers.
The great rivers awaken,
slowly uncoil themselves,
devour everything, swell up, almost burst
and go back to sleep.)

The paradox that this poem presents to the reader is similar to the one that any piece of music would exhibit; that is, there is an unfolding of signifiers that make up a discourse, a story that speaks of the oppressed races of America. But, as often happens in music, the discourse advances up to a point at which it circles back; finally, when the snakes/rivers curl up to go to sleep, it is at the same place (tonality) from which it began, and this will happen time and again, perpetually. With a more careful reading we will notice that we needn't wait for the last line before we can verify the double value that Guillén's text suggests. For example, the second stanza offers a vectoral reading (children throwing things into the river), but it also proposes a circular reading, a self-referential one, in which children, as if feeding the river, or its sign, throw into it its own referents (islands, forests, even "manned canoes and other rivers"). Moreover, we can read the snakes from the outset as ambiguous and unstable animals, circular when asleep and straight when "they awaken" and "unwind themselves." If we take the metonymic path, we have it that the snakes sleep, are awakened, unroll themselves, devour everything, and then go to sleep; if we follow the metaphor's trail, the animals send us the old self-referential sign known as "the serpent that bites its tail"; if we should read both together at once, we do not find a synthesis derived from a simple dialectic, as we have been wont to discover in Guillén, but rather an insoluble paradox: the rivers/snakes are both circular and straight, neither circular nor straight; that is, they are music.

Now if we take another step in our analysis, we see that the very idea
of taking the Mississippi and the Amazon as rivers that are both different
(one has "*negros*" and the other "*indios*") and also the same, expresses, from
the outset, the poem's musicality, since both may be seen as "voices" inter-
preting a song. It is important also to point out that, even when the two
rivers seemed to make their differences vanish through their becoming a
musical whole, this "whole" will always be absent, since the poem itself
does not name the river that could represent the "*blancos*," this latter being
the word necessary to the idea of there being "*negros*" on the Mississippi
and "*indios*" on the Amazon. In truth we could say that the poem flows
around this hidden voice—the voice of the white master—which makes
itself present (resonates) quite powerfully in its presumed absence, as it
was the Europeans who "discovered," conquered, baptized, and colonized
the Indians of America, and it was they, too, who initiated the transoce-
anic trade in Africans, whom they enslaved, renamed, and taught to speak
their language. If we keep this in mind, the poem soon proposes to us
that we search for the voice that is hidden, or rather, absent in its presence.
We might think that this voice is that of the children who feed the snake
through the bars of its cage. But we can see right away that this is not so.
A group of children who laugh and care for the animals does not suggest
for a moment the White Father's exalted voice. In fact one would have to
conclude that this Great Father's voice issues from somewhere "before or
after" the poem's immediate referents. In any case we already know that
there are four voices in the choral ensemble: the Indians', the Negroes',
the children's, and the Great White Father's. But the first three voices have
much in common. It is true that the Indians' and the Negroes' parts are
sung by caged animals, while the third is that of the children visiting the
zoo. However, animals and children have been linked metaphorically from
mythological times down to the Disney era. Furthermore, both groups
are objects of power, in that their individual members may be defined as
captives (in school, institution, asylum, home, kennel, cage, zoo, etc.) surrounded by prohibitions, while at the same time subjected to a regimen
that assigns their hours of eating, sleeping, learning. Remember that in the
word *zoological,* as in "zoological garden" (zoo), the "zoo" refers to that
which is relative to animals and the "logical" to discourse, wit, knowledge.
So the zoo can be defined as the place where the animals are exhibited
for purposes of knowledge, study, scientific discourse—that is, to be read
and annotated by those who have seized the power and held it.

Zoos, however, like other institutions that control and examine individuals, are far from perfect. The mechanism of power, the zoo or, let's say, the military academy, is a failure in itself, an impossibility, as Foucault has shown.[23] It interrupts the captive's free flow, but incompletely. It presents itself as perfect, yet knows better than anyone that it is far from being so. No matter how hard it tries to reduce the captives' freedom of movement, it never achieves this completely. Furthermore, its own desire moves toward the infinite. It is precisely this unsatisfied desire to wield total control, total vigilance, and total discipline that fuels it. The power mechanism moves thanks to its impossible desire to keep on knowing and transforming the captive. That the captive stays in jail, or in the aquarium, or in the hospital or the school does not spell victory for power; on the contrary, it certifies its failure. Granted, it is only a partial failure: the failed success of the judicial machine, the political machine, the ideological machine, the economic machine, the educational machine, the military machine, the family machine, and even the revolutionary machine when it connects itself to power. Thus the power relationship never manages to be entirely a hierarchical monologue, which is the machine's total desire. It can be understood rather as a counterpoint of flows and interruptions between subject and object which, in continual transformation, moves off toward the infinite.

Now let's return to the poem's singing group of captive voices. How shall we define this song? In terms of its words, I hear it as a song that expresses a common desire for freedom. This would reduce the poem's overall song, in the harmonic sense, to two voices: that of the snakes-rivers-Negroes-Indians-children, sung in unison and inscribed within the poetic, and that of the Great White Father, sung from "outside," before or after the poetic, in a theoretical, scientific, epistemological space. And so, in Guillén's *El gran zoo*, the snakes-rivers-Negroes-Indians-children are poetic texts that organize a counterpoint to the Great White Father's voice, the voice whose theme, as we know, expresses the desire to increase his knowledge-power over the captives, the Other. Clearly, such a desire will never be exhausted, since for this to happen the Great White Father would have to take up the Other and share its captivity. And this impossibility does not matter; the Great White Father, in his song, will read the snakes' text time and again, will correct it time and again, though it will never mean what he wants it to mean. It's easy to see that his hope and perseverance are implicit in the desire to escape shown by those who are the objects of his power. This is the double irony that the poem contains.

Certainly the idea of opposing poetry to the machine is nothing new. It is sketched out even in the poem of Agustín Acosta's that we looked at, and also in Guillén's first books. But can we even be sure that the poem "Los ríos" tries to confront technology? According to the theory I have just presented, the answer to this would be: not completely. What stands in the way of confrontation is, precisely, the version of the book that Guillén gives us, that is, the book-zoo in which each epigram is an animal held in either a cage or an aquarium. In "Los ríos" the crucial element does not lie with the snakes but rather with the cage. The cage, in its capacity as a mechanism of power, is the signifier that mediates between the poetic and the theoretical, keeping the acts of both opposition and synthesis from being consummated. The cage, like Las Casas's *piedra solimán,* can kill and it can also prolong life; it can be an icon of the madhouse and also of the girl's boarding school, of the jail or the hospital, of the kindergarten or the nursing home, of the womb or the coffin. The cage lends itself to everything and is compromised by nothing. It is triumph and defeat at once. It is writing. It is, above all, desire. It is something immoveable and porous that interposes itself always, maintaining the distance between the subject and the object, something that, with each step that one takes toward it, recedes a step away along an endless corridor, something that concedes an entry but stands in the way as a transparent, ghostly presence, something that's *there,* always *there*.

In "Los ríos," the cage speaks of power relations in abstract terms— poetico-theoretical ones—and also concrete ones; let's call them Caliban/ Prospero. We've already seen that the White Father (we'll call him Prospero) was outside of the poem (outside of the cage), although he was still *there,* putting himself forward from his position of power as scientific language, knowledge, center, origin, etc. Of course he is actually a usurper, an impostor, a mask; he is, in short, the Other Father. Such an imposture is precisely what has led me to identify the White Father with Prospero and the snakes with Caliban. But one has to conclude that Caliban here is not a coherent entity or a stable pole opposing itself dialectically to Prospero's; he is, rather, as we saw, a paradox containing a dialogue of differences and continually postponing its own ending. Caliban is the impossible knot that a linear serpent makes when combined with another, circular one; he is the ambivalent, deterritorialized being who would like to be in the place that Prospero occupies outside the poem—a place that he has begun to comprehend through his process of domestication, colonization, and dependency—that is, the space invested with the marvels of technology, historical and epistemological space, the European and monological space that the Great White Father administers. To what end? To the end of recovering, outside of the cage, his true genealogy, his ancestral innocence, his poetic language, his original habitat, his lost paradise of green islands and parroty forests. This is his inconsistency.

Guillén's Caliban is an attempt to represent the impossibility of poetry, since he cannot renounce the desire to occupy the place of history, of politics, of economics, of technology. But from the other side of the cage things are not turning out any better. Prospero too is an ambivalent being, for he would like to slip through the bars of the cage to dance a zoophilic rumba; he'd like to be within the cage, disguised as a snake and given over to the frenzy of the ancestral drums and knowing all there is to know about rivers and their metaphors, while the children toss him their laughter and their birds. Yes, certainly, Prospero controls and watches over Caliban, but he would like to return to Caliban's world, an Edenic world that once was his and that he can't return to. Of course Prospero is wrong. He takes Caliban, because he is on the other side of the cage, to be a solid, coherent savage, all innocence and poetry. Caliban, in turn, is also mistaken; Prospero is not what he pretends to be, nor is he where he says he is. Thus both Caliban and Prospero are double signs that do not manage to exclude each other mutually, since each would secretly like to be in the other's place. The difference between them does not lie in their respective natures, but rather in the space-time that they occupy: Indo-America and Afro-America on one side of the cage, Euro-America on the other. It is easy to establish binary oppositions between them, as Guillén himself was once wont to do, but also, as he does here, it's not hard to dismantle those oppositions in favor of a global ensemble of differences that might underwrite imperfect relations of coexistence in continuous transformation.

What concretely can this abstraction give us? Well, we might conclude that what Guillén here proposes will leave no place for his old idea of an American *mestizo* synthesis. The poem doesn't mention *mestizos* or *mulatos,* but rather *indios* and *negros,* and it never even alludes to the first two groups. America is the Great Zoo, with its North American and South American rivers, its Indians and Negroes, its forests and islands, its poetic children and its White Fathers. America is, above all, a book of impossible poems for impossible readers; it is *El gran zoo,* speaking of itself and of the Other, in itself and in the Other, for itself and for the Other; it is a never-ending dialogue of differences that curves back over itself as a perpetual symphony or as a paradoxical figure of power relations. It's not that Guillén expressly denies the unity of history and poetry, but rather that he places them within the cages, in mediated spaces that allow a degree of coexistence with their apparent contraries; that is, a dialogic space that, instead of leading only to a synthesis, leads toward the turbulence of doubt, toward chaos.

What do we now make of Guillén's ego? Well, it's easy to see that he has now removed the mask of the mulatto, of the ambassador who represents a *mestizo* America. He continues to wear the mask of Caliban, but it's a Caliban split in two by his own duplicity. He is now the mask of Hermes, or, better, to stay within the Afro-Caribbean contexts, of Elegua. Elegua, as we know, is the mediator between the Supreme Being and the *Orishas,* between the *Orishas* and the living, between the living and the dead; it is he who carries the word (the offering) for good or for ill, who presides over thresholds and crossroads; it is he who deals with everyone and is aware of everything; in his avatars he is at once a child and an old man, he makes things feasible and he complicates them, he is gregarious and solitary; in short, he is a double being par excellence, the Eternally Masked, the Messenger of the Word; he is the Poet.

The subversive poet

In 1968 Guillén published, in Mexico, his famous poem "Digo que yo no soy un hombre puro" ("I tell you I'm not a pure man"). Keep in mind that at that time the Cuban governmental machine was claiming to produce a "new man," a man apparently unpolluted by material cravings, a man as homogeneous and standardized as a grain of refined sugar. Remember also that on this date the so-called "revolutionary offensive" occurred, directed toward eradicating every desire, every libido that might disrupt the practice of inoculating the masses with self-censoring ideas to favor the narrow ideology of material renunciation that the regime had imposed.[24] His public support of the government notwithstanding, Guillén in this poem denounces the mystical irrationality that means to take the entire Cuban people along the path of "purity." To the politics of frugality, Guillén replies: "and I like to eat pork with potatoes, / and garbanzos and *chorizos,* and / eggs, chickens, mutton, turkey / fish and shellfish" (vol. 2, p. 297); to the politics of sexual repression he responds—with the most daring line he was ever to publish—that he mistrusted the "purity of the woman who never licked a glans. / The purity of the man who never sucked on a clitoris" (vol. 2, p. 298); to the politics of restricting consumption of alcoholic drinks and of closing down the bars, he answers: "and I drink rum and beer and brandy and wine" (vol. 2, p. 296); in short, to make his noncompliance quite clear, he answers: "I'm impure, what do you want me to say? / completely impure. / Nevertheless, / I think that there are many pure things in the world / that are no more than pure shit" (vol. 2, p. 296).

Four years later, with the publication of *El diario que a diario* (The Daily Daily, 1972), Guillén's poetry announces itself as a purgative or vermifuge to remove the long worm of history from the belly, concretely, the worm of Cuban history, the history of the Plantation. So the book can be read as a prescription for freeing Cuba from its laborious intestinal history and, at the same time, as Guillén's attempt to rid his own poetry of the parasitical presence of the island's sugar-producing history, a presence that had been giving meaning to his work for more than forty years. One might easily say that *El diario que a diario* is a scatological, terminal, residual, anal body (these are the terms that come to mind). As a reader, I seem to be listening to Guillén as he lays out his strategy: only by defeating history, expelling all at once its endless extension of rings and hooks, can poetry again be what it once was, that is, what it was before history began. Thus, what we read in this singular, perhaps unique book is not necessarily a succession of poetic texts, but rather history's cadaver, its decomposed archive or its incongruous skeleton. We're dealing, of course, with a profoundly subversive book, in many senses.[25] In the first place, Guillén here carries the genre of poetry to its most extreme limits, since poetry resides "outside" of the book. Certainly it is inside as well, but only as an index, a cause, a will to discard history. It is true that, amid the expelled material there can be found, here and there, some threads of poetry, but this had to be so, given the parasite's tenacity and the violence of the cure. Beyond that, the book does not put itself forward as a totality, but rather as a dismembered body, now quite incomplete and decomposed, of the historical discourse that spoke about Cuba. Once this intestinal discourse has been torn apart and brought to light, one can examine it at leisure: what we have here is an unforeseen, heterogeneous, chaotic organism, which if classified would fall short of or lie beyond words and things. Here is Cuba's true history— this is what I hear Guillén's saying—if there exists something that's true and can be called history; as you can see, it was not an epic or coherent system that kept on unfolding itself in spirals toward Utopia; in reality it was nothing but a long annelid parasite that we carried in our bowels and that stole our food from us: "the great thief / orders a public report / in order to know / what he can take from each" (p. 374), he says in the book's introductory verses.

What is Guillén's strategy in telling us about the impossibility of history?

Here I'd like to defer to Borges's famous and useful essay "El idioma analítico de John Wilkins" (The analytic language of John Wilkins).[26] You will remember that in this text Borges speaks of a presumed Chinese encyclopedia that classifies the animals in the following way: "A) belonging to the Emperor B) embalmed C) tame D) suckling pigs E) mermaids F) fabulous G) stray dogs H) those included in this category I) those that twitch like madmen J) innumerable ones K) drawn with a fine camel's hair brush L) et cetera M) that just knocked over the pitcher N) that look like flies from a distance." This apocryphal quotation allows Borges to expound the idea that any attempt at classification is necessarily arbitrary and conjectural, since we don't know anything about the totality of the universe that comes first in the hierarchy and contains the group that we are classifying. On reading this essay, Michel Foucault observed that the thing that makes the table of animals absurd is the excluding function, that is, the division into classes A, B, C, etc., by which, for example, "mermaids" stay separate from "fabulous animals" and "suckling pigs" apart from "those that twitch like madmen." In fact, one soon asks, what coherent space can contain this classificatory scheme? Certainly there is none other than language itself, which is a space without location. Foucault, however, doesn't stop at this point. He goes on to tell us that the table suggests something more disquieting than incongruity. This suggestion roots itself in the notion that there are fragments of a great number of possible orders coexisting in a space that has no law and no geometry: the space of the heteroclitic, of chaos.[27] This is where things exist without a common organizing center, or an origin, or logos, or universe, or Utopia that we have constructed with a story spun by our desires in the discourse of language. This space, where everything is hopelessly confused, is the antidiscursive (anti-Utopian) space of what Foucault calls *heterotopias,* that is, the (dis)ordered territory where the Other resides. Well then, *El diario que a diario*, like much of Borges's work, is a heterotopia destined to subvert history in general and the positivist version of Cuba's sugar-producing history in particular. The book begins with a "Not strictly necessary little Prologue," in which Guillén presents himself as follows:

> Primero fui el notario
> polvoriento y sin prisa,
> que inventó el inventario.
> Hoy hago de otra guisa;
> Soy el Diario que a diario

te previene, te avisa
numeroso y gregario.
¿Vendes una sonrisa?
¿Compras un dromedario?
Mi gran stock es vario.
Doquier mi planta pisa
brota lo extraordinario.

(In the beginning I was the notary,
   dust covered and in no hurry,
   inventor of the inventory.
Today I play a different part:
I am the Daily that daily
forewarns you and puts you on guard,
I am numerous and friendly.
Is it a smile you are selling?
or a dromedary you want to buy?
My large stock has everything in ready supply.
Wheresoever my foot touches the ground,
   extraordinary things can be found.) *

And so Guillén puts the reader on notice that if earlier he may have been the poet-notary who invented history (the "inventory"), he is now a different kind of poet: the one who breaks history down into days for which the most suitable space is a newspaper. There everything coexists; it is Borges's place of classification, the place of the incongruous and the heteroclitic; there the sale of "a smile" is announced in the same way as that of "a dromedary," and an English word (*stock*) counts as much as an archaism (*doquier*); it is the "numerous and friendly" space of the "extraordinary."

In this way Guillén, adopting the form of the daily newspaper, gives us a space that is daily, antihistorical, offered as a table of contents. What does it contain? News items, chronicles, announcements, proclamations, popular rhymes, etc. But clearly, as I said, we're not talking about Utopian texts, but rather about heteroclitic ones. Let's take, for example, the advertisement of "La Quincalla del Ñato," a discount store, where they sell:

needles for sewing and sewing machines . . . large and small sponges
little *Morón* pancakes streamers and confetti nail polish mop handles

The Daily Daily, trans. Vera M. Kutzinski [Berkeley: University of California Press, 1989], p. 3

snap buttons prayers including the one to San Luis Beltrán against the evil eye the one to San Judas Tadeo the one to the just judge light bulbs Santa Teresa candles *ánima sola* prayers hair nets socks real peanut and sesame dough little cake horses lace and embroidery knitting needles scouring pads made of aluminum . . . toothpicks rubber balls tops magnets with iron filings.

Notice that these articles don't come forth as enumerated or ordered under rubrics, or even as separated by commas, but rather as a chaotic assortment where things refer to different orders, even at the same time. For example, the "light bulbs" and the "Santa Teresa candles" refer us to a grouping of objects that have to do with light, with illumination, but the bulbs will illuminate a room and the candles will turn on a faith in Santa Teresa. There are also "paper flowers better than the real ones picture postcards," but one might ask what the one would have to do with the other; or again, "magnet with iron filings," the attractor and the attracted, the cause and the effect. Moreover, it should be noted that other, similar texts—"Bookstore: latest arrivals from France," "Who's not?", "European slaves," etc.—appear intercalated among texts that allude to essential chapters of Cuban history, for example, the taking of Havana by the English, the Ten Years' War, the War of Independence, Jose Martí, the Cuban Revolution. At a glance, this montage recalls the technique of *papier collé*, but what exactly are the paper clippings that have been stuck here? As a matter of fact, it's not possible to distinguish them; the book is a kind of ahistorical gazette composed of clippings that speak in the present tense but refer to the newspaper's heteroclitic space. Further, these clippings' texts are ironically composed and laid out, so that they always face the reader with two or three angles. The reader finally ends up by projecting his own version of Cuban history into them, that is to say, his own reading, his own truth.

But what will happen on a second reading? I must confess that the item that "publishes" Martí's death moves back and forth within me like a pendulum as I read and reread it. This is the text: "Martí has fallen, the thinking, delirious head of the Cuban revolution" (p. 411). What party would have been represented by the conjectural newspaper that printed this news item? A newspaper that was against Cuban independence would never have recognized the existence of a "Cuban revolution," but neither would one that favored it refer to Martí as the "thinking, delirious head" of the independence movement. Then who is speaking here? How do we reconcile "thinking" with "delirious"? As we know, Martí is sacred to all Cubans, quite apart from the ideology that they may uphold. He is the "apostle" and the "master" of Cuba's civic religion. But still, what Cuban revolution does this item refer to, the War of Independence or the Marxist-Leninist-Castrist revolution, whose discourse looks for its legitimating American center in Martí's thought?[28] Well then, how do we read this short text?

Of course we could always return to a first reading, facile, literal, and answer that, chronologically, the book's version of Cuban history does not probe the epoch that followed the year 1959, the date of the revolution's triumph. In line with this reading, Cuba's history would be divided into two periods: one that encompasses nearly five centuries and another that barely covers thirty years. All historiography written before 1959 would be false, and that written afterward would be true. Thus the First of January, 1959, would turn out to be the moment of truth, and this would turn out to be the transcendental space from which Guillén would begin to write his antihistory. But the problems that right-thinking readers would have to face in establishing this "true reading" would be enormous. To begin with, Guillén writes the past in the present tense, in the terms of the latest news, and this ironizes the very space from which he writes, that is, that of the Cuban Revolution. It could be understood, for instance, that the devastating "news items" and "announcements" that allude to the enslavement of and discrimination against the Negro are directed not just at the past but also at the present moment, in which Cuban Negroes, almost half the population, are scarcely represented in the highest circles of power. So we must conclude that the antirhetoric of which Guillén avails himself—that of the newspaper—corrodes any political, patriotic, nationalist, or party-line attempt to offer a coherent reading of Cuban history (or any other history); it trivializes and atomizes it, referring it to an archive whose chaos and whose turbulence resist all editing and manipulation, to wit, the impossible archive of the Plantation, whose (dis)ordered paper trail blows through the winds of the world. Clearly, *El diario que a diario* doesn't do everything it sets out to do. It is not the miraculous vermifuge that announced itself in the newspaper as the most radical remedy, one that takes history apart once and for all. In the last analysis the history of the Plantation stays *there,* with its violence now diminished, maybe even dead and desiccated—for all to see. But its impossible ghost keeps on watching and plundering the islands' poetry. In the end, nothing and nobody can undo history, since its very undoing writes a story that is history all over again. It is certain, at least, that history's monstrousness is out in the open and the desire to suppress it lies inscribed in the fable. *El diario que a diario,* finally, is not the official and officious history of the Plantation, nor is it the antihistory; it is an "other" history.

The philosophical poet

After this radical experiment, there is little left for Guillén to do. His life is now ebbing, and there is room only for a final reflection, a last book. This is *Sol de domingo* (Sunday sun, 1982), which includes both verse and prose. In his prologue Guillén writes: "The present edition is made up of more or less unpublished and distant texts, some of which stayed out of sight for years. If they come out now and form a whole, it is not owing to the vanity of their author, who well knows the precarious worth of these works, but rather to make room for the coming of others that are better endowed and put together" (p. 4).[29] We are looking, then, at texts that were not legitimate until 1982, a date in which the poet, now an octogenarian, wishes to present himself before the bar of posterity's judgment. Surely these texts deserve a detailed study, one that might illuminate especially the manner in which they connect with those published previously, since they were sometimes written at the same time as those published ones. I'm not going to talk here about journalistic articles, some of which emphasize the Afro-Cuban and anti-imperialist thematic, while others draw together various heterodox ideas, such as the article entitled "Remembering a Curious Coincidence: Delmonte and Engels." As for the poems, they are without a doubt the finest things in the book, especially because some of them fill a new space in his varied and polemical body of work.

In any case, the poetry of sugar is represented in *Sol de domingo*, in an interesting poem entitled "Macheteros," which I here transcribe:

> Los recuerdo, de niño,
> sombras de mochas ásperas,
> piel curtida
> por el viento y el sol. Mirada
> de lejanía y de venganza.
> Eran los macheteros.
>
> Centrales: Jatibonico, Jaronú.
> Steward, Vertientes, Lugareño.
> O el Chaparra, con Menocal
> sonando el cuero.

De niño, en el recuerdo,
los macheteros.
(p. 182)

(I remember them, from childhood,
harsh shadows of the machetes,
skin tanned
by wind and sun. Look
of distance and of vengeance.
They were the macheteros.

Central: Jatibonico, Jaronú.
Steward, Vertientes, Lugareño.
Or Chaparra, with Menocal
cracking his whip.

As a child, in my memory,
the macheteros.)

Notice that, unlike the poems of *Tengo*, these verses are not constructed with a binary strategy in which the "positive" elements of the present oppose the "negative" elements of the past. Here both past and present show themselves as somber in the intemporality of memory and, above all, in the association of ideas and images that form the remembrance. The sugar-making centers are no longer Jatibonico, Jaronú, or Steward, but under their new names, given by the state, the mills are the same. General Menocal's cruel government may have sunk into the past decades before, but the Plantation, finally, must have an authoritarian style if not a despotic one. The old slave-run sugar mill gave not just a military, repressive, and racist character to the colonial government, but it also made up a necessarily antidemocratic model of governance which, beneath different ideological masks, would tend to repeat itself for as long as the plantation economy held sway. So that when Guillén remembers the macheteros, his memory refers not only to the times of his childhood but also to the present time and even to the future. We're really dealing here with a *remembrance of the future,* since in Cuba sugar always holds the same power, and the macheteros are always the same downtrodden ones. Hence the somber tone of these lines.

In 1981 there appeared a long and noteworthy poem called *El central*, by Reinaldo Arenas, which places itself solidly within the discourse of resistance to sugar. Although this is not the time for a close examination of its text, which tries, following Acosta, to knock the Plantation from its center, I want to cite a stanza to which my reading of "Los macheteros" has brought me:

> —Manos esclavas conducen los caminos por el
> terraplén polvoriento.
>   Hablar de la historia
> es entrar en un espacio cerrado
> con trajes más ridículos, quizá,
> pero apresados por las mismas furias
> y las mismas mezquindades.
>   —Manos esclavas labran cruces, cetros, cofas,
> gallardetes y cureñas; hacen funcionar las palancas.[30]

> (Slave hands drive the trucks along the
> dusty embankment.
>   To speak of history
> is to enter a closed space
> and see ourselves
> wearing the most ridiculous clothes, perhaps,
> but beset by the same furies
> and the same meannesses.
>   Slave hands make crosses, scepters, crow's nests,
> pennants and gun platforms; they make the levers work.)

And so, once again in Cuban literature, the denunciation of sugar finds expression. The history of the Plantation puts itself forward as a voyage toward progress. But in fact it is circular, always the same, a remembrance of the future.

The two last poems of *Sol de domingo* are the only ones to come with dates attached. The date in question, for both, is "May, 1978." The first one, entitled "Haikai I," reads:

> La luna sobre el lago.
> Susurra el viento.
> Rotos en mil pedazos.
> ¡Cuántos espejos!
> (p. 24)

> (The moon above the lake.
> The wind whispers.

Broken in a thousand pieces.
So many mirrors!)

The second poem is entitled "Haikai II":

El gallo se pasea.
Hinchado y rojo
un samurai parece.
(p. 212)

(The rooster promenades.
Swollen and red
he looks like a samurai.)

That Guillén's poetry—usually disguised as *son, rumba,* Afro-Cuban rhythms, sonnets, and *letrillas* of Spain's golden age—should dress itself now in the silk kimono of haiku is a very revealing change. This spare poetic form, we know, is a kind of crystal vial, minimal and exquisitely worked, made to carry a few drops of wisdom's elixir. Traditional wisdom, symbolic wisdom: the wisdom that guides the Zen archer's blind arrow to the target's center. It seems reasonable to think that Guillén imposed this rigorous form on himself during the search for expression that might be profound and didactic at once, a universal form that would at the same time quickly allow for his last and personal good-bye. Also, whether deliberately or not, he chose an Asian form, adding it to his poetry's formal interplay, giving it a Caribbean plenitude.

From among these two poems' possible readings, I choose the following: The first haiku is night, disenchantment, despair, the end of time; the second is dawn, word, phallus, desire, the beginning of time or, as it were, the sensual spur of steel and fire that, as Acosta says "carries within it the germ of no one knows what future conflagrations." The sequential connotation of both is emphasized by their having the same date of composition, the same title, and the ordinal numbers I and II. It departs, then, from death to reach life, and such a succession, naturally, implies the universal theme of resurrection. It is the spring's ritual of sacrifice, symbolized in the carnival, and this acts in two ways, one external and one internal, on the totality of Guillén's work. In the first instance it alludes to the discourse of resistance belonging to the slave who, to endure the harsh repetitive reality of the annual sugar-making cycle, would say, facing adversity: "What you have to do is not die." This saying, which is still very popular in Cuba, refers directly to the African tradition that allows the possibility of cheating death at the enemy's hands, either by transforming oneself into an animal of the forest or else, simply, by practicing a magic ritual to keep death at bay. Thus to the circular death that the Plantation inflicts one must oppose an attempt at flight: the metonymical unfolding of a prevailing and vital culture.

But the myth of resurrection is not a true break with death, rather it speaks of a postponement of death, or of the desire for a new opportunity to defy it. In any case, this desire acts upon Guillén's work, folding it back over itself in a way that allows a rereading. We must keep in mind that the title *Sol de domingo*, in its circular march, would end up as *Domingo de sol*, which has the same number of words, letters, and even the same vowels as *Motivos de son*. If this relationship seems fortuitous, notice that Guillén concludes his words addressed to the reader by saying: "having said this, here we put the *punto redondo*"* (p. 4), instead of *punto final*. And so, following the Caribbean text's paradoxical canon, this poem sends us back to the auspicious verses of *Motivos de son*, to draw a figure of hope that spins in the midst of chaos.

*TRANSLATOR'S NOTE: The words *"punto final"* (final period) mean the last period of a particular text, while *"punto redondo"* (round period) has itself no meaning; it is a play on the expected *"punto final"* that carries the idea of circularity rather than finality.

4

Fernando Ortiz:

the Caribbean

and

postmodernity

In one of Fernand Braudel's last interviews, he was asked about the difference he saw between the concepts of interdisciplinarity and interscience.
Braudel replied: "Interdisciplinarity is the legal marriage of two neighboring sciences. But as for me, I am for generalized promiscuity."[1] I think that
Braudel's answer is not just in tune with his work, and with the so-called
nouvelle histoire, but also the multidisciplinary pluralism that we see today
in the works of celebrated scholars and humanists. One must agree that
this kind of analytic coming-together, in which the most varied disciplines'
axioms are in play, is typical of our era. In fact it keeps getting harder to
swallow any given discipline's postulates, especially as they are applied all
by themselves in studying any single phenomenon. If we want to study,
for example, the planter-slave relations of some place in the Caribbean, we
now see that we can't keep our analysis within, say, a strictly socioeconomic
language, which by itself does not suffice for a reading of those relations.
We must resort, in addition, to certain later nomenclatures which might
allow us entry into areas that were thought until a very short time ago to
exist at the margin of socioeconomic phenomena, areas which we might
see as inhabited by desire, sexuality, power, nationalism, violence, knowledge, or culture—and all of these seen from such varied perspectives that
it's not rare to come upon analytic models combining the psychoanalytic
model with that of political economy, or the philosophical with the femi-
nist, or the jurisprudential with the literary-theoretical. And yet this hybrid
and multidisciplinary fire that today's researcher directs toward his elusive

subject is still, and may always be, insufficient. In any case, the scientist as well as the artist of today no longer asks himself regularly how he might represent reality through an equation or a poem, but works rather toward imparting an ever more acute sense that reality is not representable.

We keep advancing into an era that recently began calling itself postmodern, postindustrial, postideological, or simply the "third wave," coming after the agricultural and the industrial revolutions which were the two great changes that humanity has gone through. If we examine Jean-François Lyotard's definition of postmodernity,[2] we notice that it springs from a resistance to accepting the legitimacy of the discourses of the disciplines, since their presumed legitimacy rests upon their arbitrary appropriations, as centers or genealogical origins, of one or another of the past's great fables or narratives, such as the dialectic of the spirit, or the hermeneutics of signification, or the emancipation of the rational or laboring subject, or the creation of wealth. And of course these meta-stories have to legitimate themselves in turn by invoking principles of "truth," "exactitude," and "justice" which we now would rather not call absolute, but rather the fruits of rude manipulations. Thus postmodernity offers itself as a philosophical attitude that seeks not to know about fables that seek legitimation, or about any prophetic destiny or origin, an attitude that rejects all metaphysics and all eschatological categories. Within postmodernity there cannot be any single truth, but instead there are many practical and momentary ones, truths without beginnings or ends, local truths, displaced truths, provisional and peremptory truths of a pragmatic nature that barely make up a fugitive archipelago of regular rhythms in the midst of entropy's turbulence and noise.

Now then, if we take it for granted that the Industrial Revolution has failed to solve many of the problems of the West, the East, and the Third World, that the ideologies pushing themselves forward as perpetual remedies, as infallible elixirs, in fact leave a lot to be desired when it comes to putting them into practice, that words like *good, unity, positive,* and *just* do not exist on their own but rather float like captive blimps to dock up next to whoever pulls the cables, that the paradoxes of mathematics and the applied sciences have a lot to do with those of language, that a work of nonfiction is rather more like literature than anything else, that we can find pleasure in riddles and in the intellectual jazz of the paralogical puzzle and the brainstorm; supposing, in short, that we live within the psychology of postmodernity, then what thinking and what canons are we going to follow when we try to conclude some things about any economic or cultural phenomena that appear in the Caribbean, a part of the world that the very philosophies of postmodernism exclude from their field of play,[3] a part of the world that hardly brushes against modernity and whose culture has doggedly held on to such things as blood sacrifice and voodoo, *santería, pocomania,* and *macumba*?

I'm not sure that this preamble was necessary to my bringing up Fernando Ortiz's *Contrapunteo cubano del tabaco y el azúcar,* but it is a fact that this text proposes a Caribbean response to the matters of modernity and postmodernity. In any case, anyone wishing to reject Ortiz's planting of these issues—which I will get around to analyzing soon enough—would not be alone by any means. Take Manuel Moreno Fraginals, for example, who says of the *Contrapunteo,* in the annotated bibliography in the second edition of *El ingenio*: "Many of his affirmations are quite brilliant and suggestive; many others do not stand up to the slightest critical analysis."[4] Of course Moreno Fraginals speaks to us through his lens as a modern sugar historian, and this implies that there is a scientific "truth" and an ideological "truth" as well. Whatever of Ortiz's affirmations that coincide with these "truths" must be "brilliant" and "suggestive"; what does not conform will not survive "the slightest critical analysis." This is the typical judgment of a modern social scientific investigator, the judgment of a voice specialized, ideologized, authorized, and legitimized by its fidelity to certain of modernity's meta-narratives. And I say this without irony. Everyone knows that *El ingenio* is one of the most fascinating texts that the literature of sugar has given to the world. But certainly the *Contrapunteo* is equally so, and especially if we don't read it only as a socioeconomic study of tobacco and sugar, but rather as a text that tries to speak to us about Cuban, and by extension Caribbean, experience.

The Contrapunteo *as a postmodern text*

Perhaps the first thing in the *Contrapunteo* to draw our attention is the index or table of contents. There are what we could call two parts. One of them is called "Cuban Counterpoint of Tobacco and Sugar" and the other "Transculturation of Havana Tobacco and the Beginnings of Sugar and of Negro Slavery in America."[5] This second part is composed of twenty-five chapters, the first of which is entitled "On *Contrapunteo* and Its Complementary Chapters." On reading this chapter, which contains certain general arguments and explanations concerning the work itself, we quickly ask ourselves why it didn't come at the very beginning of the book, perhaps right after

Bronislaw Malinowski's introduction and as a kind of author's note. There is no telling what Ortiz would have said about this. But we have to conclude that, as far as he was concerned, any judgment of the author's about his own book ought to be read as just another chapter of the book, not as an *a posteriori* pronouncement to be signed with the author's name, or dressed up with the author's initials, or just followed by the words "The Author." Ortiz's decision to offer his opinions about the "Contrapunteo" within the *Contrapunteo* and not in a signed author's note or preface touches on several of the interests of postmodern criticism. One of them is that there is no reason to establish a relation of semiological hierarchy between two texts, since there is really no text that can encompass the reality that it wants to express. This opinion would justify Ortiz's including this singular chapter within the same category as his chapter 6, which deals with tobacco and cancer, or his chapter 24, entitled "Concerning the Enemy Beet." Another of postmodern literary criticism's concerns lies in demystifying the concept of the author, and erasing the "creator" aura with which modern criticism endows him. For the poststructuralist critic, looking at the literary task from the postmodern standpoint, the author, far from being a creator of worlds, is a technician or artisan whose job is controlled by a preexisting practice or discourse; he is, simply, a writer. In the sustaining of this opinion, any writer's preface would lack the requisite authority needed to take over a space, within the book, that is any different from that of the text that he has written, and therefore his explanations could just as well appear within one of the work's chapters.

But now let's take a look at the type of explanation that appears in this first "complementary" chapter:

> The "Cuban Counterpoint of Tobacco and Sugar" is an essay of a schematic nature. It makes no attempt to exhaust the theme, nor does it pretend that the marked economic, social, and historical counterpositionings between both of these products of Cuban industry are all so absolute and cut and dried as they sometimes appear to be when contrasted with one another. Economic and social phenomena are quite complex in their historical evolution, and the multiple factors that determine them make them vary considerably in their trajectories, now bringing them close together in their similarities just as though they were of the same order, now separating them for their differences until they come to seem antithetical. In any case, for the most part, the contrasts here noted will sustain themselves. (p. 91)

In my reading of this paragraph, the first thing that I notice is that the "Contrapunteo" does not bring itself forward as an authoritative text, but rather as a vehicle that knows itself to be insufficient before the fact and makes no attempt to "exhaust the theme." To put it another way, we're dealing with a text here that is conscious of itself and communicates to us that those things that we might take to be truths are, rather, arbitrary decisions made to shape the strategy of the discourse. Such a strategy—we read—would consist in making something "cut and dried" out of the "economic, social, and historical counterpositionings" of tobacco and sugar, when in fact they do not inhabit such extremes. This takes us to what lies at the heart of postmodern literary analysis: a questioning of the concept of "unity" and a dismantling, or rather unmasking, of the mechanism that we know as "binary opposition"—the thing that sustains, to a greater or a lesser degree, the philosophical and ideological edifice of modernity. According to what we read here, all such concepts are nothing but appearances that make use of economic and social processes in their being born, and therefore take up the disciplinary discourses that refer to such things. In fact, these phenomena may well be related to one another through their similarities, or they might just as well deploy themselves as antithetical, antagonistic poles. And this relationship is possible thanks to the "multiple factors" (read *differences*) that come into play when the phenomena are being formed. So binary opposition is not really a *law* but just a discursive strategy, for the unity of the respective poles that set themselves up in opposition is there to be seen and is also subverted by the presence of "multiple factors," that is, by differences. Thus Ortiz plainly confesses that he has manipulated those differences, excluding the ones that wouldn't make the counterpositionings of sugar and tobacco seem "cut and dried." In the end, I'm drawn to the sentence: "In any case, the contrasts maintain themselves substantially as shown." A lapidary and unavoidable phrase, in that it marks exactly the limits of postmodern textual analysis: in spite of all that's been said, one must use analogies and establish oppositions in order even to establish the postmodern point of view. And it therefore remains necessary to keep them on hand, if not as truths any longer then as options of strategic value to be taken as more instances of the infinite play of impossibilities.

Finally, to finish with this singular paragraph, I would point out that the four hundred printed pages that make up these complementary chapters are, as Ortiz says, annotations to the eighty pages of the "Contrapunteo." That, naturally, constitutes a serious transgression even within the most tolerant limits of modernity's socioeconomic discourse, and this not just because it brings this discourse closer to the novel, but also because it unmasks the hierarchizing and exclusive strategy of the modern discourse of the social sciences. The "Contrapunteo," a social-scientific essay, refers publicly, in the book itself, to an enormous, extremely varied, and dense field of observations which, in turn, bring into play innumerable references, annotated or not, that extend throughout a group of works whose central themes correspond to those of all the arts and the scientific disciplines. This network of immeasurable connections does not, nevertheless, appear to be constructed according to an encyclopedic model, but rather according to an undecipherable code whose (dis)order resists any modern attempt at systematization. For example:

> The trickster Don Juan must have smoked tobacco and the nun Doña Inés must have sucked on almond candies. Faust, the nonconforming sage, would have savored his pipe as well, and the sweet, devout Marguerite her sugar candies. The characterologists would find an endomorph in sugar; in tobacco an ectomorph. If sugar was the desired taste to Sancho, the gluttonous peasant, tobacco could be such to Don Quixote, the dreaming hidalgo . . . Nietzsche may have thought sugar Dionysiac and tobacco Apollonian. The former is the mother of all alcohols that furnish sacred euphoria. In tobacco's smoky spirals there are illusory beauties and poetic inspirations. Freud, in his old age, may have begun to ponder whether sugar is narcissist and tobacco erotic. If life is an ellipse whose two foci are the belly and the sex organs, then sugar is food and subsistence, while tobacco is love and reproduction.
> (pp. 22–23)

How are we to organize these lines' referents when Ortiz doesn't establish differences between Sancho's gluttony and Nietzsche's Apollonian, or between Freud and Doña Inés?

In short, as Ortiz (dis)organizes the *Contrapunteo* in "a certain kind of way," he alludes to the extremely vast heteroclitic archive from which his essay "El contrapunteo" emerges. Further still, he makes the "Contrapunteo" the unreachable center of his entire work, not just that which had been published to date but even including what he would publish in the next two decades. Don't forget that it's in this book that he introduces his famous notion of "transculturation," which alludes to Cuba's supersyncretic archive, especially in everything that touches on Afro-European syncretisms. This chaotic and materially unrepresentable archive, whose

promiscuity keeps it quite far from being able to provide a stable and cate-
gorical imprint, is also, in a wider political, economic, and social sense, a
metaphor for the Plantation's impossible origins.

Such a demythifying strategy, analogous to what Guillén would follow
later in *El diario que a diario*, not only makes one think about a possible
"proto-postmodernity" in Ortiz, but also about the obvious and important differences between the *Contrapunteo* and any other modern social-
scientific text that mentions sugar in Cuba: *Azúcar y población en las Antillas*,
Azúcar y abolición, *El ingenio*, *El barracón*, etc. It is not hard to establish that
these books, all of them admirable, have been written from within a positivist ideology. The last three declare outright that their focus is Marxist. I
ask Ortiz's readers: What is the *Contrapunteo*'s ideology? There's no quick
or short answer to this. Yes, every text, as Barthes would have it, necessarily
invokes an ideology,[6] and the *Contrapunteo* is no exception. It's just that
the ideology that informs it can't be clearly identified, since we're dealing
with a heteroclitic summa of ideologies, that is, a deideologized ideology.
This difference, I repeat, is of the greatest importance, since the other texts
listed above all show the seams of their own arbitrariness, their own self-
segregation, their own self-censorship. They try fruitlessly, like all modern
texts, to quash the traces of their own arbitrariness with a noisy attempt at
legitimation; they will adduce *Das Kapital*, or any other famous and solid
account that might align itself for or against a meta-system of power (a
theme that the modern social scientist can't easily evade), and they ignore
the huge and necessarily promiscuous archive that has been manipulated
and severely edited by the "authors" of the narratives that they have chosen
to be their foundational texts. Furthermore, they construct themselves as-
tutely within a "coherent" and "authentic" fable of legitimation which
inserts them directly into the discourse of power, either to repeat its state-
ments or to displace them. And so, judging by what we've said up to here
about the *Contrapunteo*, we might take Ortiz, along with Borges, as a precursor of postmodernity.

Nevertheless, the interest that the *Contrapunteo* holds for me—the
"Contrapunteo" and its complementary chapters—does not lie in its ability
to evade the canon of legitimation and binary dialectic, the "for or against"
or "true or false" that characterize the analytic models that modernity uses
most. I'm interested in the *Contrapunteo* because I think that it's one of the
most revealing books ever written about the dynamics of the Caribbean—
a judgment that I extend to Ortiz himself and the rest of his (dis)ordered
work—and also, especially, because it offers a method by which one can

conduct a reading of the Caribbean that has an outcome different from any that might have been done from the perspectives either of modernity or of postmodernity, which are, finally, strictly Western perspectives and Western readings.

But let's leave behind this productive paragraph from the first complementary chapter, and get into the "Contrapunteo" itself. What we see right away—as many have noticed—is that the text does not seek its legitimation within the discourse of the social sciences, but rather within those of literature, of fiction. That is, it puts itself forward from the outset as a bastard text. Its discourse begins from the "battle that Don Carnal had with Dame Lent,"[7] from Juan Ruiz's *Libro de buen amor* (1330): "Perhaps the famous controversy that this great poet imagined could be the literary precedent that now allows us to personify black tobacco and white sugar, and to enter into the fable to experience its contradictions" (p. 11).

Up until this point, the *Contrapunteo* is coming to us rather like an early postmodern text, conscious of its postmodernity. Except that we soon read:

> But, furthermore, the contrasting parallel of tobacco and sugar is so curious, like that of the characters in the dialogue set up by the Archpriest, [Juan Ruiz] that it goes beyond merely social perspectives to reach the horizons of poetry . . . Finally, this dialogic genre that takes the dialectic of life to the art of drama was always there among the ingenuous muses of the people, in poetry, music, dance, song, and theater. Let's remember its most flourishing manifestations in Cuba in the antiphonal glories of the liturgies, those of both whites and blacks, in the erotic and rhythmic dialogue of the rumba, and in the versified counterpoints of the *guajirada montuna* and the Afro-Cuban *Currería*. (pp. 11–12)

Well then, such are the promiscuous origins of the "Contrapunteo": the *Libro de buen amor*—which is cited throughout the text—both "white" and "black" liturgical rituals, the rumba, popular music, song, and theater. And there's one more thing: the complementary chapters, that is, the demythologizing allusion to the "Contrapunteo"'s economic, social, and historical archive. All of these things make up the *Contrapunteo*. And so Ortiz's text doesn't offer itself as a monological fable, coherent and true in the modern fashion; neither does it offer itself as a postmodern investigator's narrative, which would have a legitimating *praxis* of establishing differences and referring to the small maneuvers—*petit récit*—of fractal mathematics and the paralogical world. Such a narrative, necessarily, would have to have been constructed with an epistemological language proper to the scientific knowledge that the narrative itself wishes to demythify (the great paradox of postmodernity). And this scientific language would of course throw away the rumba and the Afro-Cuban liturgies because they construct some enunciations of the language of the Other, propositions belonging within another form of knowledge which, because of their pre-modernity, cannot enter into the play of postmodernity. Then how shall we read the *Contrapunteo*? My suggestion would be: read it as a dialogic and uncentered text, in whose plurality of voices and rhythms the most varied disciplines and the most irreconcilable ideologies come forward along with enunciations that correspond to two very different forms of understanding, of knowing. I would say of the *Contrapunteo* that it is a text having much of the promiscuity proper to pagan cosmogonies, and yet it does not discard theological monism, as may be seen for example in the cult of the Regla Kimbisa del Santo Cristo del Buen Viaje, native to Cuba, which makes room for Christ, the Virgin, and the Catholic saints, without relegating the Congolese *nganga,* the *nkisi* of the Abakua, or the *orisha* of the Lucumi to a second level. Or perhaps the *Shango* cult, native to the island of Trinidad, which relies on more than sixty gods or great spirits, which are called *powers* by the believers. Of these gods, more than thirty can be identified as African deities, mainly Yoruba; about twenty are of Catholic provenance, that is, hagiographic; three of them (*Samedona, Begoyana,* and *Vigoyana*) are of Indoamerican origin, having reached Trinidad through the Guianas; another two (*Baba* and *Mahabil*) were brought to the island by identured servants from India, and one of them, named *Wong Ka*, comes from China. In addition, the cult has shown observers certain elements coming from the Baptist church and from medieval European witchcraft.

I have the impression that it's exactly this transgressive trope, this densely promiscuous form which, according to the perspective of modern thought, "doesn't survive the slightest analysis," and which, according to postmodern thought, would be a case of "another" game that has nothing to do with the Game. And yet I think that it's the form that best represents the Caribbean. When Ortiz says that "to study Cuban history is fundamentally to study the history of sugar and tobacco as the visceral systems of its economy" (p. 13), he is suggesting to us "another" mode of investigation whose prototype would be that of the *Contrapunteo*. In the pages that follow I'll try to comment on this proposition in more detail.

Between voodoo and ideology

Of course, according to the canons of Western scientific thought, much of what there is in the *Contrapunteo* is absurd, irrational, fantastic. But one must admit that the same could be said from the other side, if one looked from the periphery toward the centers of disciplinary power, although the periphery, it should be said, tends to be tolerant. Nevertheless, given its logocentric character, Western theoretical thinking discards any relativist schema and says merely that certain Caribbean points of view "don't hold up under modern analysis" or are marginal to postmodernity's "brainstorm." One example among many possible would be the importance that Ortiz gives to the impact of African beliefs in the Caribbean. Let's explore this aspect briefly before proceeding with the *Contrapunteo*.

When we look out over the complicated and obscure panorama of beliefs that the African slaves introduced into the Caribbean, we must bear in mind that these not only went into the forming of supersyncretic cults like the Regla Kimbisa del Buen Viaje but they had as well a decisive influence upon spheres that are quite distinct from the strictly cultural. They affected many fields which are studied, as referents, by a whole array of disciplines of knowledge that are distinct from ethnography, cultural anthropology, and the like. We can understand this better if we see that African beliefs don't limit themselves to the worshiping of a given group of deities, but rather inform an authentic body of sociocultural practices extending through a labyrinth of referents as diverse as music, dance, theater, song, dress, hairstyle, crafts, oral literature, systems of divination, medicinal botany, magic, ancestor cults, pantomime, trance states, eating customs, agricultural practices, relations with animals, cooking, commercial activity, astronomical observation, sexual behavior, and even the shapes and colors of objects. Religion in black Africa is not something that can be separated from knowledge, politics, economics, or the social and cultural spheres; it can't even be distinguished from history, since it is, in itself, history; we're dealing here with a discourse that permeates all human activity and interferes in all practices. In black Africa, religion is everything, and at the same time it is nothing, for it can't be isolated from the world of phenomena or even of Being. Keeping this in mind, we can affirm that the influence of Africa upon the nations of the Caribbean is, in the final analysis, and in the totalizing sense that we've just spoken about, a predominantly religious one. So a scientific model applied to investigate Caribbean societies and to predict their movements and tendencies would turn out to be grossly inadequate if it were to try to do without the input of beliefs formed under the African cultural impact.

It's easy to demonstrate, for example, that such beliefs furnished the unifying forces—myth, ideology—that made the slaves' prolonged collective resistance to the plantation system possible. It was these beliefs that sustained the uprooted lives of millions of men and women, providing bonds of solidarity between them, and above all, uniting them in their conspirations, their running away, and their organized rebellions.[8] Take for example the Jamaican rebellion of 1760, one of the best known Antillean revolts. The uprising involved only the Ashanti Negroes of the Akan linguistic group. Their leader, who was called Tacky, counted on the services of an *Obeah man* whose role in the conspiracy was that of its religious leader, and whose delegates spread out among plantations to supply the slaves with a magic powder to make them invulnerable to the whites' weapons. At the same time, they spread the notion that Tacky would be able to grab his enemies' bullets in midair. When this informational phase had ended, the conspirators all took the Akan oath, a blood pact, in which they promised to keep the strictest secrecy regarding the desired rebellion. This sort of organizing work, extending from east to west throughout the island, lasted for an entire year. Even so, not a single slave betrayed the secret, and the uprising went off according to plan. The rebels wiped out several plantations and put up a fierce resistance to the colonial forces, but they were finally subdued. When the episode was over and the leading conspirators, the *Obeah man* among them, had been hanged, the authorities issued a law that punished "any Negro or other Slave who shall pretend to any supernatural Power, or be detected in making use of any Blood, Feathers, Parrots, Beaks, Dogs Tooth, Alligators Tooth, Broken Bottles, Grave Dirt, Rum, Egg-Shells or any other Materials relative to the Practice of Obeah or Witchcraft, in order to delude and impose on the Minds of others."[9] This text offers the greatest proof that, contrary to what many social scientists think today, the practical men who then ruled Jamaica took the political and social importance of African beliefs very seriously.

But if Tacky's rebellion is illustrative in this respect, the most spectacular cases happened in Haiti, or rather in Saint-Domingue, before independence. First of all there is the legendary Mackandal, from Guinea. In addition to his being a fearsome authority on the toxic properties of plants, he claimed to have the power to predict the future, to transform himself into any animal, to converse with invisible beings, and to be immortal. He wandered for six years through the plantations, organizing slaves for a general rebellion, and along the way poisoned some white colonists and a few hundred head of cattle. His prestige among the Negroes was enormous, and great numbers of them awaited anxiously the date set for the great uprising. He had a simple but chilling strategy. The slaves were to poison the whites' drinking water, then the plantations would be set on fire as they died. In 1758, on exactly the eve of the date set for the revolt to begin, in the midst of a ceremony of propitiation that was saturated with ritual sacrifices, libations, drums, dances, and exalted songs, Mackandal was captured, jailed, and finally brought to the stake. Nevertheless, his being able, for a moment, to get loose from his bindings and leap over the flames was enough to convince the thousands of slaves who had been rounded up to witness the execution that his magical powers had triumphed in the end. Because the plaza was in an uproar, the Negroes did not see that Mackandal had been tied up again and put finally to the fire; the myth of his immortality prevailed for many years.[10]

There is no historical proof to the effect that the Haitian Revolution of 1791 had a direct antecedent in Mackandal's conspiracy, but one must agree that the myth of his invincibility had a positive psychological influence. In any case, it's known with complete certainty that Boukman, who would start the insurrection in the north, was a powerful *houngan* or voodoo priest. It is known as well that on the night of August 21, 1791, on a mountainside near the city of Le Cap, the leader organized a huge voodoo ceremony, at which he declared a war to the finish against the white power. The next day, at the urging of the greatest voodoo *loas,* the revolution began, and 40,000 slaves, taking orders from Boukman, started on the long and bloody road toward independence.[11]

At Boukman's death, the leadership of the rebel forces fell to Jean François and Biassou, and in the south and west upon Docoudray and Halou. All of them, to greater or lesser degrees, commanded their troops from magico-military positions, if you will permit me this term. Jean-François assured his men that if they died in combat their bodies would be reborn in Africa. Moreover, there were many voodoo initiates in his forces, and his own person, profusely adorned with ribbons, insignia, medals, and all kinds of amulets, suggests nothing else.[12] Biassou, for his part, lived wholly immersed in voodoo, and his field tent was always crowded with high initiates and magical artifacts, including human bones and cats of all colors.[13] Docoudray, another great revolutionary chief, routed the national guard's dragoons at Croix de Bouquets with a famous charge at which, waving a sacrificed bull's tail above his head, he shouted out to his troops that they were sure to be victorious because the Frenchmen's bullets would dissolve in midair.[14] Another great leader, Halou, always took a white rooster with him, through which he spoke to the voodoo spirits, to know what they wanted and to act accordingly.[15] Finally Toussaint L'Ouverture himself, when he fought in the army of Jean François, held the important post of troop doctor, for which he necessarily had to be linked to the voodoo priests and to traditional African medicine, which was based on the curative powers of plants and on shamanistic practices involving invocations, trances, faith healings, and spells. Any other kind of medicine, any "white" medicine, would surely be rejected by a soldier born in the Congo, in Angola, in Dahomey. Later on, when L'Ouverture had a place at the head of the revolution, his soldiers called him Papa Toussaint and associated him with Papa Legba, one of the principal *loas* of voodoo and of the Haitian Revolution as well, since he took charge of selecting the right course and following it through. When victory seemed assured, L'Ouverture prohibited voodoo in his ranks. He did this surely for foreign policy reasons, for we know that he wished ardently to be recognized in Europe as a civilized man in the Enlightenment mold.[16] It seems likely to me that more than one old soldier from the times of Boukman and Jean François would have regretted that a leader who was so exceptional, so lauded by the *loas,* should turn against his people's traditions in order to adopt the usages of the whites, something that in the end brought him a humiliating imprisonment and an inglorious death far from his own.

Of course voodoo didn't die, and today we can see more clearly the role that it played in the Haitian Revolution. The slaves rebelled not just because they had unbearable living conditions or because the National Assembly's decree that freed them was revoked, but also because the greatest voodoo *loas* (Legba, Ogoun, Damballah) had willed it so. As the war of independence ended, in 1804, it is thought that the Haitian troops totaled nearly half a million men, the great majority of them born—as we have seen in an earlier chapter—in Africa. It seems quite unlikely that so many people, born deep within such different African cultures and linguistic groups, could have agreed among themselves to launch the bloodiest war of liberation in America if they were following the impulse of an ideology of the Western sort. And so I don't see how we can do without voodoo in the historiographical, social-scientific, and political science models purporting to study Haitian nationalism and revolution. Voodoo, as I see it, with its vast network of relations, which includes all of the activities of social life, had to be one of the first factors to fill the ordinary slave's ideological space, contributing its dense Pan-African and Afro-European syncretism toward maintaining the solidarity of hundreds of thousands of people during the times of slavery and rebellion.

We must conclude then that in Haiti, and by extension in the most Africanized Caribbean nations, supersyncretic beliefs make up a discourse that stays in contact with many other discourses; that is, they organize themselves within a discursive network that connects surreptitiously with the knowledge of the disciplines and the professions. It's not hard to find doctors, psychologists, pharmacologists, naturalists, sociologists, and anthropologists who have been initiated into Afro-Caribbean beliefs, whether from genuine conviction or from the desire to learn, in depth, some secrets, practices, and drugs of which the scientific world is ignorant. But the disciplinary discourses are not the only things that connect to Afro-Caribbean beliefs. Political power does as well. Caribbean history, since the times of Henri Christophe, has been filled with presidents, leaders, caudillos, dictators, and influential men who, attended by high initiates, achieved power and maintained it.[17] I don't mean to say that they were all true believers— although surely many were—just that their desire for power necessitated a more or less public alliance with these beliefs so that they might be settled in the group mind as political figures. Just as in the Western world no presidential candidate should declare himself an atheist nor could any Soviet statesman (until recently) fail to do so, no Caribbean politician can afford to seem opposed to the supersyncretic beliefs that live in among the official religious forms, which include atheism. Yet the two cases are very different.

It has been two centuries now since Christianity ceased to intervene effectively in the politics of the West; its great authority within the Western political, social, and economic spheres was reduced, in battle after battle, to the size of the cultural sphere alone; it surrendered its power, for better or for worse, to Cartesian rationalism, to the Enlightenment, to sociological positivism, to existential agnosticism, and to the new scientism of our era. But the Caribbean for the most part is not like this, or at least not entirely like this. The Caribbean should be seen not just as a stage where syncretic musical and dance performances are put on, but also as a space invested with syncretic forms of understanding that connect to political, economic, and social power. It is quite possible that, in time, the importance of Afro-Caribbean beliefs will be reduced to the cultural orbit alone, as happened to religion in the West. But in this book I'm not interested in futurology; as I see it, the moment of that reduction has not yet arrived—not even in

Cuba—and my interest here is simply to comment on the area's sociocultural state, or rather to present an updated reading of the things that keep occurring time and again in the region.

To underline the importance that Afro-Caribbean beliefs still have in the structures of political power, I'd like to return to the Haitian sociocultural context. As we know, the enigma of the zombie has recently been peeled away to some extent. Furthermore, thanks to Wade Davis's investigations—see his book *Passage of Darkness: The Ethnology of the Haitian Zombie* (Chapel Hill: University of North Carolina Press, 1988)—it is possible today to appreciate the vast political and social implications of the phenomenon known as zombification. After documenting the zombification of Clarivius Narcisse, Davis recounts the results of his contacts and interviews with various *bokors* (wizards) from different parts of the country. He directs his attention first to the powders that work as a venom to change a normal person into a zombie. The most active toxin in this compound—which has ingredients from human corpses and bones, from lizards, snakes, toads, tarantulas, poison ivy, ground glass, etc.—is tetrodotoxin, found in the skin and entrails of certain poisonous fish (mainly of the genera *spheroidos* and *diodon*) of which the Antilles are swarming. This toxin is so powerful that the liver of just one of these fish would be enough to kill thirty-two humans. Tetrodotoxin acts on the nervous system to produce total paralysis, loss of pulse and respiratory rhythms, and a sudden reduction in the metabolism, symptoms that might be easily interpreted as those of death. In any case, after the individual is poisoned and buried, his body is then exhumed and rubbed down with an antidote. Then he is fed a plant called *concombre zombi* (*Datura stramonium*), which produces confusion, disorientation, and complete amnesia. At the end of this procedure, the person has been changed into a zombie and is then taken to some other part of the country to serve as a "living corpse" in some cane field.

Curiously enough, Davis had no difficulty in getting the formulas for all of the venoms and antidotes from the *bokors*. For them, the crucial element doesn't lie in the chemical makeup of the powders and potions but rather in the complex magic rituals that surround the venom—and antidote— production and administration stages, as well as the "resurrection" stage. Without them, of course, zombification would never occur. It might also be of interest, to the reader who doesn't know about voodoo practices, to remark that there are two types of zombies: one spiritual (*zombi astral*) and another material (*zombi corps cadavre*), which I have referred to earlier. In the first case, the *bokor* captures the subject's vital force (called *ti bon*

ange), keeps it in a receptacle, and uses it whenever he wants in matters
of cosmogonic relevance. According to voodoo beliefs, nobody can live
without his *ti bon ange,* so that when the *bokor* takes it the person dies. The
second type of zombie, though, has a different use: to capture the *ti bon
ange* and then to preserve the empty body in which it used to reside, the
body then being handed over by the *bokor* to third parties who may benefit
from its work. Of course the *zombi corps cadavre* is difficult to produce, since
it requires minute and complicated magical practices in which the slightest
carelessness can spoil the procedure or kill the individual. This is why the
bokor prefers the *zombi astral* to the *zombi corps cadavre.*

But what I've dealt with up to now concerning Davis's investigations is
not the most important thing. What motivations are at work making the
bokor want to practice his dark trade? The answer to this question is, in my
opinion, the most interesting part of Davis's revelations. To begin with,
if a person is zombified, it's not by chance or in the service of some private act of vengeance. In reality, zombification is a punishment, or rather
a sacrifice, carried out to benefit the social group. The zombie, whether
astral or *corps cadavre,* is a sacrificed one (*sacré*). In general it's a case of an
individual who has upset the order of his native village or town, a person
who has violated the local group's mores. This violation may or may not
be an offense according to the legal dispositions coming out of Port-au-
Prince, but that's irrelevant. What matters here is that there was an affront
directed against the popular tradition's order of things, as laid out in the
Haitian peasantry's operative codes, that is, the codes of voodoo as a form
of social life. We are, then, in the presence of a "pagan" judicial process,
alien to the juridical system established by the Haitian constitution. Clarvius Narcisse, for example, appropriated lands that did not belong to him,
thus doing injury to his brothers and his father. And so Clarvius Narcisse
was judged and condemned to be a zombie. By whom? By the enormous
power invested in the system of secret societies which are called Bizango.
One of these societies—whose everyday name is Order and Respect for the
Night—tried Narcisse, found him guilty, and punished him.

As members of these secret sects, whose practices are almost wholly
magical, there are counted not only many *mambos, bokors,* and *houngans,*
but also men and women of quite varied professions and income levels,
including people who are influential in the country's governing circles.
Within the sects the members are ordered in a hierarchy of dignitaries, that
is "emperors," "kings," "queens," "presidents," as well as cabinet ministers,
diplomats, army officers, and soldiers, thus forming a kind of secret and

nocturnal government, often more stable than the official one. Once a year, during Holy Week, the local sects' members march disguised in procession through the villages, issuing warnings and threats of punishment to anyone who flouts the life pattern expected of him by the community. This sort of inverted carnival is known as the *bande rara,* and I myself have witnessed it among the Haitians who crossed over to Cuba's eastern provinces to work in the sugar harvest. This shows that the Bizango's roots are so deep within the people that it shows up even among the rural emigrants. But as I have mentioned, these societies do not include peasants alone. There are indications, for example, that they have been partially controlled by the *tontons macoutes* during the Duvalier era, and that Papa Doc himself was very close to the hierarchy. Furthermore, the fall of Jean-Claude Duvalier's regime was due largely to his losing the favor of the Bizango societies. Anyone who thinks that the recent Haitian revolution has put an end to these sects' ramified powers is ignorant of the workings of the Caribbean dynamic. The network of cultural power that these societies have built is extremely vast, and its subterranean, or rather rhizomatic, connections to the webs of political, economic, and social power are strong and manifold, as we've seen. Bear in mind that the societies were founded by slaves and runaways at the end of the eighteenth century, and their prestige is enormous. Like the zombie, they will not rapidly disappear from the social picture.

In the specific case of the zombie, it's worth noting that we're not dealing just with a pathetic shadow that is present in voodoo's social realities, art and literature among them; it is also part of the Haitian tradition and way of life; it is the *sacré* that guarantees, sometimes better than any Western inspired law, that the peasant masses will live within the kind of order and respect that their ancestors established. Finally, the zombie cannot be removed from Haiti's social surface, because it is culture. Its confused self-presentation cannot be studied or explained properly by any discourse, for it is the simultaneous product of a toxin, which has been isolated scientifically through psychopharmacology, and the most secret manipulations of magic and folk-botany. And above all the zombie escapes our discourses because it is the product of a vehement psychological predisposition that all Caribbean cultural phenomena carry, which is another of the region's regularities. This ardent way of conceiving culture can probably be explained in several ways. In my opinion, though, it owes a lot to each Caribbean person's knowing more or less intuitively that finally the only sure thing that history's undertow has left to him is his paradoxical culture, and nothing more.

A danceable language

In a succinct and illuminating paragraph of *The Postmodern Condition*, Lyotard distinguishes between the two kinds of knowledge, or knowing, to which he has referred:

> In the first place, scientific knowledge does not represent the totality of knowledge; it has always existed in addition to, and in competition and conflict with, another kind of knowledge, which I will call narrative . . . I do not mean to say that narrative knowledge can prevail over science, but its model is related to ideas of internal equilibrium and conviviality next to which contemporary scientific knowledge cuts a poor figure.[18]

I accept this statement in principle, but what exactly is it that Lyotard calls "narrative" knowledge? It has to do with the kind of knowledge proper to societies that are undeveloped in the epistemological, theoretical, technological, industrial, imperialist, etc. senses. That is, societies that I have termed "Peoples of the Sea" in my introduction, perhaps carried away by the deep original genealogy that a marine provenance brings out: the torrential rains of the geological (and mythological) flood, the saline sediments, the lightning and thunder of the Creation, the first protein in the oceanic womb, the fetus floating in the physiologic whey, the act of parturition, cosmogonic society, Orehu the Arawak mother of waters, Obatala the Yoruba mother-sea . . . In any case, the discourse that can explain the world through the modality People of the Sea has always existed, but the West left it irrecoverably behind following a process that extends from the Greeks to Gutenberg, whose invention of movable type in 1440 marks the point of no return, since, using it, scientific discourse could then propagate effectively, through its very transmission, the "proofs" that brought credulity and certified legitimacy.

I have written "proofs" to emphasize the ironic charge that I give to the word. Scientific discourse, in order to say that reality cannot be definitively proven, must summon definitive proofs that reality is this thing or another within a rhetorical game of legitimation. Clearly, in the end, what counts are not the proofs in themselves, since the only thing that can be proved is that which is unknown; what really matters here is the fable of legitimation. Moreover, we must conclude with Lyotard that all knowledge, in the West as well as among the Peoples of the Sea, must show its competence by means of a fable of legitimation. Given all this, it's not hard to see that it is precisely the rhetorical modality through which such a story is told, that is, its *praxis,* that most separates Western knowledge from that of the Peoples of the Sea. I take it for granted that we are all well versed in the protocol—authorized voice, hypothesis, proof, discussion, consensus, etc.—that rules the story of scientific legitimation in the West. I am not so sure, though, that we are in common accord on the procedure that the Peoples of the Sea follow, since it has been observed by a vast constellation of "authorized voices" with extremely variable and at times divergent results (how do we reconcile Lombroso with Spengler, a problem that Ortiz had to face?). In any event, what is of interest here concerning the knowledge of the Peoples of the Sea is its relation to rhythm. I will begin with the criterion that Lyotard sets out, that is, with a postmodern point of view:

> Narrative form follows a rhythm; . . . nursery rhymes are of this type, and repetitive forms of contemporary music have tried to recapture or at least approximate it. It exhibits a surprising feature: as meter takes precedence over accent in the production of sound . . . time ceases to be a support for memory to become an immemorial beating that, in the absence of a noticeable separation between periods, prevents their being numbered and consigns them to oblivion . . . A collectivity that takes narrative as its key form of competence has no need to remember its past. It finds the raw materials for its social bond not only in the meaning of the narratives it recounts, but also in the act of reciting them . . . Finally, a culture that gives precedence to the narrative form doubtless has no more of a need for special procedures to authorize its narratives than it has to remember its past . . . In a sense, the people are only that which actualizes the narratives: once again, they do this not only by recounting them, but also by listening to them and recounting themselves through them; in other words, by putting them into "play" in their institutions—thus by assigning themselves the posts of narratee and diegesis as well as the post of narrator.[19]

All of this is to say that the narrative practice of the Peoples of the Sea is very different from the West's narrative of legitimation, since in the latter the problem of legitimacy is the subject of an extended process of inquiry, verification, and comment, while in the former the story itself instantly provides its own legitimacy whenever it is spoken in the present moment in the narrative's rhythmic voice, whose competence lies only in the speaker's having listened to the myth or the fable issuing from someone's mouth. Nevertheless, Lyotard's explanation is too general to be our focus. Let's take a brief look at those narrative practices of the Peoples of the Sea that had the greatest influence on Caribbean culture; that is, the practices of black Africa and India.

In the case of India, we ought to remember that Shiva, the third god in the Hindu *trimurt,* is a dancing deity whose steps and gestures interpret the rhythms of the universe, of Nature, of the cosmogony. Thus, his eternal dance may be seen as a complex text—in fact, that's how the religion sees it—whose signs are coded messages that Shiva left for humanity to read; that is, they are a kind of Testament codified in dance. Hence the importance to the Hindu ritual dance—and even to Indian popular dances—of the different percussive rhythms and the many visages executed by the performer's feet, legs, trunk, arms, fingers, neck, head, mouth, and eyes. Black Africa has an even greater dependance on rhythm. Remember the definition of rhythm that Senghor gives (see Chapter 1): rhythm is the "effective word." We're not dealing here with rhythm Western style, that is, with a signifier without a referent; nor are we dealing with the common everyday word—ours—that never manages to mean what it wants to mean. We're dealing here with Rhythm-Word. It shouldn't be surprising then that the African languages are so rhythmic and sonorous that they can be imitated by the *dun-dun,* the talking drum, whose skins, in a way analogous to the speakers in a large amplifying system, make communication possible between one village and another, without the mediation of any alphabetical code. One has to accept that in Africa, on hearing the *dun dun,* anyone can dance the language. In reality, it can be said that African culture's genres have been codified according to the possibilities of percussion. African culture is, above all, a thicket of systems of percussive signifiers, to whose rhythms and registers one lives both socially and inwardly. When a Yoruba dances the dance of Shango, for example, he is not just dancing the language of the gods; he is, at the same time, creating the deity himself through the dance. The accentuated hip movement, proper to this ritual dance, refers at once to Shango's erotic character in the Yoruba pantheon and also to his warrior attributes: the two-headed axe in the shape of a pelvis. It also refers to the color red, to blood, to fire, to anger, to pleasure, to nonreflection, to the *fiesta,* to wine, to transgression, to incest, to suicide, even to the plantain, the phallic fruit that is one of his favorite foods. Furthermore, Shango's dance carries within itself the profuse cycle of myths, legends, and proverbs that tell about Shango, and whose purpose in the Yoruba culture is a double one: to provide the child and the adolescent with didactic examples of what he should and should not do according to tradition, and to serve as a referent to the divining system of *diloggun,* based on invocations and on successive tosses of the *cauris* (a kind of shell) on a magic board; that is, narratives that serve as referents to the past and future at once. But, clearly, the dance in itself would count for little, since what makes it possible is the beat of the sacred drums, in this case the rhythm of Shango. Thus the individual, who is dancing Shango and incorporating him through the dancing spell into the group of participants, takes the place of "reader," "thing read," and "reading" in everything that touches on Shango. It is easy to see that with the existence of a great number of *orishas,* each one with its rhythm, and with their interacting in a permutational way in the *pataki* or narrations, the sum of this cosmogonic "book" is an inextricable rhythmic network to which one can only allude the mode of a deeply complex percussive language. Beginning with the idea that religion is, as we have seen, something that in traditional Africa permeates all of the discourses, I think that any definition of African culture that aspires to being functional cannot do without two words: polyrhythm and metarhythm. Thus the African practice of immediate (transhistorical) legitimation does not confine itself merely to the polyrhythmic narration of the *griot,* or storyteller—as Lyotard seems to suggest—but rather extends throughout the entire sociocultural superstructure with the result that each act, each utterance refers in one way or another to a *rhythm-langue* that underlies everything, that precedes everything, that places itself in the very root of all processes and things.

But to exempt the West from rhythm, as Lyotard does, does not seem right to me. If scientific knowledge not only coexists with music but also, at the same time, decodes it through a discipline (musicology), through a technology (sound engineering, production of musical instruments, reproduction by publication and recording), and through institutions (conservatory, theater, philharmonic orchestra, etc.), there must be some reason for this. How then are we to distinguish between a Western rhythm and an African one? I would say that, basically, scientific rhythm is a residual product, domesticated and systematized by the history of the West. Of course there was a time when this was not so, but the rhythm was emptied of cosmological and social signification during the European process of political Christianization. That is why, with its pagan noise silenced and converted into a simulacrum of what it once was, its signs would remain subject to a reduced number of rhetorics—music, dance, poetry—that prearranged their differences, making them so predictable that from that point on they could be inscribed in the musical bar according to the reigning notations and conventions. African rhythm, though—as we have seen—cannot be written down in the same way; it is ubiquitous, fluid, and it responds to a symbolic poetic like those of the societies from which it issues; its discourse in the present tense carries the group's law, myth, history, and prophecy; it is the immemorial attempt to capture the cosmogonic together with the social, and it is, in itself, the ritual sacrifice (not its simulacrum) which is there to forget past, present, and future violence. But clearly it is much more as well: it is found in every possible human activity and it can be danced when Nature is listened to. This is why, to Senghor, African rhythm is "the effective word," and why Lyotard finds the rhythmic narrative of the Peoples of the Sea to be related to "ideas of internal equilibrium and coexistence, next to which contemporary scientific knowledge [that is, its rhythm] cuts a poor figure." In short, for the Peoples of the Sea, before Rhythm there was Chaos; after it, Order, except that, in time, in the West, such Order came to be seen as (Dis)Order.

Knowledge in flight

It is evident to the reader of the *Contrapunteo* that the presence of tobacco and sugar in the text does not refer to these products only in the narrowest sense.[20] Tobacco and sugar have a metaphorical value that touches also on myth and history, black and white, slave and planter, art and machinery, rural smallholding and *latifundio,* intensive cultivation and extensive culti-vation, quality and quantity, national capital and foreign capital, *criollismo* and cosmopolitanism, independence and dependence, agricultural, indus-trial diversification and monoculture, monoproduction, sovereignty and intervention, the discourse of power and the discourse of resistance, desire and repression, the revolutionary and the reactionary, coexistence and vio-lence.

But, clearly and obviously, tobacco and sugar refer as well to the fables of legitimation set forth respectively by the Peoples of the Sea and by the West. For example, Ortiz asserts, to underline tobacco's ritual character: "In tobacco there is always a touch of mystery and sacredness. Tobacco is something for grownups, who are responsible to society and to the gods. To smoke tobacco for the first time . . . is like a rite of passage, the rite of tribal initiation" (p. 20); or "In tobacco smoking there is a survival of religion and magic . . . the slow-burning fire is like an expiatory vehicle.

The smoke rising to the heavens seems a spiritual evocation. The smoke, more enchanting than incense, is like a perfume that purifies" (p. 25). He also emphasizes the idea of social harmony and the wish to exorcise violence, as when he says: "To smoke from the same pipe, to inhale snuff from the same pouch, to exchange cigarettes, all these are rites of friendship and communion, like drinking the same wine or breaking the same bread. This is true among Indians from America, white from Europe, and blacks from Africa" (p. 21).

The narrative of sugar, though, is quite different: "The sugar economy was always capitalist, from its inception, unlike that of tobacco. This was exactly how they were seen, from the first days in which the economic exploitation of these West Indies, by Columbus and his successors in settlement" (p. 50). Ortiz also observes, in alluding to the type of rhythm inscribed in the capitalist sugar narrative, that

> In the production of sugar everything is measured, almost always according to standards with universal [read *Western* or *scientific*] value: units of surface for the cane fields, of weight for the stalks and the sugars, of pressure for the *trapiches,* of vacuum for the pumps and evaporators, of volume for the liquors and molasses, of heat for the ovens and boilers, of viscosity for the crystallization points, of light for polarization, of loss for transportation, of algebraic proportion for the extractions, the yields, and the economy of every step in the agro-industrial process, all according to the analyses of a profuse accounting. (p. 40)

Thus tobacco is carnival, the word-rhythm, ritual sacrifice, sacred dance, the drum that talks and unites, the possibility of dancing the language, immediate sensuality; it is the realm of *Don Carnal* in the *Libro de buen amor*, the territory of art, of the imagination, of the poetic; it is the super-signifier that refers to the oldest traditions of Africa, Asia, America, and Europe. And sugar calls up the binary rhythm of law and work, of patriarchal hierarchy, of scientific knowledge, of punishment and discipline, of superego and castration; it is the space of *Doña Quaresma* (Dame Lent) of the *Libro de buen amor*, the space of production and productivity, of rule and measure, of ideology and nationalism, of the computer that speaks and separates; it is, above all, the signifier that offers itself as center, as origin, as fixed destination, for that which signifies the Other.

Nevertheless, as I have said, the Caribbean, to Ortiz, does not exist exclusively in tobacco or in sugar, but rather in the "counterpoint" of tobacco and sugar. By means of this singular proposition, Ortiz avoids falling into the trap of binary opposition and establishes—in a manner unlike that of modernity—a relation that would seem postmodern to us. Such a relation, now enunciated, merits a second commentary.

To begin with, Ortiz has recourse to the term *contrapunteo,* which sends us in the direction of baroque music, that is, to a sonic architecture of an excessive and off-center character.[21] But, concretely, he refers us to a musical form in which the musical voices not only confront each other but also superimpose themselves upon one another, in a parallel fashion, interacting with each other in a perpetual flight. I am speaking here, naturally, of the fugal form, in this case interpreted by the voices of tobacco and sugar, or rather by their metaphorical values. These voices, as in the fugue system, do not mean the same thing. Voice S (Sugar), which is the second to enter, tries to exert dominance over voice T (Tobacco), the one that began the theme. Note that if the fugue exists it is only because the second voice is present; it is this one that properly speaking generates the counterpoint and makes it possible as a polyphonic genre. It might be said the S carries a *praxis* or mechanics of a technical sort that T does not possess. But, as I have said, it would be an error to think that T and S relate to each other only in an antagonistic or exclusive way. I would say that they relate also in the complementary and diachronic sense of mutual interdependence that recalls the complexity of power relations. In the kind of fugue that the *Contrapunteo* establishes, this kind of relationship suggests a socioeconomic interplay of a genealogical character, in the sense that first there was the Mother ("primitive" society's mode of production) and then the Father (the capitalist mode of production). That is why Ortiz, in setting out the scientific narrative of sugar, should speak of the tremendous socioeconomic power accumulated by the sugar mill:

> The modern center is not a simple agrarian exploitation, nor either a manufacturing plant with the production of its raw materials next door; today it is an entire "system of lands, machines, transports, technicians, workers, monies, and populations for the production of sugar"; it is an entire social organism, as alive and complex as a city or municipality, or a baronial castle with its feuded environs of vassals, nobles, and commoners. The *latifundio* is nothing but a territorial base, its established mass. The sugar mill is vertebrated by an economic

and juridical structure that combines masses of lands, masses of machines, masses of men, and masses of money, everything furnished for the integral magnitude of the sugaring organism. (p. 53)

When he speaks of tobacco, though, Ortiz discards all allusions to its measure of capitalist power, to characterize it only in terms of prestige; it is a matter then of prestige without economic power, the old and secret authority of the Mothers of the Rivers, of the mother lode, mother earth, the mother tongue; a vaginal, humid, vegetative prestige, the prestige of Gaia, Isis, the Lady of the Plants. To Ortiz, tobacco is smoke and humus, telluric ash, Taino word, sacred aroma, and it never stops residing in the hands of the *behique* (shaman) who once sustained it. It is from here that there emanates tobacco's never-to-be-overthrown prestige against sugar's power to detract, the power of the *nouveau riche,* of the bourgeois who passes himself off as a nobleman. The Cuban can be the "best in the world" in terms of tobacco alone, not sugar, since the quality of sugar, refined or not, is alike the world over.

> It is proverbial among all nations that *Cuba is the land of the best tobacco in the world* . . . *Havana tobacco* is the prototype of all other tobaccos, which envy it and make an effort to imitate it. This opinion is universally held . . . Havana tobacco's universal fame is so assured that the word *Havana* has passed into the vocabularies of all civilized peoples in not only its accepted meaning of "from Havana," but also meaning "the best tobacco in the world." (pp. 431–33)

It's clear that Ortiz's counterpoint, which is the relationship between the narratives of tobacco and of sugar, does not imply a parity, or even a synthesis derived from the contradiction of *thesis/antithesis,* but rather there is another kind of difference here, specifically the difference between power and prestige, between history and myth, between machine and hand, between Industrial Revolution and Agricultural Revolution, between mass production and artisanship, between computer and drum. It's a question of voices that come from different centers of emission, from differing moments and discourses, which coexist beside each other in a complex and critical relationship, one that is impossible to clarify entirely.[22]

In the *Contrapunteo*'s last pages (p. 88), Ortiz clearly expresses the nature of this singular relationship, as, by means of a consciously ironic trope— the text "ought to have a fairytale ending"—tobacco and sugar get married and conceive "alcohol." This new sound, far from being a stable element, is a system of differences in itself and forms what Ortiz calls the "Cuban trinity: tobacco, sugar, and alcohol."[23] So at any given moment there would be a resulting sound that was unable to dispense with the first two, and yet would be neither one of them but rather their difference. None of these sounds could exist by itself within the fugue or in any polyphonic system; none is an irreducible unity within the counterpoint; they form among themselves a harmonic ensemble of themes and responses that unfold, in opposition, in alliance, juxtaposition, and pursuit, until the piece's end, an end that in a fugue is always arbitrary.

I think that a postmodern philosopher, on reading the *Contrapunteo*, would have no trouble accepting this Bakhtinian dialogic form, whose result (its "alcohol") would be not just polyphonic music but any literary piece that expresses itself through a carnivalesque plurality of voices. Its system of differences puts into question the consistency of binary opposition, and refers genealogically not to some past socioeconomic meta-narrative, but to the *Libro de buen amor*, a fictional and a-centric text. In the rhetorical sense, one would have to say that the *Contrapunteo* meets another important canon of postmodernity, for its story of its own competence legitimizes itself through its very own paralogical value, in its signifying in the form of new and unexpected movement within the discourse of the social sciences. Furthermore, we must conclude that the *Contrapunteo* furnishes an infinite space for coexistence, that is, a space where the signifier is never "one" since what we listen to (we read) is the always incomplete superimposition of voices that continue on ad infinitum. Finally, we also have the indisputable fact of Ortiz's seeing himself as a writer, not as an "author" of texts.

But, at the same time, I think that the hypothetical postmodern philosopher whose opinion we have solicited would be confused on listening to the fugue proposed by the *Contrapunteo*. Even more, it's possible that he might deny its formal validity as a fugue. This could happen because, as I said at the outset, if he could well be impressed with its system of differences and the show of ideological and multidisciplinary promiscuity that its text unfolds, he could not systematically conjoin the epistemological narrative of sugar with tobacco's cosmogonic myth. And it is a fact that, in the canvas of generalized promiscuity that Ortiz offers, Afro-Caribbean beliefs appear together with the *rumba* and the *carnaval* as forms of knowledge as valid as those proper to scientific knowledge.

Arguing on behalf of Ortiz's prescience, one would have to say that the *Contrapunteo*'s full title establishes differences with respect to any other kind of counterpoint, whether proceeding from the European polyphonic tradition or the African polyrhythmic tradition. Remember that the adjective that defines and nationalizes the *Contrapunteo* is *Cuban,* which should be read as *Caribbean.* So the initial question concerning how to read Caribbeanness from the West is answered by Ortiz with the *Contrapunteo* itself, with a model that once was that of modernity and "something more and something less," that now is that of postmodernity and "something more and something less." I mean by this that, in traditional as well as scientific language, the fable of Caribbean legitimation has always been, is, and will be, at once excessive and insufficient; it will never entirely be able to shed the "originating" rhythms of the Peoples of the Sea that contributed to its founding, nor will it manage entirely to assimilate the scientific-technical rhythms that capitalism introduced, as Ortiz puts it, through "Columbus and his successors in settlement." In other words, the *Contrapunteo Cubano del tabaco y el azúcar* says that Caribbeanness should not be looked for in tobacco or in sugar, but rather in the counterpoint of the myth of the Peoples of the Sea and the theorem of the West, a counterpoint whose sound, according to Ortiz, suggests "fire, force, spirit, drunkenness, thought, and action" (p. 88), attributes that in the end mean everything and nothing.

5

Carpentier and Harris:

explorers

of

El Dorado

Years ago, in his famous essay "Problemática de la actual novela latino-americana," Alejo Carpentier rejected the idea of our narrative's following the *fin de siècle*'s naturalistic model of construction, in that such a choice entailed "choosing a certain ambit, informing oneself about it, *living* it for a time, and then setting out to work on the basis of the material collected."[1] And then he added:

> The weakness of this method lies in the writer's having to trust too much in his own power of assimilation and understanding. He thinks that after having spent two weeks in a mining town he has understood everything that's happened in that town. He thinks that by having attended a typical *fiesta* he has understood the motives, the remote reasons behind what he's seen . . . I don't mean to insinuate by this that our novelists lack the culture necessary to establish certain relations between events and to arrive at certain truths. But what I do mean to say is that the naturalist-nativist-localist-vernacular method applied, for more than thirty years, toward the elaboration of the Latin American novel has given us a regional and picturesque novelizing that in only a very few cases reached the bottom—the truly transcendental nature—of things. (p. 11)

One might think that Carpentier meant to exclude his own works from this critical pronouncement. But he didn't. His reproaches were directed also, and expressly so, toward his own first novel, *¡Ecue-Yamba-O!* (1933):

"After twenty years of research into Cuba's syncretic realities, I realized that everything deep, true, universal in the world that I had attempted to paint in my novel had remained beyond the reach of my observation" (p. 12).

It's obvious that these misgivings would apply equally to his second novel, *El reino de este mundo* (1949), which was born just after a short visit to Haiti in 1943. And they would also work against one of his most important works, *Los pasos perdidos* (1953), whose writing, as we know, was linked to that of *El libro de la gran sabana*, an unfinished text in which Carpentier tried to mold the experiences that he accumulated on an aerial excursion over the upper Caroní and the Roraima region (1947), along with a brief journey through the Orinoco (1948).[2] Thus *Los pasos perdidos* shares not only the jungle thematic with such novels as *La vorágine* and *Canaima*, but also their models of construction, derived in large measure from the French naturalist novel.

We might notice how Carpentier, in his criticism, seems to allude directly to *Los pasos perdidos*. When he's disparaging the so-called "jungle novel," he says: "I know many of its authors, I know how they gathered their 'documentation.' *There's one who has written a jungle novel after having looked at it for a couple of days*" (p. 12). The words that I've underlined probably refer to his own jungle "explorations," which were the objects of mirth on the part of some writers in Caracas.[3]

But the thing that turns out to be unexpected in Carpentier's essay is that the method that he proposes for the future is that of the "city novel" in the manner of Joyce's travels through the streets of Dublin. That is, after negating the strategy that served him in his first three novels, and that led him, by the way, to the notion of the *real maravilloso,* he suggests to us that we undertake the urban voyage which he himself would take in his fourth novel, *El acoso* (1956).

It seems clear now that Carpentier's essay stems from his reflection on his own career as a traveler/novelist. But is an urban voyage a real solution? Let's look at his own conclusion:

> I had lived for two years in Caracas and I didn't even know Caracas. To understand Caracas it's not enough to walk its streets. You've got to live it, to deal every day with its professionals, its businessmen, its shopkeepers; you've got to know its millionaires, as well as the people dwelling on its miserable hillsides; you've got to know the habits of its military caste; you've got to have visited the old palace of Miraflores,

discovering, with astonishment, that its interior decoration . . . is the work of Vargas Vila. (pp. 12–13)

Thus the city turns out to be just as inaccessible as the jungle, if not more so, a fact that Carpentier himself recognizes: "Our cities, because they haven't yet entered our literature, are more difficult to handle than the jungles or the mountains" (p. 12). This, following Carpentier's own line of reasoning, would also close the door on the method that gave rise to *El acoso*. What's left then? A final attempt:

> To leave the characters free, with their virtues, their vices, their inhibitions . . . starting from the profound truth which is that of the writer himself, born, suckled, raised, educated in his own ambit [which invalidates the method Carpentier uses in *El siglo de las luces* (1962), his last novel to this date], but lucid only on the condition that it get to the bottom of the surrounding *praxis*'s operations, a *praxis* which, in this case, can be identified with Sartre's contexts. Contexts which it would be fitting to enumerate here, even though the enumeration might be something like a catalog of ships or conquistadors' horses. (p. 19)

Nonetheless, we read right away that adopting the Sartrean method, whose "contexts"—political, cultural, economic, etc.—are here slightly ridiculed in being compared with silly catalogs, does not itself lead to a truthful definition of Latin American reality either. What happens, Carpentier concludes, is that the people of our countries have yet to jell, and they are "waiting for a synthesis—still distant, situated beyond the lives of those now writing" (p. 19). So that, for Carpentier, the problematic of our novel lies outside itself, that is, in its Latin American referents. The problem would be resolved at some vague moment in the future, when our socio-cultural spectrum's chaotic dynamics order themselves in a "synthesis" that can be read, interpreted, and represented textually by Latin American and Caribbean writers.

The voyage there

Naturally it's easy today to conclude that Carpentier—at least in 1964, the date of his essay—was following a faulty criterion for judging our novels, including his own. In the years immediately following, the boom of the so-called "new Latin American narrative" would explode, and it would knock his pessimism completely for a loop. There was no need to wait for the improbable sociocultural synthesis that he had situated "beyond the lifetimes of those now writing" for Latin America and the Caribbean to come up with a novelizing practice of the highest quality that would find many readers throughout the world. One has to agree that if we take any given novel to be deserving of an adjective, such as *infamous, subversive, tremendous, vulgar* (to list a few common ones), we do it according to standards that don't offer their referential authority in anthropological or sociological terms, as Carpentier had been proposing. It is now more or less generally taken for granted that there are no substantial reasons for subordinating the language of the novel to any other language. The eras of rationalist metadiscourse, of titanic systems that belonged to Romanticism and to the pseudoscientific mania of positivist thought, now seem more and more distant. To me, it is clear enough, as I said in the previous chapter, that a part of the world is beginning to leave so-called "modernity" behind and to enter a new and unforeseen era that defines itself as "postmodern," that is, having an incredulous attitude toward the effectiveness of any metadiscourse.[4] In that sense, it now seems banal to many of us to seek the legitimation of any novel's discourse within any of the great philosophic, economic, or sociological fables of the past. We are now in the era of *Blow up.* The terms *unity, coherence, truth, synthesis, origin, legitimacy, dialectical contradiction,* and others of the sort break down in the computers of the postindustrial laboratories as they are divided into squares and then each square amplified as though it were a photograph. A point is reached at which the "original" representation falls apart—it always falls apart— and then the various grains of color come under scrutiny, in their hidden regularities and especially in the empty spaces separating them, that is, the spaces of nothingness. Everything seems to come down to fiction, game, experimentation. For many, it is the sign of a new era.

It is plain, moreover, that the travel book, a genre much earlier than the novel, and which Herodotus began with his *Histories*, starts from a model quite similar to the one systematized by the French naturalist novel. It's also clear that famous globetrotters like Marco Polo, Columbus, Pigafetta "trusted too much in their powers of assimilation and understanding," as Carpentier puts it. Nevertheless, the profound semiological problems that they encounter on their adventures and their crossings haven't kept readers from reading their works, which had some force not only in the past but have it still today, when we read them as we would a novel, with curiosity and pleasure.

Today's travel book has not lost the enchantment of its predecessors. I might adduce Cousteau's accounts, or the many reconstructions of the journeys of the ancient pilgrims, of the transcontinental caravans, of the mysterious seafarers and conquistadors of the past. But we also keep on being interested by contemporary texts that take on a search, a voyage, into a kind of life lived in a cultural space quite different from our own, in an "other" society. Among the many books of this kind written by modern travelers, I would like to settle on one of them, more than anything for the relation that it establishes with the essay by Carpentier that we've just looked at. I'm speaking of the book in which Roland Barthes tells of his visit to Japan. Barthes writes, in a kind of brief preface appearing under the title of "*Là-bas*" (over there, yonder, faraway):

> If I want to imagine a fictive nation, I can give it an invented name, treat it declaratively as a novelistic object, create a new Garabagne, so as to compromise no real country by my fantasy (though it is then that fantasy itself I compromise by the signs of literature). I can also— though in no way claiming to represent or to analyze reality itself (these being the major gestures of Western discourse)—isolate some- where in the world (*faraway*) a certain number of features (a term employed in linguistics), and out of these features deliberately form a system. It is this system that I shall call: Japan.[5]

We might say that Barthes has purged himself ahead of time by estab- lishing the enormous limitations of his text in regard to the describing, representing, or properly commenting on present-day Japanese society. Still I think I can point to another intention in Barthes's words, perhaps an ironic postmodernist commentary. If we approach his notion of "*Là- bas*"—which I prefer to translate as "*over there*"—we see that it attempts to reveal (re-veil) the experience of the traveler who leaps outside his own space to land in the space of the Other, whose codes he assumes he will be unable to decipher. The idea invokes a paradox: that the traveler "read" the signs of a sociocultural space different from his own, which actually are opaque to him, and that, by putting together a few odds and ends he should form judgments about that space. These judgments, after being ar- ticulated with all deliberation, will constitute a new system, a necessarily fictitious one, which the traveler will attempt to narrate with a vehicle that partakes of all kinds of complicities and manipulations but that, finally, can lead nowhere but back to itself: to writing.

The notion of "over there" involves the following irony: it's all the same whether the traveler knows or doesn't know that he doesn't know the Other's code. In the first case the resulting text might be a deconstruction of itself—as Barthes's is—and in the second case it will turn out to be a text that naïvely attempts to set itself up as a representation of the Other's. And of course in neither case will the traveler's account give a true image of the referent. This is not just because the readings have necessarily been mistaken, but also, and especially, because the result must be a *text,* that is, a signifier that has to fall short of signifying the Other. That's why Barthes starts out by offering to imagine a fictitious nation and to treat it openly as a novelistic object. It doesn't really matter, since the "over there" operates in all possible writing, regardless of genre or rhetoric. In fact reportage, just as much as any chronicle, account, travel book, letter, diary, biography, history, or even novel, must find itself at an unbridgeable distance, *over there*—or simply *there*—from the threshold of the Other; or, as Carpentier concludes, in his lucid innocence: "beyond the lives of those now writing."

I remember the book written by a haughty Englishwoman who traveled to Havana in about 1840. She affirms emphatically in her book that Cuban fruits are nauseating, though she has never condescended to try one. She bases her radical judgment on their being eaten not just by the locals but also by the pigs. It is precisely here, in this obviously mistaken reading, that we recognize Marco Polo, Columbus; also Don Quixote. But finally we're not in a better position ourselves. For them, for us, the Other's system will always be *there,* because the act of reading it supposes also the act, conscious or not, of projecting *our* meaning toward the Other's fugitive meaning, whether it's called Japan, America, El Dorado, myth, novel. Finally Barthes warns us that his travel book will be as arbitrary, as fictitious, as much *his own,* as any other book that he might write or have written. We have to agree that this singular quality shapes an uncertainty that is not recent at all, which is already visible, for example, in the paradox of Achilles and the tortoise: the goal—what the Other means, the total movement of all its meanings—lies always at an unreachable point, at the edge of the infinite, *there,* in a space that shifts continually from the possible to the impossible.

The Path of Words

The perplexity of the writer who, with a clear head, travels into the Other's world—the unpleasantness of deliberately naming what he knows to be beyond his ken—marks his writing in some way. I think that Carpentier—whose only limitation was to judge our novel as immature without realizing that all novels, all texts are necessarily immature, and that this has nothing to do with their aesthetic value—is one of the great contemporary authors in whose works the tension of the *there* is most notable. With his life's history trapped between Europe and America, he comes to the islands and rain forests in a way that reminds one of Moses and the Promised Land, or, in his last novel, Columbus[6]; that is to say as a "discoverer" of a world that he has already conceived, that was *his,* and that has been thought up, imagined, and desired ahead of time by Europe. His most typically baroque style—a formula that proved very effective in his break with nativist naturalism—has an almost-admitted origin in the space that would be given to an "Adam who gives things their names" (p. 39) and, on the other hand, in the disquieting certainty that in losing *his* Paradise he brought down upon himself the punishment of being made to forget the names of things.

Carpentier's baroque shouldn't be seen as a will toward ornamentation, nor as an evasion or a disinterested break with *criollista* literature. To Carpentier, the American reality, including the Cuban, is only his in part. In his descriptive discourse, whether this be essayistic (such as in *La ciudad de las columnas*) or fictional (as in *Los pasos perdidos*), there is much of the stupefaction proper to a traveler getting ready to storm the Other's golden citadel. This sort of spiritual state leads him, remember, to elaborate his notion of *lo real maravilloso* after he has made contact with Haiti's (dis)ordered codes. But, above all, it moves him to name one thing after another, like an explorer marking a trail on the tree trunks that he leaves behind him. Carpentier's baroque is unique in that it assumes its own formal marginality, while being at the same time a course; it is the textual representation of the labyrinth that surrounds and leads to the fugitive center of his own Caribbean Otherness; it is Ariadne's thread, which, because it has been extended (named), can grant him a return path to this side (*here*) of his desire, which is Europe, after a frustrated voyage to the other side (*there*) of that same desire, which is America. But of course in the last analysis Carpentier is a child of America also. Europe can't be his final destination, and his search for identity will always go back and forth between the figures of *Juan el romero* and *Juan el indiano,* between the Musicologist and Rosario, between Víctor and Sofía, between the harp and the shadow. His baroque is not the outlandish and turbulent metalanguage of a spiral; it is vertical, metonymic, a linear sum of aggregates; it is the constancy of his existential route, of his pendular oscillation between two worlds; it is, above all, the Path of Words that tries to link Europe with America, *his* Europe and *his* America.

It is true that a path can open itself to adventure (like the retrograde and magical discourse of *Viaje a la semilla*—which we will get a close look at later—or the protagonists' voyages in "El Camino de Santiago," "Semejante a la noche," *Los pasos perdidos, El acoso,* and *Concierto barroco*), but in the end he always returns, like Columbus, to the starting point, the labyrinth's anteroom, on the side that's safe, politic, that touches on the tricky path that leads to chaos. His voyage toward his own Caribbean Otherness has something about it of the calculated risk, and in this element of caution, proper to Odysseus and Theseus, there might lie the difference between Carpentier's baroque and those of other Caribbean writers, such as Lezama Lima, García Márquez, Sarduy, Cabrera Infante, Arenas, Rodríguez Juliá, the forgotten Enrique Bernardo Núñez, or the Guyanese Wilson Harris, whose work I will discuss shortly.

It's obvious that the Path of Words between Europe and America becomes much more assured when one goes out parallel to some famous explorer. This consideration leads Carpentier to adopt, like a map or navigational instrument, the authoritative rhetoric of the ones who preceded him. Thus *El reino de este mundo* owes much to the observations of Moreau de Saint-Méry, *El siglo de las luces* to Humboldt's scientific and political perspectives, *El arpa y la sombra* to Columbus's papers, and *Los pasos perdidos* to Richard Schomburgk's book on Guyana.[7] I want to linger a while here over this last case. It has been shown elsewhere that *Los pasos perdidos* includes not just some versions of various passages in Schomburgk's book, but also various appropriations of his semantic attitude when faced with an unsystematized and not entirely comprehensible Nature.[8] Carpentier wants his novel's text to have its return passage guaranteed, and to this end, rather than relying on the crazy metaphors that might send him off irrecoverably into the labyrinth surrounding the Other, he chooses to reinvent the jungle through a reelaboration of Schomburgk's romantic language.

But why Schomburgk and not Humboldt, especially if we take into account that Carpentier's journey down the Orinoco duplicated part of

Humboldt's voyage and not that of the Schomburgk brothers? I concur with González-Echevarría that Richard Schomburgk's text—though not his brother Robert's—[9] is much more literary than Humboldt's,[10] and therefore a more fitting rhetorical model for *Los pasos perdidos*. But there's more to it. To Humboldt, nature in America is simply part of Nature, part of the cosmic metadiscourse in which he believed and to which he reduced every other discourse. To Humboldt the Grand Savannah was no more than a paragraph of his work called *Cosmos*. His trip down the Orinoco was not, for him, a "descent," or a recovery of the Earthly Paradise, or a return to the fourth day of the Creation. Humboldt, unlike Carpentier, did not travel in order to revisit the *there* of his identity. His goal was simply to establish statistically that Nature is a regulated machine which, if it is immense and complex, can be disassembled and understood. We might almost say that Humboldt didn't travel through the Americas, but rather that the islands, jungles, mountains, and rivers traveled through him. His voyage is not an attempt to establish a dialogue with the Other, for he has already foreseen (through his *reason*) whatever the Other might have to say. As he enters the Orinoco through a place inhabited by jaguars, giant reptiles, and saurians, his guide compares the place to Paradise. But Humboldt won't let himself be impressed by the place's virginal and wild appearance, and right away, as a response, he makes an ironic comment on the "goodness" of that Paradise. Later, as he reaches the Río Negro and starts to penetrate the legendary Amazon region, he comes out with the opinion that this territory might be developed economically by means of a system of canals that would allow commercial exchange with the Caribbean coast. (This, of course, would provoke a wail of protest from the protagonist of *Los pasos perdidos*.) With regard to the Amazon legend, Humboldt believed that the first European voyagers had a tendency to dress the New World's remote places in the mythic clothing that the Greek classics would place in exotic lands. In short, one never finds, not anywhere in Humboldt's work, a shiver of "*lo sublime*" or the epiphany of "*lo real maravilloso*."

In reality, the difference that exists between Humboldt's and Schomburgk's prose is owing to their having made their explorations at different dates. Between the former and the latter there lie forty years of Romanticism. The voice that narrates *Voyage aux regions équinoctiales* retains much of the equanimity and discipline of neoclassical scientific prose, while on the other hand, the voice that narrates *Travels in British Guiana* is decidedly romantic, and therefore better suits the neoromantic spirit of *Los pasos per-*

didos. Let's take a look at Carpentier's reading of Schomburgk contained in one of the published chapters of *El libro de la gran sabana*. Carpentier writes:

> When Sir Richard Schomburgk . . . reached the Roraima, in 1842, he declared himself overwhelmed by his own insignificance before "the sublime, the transcendent, implicit in that marvel of nature." With the rhetoric of a man who would call his black servant Hamlet, and who when faced with the Arekunas crowned with leaves would think of Birnam Wood come to Dunsinane, the romantic discoverer affirms that "there are no words to paint the grandeur of this mountain, with its noisy cascade splashing from a prodigious height." [11]

In another published chapter from his unpublished travel book, Carpentier cites Richard Schomburgk once again: "Richard points out, with feeling, that 'because they didn't know the amorous delicacies of a pair of *psittacus passerinus,* the German poets erroneously chose the cooing of two doves to symbolize an idyll.' Later, they reach a place that they call 'the paradise of the plants.' " [12] Here you find some of the strong romantic antecedents of the Carpentierian prose of *Los pasos perdidos*. But, as I've already said, what we have here is a European-style lyricism, a lyricism constructed out of ready-made expressions and adjectives, all of them quite deliberately imposing Europe's signified upon America's signifier. It is the Path of Words along which one may march back and forth with no risk of losing one's footing and falling into the turbulent abysses of a poetic death.

The trip to El Dorado

The reader might think that perhaps I'm denying Carpentier's "Caribbeanness." But that's not the case. Quite the contrary. All I want to do is to differentiate it from other forms of experiencing the Caribbean. As I see it, Carpentierian discourse is an ambivalent thing which, though controlled by the firm presence of Europe as the Father's cultural origin, carries out one of the Caribbean discourse's most visible tasks. I mean that one of the most clearly and frequently seen regularities of the Caribbean novel is its reiteration of the theme that has come to be known as "the search for identity" or "the search for roots." Critics have looked at this dynamic from all angles, and for that reason I don't want to jump now into what would turn out to be a history of the Caribbean novel. It is enough just to remember that the persistent discourse that travels toward a rediscovery of the divided Self, or better, toward a Utopian territory with an Arcadia where one might reconstitute his Being, might all be explained in relation to the known cultural fragmentation which, because of the Plantation, is the experience of every man and woman in the Caribbean.

Now, it is easy to see that this search that the novel of the Caribbean undertakes strongly recalls the search for El Dorado. It is taken in like manner along many and varied routes by various means of traveling toward a hypothetical center or origin. This imaginary point, which is fashioned by desire, is neither static nor localizable, but rather in continuous displacement, as Humboldt observed when he mapped out for himself the routes taken by various expeditions that went out looking for El Dorado. And it is right there, in this fugitive place, where Caribbean Being, violently fragmented and uprooted, intuits that it can recover its lost form. Such is the inexhaustible treasure so fervently sought in this place at once both mythic and utopian.

Every more or less serious effort at writing a novel from the Caribbean— *Los pasos perdidos, Paradiso, Cien años de soledad, Tres tristes tigres, De donde son los cantantes, Cubagua, Cuando amaban las tierras comuneras, La guaracha del Macho Camacho, El mundo alucinante, La noche oscura del Niño Avilés, Los pañamanes*, etc.—usually implies this search. Nevertheless, as happens throughout the long history of expeditions to El Dorado, there are some travelers/writers who come back from the adventure affirming its impossibility. These are travelers whose extreme theoretical lucidity has kept them from going deeply into the deceptive route, saturated with poetic mirages, that the journey presents. These are epistemological voyagers of the Barthes type. There exists a second category which, like Philip de Hutten, who was to see the golden towers of the city of Manoa—the city of El Dorado—did manage to catch a shattering vision of this marvelous space, but only for an instant, and never managed to repeat the experience. Finally, there exists another, reduced, class of explorers who come back from the jungle without their sanity—which is the same as not returning—for they claim not just to have reached El Dorado but also to have kept the vision with them in such a way as to carry it inscribed on their Being. Among the Caribbean writers of the second category we would find Carpentier; among those in the last one, Wilson Harris.

Concerning Harris, I am interested above all in his novel *Palace of the Peacock* (1960), so rightly admired in the English-speaking Caribbean.[13] Its subject is very like that of *Los pasos perdidos*. The action takes place in the Guyanese jungle. A white planter, named Donne, undertakes a voyage, in a motor launch, to look for the native workers who have run away from his plantation because of his harsh treatment. The boat ascends one of the big rivers leading into the heart of the jungle. Its crew is made up of men of diverse races and mixtures. This is a region that the Schomburgk brothers explored, and it's no accident that one of the crewmen, the eldest of them, is named Schomburgh—the same surname spelled in English— and that his *mestizo* lineage was formed through the union of a German great-grandfather and an Arawak great-grandmother.[14] In any event, the object of the expedition is to reach an indigenous village, a mission in the jungle's heart. Donne suspects that it is to this place that his fugitive peons have fled, and he has it in mind to make them return to the plantation by force. But when the boat reaches the village, the inhabitants flee upriver in their canoes. Why? The natives remember that in a former time those same men drowned in the rapids and great waterfall that the river goes over near the village. So the character who narrates the story, a brother of Donne's named Dreamer, is dead, and along with the rest of the crew he is traveling toward his second death. In fact, after passing the abandoned mission, the death trip is taken up once more, this time with a new member, an aged Arawak woman who had been wandering among the empty huts. Finally, not without fatal accidents, they cross the dangerous rapids and reach the waterfall, a monumental drop that cuts off the possibility of continuing the upriver climb. The crewmen have continued to disappear—dying all over again—and the ones still awaiting their second deaths begin to scale the ancient rock cliff amid the thunder of refracting and vaporous water. Thus they ascend painfully until they reach the Palace of the Peacock, the rainbow's spectrum, a place where the colors' identities are generated as the light's rays decompose. It is here, in this primal and poetic space, that the crew reencounters itself in death to be once again reborn.

But *Palace of the Peacock*, like *Los pasos perdidos*, is of course much more than just a telling of its story. There are, for example, concrete references to the search for El Dorado—exactly as in Carpentier's text—and to the difficult and violent conquest of the territory, which was stubbornly de- fended by the aboriginals. There is also mention of the subsequent arrival of the Africans, and of the Asian Indians and the Portuguese, as conse- quences of the plantation economy. It's evident that Donne, whose name has Jacobean resonances, stands for the earliest English colonizer to have stolen the land from the natives and forced them to work for him. It is also clear that the men who make up the boat's crew, whose blood is profusely mixed, represent, along with the aged Arawak woman (the Great Arawak

Mother), Guyanese society as it now exists. Taking all this into account, we see right away that the search of Donne and his companions is the historic search of Guyanese society, looking for a root to link it to the country's vast and intricate land. Such a search must necessarily direct itself toward the jungles and savannahs of the interior, since that's where El Dorado is found. It might be thought that I'm referring here only to the times of Walter Raleigh and the first European settlements, times when El Dorado was the explorer's most desperate dream. But that's not the case. In reality the search for El Dorado continues, and will surely continue for many years. It is now carried out by present-day Guyanese society beneath the slogan of "repossessing the interior," which refers to the economic exploitation of the inland territory, potentially rich in natural resources, as well as to the discovery of a collective psychic state which would allow a feeling of cultural identity, extended toward the hinterland, which Guyanese society has lacked.

Michael Gilkes,[15] a scholar of Harris's work, connects the expeditioner's boat in *Palace of the Peacock* to the following metaphor, stated by John Hearne: "The people of the Guyanese coastland inhabit a narrow boat filled with carefully nurtured earth and anchored at the middle of the boundary lines between two oceans."[16] And in fact this is the case. For centuries Guyana, like the other continental nations in the Caribbean basin, has defined itself according to the narrow terms of a coastal fringe that mediated between the sea and the deep interior jungle where the Indian, that is, the Other lives. And so we may read Wilson Harris's text as a voyage to establish contact with the Other, who holds a legitimate right to the earth and with whom one has to come to terms before one can have a roomier sort of nationality, one that fits the country's territorial boundaries.

Of course it's always possible to try to wipe the Indian out, which unfortunately would be nothing new in America. But nothing of this kind could be the theme of a Caribbean novel. The ordinary thing, the almost arithmetical constant in the Caribbean is never a matter of *subtracting,* but always of *adding,* for the Caribbean discourse carries, as I've said before, a myth or desire for social, cultural, and psychic integration to compensate for the fragmentation and provisionality of the collective Being. The literature of the Caribbean seeks to differentiate itself from the European not by excluding cultural components that influenced its formation, but rather, on the contrary, by moving toward the creation of an ethnologically promiscuous text that might allow a reading of the varied and dense polyphony of Caribbean society's characteristic codes. This is why, in *Palace of the Peacock*, Donne's patriarchal and logocentric figure cannot dispense with the indigenous element, but rather he must go out looking for it. Furthermore, the Great Arawak Mother herself, the mythical Orehu, Lady of the Waters, embarks with him on his boat.

At the same time, as also occurs with *Los pasos perdidos*, the trip upriver is an interior voyage as well, a psychic journey. The voyage goes on for seven days, that is, for the period of the Creation. Time begins with the time spent in the deserted mission. The crew begins to understand itself as being like the other crew, the one that died in making the same trip. Thus it knows that its trip toward death is also toward a rebirth, toward a second chance on earth, and this regeneration implies a psychic integration aiming to reduce the distance between the ego and the unconscious.

But this does not exhaust the novel's allegorical meaning. As Gilkes says, the seven-day journey points us not only to a second creation, but also to the seven stages of the alchemical process through which the *massa confusa* or *nigredo* transforms into *aurum non vulgi* or *cauda pavonis,* a state of spiritual perfection. As such, *Palace of the Peacock* may also be read as a Faustian text. We must remember of course that the true alchemist would not see his Great Work as residing in the transmutation of certain common chemical elements into gold—a merely accessory result—but rather in the transmuting of his own self, step by step, with the most exemplary perseverance, in the hope of reaching a state at the limits of human experience where he might achieve a spiritual liberation. The rule was to keep working tirelessly, to suffer in one's body the effect of all the burnings, the explosions, the toxic vapors, and to suffer, in the soul, all of the desperation of the search and the torment of losing one's way. In the course of the alchemical process the initiate had to count on Hermes' favor and, at the same time, he had to guard himself from the "dark" side of Hermes' dual nature, the side tending toward trickery and confusion. At the end of the alchemical voyage, one would reach a magical area that floated above all contradictions, all differences; there the veils would all fall away and spiritual freedom would be found.

Don't think that this Faustian reading of Harris's novel is the product of some adventurous speculation. On the contrary, such a reading turns out to be rather obvious, like the one in *Los pasos perdidos*, where the protagonist narrates his successive initiations during his transit toward the source.[17] In *Palace of the Peacock*, for example, it becomes evident, from the text's very beginning, that Donne and Dreamer are two parts split off from the same entity. The novel begins with Dreamer dreaming that Donne has been knocked off his horse by a gunshot, to fall dead at his feet. Dreamer's vision is soon blinded, and he realizes that he is seeing through Donne's dead eye; that is, Donne's dead eye, which is material, dominates Dreamer's spiritual and living eye: "his dead seeing material eye" / "my living closed spiritual eye" (pp. 13–14). Also, it has been established from the outset that Donne is the abusive and power-hungry side of this entity. He rules despotically over the savannah, and he holds in his fist the Arawaks who work for him, among them a young woman named Mariella, whom he has coerced into being both his servant and his lover. Consequently, the trip toward the Palace of the Peacock may be read as the difficult and long-suffering transit of the divided self toward an integration, toward a reconciliation of its opposing sides, toward a liberating, alchemical process of perfection. Moreover, we must note that the search for reconciliation is a recurrent theme in Wilson Harris's work. See, for example, what Harris says about this subject in one of his better-known essays:

> I have lived for long periods in savannahs so much exposed to heat and fire, that the sun has become an adversary—one of two antagonistic principles—night and day—and only an association of these two principles provides release. The architecture of release which would bring the forms that are bound in a principle of subjection . . . must find truly that the sun has no stationary hold over its subjects like a feudal lord over his serfs.[18]

In *Palace of the Peacock* the solar principle that Harris alludes to is represented by Donne. As a character, his content is phallic, practical, materialist, rationalist, logocentric, Eurocentric. Dreamer, of course, is everything opposite, except that his poetic looking has yet to awaken entirely and still finds itself imprisoned within Donne's look.[19] At voyage's end, when the second death at the waterfall occurs, Dreamer, who is now "awake," does not conquer Donne in any of the terms of domination, as would happen in mainstream European literature (the subjugated hero who manages to free himself and subdue his oppressor, the triumph of good over evil, the ego's dominion over the unconscious, the victory of order over chaos, the proletariat's victory over the bourgeoisie, etc.). What happens on this voyage is that, gradually, Donne has become more and more humanitarian, more sensitive, more spiritual, more complete. When he hazards his first step up the stone wall over which the waterfall spills, the memories of the house he built on the savannah and his colonizing past return to him like a hell whose purpose was to dominate the earth. As he continues his ascent toward the exalted Palace of the Peacock, these memories crumble and fall away forever into the abyss.

But the resurrection waiting in the palace's ineffable music and iridescent light is not a new beginning for Donne only, but also for Dreamer. It is up there, on top of the cascade, that they will both be united into a single Being, a union which, moreover, had always been poetically possible, had always been *there*. Naturally, it's clear that this union that Harris proposes extends to all Caribbean societies. In reality the expeditioners' boat in *Palace of the Peacock* is the very boat on which the Virgen de la Caridad del Cobre floats.

Concerning the three voyagers

Given the thematic polyvalence that the voyage theme takes on in *Palace of the Peacock*—in line with the Caribbean's own density of codes—we might now establish certain relationships between Harris's text and those of Carpentier and Barthes of which I spoke earlier.

It is apparent that Carpentier—at least when he wrote his "Problemática de la actual novela latinoamericana"—did not think like Barthes, since he still held to the illusion that a novel could properly name the Other, that is, could travel to the Other and discover El Dorado geographically. Clearly, his own experience told him that neither he nor the writers who came before him had ever realized this feat. Its very impossibility led him to conclude that the reasons that we cannot read the Other fully are rooted in our own society's need for a synthesis to make it legible and susceptible to being interpreted and represented. With matters in this state, our novel would have to remain immature until its sociological referents could cross the threshold leading from chaos to order. Since this immobilization, or negative entropy, did not show itself as near in time, Carpentier was led to affirm that it would stay distant not only from the present moment but even "beyond the lives of those now writing."

Carpentier's positing of the insufficiency that inheres in all texts in the terms of the novel and its referents leads one to think that he saw the society and the novel of the Western world as coherent poles that made for mutual relationships characterized by maturity and stability. This in turn assumes that Carpentier's ego would see itself as something structured by a binary opposition, whose simplest form would be in the form of Europe/Caribbean, with the first term dominating the second. This would explain—as I insinuated at the start of this chapter—why Carpentier's ego should see itself narcissistically in certain characters whom, like portraits, the West's historico-cultural discourse presents out of its vast gallery: Ulysses, Sisyphus, Oedipus, Herodotus, Marco Polo, Columbus, Don Quixote, Humboldt, Schomburgk, and so many others. The specific quality they share is that their essences are defined by passage; they are all born through their journeys and brought down by their journeys, and they exist as functions of their journeys. In writing of Juan de Flandes, who oscillates between his aspects belonging to Juan el Romero (the pilgrim) and Juan el Indiano (the settler),[20] Carpentier gives us his ego's self-image. It's not hard to see that within this system of representation, structured as it is over the Europe/Caribbean opposition, there is space for doing nothing other than swaying back and forth like a pendulum, for Europe's dominating presence hinders any indefinite stay within his Caribbean Otherness.[21] The final chapter of *Los pasos perdidos* is quite illustrative in this respect:

> The truth, the crushing truth—now I realized it—was that these people had never believed in me. I was there on loan. Rosario herself must have looked on me as a Visitor, incapable of staying on indefinitely in the Valley where Time had Stopped . . . Those who live there did not do so out of any intellectual conviction; they simply thought this, and not the other, was the good life. They preferred this present to the present of the makers of the Apocalypse . . . I had travelled through the ages . . . without realizing that I had come upon the hidden straitness of the widest door. But in association with the miracle, the founding of cities, the liberty encountered . . . were realities whose grandeur was perhaps not scaled to the puny dimensions of a contrapuntalist, always ready to employ his leisure in seeking victory over death in an arrangement of neumes . . . There the year in which we live can be forgotten, and they lie who say man cannot escape his epoch. The Stone Age, like the Middle Ages, is still within our reach . . . But none of this was for me, because the only human race to which it is forbidden to sever the bonds of time is the race of those who create art . . . Marcos and Rosario were ignorant of history. The Adelantado stood at the first chapter, and I could have remained at his side if my calling had been any except that of composing music . . . Today Sisyphus' vacation came to an end.[22]

I think that this passage, which Carpentier has fished from the main stream of the Western novel, serves him as a mirror for focusing the image of his own problematic. The dominant pole is seen as anchored in time, in the space held by the West's historico-cultural discourse; the dominated pole of his Caribbean Otherness—defined by another natural world, by another woman, by another time, and by another culture—speaks of itself as able to be visited or lived only in a transitional manner by the Self, by Being. It is Dreamer's "alive" look seen through Donne's "dead" and dominating regard; it is the counterpoint of traditional knowledge and scientific knowledge, just like the counterpoint that Ortiz composes.

It turns out to be quite clear that the voyage of the anonymous musicologist of *Los pasos perdidos* refers to codes identical to those invoked in Donne's trip in *Palace of the Peacock*. In truth, both characters have the same problematic: to reach a fleeting goal, the "center." It is there that the antagonisms that separate Self from Other must be reconciled, whether this poetic space is called El Dorado, the Signified, Resurrection, Utopia, Paradise Lost, the Philosopher's Stone, the Great Mother, the Mandala, Santa Monica de los Venados, or the Palace of the Peacock.

In the same way that Dante particularizes the ideal of Beatrice to confer the feminine upon the Other's empty and unknowable face, Carpentier and Harris particularize Rosario and Mariella. I intend to limit my drawing of parallels between *Los pasos perdidos* and *Palace of the Peacock* to a commentary upon this metaphor.

In *Los pasos perdidos*, the protagonist enters the jungle along with Rosario, and as they advance toward the most recondite and inaccessible areas —moving also toward Genesis—Rosario becomes increasingly the spokeswoman for the Other. Finally, on their arrival at Santa Monica de los Venados, they adopt a biblical style of life, to the extent that they represent the Edenic couple. There, Rosario is the Other, and she calls herself "Your wife." The binary opposition is annulled for an instant when the text insinuates that the protagonist has impregnated Rosario. But right away he abandons the place in an unexpected airplane, which was out looking for him in the jungle. The novel ends some time later, when the protagonist vainly attempts a return. In the anteroom to the labyrinth of spouting jets that guards the entrance to Santa Monica de los Venados, he learns that another man is now living with Rosario and that his son has been considered this man's son. So he will never be the real father, just as Prospero is not Caliban's.

In *Palace of the Peacock*, the situation at the outset is that Donne possesses Mariella and disposes of her "like a fowl."[23] The young girl even lives in a cabin, apart from Donne's house, and the novel's discourse picks her up when she feeds the chickens; that is, she forms an almost undifferentiated grouping with them, or, if you like, functions as a hen. Then there follows the flight of the Arawaks who work for Donne, in which Mariella presumably has participated. At the beginning of the trip to the mission, where Donne believes the fugitives to have gone seeking refuge, the reader is surprised to learn that the village's name is also Mariella, certainly a more than improbable name for this kind of establishment. This unexpected relationship is what makes us see that what is looked for, the Other, is sought under the feminine form of Mariella. If there were to be any doubt about this, it would be dissipated in the novel's following chapters. When Donne resolves to go upriver again in search of the mission's fugitives, as I've said, an old Arawak woman appears, wandering among the huts, and Donne decides to take her with him. Of course, we're dealing here with Mariella. The text itself confirms this when, with the boat's having reached the rapids, the old woman takes on the appearance of a beautiful maiden. Finally, when Donne's second death occurs at the waterfall, and while he lives in a brief limbo preceding his resurrection in the Palace of the Peacock, he has a vision: Mary and the Baby Jesus. *His* Mary and *His* Baby, the last manifestation of Mariella (Mary/ella). The novel ends with the following sentence: "Each one of us, finally, now had in his arms that which he had always been looking for [that is, Mariella] and that which he had always possessed" (p. 152).[24]

What symbols do Rosario and Mariella represent? I think one can read in them the archetypal ideal of the feminine, that is, the *anima,* the agent through which the masculine self reaches psychic equilibrium between his conscious and unconscious planes; also, passing from Jung to Freud, they might refer us to Oedipus, as objects of the Son's desire, and whose possession by means of rebellion against the Father (West) and the transgression of incest would permit the founding of a new patriarchal family in them, with which history might begin again.

Nevertheless, the metaphors that most stand out are not exactly of a psychological or psychoanalytic order. In my opinion—perhaps because I am a Caribbean reader—the most vigorous signifiers refer to the myth of integration proper to the Caribbean of which I have spoken earlier. This is especially so if one considers that both protagonists are ethnically Caucasian and represent Europe, while both women are dark-skinned and represent the autochthonous (Rosario has European, African, and Indian blood; Mariella is Arawak or *mestiza*). Evidently the myth, in its patriarchal version, desires a dismantling of the binary oppositions of the racial, cultural, economic, social, and political type that historically have fragmented and isolated the peoples of the Caribbean. The respective fecundations of Rosario and Mariella legitimize a new patriarchal right on earth and permit the advent of a new era and a new family, of a new economy (not a plantation economy) and a new society (not racist), and at the same time, a new collective ego and a new culture where Western values might make room for the aboriginal, African, and Asian traditions that are disdained by the colonizer's language.

Given all this, one must conclude that the Carpentierian version of the myth is more despairing than that of Wilson Harris, whose novel does not limit itself to visiting El Dorado but manages to transmute itself into an intense poetic text as it penetrates fully into a resplendent ambit to reside in its *thereness*.[25] Nonetheless, it would be an error to think that, given this difference, Carpentier's novel is less Caribbean than Harris's. What counts here is the voyage, the search, and above all, the collective nature of the desire to find El Dorado; that is, that in the enterprise there should participate actively the ethnological factors that are in play within the nation, a pluralist specificity that is not present in the voyages of Humboldt and the Schomburgk brothers to the territory of Caribana,[26] nor in Barthes's voyage to Japan.

In any event, the desire for total integration that the Caribbean myth carries will never, of course, be realized in terms of a linear equation, of Euclidean geometry. As Barthes illustrates in his preface, "*Là-bas*," the impossible voyage toward the Other can be read only in terms of a fictitious voyage, and if it should happen that we think we are reading a truth in his book, it is because everything can happen in language and literature. Nevertheless, we must bear in mind that Caribbean culture provides roads of water and smoke (rhythms) of a poetic kind, through which El Dorado may be reached and experienced. There is nothing magical in this; it is just a matter of handing oneself over publicly to the polyrhythmic (dis)order of the rumba or the *carnaval*, or the liturgy of some Afro-Caribbean cult, or simply a reading of life in a "certain kind of way." In any event, we cannot discount the possibility that this experience might become so genuine that it manages to create, within the context of material reality, the thing that it has been desiring.[27] This is what has happened, precisely, with El Dorado, whose incalculable riches in diamonds, emeralds, and precious metals have appeared suddenly in our time.

■ *PART 3*

THE

BOOK

6

Los pañamanes,

or the memory

of

the skin

At a symposium on Caribbean culture that I attended some years ago, the late Jamaican historian and novelist Victor S. Reid began his talk with these words: "We, the people of the Caribbean, are today the last cultural conglomeration to call attention to itself. In this corner . . . of sea one finds a significant number of the earth's races, as well as some hybrids that have never flourished anywhere else on earth."[1] These words, in themselves, were nothing new. The interesting thing about them was not their originality, but that Reid would use them to mobilize and direct his reflections on Caribbean society. Here is an intellectual—I thought—who organizes his definition of the Caribbean without starting from political, ideological, or economic premises; here is a historian who doesn't talk about history, as we might expect; here is a writer who doesn't talk of literary works, but rather of "races" and "hybrids" and their relationship to culture. Here is a perfect *Caribeño*.

In fact, in the Caribbean area, scene of the most extensive and intensive racial confluence registered by human history, it is imprudent to relegate such disciplines as anthropology and ethnography to a second order. This is so because every race and every hybrid (to go along with Reid), under the banner of its skin, bears cultural components that are to a greater or lesser degree its own, and, furthermore, it carries a local history, a sociology, and an economics, which, if quite different and out of phase in relation to one another, feature a common turbulence. In the Caribbean, at whose ports arrived millions of African slaves and hundreds of thousands of Asians to build and sustain the plantation economy, the discourses of cultural anthropology and ethnology cut through a multitude of discourses, including the economic. That is why, within this vague geographical orbit, delimited by the maritime routes, the concept of "social class" is usually displaced by "race," or in any event by "skin color."

To simplify these differences by building up a contradiction, with European/African migratory poles, is not just futile but also an act that must confound any attempt to reach an image or definition that could answer at all to the Caribbean's ethnological complexity. There are countries, such as Belize, Guyana, Venezuela, and Colombia, where the presence of the Indoamerican cannot be avoided. And this is true without even taking into account that the indigenous people themselves fall in behind no coherent cultural pole. What does a Mayan have to do with a Maquiritare, or a Miskito with a Goajiro? In other nations, such as Guyana and Trinidad, the weight of the Asian populations is enormous. One has to keep in mind that, between 1838 and 1924, there came into the Caribbean, mainly in the English colonies, a half million indentured servants from India. They came for five years—as we have seen in another chapter—destined for the sugar plantations, needed as cheap manpower after slavery had been abolished in the English dominions. The vast majority of them stayed around, to introduce new cultural, economic, and social components, but also new forms of racial mixing and, in passing, racial tensions that have stayed alive to this day, especially in Guyana. Asian immigration, as we know, did not come only from India. In Cuba, for example, the contract laborers came from the south of China, and they eventually made up 3 percent of the population by the second half of the nineteenth century. These *coolies,* who contributed generously to the independence struggles, created the demographic and sociocultural base that made possible, in our century, a sustained immigration of agriculturalists and merchants. Very quickly, Havana had a notable Chinese quarter, with its theaters, restaurants, and traditional shops, and its cultural influence was quickly seen in cooking, pharmacology, music, local language, and a gambling scheme called *la charada china* that competed with the official lottery. But, above all, an unforeseen racial type began to grow up in Cuba: *el mulato chino.* In Surinam, the population of Javanese origin, introduced by the Dutch planters, now dominates, together with the Indoamericans, over the other ethnic groups. With regard to "hybrids that have never flourished anywhere else on earth," there are the black Caribs[2] of Belize and the "bushmen"[3] of the Guianan rain forest, and there are as well modalities of *mestizaje* involving these three races in almost all of the Caribbean nations.

You will say that this multiracial concentration is not unique, as there are countries, the United States for example, whose populations can be taken as a true showcase of the nations of the world. This of course is unquestionable. The difference lies in the United States' having arisen out of its colonial past as a significantly "white," Anglo-Saxon, Protestant country. By this I mean that under the Declaration of Independence there are no signatures that lead us to Africa, Asia, or Indoamerica; nor were there in the Union army any squadrons of Chinese cavalry, or regiments of black grenadiers or Pequot artillery; nor did George Washington's general staff have any Islamicized Mandingo colonels, or Hindus, Buddhists, or Mohicans who might invoke the spirits of their ancestors.[4] The United States, on breaking its colonial yoke, assumed its role as a nation in European terms, and under the canons of European thought and traditions, which it has followed ever since. The North American nation regards its own African, Asian, Latin American, and even Native American populations as "minorities," that is, as ethnic groups alien to its essentially European nature.

In the Caribbean, however, the work of defining nationality and reaching independence was the common effort of men and women already divided by racial and cultural differences—even in the case of Haiti, where the tensions between blacks and mulattos showed up even before the revolution and continued during and after the revolution, down to the present day. Thus, in the Caribbean, skin color denotes neither a minority nor a majority; it represents much more: the color imposed by the violence of conquest and colonization, and especially by the plantation system. Whatever the skin color might be, it is a color that has not been institutionalized or legitimized according to lineage; it is a color in conflict with itself and with others, irritated in its very instability and resented for its uprootedness; it is a color neither of the Self nor of the Other, but rather a kind of no-man's-land where the permanent battle for the Caribbean Self's fragmented identity is fought.

The puzzle's next-to-last piece

The literature of the Caribbean, as I said before, refers itself generally, in one way or another, to this double conflict of the skin. Every island, every strip of coast has seen the creation of poetry, drama, essay, story, and novel on the basis of ethnological differences present in their respective locales. In this way, little by little, a literary geography of the Caribbean has been taking shape, one that attends to the theme of skin color, or rather, to the theme of its irreducible memory, expressed in ethnographic, economic, political, and sociological terms. At present, it can be said that the works that form the biggest pieces of the Caribbean puzzle are available to the reader. Nevertheless, there are still some important gaps to fill. Clearly, it is already known that we are dealing with a puzzle which, strictly speaking, is impossible to complete, since it lacks a frame, properly speaking. But, even if we were to make use of a less furtive geography, we would still have to recognize that there still remain certain islands to be fitted into place, and certain cities and ports and coastal stretches, peninsulas, and gulfs whose absence lends its shape to some irregular hollows in the Caribbean's turquoise blue surface.

One of the fragments most recently put into place represents, in itself, a minuscule archipelago, situated about one hundred miles east of Nicaragua and known by the name of San Andrés y Providencia. This rare piece of the Caribbean puzzle has been fitted into place thanks to *Los pañamanes*, a novel by the Colombian Fanny Buitrago.[5] A narrow version of these islands' history would say that Providencia (earlier Santa Catalina) was colonized in 1629 by well-born Puritans, among them Lord Brooke (the viscount of Saye-Sele), the Count of Warwick, and John Pym (the latter two appearing as ancestors of one of the novel's characters). The Providence Company, as the colonizing enterprise was called, settled not only Providencia but also, shortly thereafter, San Andrés, situated forty-five miles away, and also the famous island of Tortuga, near the northwest coast of Hispaniola.[6] Its first inhabitants founded a hardworking and austere community, which quite soon dedicated itself to growing cotton, maize, and tobacco. They brought Africans to perform the labor. In 1638 there was a slave rebellion—probably the first to erupt in the English Caribbean—but it was quickly put down. As the years went by, however, the Puritan colonists realized that the brief archipelago's geographical position greatly facilitated incursions against the Spanish cities of the neighboring islands and coasts, as well as attacks against the great galleons and coastal trading boats which, thanks to the precautions of Menéndez de Avilés, made up the traffic between the Mosquito Coast and the Gulf of Honduras. And so, relegating the plantation business to second place, they changed their habits and adopted a riskier style of living, sending out armed expeditions again and again to attack the nearest Spanish colonies. This activity, of course, could not go unchallenged in a sea that Spain then considered to be her own exclusive property, and one morning the renegade colonists found themselves surprised by cannons booming from Spanish ships. With the archipelago then temporarily taken over and its inhabitants put to flight, the inexorable law of the Caribbean fell upon this little clutch of islands and keys, which then were occupied in succession by Portuguese, Frenchmen, Dutchmen, pirates, and buccaneers before passing once more into British hands. Among the islands' best-known visitors during this turbulent epoch we find Henry Morgan, of whom legend has it that he left buried in San Andrés—another version says Providencia—the treasure he got from the sack of Panama, and also the famous Captain Bligh, who introduced the breadfruit and who has been lastingly enacted on-screen by Charles Laughton, Trevor Howard, and Anthony Hopkins in connection with the celebrated mutiny on the *Bounty*. Finally, by virtue of a treaty, the islands were ceded to Spain in the eighteenth century, eventually becoming part of Colombia in 1821. Today, any tourist leaflet would tell us that San Andrés is a free port, that there are good hotels and high plantations of coconut palms, that gambling is permitted, that there are marvelous beaches, beautiful reefs for diving, moderate prices, and access by air from the United States, Colombia, and several Central American countries. It is suggested that tourists drink mineral water and that instead of renting a car they travel through the island on a bicycle.

Nevertheless, the manuals of Caribbean history and the tourist agencies' propaganda leaflets are insufficient to the effects entailed in describing San Andrés's daily life, its inhabitants' psychology, its contradictions, its dreams and miseries, its achievements and frustrations, in short, the problems of skin color. *Los pañamanes* tries to fill this space with the fluid substance of the novel's discourse.

Both Enrique Bernardo Núñez and Alejo Carpentier have said that in the Caribbean orbit one historical stage does not cancel the earlier one as happens in the Western world. Such a peculiarity, that of living history synchronically, does not depend on the will of the people of the Caribbean; it is a circularity imposed by isolation and, above all, by the implacable repetition of the economic and social dynamics inherent in the plantation system. There is not a single country in the Caribbean that has ever been able to break away completely from the repetitive Plantation mechanism. The production of sugar, coffee, cacao, tobacco, fruit, including coconuts, in San Andrés is a thing that in the Caribbean is always there, as if established at the beginning of time through the very nature of the meta-archipelago. As we have seen, it is possible to say that the Caribbean's history, in good measure, is the history of the plantation system in the New World, since the mother countries that exercized their economic power in the area organized the territories, in all their diversity, whether insular or continental, according to their own profit motives, and in the Caribbean there was no business more lucrative than the plantation. Whenever an island was taken by force of arms, or through negotiation, by a rival colonialist power— there is not a single Caribbean island administered uninterruptedly by the same European nation—the existing plantation would never disappear, rather it would be reorganized according to the new mother country's mercantile characteristics. This would imply no profound changes at all. It can be said rather that the old structure remained as a component of the new structure; that is, there was no substituting of the new for the old, but rather there was a coexistence, relatively critical or not, within the same historical space. Thus the past was linked with the future through differences of a circular nature, like the steps of a spiral staircase.

Fanny Buitrago's text assumes this focus perspicaciously. It shows us the inhabitants of San Andrés grouped in three sociocultural sets, each representative of the mother country that set it up, that is, England, Spain, and Colombia. The order of their disposition is purely accidental; it is a consequence of the accidents of Caribbean history.

According to what the novel itself tells us, when the Spaniards arrived in 1793 there were a total of 446 inhabitants of the island, 278 of them slaves. Most of the colonists descended from Englishmen who had emigrated from Jamaica—it is unlikely that there were many whose lineages went back to the original Puritan colony. This Jamaican immigration came about in the years that followed the Treaty of Madrid (1670), through which England committed herself to putting an end to piracy and an end to the sponsoring, in Port Royal, of men like Henry Morgan and his pirates of the Brotherhood of the Coast. It was a society which, beyond its fundamental differences in language and religion vis-à-vis the new mother country, had itself been formed in the rule of hatred toward Spain, of public and private warfare against her fleets and her Caribbean possessions, a society which, possibly, had left Jamaica for reasons having to do with the prohibition of privateering and piracy.

It is logical to think that the Spaniards who arrived on the island in 1793 would look suspiciously at these Englishmen. Surely they would have called them "heretics" and avoided dealing with them as much as possible. Of course, this feeling must have been reciprocated in spades by the islanders who, sunk in the bitterest disappointment, would have cursed protractedly the false monarch who so easily had delivered them over to become subject to the odious "Papists." The term "Spanish man," by which the islanders designated the new arrivals, went on to mean more than foreigner, and something more even than intruder. To a former English subject—white, Negro, or mulatto—"Spanish man" came to mean an opprobrious man, a man without caste, living in the lowest condition to which a human being could sink. When Colombia replaced Spain in ruling the islands, the term could be reapplied with renewed scorn to the Colombians who, after the ruinous independentist period, emigrated to the place in hope of sinking roots there. Over the years, by means of the Caribbean's apocopation, "Spanish man" would shrink to "*pañamán.*" Hence the novel's title.

Displacement toward myth

Fanny Buitrago, as it happened, followed a nonhistorical path to explain the connotations of the word *pañamán*. She employed—as might have been expected in a Caribbean novel—the form of myth. This deliberate ahistoricity allows the island of San Andrés to appear in the text with the name San Gregorio, and Providencia as Fortuna, although more than enough information is offered at the same time to reveal both islands' real names. But let's take a look at the myth of the Spanish man as the text tells it:

> A shipwrecked Spaniard—the Spanish Man—emerged from the waters of the neighboring island of Fortuna, imposing himself with his regal bearing upon the descendants of a prosperous Puritan colony whose traditional spirits continued to practice discrimination between Negroes and whites, dividing into separate populations, although the majority were colored dark brown. The harsh course of the Spanish empire in the slave trade, the panic of its inquisitors before the followers of the Reformation, and his precarious position as a stranger did not keep the Spanish Man from adding to his vocabulary enough English words to enable him to seduce a woman. The process that allows the semen to fertilize an ovum and to transform it into a fetus completed its cycle normally, under a guilty, dishonorable silence. In the strife of childbirth and the anger brought on by her certain death in the process, the woman shouted a choleric "the Spanish Man!" in

a contained rage, which sounded like *pañamán* as it came squeezed out through her hoarsened throat. A shout that was to supplant all of the expressions of rejection and contempt hurled against the Colombian immigrant—Turk-Jew-yellow-white—in all respects a strange invader. The Spanish Man . . . *pañamán,* son of a wicked mother—in memory of a man who would be hunted like a weasel and hanged as an example to the ungrateful guests. (pp. 21–22)

The characteristic language of myth lets itself be heard especially in the first part of the paragraph: "a shipwrecked Spaniard" (a parvenu Spaniard, without ancestors, with white skin, in opposition to the dark brown skin of most of the islanders; a man who comes from the Caribbean, the Spanish sea, the sea of the Other, or rather the sea of evil, the sea that must be conquered by religion and by arms; the Devil); "emerged from the waters of the neighboring isle of Fortuna" (read Providencia, cradle of the first colony—the Devil shows up at the Origin, the Serpent at the Earthly Paradise); "imposing himself with his regal bearing" (the beauty of Death, the seduction of the Evil One); "upon the descendants of a prosperous Puritan colony" (which alludes to a putative uninterrupted genealogy going from 1629 to 1793). The narration mythifies the legitimacy of the island society, annulling the destruction of the Puritan colony and the occupation of the island by the Portuguese, the French, the Dutch, and the buccaneers; the adjective "prosperous," applied to this first colony, suggests the idea of Arcadian times—Eden—which must have preceded the Spaniards' appearance. "Whose traditional spirits" (the *dupys* to which the novel's text abundantly refers, that is, tutelary spirits according to the syncretic belief of the Adventist type so common in the English-speaking Caribbean) evidences the myth's African root, its indisputable Caribbean filiation. That they "continued to practice discrimination between Negroes and whites" spells out the presence of racial antagonism and sexual taboo from the time of the Origin; remember that the Puritans imported slaves from Africa and that the latter rebelled and were suppressed in 1638; that the black and white "tutelary spirits" favor discrimination, which makes it seem a legitimate and necessary form of social relations, constituting the islands' black/white tradition. "Dividing into separate populations" (notice that slavery is not mentioned): the Negro appears historically free, living apart, the ideal maroon; the white also lives apart, excluding the Negro from his precincts; there is no doubt that the myth answers to the islands' interests in general, those of the blacks as well as the whites, in an attempt at silencing the social violence set up by the Plantation. "Although the majority were colored dark brown" is a critical clarification and expresses two desires; it alludes to miscegenation as a way of annulling racial tensions but, at the same time, it denies this possibility, since the existence of a "majority" necessarily invokes a lighter-colored "minority," which is enough for the *dupys,* the guardians of tradition, to distinguish between one group and the other and to prolong the conflict between them indefinitely. Here the myth picks up the social projections of the divided settlers of the island: the "Negro" group aspires to a social equality, while the "white" one, whose skin in general is not white, declares itself to be white by self-definition and denies with this the perspective of a racial and social synthesis as a solution to the conflict. Then, in the midst of this critical form of coexistence, there appears the Spanish Man, the Other, the violator, the transgressor against the rights of the blood. His death on the gallows is a warning to those islanders who might dare cross their old dark-brown skin with the foreigner's new skin, but it also constitutes a sacrifice; the hanged *pañamán* is the scapegoat who channels the excessive violence and from whose dying body there emanates the power that guarantees the continuity of the island's racist tradition. Such is the desire that the myth carries.

In any event, the text just quoted—whether constructed by the author or collected from the island's folklore—should be read as an area of the book that cannot be sidestepped. This to the extent that, among the many possible strategies for analysis, it can be taken as a key with which to open the novel, which then reveals itself as a narrative of a succession of cycles, each one of which contains the fatal operations of circular form and the desire to conserve the old order, projected in the myth of the *pañamán.* These cycles, of course, would not be metaphorical in the sense of supposing a substitution, but rather metonymical, and they would sketch the figure of a signifier that unfolds along the line of three generations in San Andrés, which refer in turn to the island's three sociocultural groups (English, Spanish, Colombian). With the myth fulfilled for the last time in the third generation, those who will be born in the future would then see themselves freed from its fatal workings.

The first generation, to which the first cycle refers, is represented in the text by two kinds of characters: those of island descent and those of Colombian origin. Within the first category, those who stand out for their degree of participation in the novel are the island's four matrons: Maule Lever, Marsita Allen, Prudence Pomare, and Lorenza Vallejo. A brief description of these four characters would give us the following biographical index cards, containing data that allow us to read the fierce process of *mestizaje* that occurred on the island:

Maule Lever: Descendant of William Lever and his wife Elizabeth, one of twenty-seven married couples the Spaniards encountered upon taking charge of the island in 1793. Through her veins there flows the blood of the first Puritan colonists along with that of slaves of Masai origin. She practices the Adventist religion with extraordinary zeal. Among her grandparents we find "Count Warwick and the famous John Pym, pioneers of the island's commerce and its Protestant religion" (p. 39). The novel's action picks her up when she is already old, a widow, and the mother of Nicholas Barnard Lever.

Marsita Allen: Descendant of Charles Allen and his wife Jane, and also of "Poles, Scotchmen, and Lithuanians, none of said family members ever having mentioned the slaveholding inheritance" (p. 26). She is white and Catholic, the mother of Jerónimo Beltrán and of three unmarried daughters.

Prudence Pomare: Descendant of André Pomaire, a Frenchman who dreamed of converting the island into a vast cotton plantation. As this colonist does not appear in the census of 1793, he must necessarily have arrived on San Andrés after this date, although perhaps by just a couple of years, for it is likely that he formed a part of the exodus provoked by the Haitian Revolution. As for Prudence, she lived for half her life facing the police station and, as a consequence of her ardent temperament, she produced an extensive and multiracial descendancy prior to her marriage. She is the mother of Terranova González, Epaminondas Jay Long, and Pinky Robinson, among others.

Lorenza Vallejo: She was the mirror of the island's population. Among her ancestors would be found a "Portuguese slave trader, an Adventist pastor of old-time English origin, a Russian-Jewish peddler, a Catalonian teacher, a descendant of a Dutchman and a Jamaican quadroon, a Swedish sailor, and a Chinese cook's daughter" (p. 146). Her paternal great-grandfather was a Spanish tinker "wildly in love with the Caribbean Sea, obsessed with acquiring lands, an elegant man of fifty who managed to marry one of the Mays (or one of the Flowers) and, with a silky arm, enter the nucleus of the island's aristocracy" (p. 157). Against the will of her father, Don Carlos Vallejo, she married Doctor Campos Elías Saldaña, a *pañamán;* her only child, Emiliano G. Saldaña, died with his wife in a fire; her grandson Gregorio Saldaña is the novel's main character. She knows everything that happens on the island and knows all of the island's oral folklore by heart.

Of the four matrons, two violate the skin color taboo and marry *pañamanes:* Marsita Allen and, as just noted, Lorenza Vallejo. Marsita swallows rat poison after having been spurned by Etilio Beltrán, who wants to divorce her after falling in love with Sabina Galende. On the other hand, Lorenza Vallejo takes her son's accidental death as a punishment for having opposed her father's wishes in marrying a *pañamán*. As a consequence of her guilty feeling, she separates from her husband and lives alone in her family's house, buried in remembrances, old traditions, and a tide of visitors from whom she learns everything that happens on the island. She lives in pain.

The *pañamanes* who marry Marsita and Lorenza experience in turn some of the tribulations associated with the legendary Spanish man. Etilio Beltrán, after abandoning his home to run off with Sabina Galende, is thrown out by her in turn and stripped of all his property. He dies a beggar, old and sick. Campo Elías Saldaña has no better luck: he gets stripped of his post as quartermaster because of political intrigues, and he dies embittered and alone, his body wasted by white rum.

The fatality of the myth's second cycle falls again on Marsita's and Lorenza's offspring, that is, on Jerónimo Beltrán and Emiliano G. Saldaña. The former bears the guilt for the suicide of Jane Duncan, spinster, the mother of his son Nicasio Beltrán; he is a man worn out from all-nighters, gambling, drugs, and alcohol, who achieves nothing of what really matters to him in life: Sabina Galende's love, the lands of El Arenal—where he would like to build hotels and gambling casinos—and a way to live in a family with his son Nicasio. After being abandoned by Sabina Galende, he dies when she arouses, in Nicasio, the irrational passion of which he himself was a victim. As for Lorenza's son, Emiliano G. Saldaña, he dies beside his wife in the fire at the district office.

The sons, Nicasio Beltrán and Gregorio Saldaña, who are Marsita's and Lorenza's grandsons, find true love with the *pañamanes* Sabina Galende and Valentina Cisneros. But they both die by drowning in the Caribbean, thus ending the cycle of the third generation. Significantly, their deaths are a return to the sea from which the Spanish Man emerged. With this ending, with the myth's tragic and fatal action annulled by Nicasio's and Gregorio's marine deaths, the succeeding island generations will live free of the skin-color taboo. So the text of *Los pañamanes* begins with a Caribbean myth, fulfills it, cancels it, and sets itself up in a new myth: the possibility of arriving at a Utopian time in which conflict over skin color does not take place, that is, where skin loses its ancient memory and erases the whiplashes and branding irons, the plantation's stock and shackles; where it washes out its guilty stains, the stains of the slave trade, of the terrible middle passage, of the buying and selling of flesh, of the master's house and the slave barrack.

In any case, *Los pañamanes* lies within the most repeated literary tradition of the Caribbean: the novel-myth, but not an epic myth, rather a myth of the uprooted one who dreams of reuniting the fragments of his dispersed identity beyond the confines of the Plantation. *Los pañamanes*, like many other Caribbean novels, is a double performance, a representation containing another representation. The first, or rather the most visible, is directed toward seducing the Western reader; the second is a monologue that returns toward the I, toward the Caribbean Self, intending to mythify and at the same time transcend symbolically its unnatural-natural genesis, that is, to assume its own marginality vis-à-vis the West and to speak of its Calibanesque Otherness, an Otherness deriving from the violence of conquest, colonization, slavery, piracy, war, plunder, occupation, dependence, misery, prostitution, and even tourism. The result is San Andrés:

> At the foot of the sea wall and all around the dock-warehouses an impatient and loud multitude is continuously formed. Cut haphazardly by honking late-model automobiles and noisy motorcycles corroded by saltpeter. Sailors of diverse nationality, smugglers, fishermen, sunburnt adventurers, drug pushers, beggars, and drifters. A parade of haughty islanders with honeyed skin and luminous blue eyes, athletic Swedes lit up by the tropics, active and sweaty merchants, longhaired vagabonds with wild eyes, fanatical Bible-thumpers and—every now and then—startled tourists who have lost their touring companions along with the diversions detailed in the National Tourism Corporation's elegant brochures. The hawkers announce exotic pomades, medicinal roots, garlic braids, magnetic wristwatches, and concentrated syrups tinged with violet, mandarin, and vermilion. In the stands, covered with zinc sheets, the fruit sellers move with a somnolent air, as though doped by the furious flies' buzzing. There is traffic in girls, copra, acid, foreign exchange, public employment, frozen meats, construction materials, electric artifacts, perfumes, and adulterated whiskey. There are fortune tellers, Negresses with silvered fingernails, storytellers, tireless politicians. And all those who, ignorant of the

island's legendary past, emerge from the muck of history. All of them. United by the common language of shouting. In Spanish, Patois, English, Arabic, Russian, Yiddish, Italian, Hebrew, Chinese, and Portuguese. Their scents mingled into the rotting vapor of stagnant tides. (p. 13)

This is surely not the scene that one finds described on some multicolored travel-agency poster, and yet it is one of the faces of the Caribbean, from San Andrés to Cartagena.

The "other" Caribbean city

Every Caribbean city carries deep within it other cities, which live as fetal, minuscule nodules of turbulence that proliferate—each different from the last—through marinas, plazas, and alleys. They can be grouped into large classes. Only two of these interest us here, the yard, or *solar,* and the dockside (*muelle*) whose description we have just read. But what is a *solar?* We're talking here of a common patio—sometimes belonging to a crumbling colonial mansion—access to which is given to a series of squalid rooms which have no running water and whose electricity is illegally tapped. Of course, the whole is much more than this; in reality it is a variegated social cell, a dense melting pot that cooks together several religions and beliefs, new words and dance steps, unforeseen dishes and musical styles. Here the Negro race usually dominates, but one almost always finds representatives of other ethnicities and hybrids of every sort. In no way should this cell, this umbilicus, that spreads itself throughout the city be confused with the rental housing that proliferates in the capitals of the world. The yard, or *solar,* is a result of the plantation, and it is at once the anti-plantation. I will explain. This kind of living arrangement was organized for and among a marginal population of freedmen, that is, Negroes and mulattos who, whether because they bought their freedom, or ran away, or were manumitted, or were free for any other reason, came to the city to earn a living. Later the yard or *solar* made room for the Asians—Chinese, Indians, Javanese—who had completed their work contracts and decided to stay in the Caribbean; it was also a place for the "poor white," the *petit blanc* of the French colonies, and for successive immigrations of Portuguese, Arabs, Galicians, Jews, Slavs, Yucatecans, Antilleans from other islands, in short, all those who left behind hunger, pogroms, war, jail, debt in order to seek their fortunes in the Caribbean ports.

What are these people's occupations, what do they live on? To begin with, they are not malefactors; they do not constitute what is usually called "the scum of society" (*la escoria*) or the "lumpen." They are people who are rarely employed in factories, offices, or stores. Their refined individualism and their peculiar sense of freedom would make such a thing improbable. In general, they are self-employed workers: washerwomen, dressmakers, midwives, tailors, cobblers, confectioners, fishermen, freelance masons and carpenters, fortune tellers and healers, including *iyalochas* and *babalochas* of the Lucumí order or voodoo *houngans;* in short, sellers of everything and buyers of nothing, *bricoleurs,* as Lévi-Strauss would say. They almost always own drums, harmonicas, and guitars, for they like to make music, to sing, and to dance. The common courtyard serves as a stage for these performances, and also as a park for the children; this is where the costumes for the next carnival masquerade are designed, political meetings are held, dreams are interpreted through the African codes or the *charada china,* and the future bolero or reggae stars are trained, as well as future boxers and baseball, soccer, or cricket players. People are born and they die there, they recite verses and they argue, they listen to the radio and they play cards or dominoes.

There is almost always a man of some years who acts as mayor and wears a hat and carries a cane or an umbrella; there are also old men and women, who, without entirely intending to do so, transmit kitchen recipes, infallible prayers, advice for the lovelorn, powerful medicinal formulas and tricks to cure sleepwalking and rheumatism, dandruff and indigestion; they also perform the function of African *griots,* and they prolong the course of ancient traditions from generation to generation; they know by heart the suspicious genealogy of the "white" aristocracy, the secret workings of whatever intrigue, crime, or spectacular event has occurred in the city; they talk about the times of slavery, about wars and revolutions, about ghosts, comets, hurricanes, and earthquakes that heralded good or calamitous times. Their stories, (dis)ordered, (un)wound, and (un)authorized, whose discourses spring out of mutilations and abusive practices that happened in all of the times and spaces of the world, are here drained of all the social violence that they carry, put on an equal ahistorical plane, and heard as homogeneous and legitimate signifiers that constitute knowledge itself. In passing into the genres of literature, this "other" discourse helps to inform modes of expression now known as magic realism, the neobaroque, the *real maravilloso;* forms of expression which at bottom are the same, which in the case of the Caribbean refer to the same sociocultural space, trying to decenter the violence of their origins with their own excess, looking for legitimation in their own illegitimacy.

Of course, the yard or *solar* does not lie in the city's commercial center, or in the rich and middle-class residential neighborhoods. It has its enclave in the "old city," the colonial section out of which the Caribbean city grew, the old neighborhood now menaced by new streets and avenues leading to the elegant suburbs. In any event, there is in *Los pañamanes* an area of the city where this sort of Antillean institution still maintains itself: it is the Negro quarter known as El Arenal. Its survival hangs by a thread, for the place is coveted by a developer intending to raze it to put up a complex of hotels, casinos, restaurants, stores, and bars for the growing tourist industry, which is thriving on the island because of the low prices— remember that San Andrés is a free port—and because of its excellent beaches, the legalized gambling, and above all, the authorities' indifference to drugs, pornography, and prostitution. The text tells us about this:

> The times turned out to be difficult for those who lived in the island's Negro quarter. In the last few months this section suffered an invasion of undesirables. Not just the scum rejected by high-class casinos and brothels, but foreigners in flashy clothes and cowboy hats, coming from Miami, Jamaica, the continent, and Central America. International crooks, swindlers, pushers, dealers in acid and marijuana, famous call girls, illegal abortionists, painted fairies, and loose women. It was nearly impossible to walk through the streets at night without coming upon bands of thugs with knives and brass knuckles out looking for trouble, without witnessing heated disputes between streetwalkers and exhibitionists, or seeing the lamentable spectacle of a strung-out girl gone mad. (p. 19)

El Arenal is the axis of many of the novel's episodes. Its inhabitants are protected by Gregorio Saldaña and his companions—called *los Tinieblos*— who struggle in their own way against the forces of international tourism to stop the displacement of the people living there.[7] Gregorio Saldaña and *los Tinieblos* play all of the island's strings, making use of their deep understanding of its traditions. Sometimes by legal means and sometimes not, but always within the *Tinieblos'* code of ethics, they usually realize their aims. El Arenal's survival is their main preoccupation; they know that the neighborhood's destruction would be a death blow to the island, whose foundations have already been undermined by its being a free port and by the endless stream of tourists and undesirables. They know that generalized gambling, drugs, and prostitution would put an end to the island's traditions, an end to the legitimizing folklore that flows from its courtyards.

The text of the novel frequently picks up the flavor of the oral literature heard in San Andrés and transmitted to other Caribbean islands. There are, for example, the many stories about Anancy—Fanny Buitrango uses the apocopated form "Nancy"—which the old women tell to their friends and grandchildren. These stories radiate from the Akan culture of West Africa. Slaves from the Akan region spread this vast cycle of stories throughout the entire Caribbean area, mainly in the territories colonized by England, France, and Holland. The cycle contains stories similar to the stories about Renard, the fox of the French tradition. Their protagonist, Anancy, is an astute spider-man, who sometimes comes out a winner from his adventures and sometimes does not. The interesting thing about these stories is that, in spite of their unquestionable African provenance, they can be considered a part of Caribbean folklore, for the spirit of the tales adjusted itself to conditions proper to the Caribbean. Some of the African characters appearing in these stories underwent changes as well: thus the "wax woman" turned into the "tar woman," the latter being a more abundant material in the Caribbean, used in building and repairing ships, rigging, and docks.

Violence, folklore, and the Caribbean novel

The theme of piracy and buried treasure which, in competition with historiographic discourse, runs through Caribbean tradition and literature going back four centuries, is also touched upon in *Los pañamanes*. In San Andrés, for example, there is a belief that when someone dies he takes two others with him, since Henry Morgan killed three of his men in order to bury them, as gatekeepers beyond the grave, beside the treasure he took in the sacking of Panama. It is also thought certain that on one stormy night Henry Morgan himself anchored his ghost ship in The Cove, whereupon he disembarked in order to slit the Duncan family's throats. This bloody deed had necessarily to occur, for the Caribbean's cultural code demanded it. Morgan had visited the Duncans in dreams to show them the site where a part of his loot was buried; they could enjoy it in exchange for certain favors demanded of them by the pirate. The Duncans failed to meet their obligations to the powerful dead man, and they naturally had to pay the consequence: having their throats cut.

Behind this ghost story lies the historic violence of the meta-archipelago, which the story itself tries to dispel. Notice how the bloody crime against the Duncans is justified by their having violated their word, given to the ghost of Henry Morgan, who appears in the legend as a guardian rather than a violator of the law. This mythification of piracy should be seen as an attempt to authenticate through the narration itself—as occurs, above all, in the cases of the Creole pirates Diego Grillo, Cofresí, etc.—an entire field of allusion, scarcely explored in literary criticism, which speaks of sackings and kidnappings, of burning and booty, of buried treasure and secret maps, of the terrible black flag and of duels to the death, of coffers of jewels and pieces of eight, of the gallows and the plank, of galleons and fortresses, of muskets and culverins, of boardings and of ransoms, lookouts and alarm bells, of besieged cities and naval battles, of Tortuga's taverns and nights of frolic in Port Royal. Keep in mind that we're dealing with a distinctly Caribbean folklore whose reworked language served as primary material for *Treasure Island, El corsario negro,* and *Captain Blood.* Notwithstanding this deliberate manipulation, it has been impossible to effect a complete elimination of the violence that lies deep in the marrow of this or any other Caribbean historical theme. If someone had to define, at once, the meta-archipelago's historical novel and its folk narrative, using just two words, these would be, unquestionably: *revelar* (to reveal and to re-veil in Spanish) *violencia.*

Even religion shows itself intermixed with violence in the area's folklore, especially in everything that touches on the stories of "heretic" pirates and "Papist" Spaniards. It occurs, in a parallel fashion, in an early example of local literature, the poem *Espejo de paciencia*—which we have already seen—written by Silvestre de Balboa in 1608, and it also happens in real life, for example in the massacre of the Huguenots perpetrated by Menéndez de Avilés in 1565. In *Los pañamanes* we see how the reverend Nathan Henry "criss-crossed the Caribbean using as his boat an imposing wooden church, which was painted an immaculate white, in time for the preaching of the doctrine of salvation through the Church of Jesus Christ of the Latter Day Saints" (p. 15). It was this very Church that hanged the Spanish Man.

Everything seems to indicate that Fanny Buitrago collected this rich folklore in the selfsame archipelago of San Andrés y Providencia. It is a question of one representative sample of the thousand and one stories through which any Caribbean person, regardless of his color, sex, or social class, is formed. This collection of traditions makes up a system of differences to which the tales of piracy, the stories of slave revolts, and the legends of runaway slaves all belong. The patriarchal, racist myth of the Spanish Man belongs here along with the myth of coexistence and tolerance that the novel's text proposes. To reduce this system of differences to the clash of contrary orders—which is too frequently done—would give us an impoverished reading of the Caribbean's folklore. In reality, this folklore, which is a very important source for the local literature (think of *Cien años de soledad*, whose myth begins with the landing of Francis Drake in Ríohacha, but remember also *Tres tristes tigres*, *Concierto barroco*, and *La guaracha del macho Camacho*) is a kind of marine soup that is impossible to pour. Perhaps the only thing that we can come away with clearly is its relationship to violence. For example, in the novel that we are dealing with the fable of Henry Morgan's three dead men gets confused with the myth of *Los pañamanes* (the one that the text offers), not just in that deaths should occur in three generations, but also in that each "outside" death presupposes an "inside" death as well within the group or generation. Thus it will be noted that the *Tinieblos* die two by two, just as their parents and grandparents did. Moreover, these deaths should be seen as sacrifices similar to that of the Spanish Man and the one executed by Henry Morgan, since all of them are propitiatory rituals for the eradication of public violence.[8] In Morgan's case, the deaths will prevent the finding of the immense Panama treasure—never found, as a matter of fact—for if it did not stay hidden it would divide and destroy the Brotherhood of the Coast's association through internecine battles; in the case of the Spanish Man it is easy to see that, if a sexual taboo had not been created with the sacrifice of his body, the rivalries between islanders and Spaniards would have bathed San Andrés in blood; and, finally, in the case of *Los pañamanes*, the immolations of Gregorio Saldaña and Nicasio Beltrán neutralize future acts of violence in two directions: in the first place they make any more blood sacrifices unnecessary, since with their deaths the last cycle of the skin-color taboo is closed; in the second place, they preserve the existence of El Arenal, the (dis)ordered center of the island culture, deferring its liquidation.

In any event, no matter what reading we make of this vast and chaotic system of myths, legends, fables, old wives' tales, and folk tales floating over the Caribbean, our reading will fall short if used as a code or genealogical vehicle to find a stable cultural origin. The same thing will occur if one relies upon systems of dance, music, beliefs, or others. Supposing it possible to stop the continuously transforming dynamics of these discourses of difference, with the object of making a total reading out of them, there would still be only flows and fluxes of signifiers which, beyond the Caribbean—like the stories about Anancy and the tales of piracy and treasure—spread out to the ends of the earth. Every Caribbean person, after an attempt has been made to reach his culture's origins, will find himself on a deserted beach, naked and alone, coming out of the water as though shivering and shipwrecked—like the Spanish Man—without any identification papers other than the uncertain and turbulent memorandum inscribed in his scars, tattoos, and skin color. Finally, every person of the Caribbean is in exile from his own myth and his own history, and also from his own culture and his own Being, now and always, in the world. He is, simply, a *pañamán*.

■ *7*

Viaje a la semilla,

or the text

as

spectacle

I think that the novel written in the Caribbean is one of the most spectacular in the world. I should make it clear that in talking of spectacularity I don't refer to the use of certain experimental techniques which we see successfully employed in novels such as *Ulysses, In Search of Lost Time, Orlando, As I Lay Dying*, or, in Spanish America, in the works of Cortázar, Vargas Llosa, Fuentes, or Roa Bastos. When I mention the spectacular nature of the Caribbean's narrative, I mean to use the strictest definition of the word *spectacle* (my Larousse says "public entertainment of any kind"). I say this so definitively because I detect in the Caribbean novel a will to set itself up at all costs as a total performance. This performance (and "something more," as we saw earlier) can be carried out under the rules of several kinds of spectacles: variety shows, circus acts, dramatic works, radio or television programs, concerts, operettas, carnival dances, or any other kind of spectacle that one can imagine.

Naturally, the characters in these novels often appear literally as singers, musicians, ballerinas, transvestites, etc., and it's easy to identify them as members of a troupe or ensemble, even a singing group or dancing chorus. But beyond these characters' virtuosity there is the text itself, the star of the show, the great performer. You will recall, for example, the very beginning of *Tres tristes tigres*:

> Showtime! *Señoras y señores.* Ladies and Gentlemen. And a very good evening to you all, ladies and gentlemen. *Muy buenas noches, damas*

y caballeros. Tropicana! The MOST fabulous night-club in the WORLD *El cabaret MAS fabuloso del mundo*—presents—*presenta*—its latest show —*su nuevo espectáculo*—where performers of Continental fame will take you all to the wonderful world of supernatural beauty of the Tropics—*al mundo maravilloso y extraordinario y hermoso:* The Tropic in the Tropicana! *El Trópico en Tropicana!*[1]

Remember the start of *Cuando amaban las tierras comuneras,* where Pedro Mir, taking on the duties of both author and stage director, calls for a curtain-raising, after which, for an instant, bathed in the spotlight, the actress-text appears, stopped in a *tableau vivant,* to begin moving when the show begins:

> Romanita was standing there facing the gutter with her back to the street completely immobile ecstatically inert without the most minimal animation to her hands or even her eyelashes being able to infringe on the norms of rigidity imposed upon her entire figure as if all of a sudden she had been crystallized as she reached the last wall of cosmic time and had been unable to adopt a more purely cadaverous pose or a more eloquent gesture of eternity.[2]

Or, if you like, Luis Rafael Sánchez's "Notice" with which he presents *La guaracha del Macho Camacho,* out of a space shared by a disc jockey's studio and a typewriter:

> **Macho Camacho's Beat** tells of the flattering success of Macho Camacho's guaracha *Life is a Phenomenal Thing*, according to information received from disk jockeys, announcers, and microphomiacs. It also tells of some miserable and splendid ups and downs in the lives of certain supporters and detractors of Macho Camacho's guaracha *Life is a Phenomenal Thing*. Furthermore, as an appendix to **Macho Camacho's Beat**, transcribed in its entirety is the text of Macho Camacho's guaracha *Life is a Phenomenal Thing*, so as to afford unsurpassed delight to collectors of all-time musical hits.[3]

Keep the first paragraph of *Cien años de soledad* in mind as well, in which Melquíades and his gypsy troupe unfold their tents and circus acts, and amid a clamor of fife and drums they make known the marvels of the sage alchemists of Macedonia as well as the "new inventions," ice being one of them.[4]

And so Havana, Santo Domingo, San Juan, and Macondo are stages, not just in terms of the things that they refer to but also as spaces for spectacular presentation, in a *sancta sanctorum* of collective mysteries, in a "sacred zone" in which one finds ritual sacrifice and representation of the mystery of Caribbean identity. Of course a text's discourse, in its performing, takes on a secular tone. But it's not hard to see, among the veils and in the creases of its trick-bag, the myth's hidden skin, the ceremonial tattoo, the cords that connect to Africa, to Asia, and to pagan Europe. Behind Farraluque, *Paradiso's* priapic dancer, there is a Greek connection; behind the tortured slipper of Cobra, Sarduy's transvestite, there lies the Chinese mania to reduce the female foot to a brushstroke; under the metaphysical solo that Cabrera Infante gives Estrella there lies the African predisposition not to separate life from death, and behind Dreamer's symbolic dream there lies, as we have seen, the unreachable Arawak. In short, the Minotaur lies just beneath each one of the masks that these characters wear. And so the text's performance is always a double one.

It's been said more than once that Caribbean novels have protagonists who are excessive, baroque, grotesque, and even that the texts out of which these characters speak are the same way. I think that all this is true, but only when it's seen from Europe. I mean by this that the masquerade that the Caribbean discourse often puts on is nothing but a concession to the bungling of Christopher Columbus, who took the Caribbean for Asia and the "*indios*" for Indians. The West's idea of the Caribbean is a product of these and other mistakes and inventions. Acceptance of certain forms of Caribbean culture—such as music, dance, literature—in the great cities of the Western world owes substantially to these forms' playing the roles of the "native," or the "picturesque Indian maiden," the "blithe Negress," the "sensual mulatress," the "baroque creole," that is, roles belonging in the farcical libretto that Europe has written about the Caribbean for five centuries. Except that behind the words in that libretto, behind the "Good evening ladies and gentlemen," behind the picturesque steps of the "one-two-three-hop," there lie codes that the Caribbean people alone can decipher. These are codes that refer us to traditional knowledge, symbolic if you will, that the West can no longer detect.

In general, as I have no doubt made known by now, I think highly of the culture of the Caribbean. Not because I think it superior to other cultures, but because I see in it a capacity for simulation (I'm thinking of those mimetic mechanisms that certain animal species use to defend themselves), a histrionic virtuosity that I do not see elsewhere in the world today. It would be an error to take the Caribbean text as just the rhythmic, flowery gesture of a rumba dancer. The Caribbean novel is this and much more. To begin with, as I said, its discourse is doubly spectacular, and not simply because it assumes its own spectacularity but also, above all, it is a discourse that, as well as being scenographic, is double in itself: a supersyncretic discourse. This discourse speaks to the West in the terms of a profane performance and, at the same time, it speaks to the Caribbean in the terms of a ritual performance; it has scientific knowledge on one side and traditional knowledge on the other. The ordinary non-Caribbean reader registers only the profane reading, although he usually gets a glimpse of "something more"; the Caribbean reader sees both, as Ortiz learned to see them. It is this scenographic (public) cross-dressing ability that leads me to think that the Caribbean text is, like the Caribbean reader, a consummate performer.

If someone were to ask me to explain what I mean by a scenographic discourse that speaks at once in terms of representation and ritual sacrifice, and then ask me to demonstrate my opinions within literary criticism's analytic format, I would proceed to point out certain regularities in a dozen contemporary novels with which I might give a picture of the Caribbean narrative discourse's complex performance. This of course would require me to fill the pages of a thick book, or even several books, and so it must remain outside this chapter's modest perspective. It is feasible, though, to choose a brief piece which has already been gilded by its many readings, and to analyze it in a spectacular and unforeseen way. I say unforeseen because such a piece—if I intend to convince the reader—ought to show a transvestite's virtuosity in a much less obvious way than those shown by the novels that I have mentioned above. Among the texts that could be examined which meet these requirements, I choose to write about *Viaje a la semilla*, by Alejo Carpentier.[5]

A canon called the crab

Before entering into the analysis itself, I ought to provide some musical information. This is necessary because a large part of Carpentier's work is built over musical structures, which both he himself and the critics have noticed.[6] In any case, the information that I need to give is minimal, and it refers concretely to the musical form known as the *canon cancrizans* (recurring canon, crab canon, etc.).[7] In this canon, which was quite in fashion in the Baroque period, the treatment of the theme reminds one of the brooding locomotion of the crab, who seems to advance by walking backward. According to what these pieces demand, the first voice enunciates a given theme while the second voice states a copy of it in reverse, that is, beginning at the end and ending at the beginning, or if you like, going from right to left. In this way one hears the first note along with the last, the second with the next-to-last, etc. The two sections of the theme's figure can be represented by the following scheme:

Theme:	fa	la	do	mi	sol	si	re
Copy:	re	si	sol	mi	do	la	fa

We notice right away that the *canon cancrizans* and *Viaje a la semilla* have something in common: there is within the text a discourse that moves in a normal progression, which I will call P, and another discourse that moves backwards, which from now on I will call R. Now I intend to take just any paragraph from the story, to observe the interplay of P and R. To differentiate the two discourses, I'll put the R discourse in italics:

> *And a splendid evening party was given in the music room on the day he achieved minority. He was delighted to know that his signature was no longer legally valid, and that worm-eaten registers and documents would now vanish from his world. He had reached the point at which courts of justice were no longer to be feared, because his bodily existence was ignored by the law.* After getting tipsy on noble wines, the young people took down from the walls a guitar inlaid with mother-of-pearl, a psaltery, and a serpent. Someone wound up the clock that played the *"Ranz-des-vaches"* and the "Ballad of the Scottish Lakes." Someone else blew on a hunting horn that had been lying curled in copper sleep on the crimson felt lining of the showcase, beside a transverse flute brought from Aranjuez. Marcial, who was boldly making love to Señora de Campoflorido, joined in the cacophony, and tried to pick out the tune of "Trípili-Trápala" on the piano, to a discordant accompaniment in the bass. Then they all trooped upstairs to the attic, remembering that the liveries and clothes of the Capellanías family had been stored away under its beams *which were recovering their plaster.* (pp. 115–16) [8]

We can see right away that discourses R and P have different functions. In fact these are two discourses whose differences would have to be established in linguistic terms the better to tell them apart. For example, I would say that discourse P is synchronic and descriptive; R shows itself, on the other hand, as diachronic and narrative. An R phrase, for example, "under its beams which were recovering their plaster," achieves its retrogressive effect not by a syntagmatic route, but rather through a perturbation of the paradigmatic or metaphoric relationship, by supplanting the transitive verb "to lose" (*perder*) with an antonym capable of inverting the verb's action in a vectoral sense (as in coming for going, approaching for receding, etc.). In the example just quoted, one could replace "lose" by "gain" or "take on," but, clearly "recover" is a better choice given the vectoral value of the prefix "re," which sends us quickly toward the past "to take on again that which was lost." It's understood that this kind of phrase not only shatters the reader's natural diegetic sense, but also, driven by the verb's active dynamic, crosses through, like a bolt of lightning that moves from right to left, the wide synchronism of discourse P. All of this can be seen clearly in the phrase that I've quoted, since its action implies years of retrocession, while the course of the evening party requires no more than a few hours of forward motion. One might say then that discourse R dominates discourse P.

Now then, regarding P's static nature, I can derive what Barthes would call a P "picture." In reading the story, we observe a series of P pictures, which line up in retrogressive order from "death" (p. 105) to "birth" (p. 131), for example, "bordello" (p. 119–20), "spiritual crisis" (p. 120), "lead soldiers" (p. 121), "the groom Melchor" (p. 126), "the dog Canelo" (pp. 127–28), etc. But this kind of disposition (from "death" toward "birth") doesn't constitute in itself a regressive dynamic; rather it is discourse R's necessary complement. The effect of retrogression that this discourse achieves, by overturning the paradigm, requires the sequence of P pictures to fall in a retrogressive order along the line of the syntagma or diachronic axis, although the action itself, within these pictures, unfolds in the regular way. Let's take for example the R phrase "the married pair went to church . . . to regain their freedom" (p. 114). As we shall see, the discourse's R movement establishes a need for the pair's "engagement" to occur after the "wedding." To look at it another way: if the P pictures were to appear ordered from "birth" to "death," they would not fall in with the R discourse, which moves only toward the past. This discourse makes sense only when the P pictures line up in the R order. This is what makes the story, including its title, possible.

With these aspects now before us, we may conclude that the text's R and P discourses correspond to the canon's R and P voices; these are analogous dynamics, functions of analogous structures. One might argue that the R function shows itself to be dominant in the text, but this does not separate text from canon: in the latter the R voice is determinative, because not any P theme that one might compose will be able to fold back on itself musically in the R sense. The R function, then, is the very expression of the *canon cancrizans,* the function that gives the canon its name.

One could argue as well that the voices R and P are heard simultaneously in the canon, in such a way that the voice that sings the theme describes a melodic line, and the one that sings its retrograde copy enters into a harmonic relationship (a duo) with it. This would be a pertinent observation, valid not just for *Viaje a la semilla* but also for Ortiz's *Contrapunteo.* But simultaneity is not possible in writing. Nor is it possible within the system of language. We can find a relative equivalence between a musical note and a phoneme, but there is nothing in music like a word, and hence a group of musical notes cannot convey a concept. Music is a language without a signified, as Lévi-Strauss says,[9] or if you like, it is the signifier's *ars combinatoria,* in which we can make out the different voices in their paradigmatic moment as they run by along a syntagmatic line. This leads the reader of music toward the continuous perception of a "totality," of an algebraic matrix that is heard at once in both its vertical and horizontal dimensions as it unfolds. It even allows us, when faced with a *theme and variations,* to superimpose our recollection of the theme over the shapes of the different variations, while at the same time superimposing our memory of a previous variation upon the one that we're hearing at the moment.[10]

But that music and writing should be two distinct formal systems in no way presupposes that certain structures can't be traded back and forth between them, insofar as these latter are dynamics with analogous structuring and transformational functions. For example, the P/R structure that we're observing shows itself not only in the *canon cancrizans* and in *Viaje a la semilla,* but also in the plastic arts (the famous Crab Canon by M. C. Escher, 1965) and again in molecular biology (the celebrated helicoid DNA molecule). In any one of these examples, what changes is not the structure, which keeps on being P/R; it is the structure's immediate vehicle that changes.[11] In any case, to get back to the text of *Viaje a la semilla,* when the R and P discourses cross vectorally, as we've seen, an effect of superimposition similar to a chord or duo is achieved. Beyond this it's not possible to go.

Now I should mention one of this structure's rare properties. If we look at the table of notes with which I illustrated the interaction between theme and retrograde copy, we observe that the middle notes of each are the same, *mi* in this case. This is not by chance. It will always happen this way, because it's understood that with the theme crossing left to right while the copy goes right to left, the two will cross each other at their respective "centers," that is, on the common note. I've put *centers* in quotation marks because it's obvious that this sort of constant unseats the very idea of center, since on arrival at the piece's very middle both voices will have to intone a sound both the *same and not the same,* for, vectorially, one voice is P and the other R, and if properly represented in writing, the notes in the example would be *mi* and *im.* This unforeseen ambivalence, apart from the interesting speculation that it might arouse, has a practical result: the *canon cancrizans* constructs itself in this hollow, or black hole, and works outward in both directions.

It is obvious that we would find the signs of this paradoxical "origin" in *Viaje a la semilla*'s signifiers. Nevertheless, given the spectacular nature of just such a find, I prefer to delay my presentation until the close of my own performance, an amateur's interpretation that needs the help of a showy final number.

Well, up to this point I've tried to take my comments on *Viaje a la semilla* along the safe and well-paved road of structuralist analysis. What I've said goes along with a first reading of the text; that is, a binary reading where R opposes P, and where their dialectical relationship will lead to a foreseeable result: a synthesis (the canon). From now on, my interests as a Caribbean reader, one generally averse to accepting any first reading as definitive, will strike out along other paths offered by the story's system of P/R differences. I'm interested, above all, in reaching a point at which, beneath the violin-viola duet that plays Carpentier's *canon cancrizans,* we see revealed the face of the Caribbean performer, the minotaur or fabulous animal created out of differences, who exhibits his forked nakedness from beneath an elegant baroque mask.

We open the door to the enchanted house

I can find a promising performer in the story's first chapter: an old, enigmatic Negro who comes onstage with a walking stick. From the lip of the stage to its depths there extends a group of scenic displays, which are probably hanging from the ceiling by nylon cords (that's how I imagine the text's setting). This group represents an old house, or rather a vast, disarticulated colonial mansion, which some workmen are taking apart, amid creaking pulleys and clouds of dust. The old man, skirting a pile of wreckage, approaches the still-erect façade and inspects it closely. Presently, on being questioned by the workmen, "the old man made no reply. He moved from one place to another, prying into corners and uttering a lengthy monologue of incomprehensible remarks" (p. 105).

The second chapter takes up the approach of night. The men have finished their day's labor, which they will take up again in the morning, because much of the house is still standing. The men disperse, and then disappear, talking and gesticulating behind the set.

> Then the old Negro, who had not stirred, began making strange movements with his stick, whirling it around above a graveyard of paving stones. The white and black marble squares flew to the floors and covered them. Stones leaped up and unerringly filled the gaps in the walls. The nail-studded walnut doors fitted themselves into their frames, while the screws rapidly twisted back into the holes in the hinges. In the dead flower beds, the fragments of tile were lifted by the thrust of growing flowers and joined together, raising a sonorous whirlwind of clay, to fall like rain on the framework of the roof . . . And the gurgling water summoned forgotten begonias back to life. (p. 107)

I propose to decode this as follows: Then the R dynamic, which had not yet begun, transmitted its retrogressive principle—having returned to the *sol* key—to the musical system's potential signifiers. The musical notes, both white and black, spread out along the lines of the staff, filling it. Under the R dynamic, the musical system's signs mobilize, cross the threshold of their possibilities, and as signifiers now, construct the canon's sonorous flow, adjusting it to the tonal framework . . . and the R voice makes its entrance.

This fragment turns out to be extraordinarily interesting. The second chapter's text does not refer just to music but also, concretely, to the *canon candrizans*. In accordance with this observation, the first chapter would not be connected to the canon's structure. This is in fact the case. In this chapter's text we find neither the picture P nor the retrogressive discourse R, which is easily recognizable. In reality, the canon's structure does not begin to show itself until the second half of chapter 2, as we shall soon see. Before this, however, I want to point out that as the old Negro becomes the mouthpiece of discourse R we are given the explanation as to why his words in the first chapter were "a lengthy monologue of incomprehensible remarks." What's happening, simply, is that the old man R has been speaking backwards. Of course, since the canon's ways haven't been established yet to provide a space for the play of R and P, the old man's words fall outside the frame of this chapter, which is narrated conventionally. As we follow the Negro's footsteps in chapter 2 we see that, after founding the R discourse, through which the house is reconstructed, or rather sung in reverse, the old man inserted "a key into the lock of the front door and began to open the windows. His heels made a hollow sound. When he lighted the lamps, a yellow tremor ran over the oil paint of the family portraits, and people dressed in black talked softly in all the corridors, to the rhythm of spoons stirring cups of chocolate" (p. 108). References to the canon are obvious here. The "hollow" sound made by the old man's heels is nothing other than the R song-discourse, which opens the house-canon with the key-keynote and establishes the P song-discourse: "people dressed in black" (the P notes) "talked softly in all the corridors" (were heard along the lines of the staff) "to the rhythm of spoons stirring cups of chocolate" (distributed in measures according to the tempo of the piece).

Right away we read (listen to) the first P picture, whose motif is the Marqués de Capellanías on his deathbed, through which the text stays connected to the workings of the canon. From now on, up to and including chapter 12 (the story's next-to-last chapter), we are going to see a systematic equivalence between the R voice and the R discourse, the P voice and the P discourse; that is, between the canon and the text. The dominant function R expresses itself in the old Negro's (the R mouthpiece's) being the animator of both discourses (R with the stick, P with the key). On a practical level, R's dominant function expresses itself more simply: of the two possible vectorial readings of the story, the conventional one, the one that moves from left to right, will force us to read it from "death" to "birth," that is, in reverse.

But what minotaur hides beneath the old Negro's mask? The Caribbean's cultural codes make for a quick identification: he is the *orisha* Elegua, our old acquaintance from the Yoruba and Ewe-Fon West African cultures, creolized in Cuba and elsewhere in the Caribbean. You will recall that among his functions is the one of watching over doors, keys, locks, and houses, and that in one of his principal avatars or "roads" he takes the shape of an old Negro with a cane. This is perhaps his most frightening manifestation, because in this guise he likes to upset everything. In Cuba, this avatar is known by the name of Eshu (Exiu in Brazil), and the *santería* cult represents him sometimes as the devil, and consequently it is said of Eshu that at times "he speaks backwards." [12] At other times, in Haiti, he is the greatest of wizards, who likes to live at night and in the darkest places; he is voodoo's Legba-Carrefour, *petro's* Maître-Carrefour. [13] There's nobody better than he at letting loose retrograde dynamics. The text that we're re-reading is then, in good measure, the performance of a trickster-devil who taps his heels with a hollow sound.

Chapter 4 draws our attention to an old Negress with divinatory powers. There are some interesting features here. The Negress *reads* the Marquesa's coming death in the water signs: "Never trust rivers, my girl; never trust anything green and flowing!" (p. 112). This is the only time that one of the story's characters "speaks." Who could this Negress be? Clearly, we can see from afar that something sinister is going to happen. And so it does; the Marquesa dies by drowning in the Almendares, the river at Havana's outskirts. Her death, its circumstances, are obviated by the R and P discourses. Nonetheless, for the Marqués, "the months of mourning passed under the shadow of ever-increasing *remorse*" (p. 111). Of course the emphasis is mine, and by this I mean to involve Don Marcial in a cloudy affair, maybe a crime, maybe his wife's murder. In any case, I'll leave this matter in suspense for now.

We close the door to the enchanted house

An unforeseen catastrophe occurs in chapter 12: the Marqués's house disappears. It is swept off to its origins by discourse R, the alarming whistle of Elegua-Eshu:

> Blinds disappeared into the darkness in search of ancient roots beneath the forest trees. Everything that had been fastened with nails was disintegrating. A brigantine, anchored no one knew where, sped back to Italy carrying marble from the floors and fountain [the notes as *parole* and the music as *langue*] . . . Everything was undergoing metamorphosis and being restored to its original state. Clay returned to clay, leaving a desert where the house [the canon] once stood. (p. 130)

This chapter, the story's next-to-last, has two parts, which are separated by a blank space, something exceptional in the text. The house disappears beyond this frontier, now let loose from the canon's centripetal machinery, which has worked only in the first part of the chapter. It is precisely in the first part where the Marqués's voyage through the text ends; it is here where Don Marcial is "born," in the last of the P pictures. On the other side of this limit, which is fixed by the action of the canon's dynamics, we find chaos: "But now time passed more quickly, rarefying the final hours. The minutes sounded like cards slipping from beneath a dealer's thumb"

(p. 129). In short, time is devoured by R, though strictly speaking this is no longer R since it lies outside the canon's interplay. In any event, on the following day, when the workmen return to their labor of demolition, they find to their surprise that the house has wholly disappeared, leaving not the slightest scrap of debris. Clearly, the abduction of the house leaves us dizzy (stopped there, alone, before the void), although our impotence brings along at least one certainty: the new signifiers can't be deciphered with our old decoding method. We are going to have to find some new keys to open up other possible readings. Here I'm going to leap over the vanished house and continue on.

Chapter 13, the story's last, remains outside of the canon's dynamics, as the first chapter also had. If we look at these two chapters together, it's obvious that they balance each other, in a strictly paradigmatic relation. Their function is plainly commutative, as, like an electric switch, they illuminate and snuff out the Marqués de Capellanías's life, and in passing open and close the canonic form. Nevertheless, notwithstanding its auxiliary function, chapter 13 turns out to be extremely interesting. In the first place, there is a workman who, in trying to explain the house's disappearance to himself "remembered some vague story about a Marquesa de Capellanías who had been drowned one evening in May among the arum lilies in the Almendares" (p. 131). This forces our return to the passage in the text where we read the old Negress's terrible admonition, for we've been given here a connection between the disappearances of both the house and the Marquesa.

Who is this woman who reads fate in water spilled from a jar? The only thing we know about her is that "she kept doves under her bed." This isn't much, but it is an indication at least. We can say with assurance that we're dealing with an *iyalocha,* who mediates between the *orishas* and the believers in Afro-Cuban *santería.* The doves that she stores under her bed may be useful in seducing a desired person. Moreover, the confidence with which the Negress deals with the Marquesa—addressing her familiarly, calling her *"niña"* (girl)—indicates that she is not just her personal slave but was also, years earlier, her nanny or wet nurse. These domestic slave women would stay by their *niñas* all their lives, and they enjoyed special privileges and a familial treatment that was beyond the reach of other slaves. From all this we might conclude that the doves are being "worked" in order to further an amorous caprice of the Marquesa's. Everything seems to indicate that the Marquesa de Capellanías wants to seduce someone. Who is it?

The old *iyalocha*'s warning occurs after the Marquesa spills a jar of water on her dress "after the anniversary ball given by the Governor of the Colony." Alarmed, the old woman says: "Never trust rivers, my girl; never trust anything green and flowing!" In these last words "never trust anything green and flowing" there is a clear allusion to the serpent, not just any serpent, but the serpent-river, the snake-river of the African and Caribbean myths. Clearly, this signifier is supersyncretic and enormously complex. It can send us to Erúkurubén-Ñangobio, the sacred snake of the Abakuá and their mythic river (Afocando Oddame Efí, Oddame Efó Yenenumio) that divided the lands of Efí and Efó in the Calabarese tradition (Calabar, now South Nigeria). This path would lead to the Sikán myth, which establishes the taboo of woman and the drum and, if we follow it we will reach the Marquesa's having transgressed and paid the consequences. What might the transgression have been? We have another path to follow at any rate, toward the myth of the founding of Da (Dahomey), achieved through the effort of the river-serpent-rainbow, that is, the dual being, straight and curved, the manifestation of eternal motion, movement outside of time, the Damballah-Wedo of voodoo. But if it is quite possible to send Guillen's poem "Los Ríos" and the *Palace of the Peacock*'s rainbow back to this Ewe-Fon myth, it does not seem feasible to link the Marquesa's death to it, since it carries the message of eternal life. Perhaps the *iyalocha* is alluding to the fearsome Mother of Waters, who lives in the rivers of Cuba, Brazil, Guyana, Haiti. From the Mother of Waters one must always expect the worst, for she is a kind of ophidian mermaid who demands ritual sacrifices. In Guyana there was once a dance called *waturmama,* and in Cuba it's quite possible that the dance called *matar la culebra* is related to this sacred creature. And so the Marquesa might have been chosen as a sacrificial goat to neutralize future acts of public violence.

Does this explanation fit? Who knows, but let's forge ahead. Well, we have to keep in mind that the *iyalocha*'s forecast might refer to the Cuban boa, the *majá,* though this wouldn't leave us with much to do, since its mythology is so ample that we'd lose ourselves among the possibilities. One of them, however, was previously explored by Carpentier himself in his story "Histoire de lunes,"[14] which is built over the close relationship between the *majá* and the moon, the *majá* and the night, the *majá* and the female fluxes, the phallic *majá* and the vaginal moon. In Carpentier's story we see a Negro who, under the moon's influence, covers his naked body with tallow and slides like a nocturnal serpent through the bedrooms of the women of the town. This intertextuality could lead us to think that the Marquesa's death occurred when she was raped by a man-*majá,* or rather a man-phallus who lay in wait for her in a thicket on the banks of the Almendares. But this is just a conjecture; we're on ground as slippery as the *majá*'s own kin.

Another path we could follow would be to consider the Marquesa's having spilt the water jar on returning from the Governor's ball. We might infer that the Marquesa was having an affair with someone she met at the ball, and that she hid her adultery behind some supposed excursions in her carriage along the Almendares. It's possible to imagine Don Marcial, mad with jealousy, saddling up his horse himself and waiting, amid the thick foliage of the arum lilies, for the light and rhythmic passing of his wife's carriage, which is surely a calèche with enormous wheels and a splashboard seat. But all of this, though novelistic, is also quite improbable. We must think of the obligatory presence of the calèche driver, namely the calèche driver Melchor, childhood playmate of the Marqués himself. Melchor turns out to be an insuperable obstacle, because he doesn't belong to the Marquesa nor would he enjoy her confidence, and he would be the last person she would pick as her accomplice in her adulterous flights. Furthermore, it is very unlikely that Don Marcial would murder her in Melchor's presence. If someone told me here that it's only a slave that we're talking about, and that Don Marcial could do what he wanted with him, even silence him forever, I would answer that, in the first place, Don Marcial is not that kind of man, and, in the second place, Melchor dies in "Los fugitivos," a story that Carpentier wrote later.[15] Nevertheless, there is something obscure about the Marquesa's death. Consider that on returning from the tragic incident "the manes of the horses harnessed to her carriage were damp with solely their own sweat" (p. 111). Hence the carriage did not fall into the river and, necessarily, the Marquesa must have stepped down or been pulled down from it before she died. And, clearly, we have Don Marcial's "ever increasing remorse," and also something more: Melchor dies on his master's sugar plantation. Why should he have been transferred from the house in Havana to the sugar mill? This was done only when a slave had committed some grave offense. What might the elegant Melchor have done? Certainly we could imagine that the Marquesa, tired of Don Marcial's limp virility (a guess), might have set about seducing Melchor. Then the *iyalocha*'s doves might work to attract Melchor, who would resist taking his master's place in the Marquesa's arms. In any event, the theme of sexual love between black and white, even between master and slave, has been worked exhaustively in the Antillean novel. But, strictly speaking, just as with the matter of the snake, the only things we have here are suspicions, uncertainties.

We are lost in the labyrinth of Caribbean codes. Concretely, we have been able to establish a point at which both the house's and the Marquesa's disappearances allude to a common term, perhaps to violence that sublimates violence: the form of the ritual sacrifice.

All quiet on the western front

After all these speculative gropings we need to start rereading the text again. There are only a few lines left. We dropped it at a point where one of the astonished workmen, trying to explain the inexplicable—the Mystery—told the story of the death of the Marquesa de Capellanías: "But no one paid any attention to his story because the sun was traveling from east to west, and the hours growing on the righthand side of the clock must be spun out by idleness—for they are the ones that inevitably lead to death." With these lines *Viaje a la semilla* comes to an end.

It is curious how the text disqualifies itself at the end. It notifies us, from an entirely Cartesian posture, that we must read life in a diurnal, solar sense, in the light of reason. Notice how the last paragraph's lines establish a new kind of writing, of rhetoric; they have something of the didactic self-righteousness of neoclassic fables. They want to convince us that the night of Eshu-Elegua, the night crossed by the history of Don Marcial and the disappearance of the house and the Marquesa, has left behind no more than the vague recollection of an unlikely dream. And so this paragraph or coda, which belongs in the Age of Enlightenment, looks upon the text that precedes it in terms of an Other; it breaks loose and distances itself from the preceding text as if this text had dealt with a turbulent and embarrassing past. The coda tries to erase the text's paradoxical, nocturnal, lunar aura in favor of an idiom that speaks of transparency, symmetry, control, stability, silence (*All Quiet on the Western Front*); it wants to tell us that *Viaje a la semilla* is nothing but a product of an intellectual exercise, a curious result coming from the application of a baroque canon's structure to a baroque narrative, in short, a *divertissement,* a display of musico-literary finesse. Yes, but this quiet performance is directed specifically toward Paris, London, Rome, New York. Such a performance, one that builds a story in reverse without departing from a strict canon à la J. S. Bach, is what the West expects from a good Caribbean story. The text's "other" performance, the one that makes noise and goes masked in a Calibanesque pirouette, expresses its desire to reinterpret, in some fashion, the fragmented identity of the Caribbean Self. Here the text folds back on itself, looks for itself in its own mirror, observes, questions, narrates, and erases itself, tries in vain to run away from its own reflection. It keeps on being a Western text: language, Spanish; genre, story; style, baroque; technique, vanguardist; current, surrealist; idea, Nietzschean. Yes, but this text that folds back on and inspects itself makes a noise and leaves a mark when it rereads itself, and it is a Caribbean mark, a Caribbean noise meant for the people of the Caribbean.

Many years later, as Carpentier was writing *El arpa y la sombra* and confessing his literary duplicity behind the mask of Columbus, he decided to issue the following monologue:

> When I search through the labyrinth of my past, in this my final hour, I am astonished by my natural talents as an actor, as the life of the party, as a wielder of illusions, in the style of the mountebanks in Italy who, from fair to fair—and they came often to Savona—brought their comedies, pantomimes and masquerades. I was an impresario of spectacles, taking my Pageant of Marvels from throne to throne.[16]

This quotation scarcely needs comment. Carpentier, now gravely ill, confesses that his Pageant of Marvels—his theory of *lo real maravilloso*—was a farce, a performance which, dressing up in a newly minted picturesqueness, enabled him to impress the intellectual thrones of the West. But of course this is not all. He soon also confesses that his work offers "another" reading, and that this is the one that counts, that tries to confront the problems that lie "within," the problems of the Caribbean Self, which in the first instance are problems of origin:

> I was the Discoverer-discovered, uncovered; and I am the Conqueror-conquered because I began to exist for me and for the others the day I reached *over there,* and since then, it is those lands that have formed me, sculpted my shape, defined me in the air that surrounds me . . . And it is because you never had a homeland, mariner: that is why you had to search *over there*—in the West—where you are never defined in terms of national values, in days that were day when here it was night . . . Any manikin from *over there* is more aware of *who he is,* in a land known and delimited, than you, mariner, with centuries of science and theology on your shoulders. Pursuing a country never found that fades away like a castle of enchantments each time you sing your victory song, you were a follower of vapors, seeing things that never became intelligible, comparable, explicable in the language of the *Odyssey* or in the

language of Genesis. You went into a world that played tricks on you when you thought you had conquered it and which, in reality, threw you off your course, leaving you with neither *here* nor *there*. Swimmer between two waters, shipwrecked between two worlds, today you will die, or tonight, or tomorrow, like a protagonist of fictions. Jonah vomited from the whale, sleeper of Ephesus, wandering Jew, captain of a ghost ship.[17]

Noise

It is obvious that the title *El arpa y la sombra* (The harp and the shadow) is a split text in itself. It is an impossible bifurcation, and Carpentier himself wants us to know as much before entering into the first part of the novel. Remember the epigraph from the Golden Legend that opens the book: "In the sounding of the harp / there are three elements; / the hand, the string, and art. / The man; the body, the soul, and the shadow."[18] So the words *harp* and *shadow* refer to two orders of things, and they form a conjunction of differences as particular and complex as that of *sugar* and *tobacco* in the *Contrapunteo*. Except that here the musical voices don't allude to a socioeconomic reality but rather to a human, ontological one.

In fact it's obvious that beneath the mask of Columbus there lies a man in pain, a man cut apart between the Caribbean and Europe, a man whose identity was shipwrecked between the cathedrals over *here* (the "harp") and the islands over *there* (the "shadow"). But Europe's sway over Carpentier's own ego—which we noticed earlier—does not disqualify him as a Caribbean man. The final measure of Caribbeanness is the search for that which is Caribbean, independently of the port or portal from which this search is undertaken. In reality, the Caribbean Self must begin the utopian voyage toward its reconstitution from a cultural space that necessarily remains "outside," whether in Europe, Africa, Asia, or America, whence comes the dominant focus of its syncretism. Such a voyage's itinerary is a kind of Parcheesi, or better, an unending game of Monopoly, where the player acquires, alters, trades, builds on, and liquidates minuscule cultural lots, amid the unpredictable roll of everyone's dice; he advances, he retreats, he comes back again and again to his starting point, he owes and is owed; prizes are awarded and fines assessed, properties are mortgaged and unmortgaged, but this Monopoly was not made for the players to lose or win but rather, simply, for them to be able to play in the belief that a victory might be possible, that it might be possible to bring together, on a single property, the colors of both "harp" and "shadow." It is easy to demonstrate—as I think I have already suggested—that one never becomes a wholly Caribbean person; one is also something more or something less, one always falls just short of or just beyond it, one is always involved for both the near and the long term in the search for Caribbeanness, and above all, one writes page after page concerning that search or the illusion of having completed it, with a "victory" that quickly evaporates. The phrase I quoted earlier: "pursuing a country never found that fades away like a castle of enchantments each time you sing your victory song" alludes directly to this impossible search. Of course it refers also to the colonial mansion in *Viaje a la semilla:* the house of mysteries, of secrets, of the pacts and founding documents of everything Caribbean. This house, for Carpentier, is the *sancta sanctorum* where the arcana of Caribbeanness are revealed, the hypostatized union of *here* and *there,* of the "harp" and the "shadow," two people in one; it is the House of the Negotiating, in *El acoso,* where the fugitive's life and death are negotiated.[19] But, in *El acoso* as much as in *Viaje a la semilla,* the house is in ruins and, above all, empty; hope has vanished in the night of both texts, and all that remains now is that which is invisible, unknowable: the "shadow." We needed to recall this before moving on.

In any event, *Viaje a la semilla* marks a limit to Carpentier's search for his Caribbeanness. He undoubtedly understood, as did Fernando Ortiz and Lydia Cabrera, that Cuba was black and white. Except that to him black and white did not suppose the criss-crossing of power relations that went beyond the Caribbean sphere and ran through the history of the world in a network of flows connected to other flows, but rather, a relationship that was exclusively antagonistic and local that one day would be resolved socioculturally. It's no accident that he availed himself of music's black and white signifiers; nor is it by chance that the R discourse should be founded by Elegua-Eshu and that it should be a narrative (myth) and should deploy itself in retrogression (the return to Africa), and that the P discourse should be progressive, should move from left to right following the Western writing system, and should make stops with pictures that describe the life of the Marqués of Capellanías, owner of a sugar mill, owner of slaves. I don't doubt Carpentier's having had a profound insight into the racial, social, and cultural differences separating black from white, but he did not see the differences that lead them to approach each other.

Carpentier's difficulties in navigating more deeply into the Caribbean start when he tries to define the Negro. His novel *¡Ecue-Yamba-O!*[20] is a genuine attempt to reveal the Cuban Negro's inner world, but, as he would later recognize, it was a failed attempt. Nevertheless, no Negro character ever appeared in his later work who got beyond the self-definition of the tragic Menegildo of *¡Ecue-Yamba-O!* I think that Carpentier, perhaps blinded by the richness of the Afro-Antillean cultural context—then a popular theme in the islands because everyone had read Spengler—fell into the error of taking it for granted that the Caribbean Negro could assume the color of his skin without experiencing any conflict. This assumption is quite curious, given that he had in hand the texts of the Harlem Renaissance and the poems and manifestos of *Négritude*, which originated, precisely, in the cry of pain and anger with which the Negro uprooted from Africa asks: Who am I? Clearly, Césaire and the poets of the Antillean *Négritude* fell into a similar error on their own, since they presumed that the Caribbean white—white by self-definition—wore his skin on the outside, as though it weren't a flag to be suspected always of showing black bloodstains spattered there by some deliberately forgotten encounter or by the planter's or slavedriver's whip. In reality, every Caribbean person, as I said in the previous chapter, feels his skin as a territory in perpetual conflict, as a trench that he must take and claim for his Self, or else surrender unconditionally to the Other. This war may be covert or open, but it is waged without quarter. Even supposing that one day the population of the Caribbean should become entirely mixed, the battle of skin color would not abate, for then the conflict would be no longer expressed in terms of "black" and "white" colors, but rather in terms of shades. In the Caribbean we are all performers. As we saw in the case of Guillén, we all try to act the roles that our skin reads out to us. This is a regularity.

In my opinion, Carpentier managed to see the inconsistencies of the white regarding the Negro—think of the embarrassing psychological moment between Sofía and Ogé (*El siglo de las luces*), or between the Fugitive and the old Negress (*El acoso*)—but he was unable to feel the Negro's conflicts with the white man's skin, or with his own skin and his own culture. In short, he could not, even intellectually, deconstruct the Negro. He saw him as the coherent pole of an ethnological confrontation with the white, and he perceived that some day "beyond the lives of those now writing" a liberating social synthesis would supervene, which in its coming would make the Caribbean novelizable in Europe's terms. I think that this is the reason that Carpentier's Negro characters don't quite jell, don't quite convince.

In *Viaje a la semilla* Carpentier faced the ontological necessity of taking an *orisha* of Yoruba origin as the carrier of the R discourse. It was the discourse of his Otherness, of the "shadow" of himself which he had to explore minutely in order to reach his Caribbeanness; it was the sacred myth of the Other, which spoke of gods in animal form and of dark sacrifices (remember the Marquesa and the serpent-river) and which, when heard from the West, flowed in reverse. But, clearly, communication with his *there* had to be reached via a Western vehicle, a kind of Columbus's caravel, that is, a written *canon cancrizans*. Nothing else was feasible, since Western language does not lend itself, as does the African, to transcription through drumbeat. So Elegua-Eshu did not descend gloriously on the holy drumbeat as he should have, but rather he came in the form of a hollow allegory, invoked by a Western voice that did not sing out *bembé,* but played chamber music instead. As we can see, the success of the ontological project was compromised from the start.

We can imagine Carpentier's doubts as he wrote out a plan for the story. Above all, as he finished his mechanical transcription of canon into writing. How to destroy the house that the black-white dialectic, begun by Elegua-Eshu, had so consciously reconstructed? Remember that the situation could have stayed as it was; that is, after the Marqués's "birth" the house could have continued to age and could then have reached the exact point of demolition at which the workmen had left it. In which case, on the following day they wouldn't have noticed anything unusual and would have kept on taking the house apart. The story then would have achieved total symmetry. But of course this was not likely. For Carpentier, the *orisha*'s retrogressive song would turn out to be more vigorous, attractive, and consequential than the song of the epistemological discourse that was playing left to right. Influenced by Spengler's ideas,[21] Carpentier saw African cultures as in their ascending cycle, shedding the hegemony of a Western culture that had entered its period of decline. And, clearly, now legitimized by Europe, his *there* side demanded recognition. This appraisal can already be seen perfectly in *¡Ecue-Yamba-O!,* whose publication precedes that of *Viaje a la semilla* by eleven years. How could it be possible to confine once more, in the canon's last note, the African discourse's powerful cosmogonic and vital forces, once they have been set loose? We must keep it in mind that, barely two months earlier, Carpentier had traveled to Haiti, and that the experience of making contact with voodoo and with the Haitian Revolution's historico-cultural testimonials had suggested the notion of the *real maravilloso* to him.[22] Of course, the canon had to be brought to an end according to its own rules; but beyond the ending he could establish a space, delimited of course by the canon's structure, in which the *orisha* could reel out all of his renovating, regenerative energy, to put things back into their "original condition" in order to begin again, to write the story anew. Bear in mind that, in returning the house's materials to their places of origin (marble to Europe and wood to the African forest), Carpentier restored at once a time prior to slavery and the Plantation: a mythic time which, given its inherent ahistoricity, provided a utopic space, past and future at once, where one could build a "total" society, a society in which the old desire expressed in the myth of the *Caridad del Cobre* would function as a synthesis and, also, a psychic state where all of the contrary sides of the Self that the Plantation had split apart could now be reconciled. The lot on which the house had stood, now a wasteland, would furnish the blank space, making it possible that such a desire, through a rewriting of history, might in the future be realized materially.

But the house's disappearance can be explained in an "other" way. As Carpentier has confessed, beneath the mask of Columbus, his ego's proclivity toward rooting itself in Europe kept him from being able to decode certain cross-rhythms, flowing from the corners of the Caribbean house, which he wanted to have for himself. This is the house in which the story of the West ("in the language of the Odyssey or the language of Genesis") reverberated, but which, above all, served as a dwelling place for the secret rituals of the Abakuá, of the *mayomberos* of the *Regla Conga,* of the *cauris* in the Day of Itá, the great day of revelation to the *lucumí* initiate. It is obvious that for Carpentier the search for his Caribbeanness was to take place *there,* in the house's shadows. Except that those dark thresholds, which Elegua-Eshu would open for any "*monicongo* from *there,*" were always an irreducible enigma to him. These thresholds, being reached, dematerialized as if he were in a "castle of enchantments." In this sense the house—*his* house—turned out to be, for him, a space as fugitive and phantasmagorical as the "center" of a *canon cancrizans* whose presence we noted some pages earlier. And so the unknowable house had to disappear in a regular way: the marble *here,* the wood *there.* Everything returned to its "original condition," but without anything being gained; the story did not begin again, and Columbus was wrecked between his *here* and his *there.* This is what we get out of our "other" reading of the house, if we can even call it getting anything. In any event, this is the reading that I think is the closest to the book, even to the paradox of the *canon cancrizans.*

This last reference, which has erupted unexpectedly in my argument, suggests to me that the time has come to find the canon's spectacular "origin" in *Viaje a la semilla.*

Directions for reading the black hole

Let's get to it right away: if of the story's thirteen chapters we take those eleven that respond to the canonic structure, and if we lay out these chapters according to the rules of the dynamics R and P, we get the following scheme:

P: 1 2 3 4 5 6 7 8 9 10 11
R: 11 10 9 8 7 6 5 4 3 2 1

A quick look reveals that the two series cross at the midpoint, 6. Well then, if we take a look at the start of the story's chapter 6, we find:

> One night, after drinking heavily and being sickened by the stale tobacco smoke left behind by his friends, Marcial had the strange sensation that all the clocks in the house were striking five, then half past four, then four, then half past three . . . It was as if he had become dimly aware of the possibilities. Just as, when exhausted by sleeplessness, one may believe that one could walk on the ceiling, with the floor for a ceiling and the furniture firmly fixed between the beams. It was only a fleeting impression, and did not leave the smallest trace on his mind, for he was not much given to meditation at the time. (p. 115)

The text has opened up in the middle to show us the empty space that generates the canon's structure. It is an exemplary performance: the reader is informed that the Marqués has an impression that the spatio-temporal continuum might be upside down, but since this in itself would have Don Marcial moving toward his "birth" according to the R dynamic, we are soon told that "one could walk on the ceiling, with the floor for a ceiling and *the furniture firmly fixed between the beams*." That is, it's not a matter of a simple inversion of the spatio-temporal planes (with the underneath part now on top and the left-right movement reversed), but rather it is a situation in which one is above and below at the same time and moving toward the right and the left at once. In reality, if the Marqués were a musical note, *mi* for example, he would be *mi* and *im* at the same time, since he is in an empty place within the canonic structure's force field, at the midpoint where the R and P voices intersect vectorially, suspended between a *here* that projects itself toward *there* and a *there* that projects itself toward *here*.

In the confessions offered by *El arpa y la sombra*, Carpentier takes for himself the Marqués's paradoxical situation: "in days that were day when here it was night, in nights that were night when here it was day, rocking, like Absalom hanging by his hair, between dream and life, without ever learning where the dream began and the life ended."[23]

These words carry a certain pathos. I say this because, contrary to what Carpentier believed, the Caribbean has no origin that stands beyond the threshold of the "castle of enchantments." There are only Afro-Cuban, or rather Afro-European signifiers whose pathways spread through Africa and Europe and then out to the whole world, canceling the past and the future, along the length and breadth of the infinite flight of signification. There is certainly no reason for Carpentier's despair. Even if he had been able to deconstruct the African side of his Caribbean ego, he would have seen that his position with respect to the Caribbean's and Europe's *here* and *there* would have remained more or less as it was. Of course, if he had decoded the unrepresentable cross-rhythms of the musical score played from the house's dark corners, he would have learned more about the Caribbean, but all the same he would not have fully arrived at his Caribbeanness. Not only because he would yet have to explore the basement where the Indian *behiques* were smoking sacred *tabaco* and the *areíto* was being danced, or for that matter the rear annex, where the strings went out of tune and the walls smelled of Cantonese rice, but because, even had he known these places, he himself would not have been more Caribbean than he was. In the end, nobody can fill materially the dense void of the Caribbean; one always perceives a lack. The voyage to *there* can always be made in terms of hope and desire, or by traveling up the rivers of poetry in the vehicles of dance, music, and belief, and even in the vehicle of writing, as we saw Wilson Harris and Carpentier himself doing. But this is an aesthetic experience, and thus more or less transitory; it is an experience which, on the strictly sensorial plane, is remembered in terms of dream, vision, epiphany. Thus the essentially Caribbean never ceases to be, precisely, the search for that golden and fleeting moment of this visitation, when all clocks are stopped. If culture, as Bakhtin would say, is collective memory, one would have to agree that the Caribbean's memory recalls only the voyage, given that over *there,* beyond the Carib and Arawak canoes, beyond the galleons of the West Indies Fleet and the slave ships that plowed the middle passage—among other passages—this message disarticulates irrecoverably and spreads out to the corners of the earth. As Ortiz said about tobacco, we're dealing with a rite of passage, of initiation; once the threshold is crossed, time past is shuffled and one of the Parthenon's columns serves as a sacred tree for the dance of Oshun and Shango. In the Caribbean, the Voyage is the *thing in itself.* This, as we have now seen, is another regularity.

Whatever else, *Viaje a la semilla* is a story that, as its title indicates, proposes to reach the origins of Caribbeanness by spreading itself out along two routes: one leading to Europe (the canon) and the other to Africa (the house). But in this double journey after signification and legitimacy the text (dis)covers that *there* and *here* are nothing other than black holes into whose vertiginous drains things keep disappearing, without anyone's knowing where they're going—torrents of cultural forms as various as those that we see on the Quincalla del Ñato's shelves; black-white "centers," finally, that flow into the void like the Marqués de Capellanías's inverted notes, *mi* and *im*. In this way, *Viaje a la semilla*, from writing's nearby proscenium, offers itself as a doubly spectacular spectacle: at once directed toward the West in terms of an excess of invention and professional competence (to make an impression, to follow the current), and also directed to the reader in the meta-archipelago, beneath a ritual language which, in its repetition, tries to interpret two performances of the impossible: to *be* a Caribbean person and to *be there* in the Caribbean.

Niño Avilés,

or

history's

libido

In 1782 the Count of Floridablanca received a manuscript entitled *Historia geográfica, civil y natural de la isla de San Juan Bautista de Puerto Rico*. Its author was Fray Agustín Iñigo Abbad y Lasierra, an ecclesiastic who had traveled to Puerto Rico in 1771 as secretary and confessor to the new bishop, Fray Manuel Jiménez Pérez. The manuscript had been printed in Madrid in 1788, and would be published several times thereafter.[1] The work comments on events that occurred on the island between 1493 and 1776.

In 1984 the writer Edgardo Rodríguez Juliá published the novel *La noche oscura del Niño Avilés*.[2] The story begins in 1797 and soon shifts to a retrospective that starts the story over in 1772. It's possible then to read this novel as a text that moves up against Abbad y Lasierra's *Historia*, penetrating it through a space whose temporal extent is four years. It can be established, moreover, that the historiographic text left its mark on the novel, something which, apart from its having been pointed out in general terms by various critics,[3] will be established herein from up close.[4] This deliberate encounter implies, naturally, that the two texts will confront each other, since, in the reader's eyes, there soon comes a need to formulate some hypothesis to explain the novel's apparent desire for or attraction to the history.

Well then—to look now at either one of these two texts—what is current historiographic opinion of Abbad y Lasierra's work? In his note to the 1959 edition L. M. Díaz Soler, director of the history department of the University of Río Piedras, characterized the book as "a precious jewel of our historical literature" (p. XVII), while Isabel Gutiérrez del Arroyo, in her excellent preliminary study, considered it to be "the source, vigorous and stimulating, of all the Puerto Rican historiography that was to follow" (p. XIX). Warm appreciation for the book has been expressed in school-texts as well. J. L. Vivas Maldonado, in his *Historia de Puerto Rico*, says: "In spite of O'Reilly's accurate description of Puerto Rico, and the accounts of Ledrú and Miyares González . . . , the most faithful, detailed, and studious observation of Puerto Rican life was made by someone else: fray Iñigo Abbad y Lasierra."[5] If we were to add to all this that the University of Río Piedras has reprinted the book four times between 1959 and 1979, which speaks of how often it is read in university courses, it's easy to see that we're in the presence of a foundational text in the island's history, that is, a text indispensable to any solid reflection about Puerto Rican origins.

What does this book have that gives it such an honored place in the local historiographical discourse? In the first place, there is Abbad y Lasierra's having had the good sense to examine carefully every important text that carried some information about the island, which allowed him to offer the first summary of Puerto Rico's historical sources. To this we would have to add that such an effort at organization resulted in an eclectic work which, as a rule, eschewed extreme judgments. In fact, as Gutiérrez del Arroyo points out, Abbad y Lasierra's text is written with a singular balance and objectivity, to the extent that it includes the opinions of the Abbé Raynal and of William Robertson, whose works were banned in Spain. The book, which was sponsored by the Count of Floridablanca, shows the eclecticism that was reached in certain circles of enlightened Spanish thought, while reflecting also the Enlightenment's rationalist pragmatism and faith in scientific and social progress.

But we should say above all that Abbad y Lasierra devotes the second half of his book to a detailed commentary, as in a didactic chronicle, on the topography, natural history, demography, agriculture, commerce, and customs of Puerto Rico, offering in the process the first modern picture of Puerto Rican society. Clearly, like any work written in its century, it reveals itself in the sparest, most precise and well-ordered neoclassic prose, which keeps its composure even when narrating the burning and pillaging of the city of San Juan during the era of pirates and corsairs:

> In 1595 the celebrated pirate Francis Drake, after having robbed and burned the coasts of Perú, Cartagena, and other provinces, pushed open the door of the City of Puerto Rico with a considerable fleet; he

set fire to the ships he found there and he sacked the city; but considering that he could not stay without abandoning the rest of his mission, he kept going, after having destroyed the place. Three years later the Count of Cumberland took over the Island in the hope of establishing himself there; but the sharp edge of an epidemic cut into his forces and took more than four hundred men from him within a few days, forcing him to abandon the enterprise; he sacked and burned the City anew, killing many of its inhabitants, and then set sail, carrying with him the spoils along with seventy pieces of artillery. (p. 85)

And so one might think, at least in a first reading, that Abbad y Lasierra's text represents a serene and auspicious, almost exemplary, point of departure for Puerto Rico's historical discourse.

La noche oscura del Niño Avilés, as we know, offers us a very different reading. Perhaps the first difference we notice is the insolent and sometimes demented baroqueness of its language. For example:

Now there came an enormous hand dragging with its index finger a hairy monkey with a human face, dressed in a nun's habit. It was a joke played by Lucifer himself that the monkey was defecating huge flying turds and that these would then change, while floating in the air, stinking up the whole place, into very serene and lovely daisies. Over there beside the Bishop there came, most genially, a miniature man, if not a hunching dwarf, and this freak vomited reptiles into the air, whose mouths were shaped like conches, and with these they were sucking, as they flew along, from the deceitful daisies. There came flying by as well, above so many wretched things, some enormous ears that rent the air with barely endurable screams. Cymbals and drums resounded, played by gray rats as large as the dwarfs, and the damned things were actually quite coquettish and show-offy, for they had the brilliant plumage of peacocks where there should have been tails. These jolly rates had faces, but no noses, so that when they breathed they seemed to shout. (p. 41)

Certainly the novel offers itself as a foundational text as well, but it's a matter of founding the Other, that is, the Niño Avilés, a predestined and monstrous being. This character really lived, although the legend cloaks him in mystery. He was a child born without arms or legs, an exceptional circumstance that led to his being painted in 1808 by the creole José Campeche. His having remained in posterity's mind as a circus attraction, a feature from a cabinet of horrors, sharpens to the point of inexpressibility the dolorous patience with which the child regards us from the canvas. Two years after the novel was published, Edgardo Rodríguez Juliá, commenting on Campeche's work, gave us his reading of the portrait:

> According to what is written below the portrait, this child of Coamo was born on July 2, 1806. He was brought by his parents to San Juan, where he received the Sacrament of Confirmation on April 6, 1808. It was then that the Bishop Arizmendi ordered this portrait from Campeche. Why might the Bishop have done this? Dávila tells us: "These demonstrations of scientific curiousity on the part of bishops, during the course of their pastoral visitations, are common in Spain and in America during the second half of the eighteenth century" . . . If such was the original intent, Campeche soon exceeded it, to turn the portrait into a metaphor of suffering . . . And this suffering has something to do with the common people: the painter's look—accustomed to capturing the habits and personalities of the creole elite and the colonial administrative caste—rests here on that which is deformed, on a son of the People . . . Avilés is bound inside his body, manacled by his organic deformity . . . The pictorial metaphor takes on a temporal expression which verbally we would define as gerundive . . . The child Pantaleón Avilés *is suffering,* his act of suffering becomes a pure expression of time . . . One feels an uncertainty regarding the child's age. Suddenly it seems to us that in reality we are faced with the woeful situation of a young man shrouded in an infant's body. His head has nothing to do with his body. He has grown older in this atrocious pain, in this furious suffering . . . The right eye seems more resigned . . . But the left eye despairs . . . In that distance between the right and left eyes lie obedience and rebellion, salvation and damnation, saintliness and pride.[6]

So this elephant man is the hero of Rodríguez Juliá's novel; he is the "other" Moses who will found, in the swamps and streams that ring San Juan, the incredible city of Nueva Venecia. A new Manoa, city of El Dorado, lost paradise or poetic vision of the Caribbean? Yes, and no. One might think that Nueva Venecia is to Rodríguez Juliá what Santa Mónica de los Venados and the Palace of the Peacock were to Carpentier and Harris, but this is true only in part: that which is Caribbean—if you will allow me this generalization—also has its *here* and its *there,* and Nueva Venecia is the Caribbean's *there,* while Carpentier's and Harris's visions refer the *here* of Caribbeanness, that is, to the space closest to the European *here*. Rodríguez Juliá, though, begins his journey from the cultural *there* of the Christian West; that is, from the Tower of Babel, from animist beliefs, from ritual incest, ancestor cults, blood sacrifices, pagan oaks, oracles, soothsayers, orgiastic ceremonies, witches' sabbaths, in short, all of the codes of exorcism. Rodríguez Juliá is not the first Caribbean person to attempt this voyage; Fernando Ortiz, to demonstrate that Western culture was more irrational than Africa's culture, had published, almost three decades earlier, his *Historia de una pelea cubana contra los demonios* (History of a Cuban struggle against demons), a book which, visibly, constitutes one of this novel's most important sources.[7] Another principal source is Hieronymus Bosch's visual imagination—Rodríguez Juliá teaches art history at the University of Puerto Rico—which could easily have painted "making use of dark visions and the most minutely detailed realist landscapes, the history of the singular settlement and its founder, the Niño Avilés" (p. 10). We have here, of course, the representation of a mythical city, the city of desire; not the desire censored by the preconscious, but the desire of the libido itself, whose vital and excessive impact builds the entire text. Such a city has been destroyed and erased from the archives and from the collective memory, and this novel, precisely, offers itself as a part of a manuscript of doubtful authenticity that narrates the city's forgotten history. Why forgotten? Because of the collective fear of a total freedom, without law or limit, where nothing is marginal. Thus Nueva Venecia can be read as the "other" Caribbean, as the subversive and "dark reverso" of the islands' manipulated history: "It was the fear that crouched within the colonist as well as the colonized . . . the danger implied in any domination" (p. 11).

Nueva Venecia, *an onion*

Naturally, Nueva Venecia exists, though in a state of invisibility. Not only does it give us the other face of the Caribbean city, the one that Fanny Buitrago recognizes and tries to demythify and remythify in *Los pañamanes*; it is also, as I've said, the unnameable city that palpitates within our mental lockups, the sight of which is repressed by the psychic mechanism of censorship. But we're barely going to scratch the surface of the psychoanalytic codes here; the codes that interest me are rather those having to do with the search for the *there* side of Caribbeanness. And on top of this we'd have to say that the chronicles of Niño Avilés attempt to reach an "other" origin which, though disturbing, is no less legitimate, in all its elusiveness, than Santa Mónica de los Venados or the Palace of the Peacock. Bear in mind that the story refers to the mysteries of Dionysus in the meta-archipelago's first age, but that these mysteries are not dealt with in Hellenic terms, but rather in terms of their Caribbeanness, and they have become more dense than ever, for all of the world's subterranean deliria have spilled out upon the islands.

Thus, Nueva Venecia, whose founding is not even entirely consummated in the action of *La noche oscura del niño Avilés*—the first book of a trilogy—[8] is the most recent attempt to draw out the dark sides of the Caribbean's *there,* dark sides that are also supersyncretic, where exorcism mixes with *"despojo"* (*Santería's* spell-breaking practice) and demonology with African witchcraft. Nonetheless, it would be wrong to think that Nueva Venecia is no more than a construction of the unconscious part of Caribbeanness. Although we don't know much about it, the text informs us of the following:

> But the truly strange thing is that the people should have forgotten that precinct where Avilés sought to establish freedom . . . We can't fault the common people with the prudishness of the creole bourgeoisie, that timorous class, depending on the colonial power that *only* [my italics] saw the Nueva Venecia that was decadent, the city of prostitution and strange Dionysiac cults, the pandemonium of heresies and demoniacal exaltations, the pigsty where dreams and deliria flourished, the market for hallucinogenic drugs and impossible communities. (p. 11)

So Nueva Venecia is not *only* the product of an objectivation of the libido, but also "something more" that moves above and below the sexual instinct and the pleasure principle. According to the text, its founding has been preceded by those of several utopian cities, and like Troy, its fragments rise above the ruins of the other cities. This monument to failed utopias is not gratuitous. Aníbal González, in his critical note to the novel, points out that each one allegorizes different readings of Puerto Rican culture. Thus one city emphasizes the African, another the Spanish, another the Creole, etc.[9] We would have to conclude that Nueva Venecia proposes itself no longer as a hierarchized and exclusive reading of the island's culture, to be relegated to the idle chatter of intellectual circles, but rather as the allegory of a culture that responds to a utopia of generalized supersyncretism.

What role does the Niño Avilés have in this? To begin with, all of the cities have been founded under his supposed sponsorship. As a victim of his helpless youth, he was carried off and appropriated by one group after another as a talismanic source of power; his body has been exhibited as an instrument of predestination, as a sign of hegemony; his body is, no more nor less, the "truth." His having been the sole survivor of a shipwreck, and his having floated all alone to the beach in his cradle, lead him to be taken as a bearer of good news or as an evil monstrosity, as a miracle or as a curse, depending on the party one belongs to. In reality, as Rodríguez Juliá says when commenting on his sad portrait, he is simply a child of the people, that is, of the People, that institution of institutions that the political power always assures us it represents in its story of legitimation. So, we can say that Nueva Venecia also constitutes a social utopia. In fact, who are those who follow the Niño Avilés in his foundational enterprise? The text answers: "slaves and runaways, workers and freedmen" (p. 12). Then suddenly we have again the myth of the Virgen de la Caridad del Cobre, or rather a Puerto Rican variant of it, but like it in setting up a complex utopian system of differences that imply a desire for sexual, cultural, racial, and social freedom. It's understood here of course that we're not talking about one sex, one race, one culture, and one class that desires its own liberation; within the meta-archipelagic perspective it is a matter of representing all the sexes, all the races, all the cultures, and all the classes in the world that want a space—"not solar," Wilson Harris would say—where liberation is possible, especially liberation from the memory of the skin color minted by the Plantation.

Clearly, such a desire does not, properly speaking, construct a utopia, but rather a heterotopia like Guillén's *Diario*, for it alludes to fragments of desires that belong to different orders and yet install themselves rather astonishingly in the same space. Nueva Venecia, yes, but also language, writing, novel, concretely *La noche oscura del Niño Avilés*, a tantalizing summa of the neobaroque: Lezama Lima, Sarduy, Arenas, García Márquez, Carpentier, Sánchez, Guillén, Ortiz, all of them tossed in here with whopping Negroes and Negresses, with archaisms, neologisms, and anachronisms, with Bosch, Sade, Rasputin, Bataille, Artaud, Buñuel, Fellini, surrealist, and neoexpressionist painting: visions of excess, the superbaroque construction of the libido and "something more."

Nevertheless, we shouldn't get too far away from the idea that Nueva Venecia is, also, a summation of cities that transgressed. I can't help associating it with Yaguana, Bahayá, and Puerto Plata, the heretical and contrabandist towns that succumbed to the torch and quicklime of the *devasta-*

ciones; and Providencia and Tortuga, forgotten seats of Caribbean piracy and libertinage; or Port Royal, the Gomorrah of the Antilles, second capital of the Brotherhood of the Coast, sunk into the sea by the 1692 earthquake, for its sins, they said; or the fabulous *quilombo* of Palmares, the most powerful and enduring city of *cimarrones* (runaway slaves or maroons) in history and, of course, Canudos, the holy city of *O Conselheiro,* wiped out in cannon fire after a memorable siege.

In any event, the sociocultural codes of *La noche oscura del Niño Avilés* refer, above all, to the community of maroons, the *palenque.* And this is true not just because the story insists, time and time again, on naming the runaway Negro—in reality a multitude of them, involved in the founding of Nueva Venecia—but because, of all the communities of transgressors possible in the colonial Caribbean, the palenque was much the most widespread, the most representative, and also the most dangerous; it was in itself the antiplantation and, therefore, the one community whose destruction was most urgently required.[10] But this point of view was held by the planters. What was the point of view of the fugitive, the one who ran away to find freedom?

Of palenques *and* cimarrones

Run to freedom . . . Why is it that in the Caribbean one always has to run away toward freedom, or rather, toward a space that the imagination paints as freedom? The answer is obvious: Caribbean societies are among the most repressive in the world. I'm not referring necessarily to political repression, although we'd have to agree that the Caribbean's history, colonial and contemporary, exhibits a gallery of governors, captains-general, dictators, and fathers of the fatherland of a hardly surpassable ironhandedness. In reality, as I have already said, the Caribbean's economic and social structures favor this type of political option. But I'm referring here to another kind of repression, and this is the one that every Caribbean person experiences within himself and which impels him to flee from himself and, paradoxically, which leads him finally back to himself. I think that this circular destiny, which starts in the individual and spreads through the collectivity, requires an explanation, or at least an example.

Let's take the case of Enriquillo, one of the first Caribbean men in the brief decades of Hispaniola's colonial hegemony. I want to review his known history as though writing an entry for a dictionary or *Who's Who,* and I'll eliminate the dates to bring it all closer to us. Enriquillo (born

Guarocuya). Nephew of the famous Anacaona and cousin of Higuemota. His father was one of the chiefs murdered by Nicolás de Ovando in the Jaraguá region. He was baptized Enrique and educated in the Franciscan monastery of Santa María de la Vera Paz. He may have learned how to use weapons at this time. Married Mencía, a baptized Indian like himself. His authority being recognized by his father's former subjects, he went with them to a *repartimiento* in San Juan de la Maguana. There he worked the lands of a colonizer and at the latter's death continued in the service of his son, Valenzuela, an overbearing and abusive man. Valenzuela, exceeding the bounds of his authority, stripped Enrique of his mount, the sign of his prestige, and attempted to violate Mencía, beating her with a stick. Enriquillo lodged a protest through the routine judicial channels, but his appeals were ignored time and again. He decided to rise up in arms with a group of followers in the mountains of Bahoruco, and there he grew stronger for thirteen years. During that time his forces were augmented through his giving refuge to other fugitive Indians, among them the well-known rebel Tamayo. He never lost a battle. He transformed the Bahoruco into a defensive system of lookouts, trenches, caves, encampments, and escape routes. His military tactics were similar to those of modern guerrillas, and he defeated Spanish forces numbering as many as 300 men. As years went by, his campaign became known as the War of the Bahoruco, and his fame grew to the extent that it was known to the Emperor Charles V. On the advice of his counselors, the emperor issued a letter of pardon. Bartolomé de Las Casas, always a conciliator, participated actively in the move toward peace. On coming to terms, Enriquillo received the title of Don and was showered with gifts, allowing him to found his own village, named Boyá, to which he retired with his people and his wife Mencía. In exchange, he was to pursue and capture runaway Indians and Negroes, being paid by the head, for which he was given the authority to appoint field constables. The historian Oviedo says that he died a year after his capitulation.[11]

Some scholars, imbued with patriotic sentiment, have asked why Enriquillo would have betrayed his own rather than remaining undefeated on the mountain. My answer would be: because Enriquillo, culturally, had both an Indian and a Spanish side; he sought to liberate his humiliated and repressed Indian side in the Bahoruco, but there he discovered that his "Indianness" was now irrecoverable, that the fabulous *areítos* that his aunt Anacaona had organized, with their delirious dances, their vast tableaux where battles were replayed among fruits and flowers, that magnificent bare-bodied paganism that his memory had kept alive and golden, could never come out of the past. I think that after long years of being victorious—years in which his dishonor had been abundantly avenged—his Indianness had started to seem like an unbearable confinement to him. And so, little by little, his Spanishness started to remember the freshness of the patio at the good Franciscans' monastery, the sweet harmonies of the mass, the lessons in Latin and arithmetic, and he soon began thinking about a flight from the Bahoruco toward the freedom *over there*. Reasons exist to support this opinion: during his campaign, Enriquillo returned large sums of money that he had robbed, and spared the lives of many captives, allowing them to return home. I mean that his Spanishness took care not to close off the return path completely. In truth, Enriquillo comes very close to the character Juan in Carpentier's "El Camino de Santiago," trapped within his recurring avatars *Juan el Romero* (the pilgrim) and *Juan el Indiano* (the adventurer), each of them desiring always to be in the place of the other. In fact, when he flees from the mountains of Bahoruco to the colonial plain, Enriquillo assumes his Spanishness, and tries to act according to its codes. Now he is simply Don Enrique. Clearly, when he chased fugitive Indians and Negroes, his Indianness ought to have made its presence known again, and perhaps he dreamed one night, panting and in a cold sweat, that he was pursuing himself along the ridges of the Bahoruco. On the night that this happened, he would have lost any certainty he might have had about his life's circle having closed, and he would have found himself again in the "labyrinth's anteroom." There's nothing strange in his rapid demise.

Of course, it has not been my intention here to judge the attitude of Enriquillo, which three centuries later would be repeated with extraordinary symmetry in the case of Cudjoe, the indomitable Jamaican maroon.[12] I have taken his story, certainly spectacular, to illustrate once again that a coherent form of Caribbeanness, even in its simplest and earliest form—the interplay of the Taino and the Spanish—is impossible, since it usually goes looking for itself, either in the body or in the imagination, in a *there* that offers itself successively as a space of liberty and a space of repression. Generally, every Caribbean person's present is a pendular present, a present that implies a desire to have the future and the past at once. In the Caribbean one either oscillates toward a utopia or toward a lost paradise, and this not only in the politico-ideological sense, but, above all, in the sociocultural sense—remember L'Ouverture's move from voodoo to the Enlightenment. That is why there are always groups that try to recover the African, or European, or Creole, while others talk of moving toward a racial, social, and cultural synthesis that sees itself as a "new" world. I think, in truth, that neither one place nor the other will ever be reached; Africa, Europe, Asia, and the creole societies that preceded the Plantation are all as irrecoverable as Enriquillo's Indianness; as for a unifying interpretation of the myth of the *Virgen,* the only thing that will ever be put into that boat is just what's there today: differences. In short, every Caribbean person, wherever he is, finds himself suspended in the void at the midpoint of *Viaje a la semilla,* that is, between a floor that travels from *here* to *there* and a ceiling that moves from *there* to *here.*

At any rate, as I've said, in the Caribbean the model of the fugitive is the runaway slave, the *cimarrón,* the maroon, and the model of the transgressive community is the *palenque*—also called *quilombo, mocambo, ladeira, cumbe, mambí,* etc.[13] The adjective *cimarrón,* which was used to designate wild cattle,[14] was applied first to the Indian and then to the Negro.[15] The word *palenque* refers to the stockade that usually surrounded a village of runaways,[16] but, in reality, the palenque was much more than runaway slaves' huts inside a stockade; it was an entire defensive system similar, although on a smaller scale, to the one that Enriquillo built in the Bahoruco. Daily life in the average Antillean palenque went more or less along the lines of what's described in the following passage:

> Inside, they establish storehouses for provisions, those needed most for sustenance, as are, to the Negro, the plantain, the yam, the *malanga* [taro root], beans, and other grains. They elect a captain, to whom they all happily subordinate themselves. To supply meat they capture the *puerco cimarrón* [wild boar] with ropes, unless they have managed to get some wild dogs, or domestic ones, which they train to hunt for them. They are also good at catching the *jutía* [hutia, a large rodent], and with the fish abounding in the rivers they get enough to eat. They require pots to cook in, and salt, and clothes, and arms and munitions for defense . . . and to provide themselves with these articles . . . they descend together on the haciendas dominated by the slaveholders and take everything that interests them, and so they keep fortifying their mountain refuges. And if they should be pursued by a party of *ranchadores* [bountyhunters] or by the Holy Brotherhood . . . they move to other places, no less hidden, of difficult access, where they also clear lands and cultivate them, and to get there they take the precaution of cutting no roads, but rather they look for paths that the rivers touch, and they wade along for miles on their march, leaving no traces of

their passage on foot . . . They take the precaution of opening, around their *palenques,* a number of false paths which they sow with sharp stakes made of *cuaba* . . . and they set traps along the roads that they've prepared for their escape . . . Furthermore, when the palenque is situated atop a mountain, they gather, for its defense, some huge boulders to be rolled down as soon as the fighting starts . . . When they find that they've gathered enough provisions, they put part of their forces to work in the wild beehives in the forest . . . The first avenue of trade in wax open to them is with the Negroes of the nearby cattle ranches and sugar mills . . . with whom they are in league behind the backs of the owners and overseers of these lands . . . and who bring it to the city on market days, where they sell it to the cunning Catalan merchant [who], without tendering any money, trades hatchets, machetes, gunpowder, flint, cloth, ribbons, salt, and other articles which these Negroes carry to a place of deposit, where the maroons come to pick them up . . . When there is a greater effort against them made by the colonial government, and it stations troops to guard the fields and put a stop to the clandestine commerce . . . they then direct themselves to the other side of the place . . . descending like falcons upon the now unguarded landowner, whom they despoil of what they need . . . They carry off slaves of both sexes, cut down or ruin the crops, burn the cane fields, and sow panic in the haciendas of the invaded zone.[17]

The history of the maroons and the palenques is a recent interest of social scientists studying the Caribbean.[18] In spite of the enormous number of documents brought to light in recent decades, their investigation is still at an early stage, that is, fragmented according to locale. Jamaica may be the country that has been most worked over in this sense, but there are still many pieces of the puzzle to be put into place within the Caribbean's elusive frame. We're dealing here with an unending puzzle, of course. I say this because, supposing that suddenly all of the Caribbean basin's archives were to yield every piece of information about this subject, and that it were to be transcribed, studied, annotated, edited, and translated faithfully into all of the official languages, then published and criticized, even then we couldn't consider the matter ended. The maroon's flight carries him far beyond the linear geography that we studied at school: maroons from Jamaica were transported to Nova Scotia and to Sierra Leone; maroons from the three Guianas (Surinam, Cayenne, Guyana) fled to the forest, mixed with the indigenous people, invented languages and beliefs, and penetrated deeply into the South American interior, how deeply no one knows; slaves from Cuba captured the schooner *Amistad* and sailed to New England, where they were tried, acquitted, and returned to Africa; runaway slaves from Florida participated in the Seminole Wars, mixed with the Indians, and left descendants whose blood now runs throughout the United States; runaway slaves from Bahía and Recife fled to the sertão's vast solitude and their descendants transformed its folklore and joined the bands of *cangaceiros;* runaway slaves from all the islands, down the course of three centuries, filled out the crews of pirate ships, privateers, smugglers, slave ships, merchantmen, and whalers; finally, it was a maroon from Panama, Diego, the protégé of Sir Francis Drake, who went beside him in the circumnavigation of the globe, a maritime feat on a world scale that carries this theme's emblematic aura.[19]

Yes, the runaway slave's flight to "freedom" has no frontiers, unless they are those of the meta-archipelago. One day, when global investigations of this theme are undertaken, the Caribbean itself will astonish everyone by how close it came to being a confederation of fugitives, of outlaws. I am not exaggerating; in the last decade of the eighteenth century there were slave rebellions and massive escapes in literally all of the region's islands and coasts. One might think that there was a huge conspiracy, of which the Haitian Revolution was only a part, the part that triumphed visibly. Furthermore, there seem to have been mysterious personages who traveled here and there carrying secret words and letters, like the famous Vincent Ogé,[20] whose fascinating character was captured by Carpentier in *El siglo de las luces*. Certainly we should go more deeply into an investigation of the runaway slave's participation in the region's independentist and social struggles. In Cuba, we have the testimony of Esteban Montejo,[21] veteran of the war against Spain, but how many fugitive slaves and entire palenques were incorporated into the army of liberation, or rather, why was this army called "*mambí*," an African word synonymous with palenque and meaning "savage"?[22] There must have been a great number of runaway slaves among those fighting against Spain for this to have happened.

We must conclude that the historiography of the Caribbean, in general, reads like a long and inconsonant story favoring the legitimation of the white planter—the tapeworm that Guillén tried to purge in the pages of his *Diario*. In any case, I think that the Caribbean's "other" history had begun to be written starting from the palenque and the maroon, and that little by little these pages will build an enormous branching narration that will serve as an alternative to the "planters' histories" that we know. The runaway slave's impact on the big city is already being studied,[23] and for some time now he has been treated in literature and film as a character representative of the Caribbean region. Of course all this is done by installing him in a precise and closed historical context, but in time I think it will be understood the codes of the Caribbean *there* have much to do with the maroon and the palenque. I'm not referring only to the instinct toward flight to "freedom" that I've mentioned, but also to defensive codes, to the extremely complex and difficult architecture of secret routes, trenches, traps, caves, breathing holes, and underground rivers that constitute the *rhizome*[24] of the Caribbean psyche. It is precisely the unrepresentable representation of this "other" city, imagined as baroque, labyrinthine, promiscuous, monstrous, free and captive, libertine and tortured, invisible and extant, fugitive and right here, that the Niño Avilés has founded with the name of Nueva Venecia.

But, of course, Nueva Venecia as a palenque or rhizome-city has discovered that its own *there* is no means of escape; it desires an escape from itself, a flight to the "freedom" *over here*. I mean that Nueva Venecia, the runaway city living in the nocturnal miasmas of the marshes beyond San Juan, would like to be San Juan; it dreams of having a capitol, a cathedral, a Morro Castle, a university, a library, a flag. For his part, the Niño Avilés, with his desperate eye and his sad one, with his minotaur's deformity, wishes to break away from his indecipherable portrait, to be simply *here,* like any child; perhaps, in fact, he spends the eternal night of his ahistoricity kept awake by his desire to submit to the discipline of father, fatherland, and school. We might well surmise that he is already more than bored with living inside his own elemental and instinctive imagination, and that he longs for a civil life, a life in *history*. Perhaps, like the axolotl of Julio Cortázar's story, he senses, with minute patience, that his *here* side, the "other" Niño Avilés, is attending the gallery where he himself sits exposed in Campeche's portrait, and he looks fixedly into his own eyes, at his scarcely perceptible stumps, at his infant's sex organ, and returns the next day, and the next, looking longer each time until the miracle is produced. For him, the regimented, hierarchical life of the society *outside* looks like the image that Segismundo, Calderón de la Barca's character, dreams of in desperation from his tower-prison. Then why not think that the Niño Avilés, without renouncing his wild and lascivious mute language, would like to write the measured and rationalist pages of Abbad y Lasierra, the ones that are studied and valued as the historiographic origin of the Puerto Rican *here*? Or, analogously, why not think that the text of *La noche oscura del Niño Avilés* would like to dance, like Cinderella, in a stately fashion, at the great ball put on by Western Disciplinary Knowledge itself? This would explain the novel's wish to penetrate the space occupied by Abbad y Lasierra's *Historia*.

Of course we're dealing with an impossibility, as the social sciences pay no attention to the fictitious. The fields seem well marked out here, and the social scientists seem more jealous of the distinction. It's worth noting that the reviews hostile to *La noche oscura del Niño Avilés* were not written by literary critics, but rather by historians who were scandalized by the novel's anachronisms, including Niño Avilés himself.[25] In reality, I think that those historians did the right thing. They acted within the canons of their professional calling, and behaved a bit like zoo keepers; that is, taking care to preserve the animals-novels, but also seeing to it that they don't run away to "freedom" and come to occupy the keepers' own place *there*. It's true that history's legitimating narratives, like those of any learned profession, are laborious, arbitrary, and paradoxical. But we must agree that they are institutionalized, a fact that gives them prestige and, above all, power. Besides, we must also agree that it is more predictable and bearable to live by the historiographic world's norms than by those of fiction, where everything that can be imagined has license to exist and to be at hand.

Nevertheless, the matter shouldn't be disposed of so quickly. A first reading of the problem, as we already know, is only step one of a long march. In any event, I propose to demonstrate that it is not just the novel that wants to change places, but that, reciprocally, the history—at least in a subliminal way—would like to occupy the novel's place. Let's take a look.

The temptations of Fray Agustín

It is easy to see that the discourse of the social sciences does not rely on a method or a precise, uniform, regulated language that would characterize it in the terms of a single voice, such as those used in mathematics, physics, or chemistry. The discourse of the social sciences, as Hayden White has proved,[26] is enunciated in a plurality of voices or narrative tropes that are found commonly in fiction and respond, in their differences, to the different ideological systems into which the texts intend to install themselves. I mean that the idea of history, as a discipline of knowledge, lacks a language to defend and expound itself as such, but is argued rather through a cluster of different ideologized and fictionalized languages—Michelet, Ranke, Burckhardt, Nietzsche, Marx, Croce, etc.—which if we were to listen to them all at once in the same space, on a stage for instance, would give us something like an incredible comic opera, in which Aida, Siegfried, Carmen, Tosca, the Duke of Mantua, Faust, Joan of Arc, and Porgy and Bess would sing and carefully act out their roles. This focus, of course, undermines the distinction between history and the philosophy of history, but it also shows a secret desire of the social sciences to keep from systematizing themselves, rather to "carnivalize" themselves—as Bakhtin would say—in a way that brings them near to the situation (place) of the novel.

Still, this is not all. Whatever the voice may be that the text chooses as most ideologically effective in constructing its story, this will not make itself heard as a single voice, but rather as an ensemble of different voices, at least a duet, attempting to sing a (dis)ordered harmony. To demonstrate this I will take Abbad y Lasierra's history as a typical case within the Caribbean orbit. In a first reading we will see its pages as an example of the didacticism and argumentativeness of the best Enlightenment prose. Nonetheless, a rereading of the text will reveal areas or arias that are sung by another voice. Compare the passage on Drake and Cumberland's landings, which I transcribed earlier, with the following:

> The Governor of Tortuga Island, Beltrán Ogeron, a Frenchman, built a warship and with 500 "filibustiers" set off to attack the island of Puerto Rico; but when he reached her coasts he was overtaken by a storm, which dashed him up against the Guadanilla islets to the Island's southwest, and although most escaped alive from the shipwreck, all fell into the hands of the Spaniards, who came out after them and set upon them fiercely; but seeing that they were defenseless and asking for quarter, they spared their lives and merely bound them. They inquired about their captain and were told that he had been drowned in the shipwreck; but Ogeron, who was there present among his fellows, feigned madness, and the Spaniards, not perceiving the ploy, untied him along with the surgeon . . . These two, at nightfall, fled into the shelter of the forest and came out at the seacoast, where they began cutting wood for a raft to take them to the island of Santa Cruz [St. Croix], which belonged to France and was nearby. As they occupied themselves with this, they espied a canoe in the distance, which was moving in their direction. They hid in the underbrush, and when it landed they saw that it carried two fishermen; they resolved to kill them and take their canoe. One of the fishermen, loaded down with fish and calabashes, set out along the path beside which

the Frenchmen were hiding; they hit him quickly in the head with a hatchet, and he fell dead; then they set upon the other, who tried to escape in the canoe; but they killed him in it, and to hide the traces of their infamy they threw the bodies into the high sea; setting their course toward the island of Santo Domingo in the same canoe . . . After they arrived at the port of Samaná on that island, Ogeron left his companion the task of recruiting all the corsairs that he could, and he himself went on to Tortuga with the same intent, to be able to return to Puerto Rico and rescue his companions and then rob and destroy the island, and since the inhabitants of Tortuga knew no other calling, he was able, within a few days, to assemble a squadron to undertake his project, and he set out on a return voyage to Puerto Rico. As soon as they perceived its coasts, they furled their topsails, using only the lowest sails to keep from being seen too quickly by the islanders; but the latter, who were bitter because of these sudden attacks, had posted good watches, and with the first warning they put themselves on the defense. The cavalry came out to oppose the landing and deployed upon the beach where the landing was being attempted . . . Ogeron brought his ships near the coast and began sweeping it with grapeshot. This forced the horses to retire into the adjoining forest, where the infantry was hiding. Ogeron, in this circumstance, and ignorant of the ambush, had no misgiving in disembarking; he therefore rushed ashore with his companions and began to march along the beach, which, covered with trees and thickets, hid the infantry; and when the latter saw the Frenchmen within range, they attacked with a fury fueled by the desire for revenge. The pirates, though surprised, attempted to defend themselves, but being unable to withstand the attack, they found themselves having to hurry back aboard their ships, leaving behind many dead and wounded whom their boats could not pick up . . . Ogeron, wounded and undone, set sail with his squadron, saddened and disturbed at having seen his two expeditions against Puerto Rico foiled, his riches gone along with those of his friends, who abandoned him, electing as their chief another pirate, called *Sieur Maintenon,* who led them to the island of Trinidad and the coast of Paria, where they committed their usual robberies and barbarities. Those from Puerto Rico, after entering the city in triumph with their prisoners, put the latter to work on the fortifications which were at that time being built. (pp. 92–94)

If I were to compare the two passages, my first question would be: Why did Abbad y Lasierra develop such a complete account of Ogeron's insignificant and hapless adventures in Puerto Rico, while doing nothing of the sort with Drake's and Cumberland's successful landings, which were serious projects that might have led to a British colonization of Puerto Rico, and which have less than half a page devoted to them? But in fact I'd have to ask other questions as well. There's the matter of the authenticity and the authority of the sources; Drake's and Cumberland's invasions were reported in the official papers of England and Spain, while the story of Ogeron's adventures derives from the testimony of one of the inhabitants of Tortuga, the buccaneer John Esquemeling.[27] And how do we explain Abbad y Lasierra's abandoning his neoclassic prose, to fall suddenly, with no transition, into a novelistic language with something in it of Sir Walter Scott, who was yet to write anything, a language that makes of Ogeron more an unlucky antihero than an enemy? Why this antididactic treatment of Ogeron?

Let's look first at the type of man Ogeron was. Tortuga, we know, was colonized by the English shortly after Providencia, except that right away it fell into the hands of the pirates and buccaneers of the Brotherhood of the Coast, who elected their own governors from among themselves until 1664. At around this time the island's rivalries and disorders, combined with its lack of any stable trading relations with Europe, put its continuity in doubt. It is at just this moment that Bertrand Ogeron, representing the interests of the French West India Company, comes on the scene, arguing persuasively and finally convincing the island's daring international population to place itself under the protection of France. His popularity and his political genius stand out in two actions that had enormous repercussions on the island. The first of these was to get the crown of France to mandate a great roundup of prostitutes, meaning to ship them to Tortuga to become the buccaneers' amorous consorts. The second was his victory over the thousands of wild dogs that lived on the island, for which he imported, for several years, enormous quantities of poison from France.[28] Thus, prostitutes on one hand and poison on the other established his prestige as a governor in the Brotherhood of the Coast, to the extent that he is taken to be Tortuga's first real colonizer. This is the protagonist of Abbad y Lasierra's narrative.

Well now, as I read Abbad y Lasierra's intercalated narration I can't help thinking of the ebbs and flows of prohibited desire, and especially this desire's tenacity and astuteness in returning time and again to install itself as something permanent wanting to make of life a perpetual act of transgression. I say this because I think that Ogeron, as something more than a historic personage, appears here in the role of spokesman for a repressed desire. Notice how Ogeron returns, as temptation so often does. He feigns madness, he escapes, he kills a local with a hatchet to the head, and then he returns in stealth; he is defeated by the Spaniards, then he's forgotten, obscure, but he returns when Abbad y Lasierra reads about him in Esquemeling's racy account, and he's brought back by the historian's pen, certainly an inexplicable return if we pay attention only to historiographic motivations.

Abbad y Lasierra says of Ogeron that "he feigned madness, and the Spaniards, not perceiving the ploy, untied him." In reality, what he read in Esquemeling's book was:

> For Monsieur Ogeron, being unknown unto the Spaniards, behaved himself among them as if he were a fool and had no common use of reason. Notwithstanding, the Spaniards, scarce believing what the prisoners have answered, used all the means they could possibly to find him, but could not compass their desires. For Monsieur Ogeron kept himself very close to all the features and mimical actions that might become any innocent fool. Upon this account he was not tied as the rest of his companions, but let loose to serve the divertisement and laughter of the common soldiers. These now and then would give him scraps of bread and other victuals, whereas the rest of the prisoners had never sufficient wherewith to satisfy their hungry stomachs.[29]

It's not hard to picture Ogeron grimacing, sticking his tongue out and jumping on the beach, grabbing a crust of bread here and a bit of cheese there, before the jesting soldiery. These are stratagems of which an amoral person may avail himself, things unforeseeable in a man who holds political power. It's also easy to imagine Ogeron within his fortress at Tortuga, master of dogs, whores, and poisons, lord of all of the flesh's pleasures and of that infamous crowd of pirates, buccaneers, and fugitives from all flags. I think that we can agree that Bertrand Ogeron is the Other, the Forbidden One, to Abbad y Lasierra, Benedictine friar and doctor of theology. He is the elemental, ineluctable, desired, and feared entity who rules the "black" side of his psyche—notice that Ogeron is an anagram of *O Negro*, The Black One—the side from which a desire for forbidden pleasure emerges. Furthermore, if Abbad y Lasierra consciously founded the historiography of Puerto Rico, his subliminal counterpart was Bertrand Ogeron, founder of Tortuga, the city of unlimited violence and pleasure.

It's quite apparent to me that in this singular pseudo-historical (or pseudofictitious) passage, drawn from the book of a chronicler who—as the footnotes attest—was on the outer margins of respectability, Abbad y Lasierra tried to legitimize the space of his always-recurring prohibited desires, giving literary weight to the Caribbean adventures of the mad libertine living on the *there* side of his Western, Christian Otherness. Here, of course, there is room for a reflection. And this is it: historical discourse, subliminally, would like to occupy the place of novelistic discourse;[30] it would like to abandon the normative canon that constructs its "true" account, to wander through the chance infinity of fictional worlds and imaginary eras, the poetic open spaces where everything can happen and come together. So we may speak of history's and the novel's secret wish to exchange places, which brings about an unforeseen kind of coexistence of the two discourses. Notice that we're talking about a relationship that is nonmetaphorical (nonexcluding); rather it is metonymic, with history and the novel traveling separately but crossing each other at their respective nodes of desire (a crab canon). In reality, when Abbad y Lasierra was writing his *Historia* about Puerto Rico, he could not keep from leaving a line open that one day would allow the text to communicate, precisely on the question of origins and the foundational moment, with the text of Rodríguez Juliá's novel. We can end by saying that Ogeron found his desired author in Rodríguez Juliá, and that the Niño Avilés found his in Abbad y Lasierra. And so the pendulum swings one more time, and San Juan, Puerto Rico, in search of the "freedom" of its *there,* completes its Caribbean oscillation between Tortuga and Nueva Venecia, between the buccaneer and the maroon, that is, between the marginality of prohibited pleasure and that of the fugitive from the Plantation. A final regularity.

The perspective of Chaos arose potentially with the emergence of thermo-dynamics, whose second law, known as the law of entropy, establishes that the universe, along with all isolated systems within it, is sliding inexorably toward a state of absolute absence of heat. Time, then, becomes an extremely important category, since its passage produces irreversible changes. Naturally, this law undercut the eighteenth century's mechanistic physics, in which time was seen as reversible in the sense that its passing did not render impossible an understanding of the system's past. Toward the end of the nineteenth century Henri Poincaré—who to many is the father of Chaos—observed that minimal causes or errors of estimation in a phenomenon's initial moments could turn out to be catastrophic later on; that is, unimportant differences could grow disproportionately to produce unpredictable results. In 1961 Edward Lorenz, in trying to predict the world's climate on a computer, accidentally arrived at the conclusion that any non-periodic physical system was unpredictable in the long term, since the tiniest error in calculation, or in the case of the climate, a bit more rain nearer to or farther away from the predicted area, could make the results vary considerably. This disproportionate effect was dubbed the "butterfly effect," named for an amusing metaphor: a swarm of butterflies beats its wings in one place and this fluttering causes a storm somewhere else. Lorenz didn't let the matter rest here and he continued investigating other nonperiodic systems, that is, ones that never repeat themselves exactly. When he fed a pendular system's data into three-dimensional functions in his computer, the results astonished him: the graphic form—a double spiral whose lines circumscribed each other without touching—indicated a chaotic system. Still, the design that he obtained also illustrated, surprisingly, the existence of a different type of order hidden inside disorder and chance. At the same time, other investigators working within varied fields of knowledge were getting similar results both in Europe and the United States. David Ruelle, in studying the phenomena of turbulence in liquids, gave the name "strange attractors" to the regularities hidden within disorder. Very soon a substantial number of scientists were looking for "strange attractors" in the most ordinary phenomena of daily life.

In mathematics, Chaos's principal figure is Benoit Mandelbrot. Basing himself in the paradoxes of Cantor and Koch, Mandelbrot founded fractal geometry—named by him in 1975—which, instead of moving between one dimension to another in the Euclidian manner, moves among points that lie between the dimensions. Mandelbrot started from the fact of Nature's producing no abstractions such as the triangle or even the straight line. The question of the length of Britain's coast, for example, does not have a single answer but rather an infinity of them. Seen from a space vehicle, the distance measured would be shorter than one made in walking along the island's irregular coast; nevertheless, seen by an ant, capable of walking in and out the rocks' interstitial cracks, the distance would be even longer. And so the smaller the unit of measurement the more complex and extended the coastline will be. We come finally to the paradox that it is infinite. Simultaneously, Mandelbrot observed that these fractured perimeters filled a space, and therefore exceeded the absence of space proper to a straight line, although, clearly, without ever constructing a flat two-dimensional figure. And so it is pertinent to say that a line that breaks continuously on a sheet of paper—that is, a fractal line—refers to a dimension that lies between 1 and 2, let's say 1.32628. Nevertheless, Mandelbrot did not remain content. In studying Nature's fractal forms, he discovered that if indeed they were disordered, they followed certain universal patterns. Even more, on widening the scale of enlargement under which such forms were observed it was established that they were self-referential and repeated themselves in different magnitudes. (See his illuminating book *The Fractal Geometry of Nature* [San Francisco: W. H. Freeman, 1982].)

Concerning Chaos, on an informational level, the reader should consult James Gleick's book, *Chaos: Making a New Science* (New York: Viking, 1987). This work has as its sources the judgments of nearly two hundred scientists from different branches of knowledge. It is an introductory work that has had a great influence on subsequent books. It has the advantage of bringing together a considerable amount of information on Chaos, including color plates and numerous illustrations, all without demanding of the reader any mathematical or scientific training. Nonetheless, it is limited by its scant attention to the scientists and philosophers belonging to the current that has developed in France. Within this perspective there lie the books of Ilya Prigogine, *From Being to Becoming* (San Francisco: W. H. Freeman, 1980) and *Order Out of Chaos* (Toronto: Bantam Books, 1984), this last in collaboration with Isabelle Stengers. Prigogine's principal interest lies in his developing the hypothesis of the reorganization of open systems within entropy, while proposing at the same time a dialogue between chaotic systems and the humanities, based on the one's being concrete and particular and therefore analogous to the problems studied by the other. As Alvin Toffler points out in his introduction to this last book, Prigogine's reflections correspond quite well to the paradigm of postmodernity, which Toffler himself has defined as that of the Third Wave, where civilization leaves behind the mechanism characteristic of the industrial era and moves into a postindustrial and postideological age that concentrates on the theory of information, paralogy, and innovation.

Since the publication of the present book in Spanish, two general books on Chaos have appeared that should be quite useful to the reader with no training in science or mathematics: Ian Stewart's *Does God Play Dice? The Mathematics of Chaos* (Cambridge, Mass.: Penguin Books, 1989) and *Turbulent Mirror* by John Briggs and F. David Peat (New York: Harper and Row, 1989). Stewart's book, as well as offering an informative and pleasant read, as Gleick's book offers as well, centers itself on Chaos's mathematical aspect. Throughout the book, Stewart emphasizes two ideas crucial to the inscribing of Chaos's discoveries within the postmodern perspective; the first is the tremendous complexity concealed by the world of appearances, so that what seems simple can turn out to be very complicated; the second, which is most important to me, says that a system, generally, exists in a variety of states, some ordered and others chaotic. These, nonetheless, far from opposing each other, make up a continuous spectrum similar to that of music, where harmony and dissonance combine productively to generate beauty. This last reflection serves too as a starting point for Briggs and Peat's book, which is the most poetic and imaginative to be written on Chaos. Its practical import, though, is powerful, for in addition to studying feedback loops through which systems organize and disorganize themselves, it attacks scientific reductionism from holistic positions like those held by ancient civilizations.

More recent is the work of Katherine Hayles, *Chaos Bound: Orderly Disorder in Contemporary Literature and Science* (Ithaca: Cornell University Press, 1990). This is a brilliant study that holds particular interest for literary critics, especially the poststructuralists. The book, after offering an introductory chapter on the history of Chaos, divides into two parts, corresponding to the two great branches into which the new paradigm organizes itself: a speculative and philosophical one that looks at disorder as a generative void from which order emerges (Prigogine), and another more linked to mathematics and the sciences that looks within disorder for the regularities of the "strange attractors" as sources of information (Lorenz, Mandelbrot). In the chapter entitled "Chaos and Poststructuralism," Hayles observes from three points of view (Derrida, Barthes, and Serres) the interrelation between science and literature, and in another chapter she problematizes the relations between the local and the global, as they are observed in Chaos, in relation to the ideas of Lyotard, Foucault, and de Man. In the next chapter she leads a "chaotic" reading of Doris Lessing's *The Golden Notebook*, offering an interesting model of textual analysis. Finally, Hayles observes that the theory of Chaos, like other postmodern theories, is characterized by the ambivalence of the present cultural moment.

A bibliography of a more specialized kind would include many works which I see no need to cite here, since most of them presuppose a knowledge of mathematics which, in general, an investigator who specializes in the humanities does not have. At least, in substantial measure, such has been my case, and for that reason this book shows no attempt to discuss, or even trace the history of, Chaos's advances in each of the scientific disciplines. Further, even supposing that my mathematical competence were to allow me completely to cross the threshold that separates the humanities from the sciences, there would always be the problem of constructing a language capable of making such a connection viable in discourse. In reality, as I said in the Introduction, I have worked on the basis of establishing analogies through certain metaphorical models. For example, the nonantithetical dialoguing that Chaos observes between order and disorder is comparable to the dialogue between the discourses of history and the novel, as I note in the book's last chapter. Or, if you like, the phenomenon known as the "butterfly effect" was useful to me in establishing that the greater or lesser degree of African components in the current culture of a former slaveholding colony does not depend on the total number of slaves that once lived there, but rather on minor variables such as the date on which the Plantation was established, or the proportion of freedmen, maroons, and domestic slaves that lived in the colony. Curiously, postmodern literary theory—as Hayles observes—has proposed models that are analogous to those of Chaos, but we must conclude that, within the former's discourse, these are usually more difficult to capture visually. At any rate, we must agree that, although following different strategies, both literary theory and Chaos try to find regularities or forms in flight within nonperiodic and unpredictable systems, because what other than this is involved in analyzing a text?

This brief bibliographical note on Chaos should include a series of basic and accessible works, having more general implications, concerning the complex relation between order and disorder, determinism and chance, localness and globalness. Nor could it do without a minimal showing of some very well-known works which, in my own experience, were useful to me in applying the theory of Chaos to the fields of social science, culture, and literature. I think that Thomas S. Kuhn's celebrated book *The Structure of Scientific Revolutions* (Chicago: University of Chicago Press, 1962) is an excellent starting point for the appreciation of the capricious history of knowledge and, above all, the effect of arbitrary and irrational procedures upon the disciplinary discourses. Concerning the scientific revolutions, Kuhn's judgment that these usually occur in an interdisciplinary and marginal space gives one reason to think that Chaos, more than a perspective, is an interscientific movement of a revolutionary nature. *La Condition postmoderne; rapport sut le savoir* (Paris: Minuit, 1979)/*The Postmodern Condition: A Report on Knowledge* (Minneapolis: University of Minnesota Press, 1984), by Jean-François Lyotard, takes off from Kuhn to make valuable distinctions between the narratives of legitimation of knowledge, very useful in comparing, especially, the paradigms of modernity and postmodernity; moreover, in defining postmodernity, Lyotard offers a report on the current state of knowledge that includes fractal geometry and the paradoxes of Chaos. Michel Foucault's *Les Mots et les choses* (Paris: Gallimard, 1966)/ *The Order of Things: An Archeology of the Human Sciences* (New York: Pantheon Books, 1971), in studying historically the connection between different disciplines, helps in understanding the relations between the discourse of Chaos and the postmodern discourses, as well as the political implications of such relations. The extensive work of Michel Serres explores the interaction between the local and the global, and the old and the new, establishing connections between science, philosophy, religion, literature, and art; the selection of essays entitled *Hermes: Literature, Science, Philosophy* (Baltimore: Johns Hopkins University Press, 1982), edited by Josué V. Harari and David F. Bell, is an excellent selection of Serres's works. *Gödel, Escher, Bach: An Eternal Golden Braid* (New York: Vintage Books, 1980), by Douglas R. Hofstadter, discusses in a didactic and creative language the implications of Gödel's autoreflexive theorem in current thought and technology, as well as the paradoxical and self-referential character of J. S. Bach's music and M. C. Escher's art; his notion of the "strange loop," as an obstructive element that impedes the continuation of a travel through hierarchical orders of an ascending or descending type, was particularly valuable to me in the analysis of *Viaje a la semilla*. (For a provocative introduction to paralogy and the study of pattern, including "strange attractors," see Hofstadter's *Methamagical Themas: Questing for the Essence of Mind and Pattern* [New York: Bantam Books, 1986].)

Entre le cristal et la fumée (Paris: Seuil, 1979) by Henri Atlan proposes that living organisms, faced with the medium's disorder and chance, modify their structures and reorganize themselves on a greater level of complexity; in accordance with this principle, the relation between order and disorder should not be seen in antithetical terms but rather as a productive coexistence. If we perhaps might criticize René Girard for wishing to extend too broadly his theory about the mimetics of desire and the regulatory function of the scapegoat, we would still have to agree that his contribution to the new perception of disorder/order is of noteworthy importance, and this not only in the field of anthropology but also, for example, in things touching on relations between myth and the novel; his work, starting with *La Violence et le sacré* (Paris: Bernard Grasset, 1972)/*Violence and the Sacred* (Baltimore: Johns Hopkins University Press, 1977), is a worthy example that allows us to observe the action of the new paradigm in fields other than those of the exact sciences. Applying Girard's theory to the phenomena of the carnival (disorder) and lent (order), Jacques Attali studies the changes undergone by music within the historico-social contexts; see his book *Bruits: Essai sur l'economie politique de la musique* (Paris: Presses Universitaires de France, 1977)/*Noise: The Political Economy of Music* (Minneapolis: University of Minnesota Press, 1985). Jean-Pierre Dupuy, in his *Ordres et desordres: Enquête sur un nouveau paradigme* (Paris: Seuil, 1982), treats the ideas of Atlan, Girard, Attali, Edgard Morin, Ivan Illich, and Cornelius Castoriades and applies them successfully to economics and the social sciences, while at the same time pointing out the advantage that the biological model holds in reaching these ends. Finally, as a complement to Gleick's book, I recommend the reading of issue number 40 of *SubStance* (1983), edited by Jeffrey Joel and with an introduction by Frank Coppay, which brings together, in a kind of debate, works by Serres, Atlan, Morin, Prigogine, René Thom, Antoine Danchin, Jean Largeault, and Claude Richard.

A final comment

I want to reiterate that this work does not pretend to offer any irrefutable truth, nor does it try to exhaust the theme of the Caribbean's literature and culture. If I have seized hold of certain models belonging to Chaos, it has not been because I think that these can manage to signify fully what's there in the archipelago; rather it's because they speak of dynamic forms that float, sometimes in unforeseen and scarcely perceptible ways within the Caribbean's huge and heteroclitic archive. These forms do not constitute any sort of essence; they are mere abstractions arrived at through the new language of computers and mathematics which, if they tell of the existence of another kind of order in the universe, never get beyond their condition as signs allowing themselves to be read amid processes of disorganization and reorganization. Still, for a literary critic who wants to find cultural specificities that might differentiate one region from another, the Chaos perspective offers great advantages; its way of looking right at noise and turbulence to find common dynamics comes up with graphic models that allow us to appreciate that a given region's flight of textual signifiers is neither wholly disorganized nor absolutely unpredictable; rather it responds to the influx of "strange attractors" in whose codes the dynamics tend to follow determined movements and, therefore, to draw certain regularly repetitive and self-referential figures. In the case of the Caribbean, I think that the most important "strange attractor" is the Plantation, which allows us to predict the continuation of a literature, a music, and an art having forms similar to those dealt with in this book.

The objection could be made that my work does not encompass all of the Caribbean. This is a justifiable objection, but if someone were to make it, my answer would be that, due to the area's extremely complex cultural spectrum (a soup of signs), no one could really claim to be a full specialist in Caribbean culture. Scholars infinitely more competent than I—Fernando Ortiz, for example—could scarcely go beyond certain themes that were within their respective language areas. The reader will have noticed as well, perhaps with some surprise, that the method of analysis I've followed here made no attempt to invalidate other readings of the Caribbean, but tried to take them all into account. This eclecticism should not be regarded as a reluctant concession but rather as a considered strategy. I think that in the end the readings that the Caribbean admits all inscribe themselves inside the three great paradigms of knowledge that I've been talking about: those of the Peoples of the Sea, of modernity, of postmodernity. And to my way of seeing things, no one of the three is suited in itself to take over the Caribbean's total cultural space, as I observed in Chapter 4. I think in fact that all of them are needed at once, since we're dealing with a supersyncretic referential space. By this I mean that if, for example, an investigator were to pay attention to nothing but the sociocultural impact of the Caribbean's complicated cosmogonies and beliefs, while ignoring all referents coming from scientific contexts, he would still be making a valid study of one of the area's fundamental aspects. Something similar would happen if one were to observe the Caribbean phenomenon in terms of the antithetical polarization of two discourses, let's say one of power—sugar—and another of resistance—the slave, the maroon, the agricultural proletariat, etc. How can we think that, in the case of the Antilles, this binary opposition is just a mirage? Yes, of course, it's a reduction characteristic of modernity, but still it's one that has remained on the scene with uncommon violence from the sixteenth century down to the present day and from which no escape seems plausible, no matter how oversimplified we might judge the construct to be. And yet the Caribbean is more than that; it can also be regarded as a cultural sea without boundaries, as a paradoxical fractal form extending infinitely through a finite world. Who can tell us that he's traveled to the origins of Caribbeanness? And this is why my analysis cannot dispense with any of the paradigms, while at the same time it will not be able to legitimate itself through any one of them, but rather only in and through their nonlinear sum.

So I haven't tried to be original but rather honest with myself. Still, as an observer and also a part of the Caribbean phenomenon, I think it would have been difficult for me to formulate such a strategy of coexistence from a perspective other than the one allowed by a postmodern dialogue, even when this also turns out to be patently limited in its application to the study, from within, of societies and cultures of the so-called Third World, the semisecret world of the periphery, the semisacred world that lives all around the centers of epistemological and technological knowledge. But in spite of this insufficiency—which extends also to the other paradigms—the postmodern lens has the virtue of being the only one to direct itself toward the play of paradoxes and eccentricities, of fluxes and displacements; that is, it offers possibilities that are quite in tune with those that define the Caribbean. This circumstance moved me to give the book the subtitle of *The Caribbean and the Postmodern Perspective*. Of course the subtitle also alludes, in its inconclusive instability, to the uncertainty that every Caribbean person must feel in trying to write about the Caribbean, especially when suspecting that any chosen rubric is never one's own but rather realizes itself wholly in some alien language, in some ordering code that comes from over *there*, whether it's called novel, history, political science, anthropology, economics, sociology, psychoanalysis, literary theory, feminism, Marxism, or rather, simply postmodernity. This insoluble paradox runs throughout my work.

■ *Notes*

1 From the plantation to the Plantation

1 The process of making the place stand out was so deliberate that around it they situated, as ornamental settings, old seventeenth- and eighteenth-century cannons, and they placed, in the tower, a beautiful and heavy bronze culverin that bore the molded figure of Louis XIV's flaming sun and an inscription that testifies to its having been forged in the royal armories of France. The story of how this magnificent piece came to wind up in the town of El Caney would set in motion the writing of one of those novelesque narrations that any contact with the Caribbean seems to suggest.

2 James Anthony Froude, *The English in the West Indies*, quoted in Franklin W. Knight, *The Caribbean: The Genesis of a Fragmented Nationalism* (New York: Oxford University Press, 1978), p. 60. Froude wrote this in 1888.

3 P. Labat, *Nouveau voyage aux Iles de l'Amérique (Antilles) 1693–1705*, quoted in Knight, *The Caribbean*, p. 189.

4 Knight, *The Caribbean*, p. x.

5 See the section "Bibliographical Notice Concerning Chaos" at the end of this book.

6 Frank Moya Pons, "Is There a Caribbean Consciousness?," *Américas* 31, no. 8 (1970): 33.

7 Sidney W. Mintz, "The Caribbean as a Socio-Cultural Area," *Cahiers d'Histoire Mondiale* 9, no. 4 (1966): 914–15.

8 The capital letter to indicate the society dominated by plantation economy.

9 Oviedo offers an illustrative description in this respect. The basis of the organization of labor was the *batea*, understood as the receptacle that was filled with sand or earth to be washed and the gold separated out. A batea presupposes the work of five Indians: two "diggers," two "porters," and a "washer." At the same time, the extraction of gold required the construction of barracks for the Indians and some farming, cooking, and

Note: All translations are by James Maraniss unless otherwise indicated.

maintenance operations. The different work assignments were given out according to
the Indians' sex, age, and physical condition.

10   Fernando Ortiz, *Contrapunteo cubano del tabaco y el azúcar* (Caracas: Biblioteca Ayacucho, 1978 [Havana: 1940]), pp. 371–72. There is an English edition, *Cuban Counterpoint:
Tobacco and Sugar*, trans. Harriet de Onís (New York: Vintage Books, 1970).

11   Eric Williams, *From Columbus to Castro: The History of the Caribbean* (New York: Harper
and Row, 1970), p. 27.

12   To avoid confusion regarding my use of the terms *creole culture* and *creole*, I offer the
following clarification. In the context of this chapter, the adjective *creole* has a basically
cultural connotation and is applied to those who were born in America—whether of aboriginal, European, African, or Asian parentage or the products of any kind of mixing or
miscegenation—who speak the colony's official language. Nevertheless, in no instance
do I use the word *creole* to designate the group that had already experienced the desire
for nationhood, in which more complex factors come into play, not just of a cultural sort
but also of a political, economic, and social nature. Thus I see the need to differentiate
between a "creole" culture, characterized by its local customs, from another, "national"
one, in which a group makes its desires transcend its minuscule place to encompass a
greater national homeland.

13   Quotation taken from Pedro Mir, *El gran incendio* (Santo Domingo: Taller, 1974), pp.
107–8.

14   I use the term "European world system" according to the usage of Immanuel Wallerstein, that is, to mean the international economic scene with foci in certain European
cities where capitalism appeared. See his book *The Modern World-System, vol. 1: Capitalist
Agriculture and the Origins of the European World Economy in the Sixteenth Century* (New
York: Academic Press, 1974), pp. 15–63. Wallerstein organizes the European world system on the basis of a small core, a vast periphery, and a middle-sized semi-periphery. The
usefulness of this classification was recognized, in its essence, by Fernand Braudel in *The
Perspective of the World*, trans. Sian Reynolds (New York: Harper and Row, 1984 [*Le Temps
du Monde*, Paris, 1979]). Braudel prefers to substitute "the European world economies"—
a less totalizing term—for "European world system," noting that the former connected
the world on different levels, carrying technological, social, and cultural changes of the
greatest importance (pp. 21–45).

15   Concerning the Genoese control exerted upon the American traffic, see new information
in Braudel, *The Perspective of the World*, pp. 164–73.

16   Franklin J. Franco, *Los negros, los mulatos, y la Nación Dominicana* (Santo Domingo:
Editora Nacional, 1970), pp. 47–49. See also Doris Sommer, *One Master for Another*
(Lanham, Md.: University Press of America, 1984), especially chapter 2 (pp. 51–92), in
which Sommer offers a reading of the novel *Enriquillo* (1882), by Manuel de Jesús Galván,
where she makes plain the Dominicans' desire to legitimate their national genealogy by
exclusive means of a Hispano-aboriginal synthesis, not recognizing, within the popu-
list strategies that speak of homeland, history, cultural heritage, race, etc., the Negro's
decisive participation in the process of forming the desire for a Dominican nation.

17   See Chapter 8 of this book for the case of Puerto Rico.

18   In Hispaniola it appears in 1598 to designate a chief of the maroons: Juan Criollo. See
Franco, *Los negros, los mulatos, y la Nación Dominicana*, p. 42.

19 Concerning the place that they occupy in the myth of the *Virgen de la Caridad*, the *Espejo de paciencia*, and the sonnets of Puerto Príncipe, see the notable essay of José Juan Arrom, "La Virgen del Cobre: Leyenda y símbolo sincrético," in his *Certidumbre de América* (Madrid: Editorial Gredos, 1971), pp. 184–214.

20 Concerning the significance of the *ajiaco* in things Cuban, see Fernando Ortiz, "Los factores humanos de la cubanidad," *Revista Bimestre Cubana* 45, no. 2 (1940):161–86.

21 Alejo Carpentier, *La música en Cuba* (Mexico: Fondo de Cultura Económica, 1972 [1946]), pp. 41–42.

22 Julien Mellet, *Voyage dans l'Amérique Méridionale, a l'intérieur de la Côte Ferme et aux isles de Cuba et de la Jamaica, depuis 1808* (Agen: P. Noutel, 1824). See Antonio Benítez-Rojo, "Para una valoración del libro de viajes y tres visitas a Santiago," *Santiago* 26–27 (1977): 280–82.

23 Williams, *From Columbus to Castro*, p. 33.

24 From *latinos,* Indoamericans who spoke Spanish; it was also applied to the Negroes. The term is used by Darcy Ribeiro in *As Américas e a Civilização* (Rio de Janeiro: Civilização Brasileira, 1970) to imply the process of deculturation suffered by the aborigine after the conquest. Here it is used to differentiate between creoles of indigenous origin and creoles of other origins.

25 Knight, in *The Caribbean*, establishes a difference between the American colonies, dividing them into *settler colonies* and *exploitation colonies*. It is not a question of a simple binary opposition, since he sees all colonies of settlers as carrying elements of exploitation, and vice versa. Nor is it a question of a positivist or nationalist division, since Knight makes it clear that neither one condition nor the other implies adjectives such as *good* or *bad*, *superior* or *inferior*. The basic difference is drawn from the greater or lesser degree to which a colonial society transfers the institutions of the mother country and converts them into its model or goal (pp. 50–66). This turns out to be a useful difference, above all for its dynamism and instability, since a colony may have begun with the form of settlement to end up with that of exploitation. Helped by Knight's judgments, I would say that in the Caribbean the settlement/exploitation change occurs in parallel with the shift from the plantation to the Plantation. This nomenclature also turns out to be functional in differentiating in bloc the Caribbean from the mainland Spanish colonies, since in the Antilles the form of exploitation predominated and on the mainland it was that of the settlement, each one with components of the other.

   Interesting as well is the well-known classification suggested by Ribeiro in the work just cited. Ribeiro divides the peoples of the Americas into three groups: *Pueblos testimonios* (theocratic civilizations of irrigation similar to that of Mesopotamia, where the individuals, after experiencing a violent process of physical extermination and deculturation, come to constitute indigenous and ladino masses); *pueblos nuevos* (basically the Caribbeans and the Brazilians, who sprang up as a result of the ethnic and cultural miscegenation of Indoamericans, Europeans, and Africans, in a situation of scarcity of labor supply); *pueblos transplantados* (North Americans, Argentines, etc., who are distinguished by their scant miscegenation and their aspiring to reproduce in America the European culture out of whose matrix they come). It's a matter of a historico-cultural classification of a structuralist type that, if useful anthropologically for a first reading of the continent, turns out to be too fixed and rigid for a deeper analysis.

26   France, *Los negros, los mulatos, y la Nación Dominicana*, pp. 64–65.

27   Williams, *From Columbus to Castro*, p. 246.

28   Concerning the Plantation's beginnings in Cuba, see Manuel Moreno Fraginals, *El Ingenio*, 2nd ed., 3 vols. (Havana: Editorial de Ciencias Sociales, 1978)/*The Sugarmill*, trans. Cederic Belfarge (New York: Monthly Review Press, 1976 [a shorter version that I am not using here]), and the work in progress of Leví Marrero, *Azúcar, esclavitud, y conciencia (1763–1868)*, vols. 9–12 of his work *Cuba: Economía y sociedad* (Madrid: Playor, 1983–1985).

29   Thomas Gage, *Travels in the New World* (Norman: University of Oklahoma Press, 1958 [London: 1648]), p. 215.

30   See Paul E. Hoffman, *The Spanish Crown and the Defense of the Caribbean* (Baton Rouge: Louisiana State University Press, 1980), pp. 175–212.

31   Williams, *From Columbus to Castro*, p. 245.

32   The presence of blood sacrifices in Caribbean beliefs ought to be related in the first place to the cultures of black Africa, but it would be senseless to discount the influences in this regard brought by other cultures that emigrated to the Caribbean, let's say, the Sephardic, the Chinese, the Canarian, and in general the substrata of certain European cultures that, like the Galician, brought over important pagan components that were assimilated by the local form of Christianity. In any case, the signal presence of the sacrifice within the present state of Caribbean culture presupposes a collective desire for the conservation of these rituals, all this without mentioning the numerous symbolic forms that, like the carnival or the burning of the *juif* (Haiti), refer directly to the sacrifice of the scapegoat. Although I have already noted it, I take this opportunity to underline the idea that such an idea of conservation obeys the conditions of acute social violence, still in effect, in which Caribbean society was set up. The relations between sacrifice and public violence have been studied by René Girard in his *La violence et le sacré* (Paris: Bernard Grasset, 1972)/*Violence and the Sacred*, trans. Patrick Gregory (Baltimore: Johns Hopkins University Press, 1977). Here Girard expounds clearly the hidden function of sacrifice: to discharge in the death of the scapegoat, in a channeled and foreseeable way, the participants' individual violence (originating in insecurity, fear, rivalry, etc.), toward the end of avoiding the collective violence that would endanger the public order. Thus it could be said that, in repeating the ritual sacrifice, Caribbean society tries to sublimate the danger of a blind sociocultural dissolution whose results are impossible to anticipate, or, if you like, to control the regime of tensions and differences, deferring the moment of the system's explosion.

33   Unlike what occurred with the slave in the sugar mill, it often happened that these Negroes bought their freedom through a legal provision called *coartación* (which limited the owner's right of possession). This contributed, in Cuba, to the proportion of slaves to freedmen being much lower than in the non-Hispanic colonies. Williams, in *From Columbus to Castro* (p. 190), assembles the following table:

Colony	Year	Slaves	Freedmen	Proportion
Jamaica	1787	256,000	4,093	1:64
Barbados	1786	62,115	838	1:74
Grenada	1785	23,926	1,115	1:21
Dominica	1788	14,967	445	1:33

Saint-Domingue	1779	249,098	7,055	1:35
Martinique	1776	71,268	2,892	1:25
Guadaloupe	1779	85,327	1,382	1:61
Cuba	1774	44,333	30,847	1:1.5
Cuba	1787	50,340	29,217	1:1.7

Notice that as the number of plantations in Cuba kept increasing, between 1774 and 1787, the proportion of slaves increases as well. Nevertheless, in the year 1787 itself, Jamaica had one freedman for every sixty-four slaves, while in Cuba the proportion did not even reach one to two.

34 Lydia Cabrera, *Yemayá y Ochún* (New York: Chicherukú, 1980), pp. 9–19.

35 In the city of Santa Clara, for example, the feast of the Virgen de la Caridad was celebrated by the Negroes in the following manner:

> They came from all of the mills in the district, and in . . . the bare land that surrounded the church, the eve of September 8, in the morning, to the sound of the drums . . . they cut the grass, which the Negresses collected, in small baskets, dancing and drinking rum. In the afternoon, in procession, the King and the Queen of the Council of the Congolese (who predominated there) filed past beneath an enormous parasol four meters in diameter which they called the *tapasolón* and behind them, under another *tapasolón,* those who were called the princes. They were followed by a great number of their retinue or vassals. All of the men were dressed in frock coats and trousers and sported derby hats; at their waists were toy sabers and they wore leather shoes. The cortège was led, in front of the great parasol, by the drums, rustic wooden trunks a meter and a half long. [Also there were] four or five drums of different sounds, which were carried between the legs. The Council had its seat in a piece of land of its own near the church . . . There the Negroes danced a kind of Lancer; lined up in two rows, the men facing the women, they executed dance figures and moved to the drumbeats . . . To play a rumba figure was absolutely forbidden. When the creoles in the congos' line insinuated a rumba figure—that was profane music—the indignation of the elders could be felt. It was typical . . . to share among the Negro participants who attended with their Kings, and also the white devotees—all in the greatest harmony—the Agualoja, a drink made from water, sweet-basil, and burnt maize. (Cabrera, *Yemayá y Ochún,* p. 57.)

It should be pointed out that if indeed the Plantation brought down the proportion of free to enslaved Negroes in the island's total population, their number continued to be much greater than in any other, non-Hispanic, colony. For example, owing to the massive slave importations, the percentage of freedmen between 1774 and 1827 went down from 20.3 percent to 15.1 percent. But this last figure was not even remotely equaled by the English, French, and Dutch colonies.

36 Williams, *From Columbus to Castro,* pp. 136–37.

37 Ibid., p. 83.

38 Ibid., p. 145.

39 Ibid., p. 146.

40 Gilberto Freyre, *Casa grande & Senzala* (Rio de Janeiro: Schmidt, 1936), pp. xxxiii. There is an English edition, *The Masters and the Slaves: A Study in the Development of Brazilian*

Civilization, trans. Samuel Putnam (New York: Alfred A. Knopf, 1966).

41 Ibid., p. xii.

42 Ribeiro, *As Américas e a Civilização*, pp. 262–63.

43 Mintz, "The Caribbean as a Socio-cultural Area," p. 922.

44 Quotation taken from Fernando Ortiz, *Nuevo cauro de cubanismos* (Havana: Editorial de Ciencias Sociales, 1974 [1923]), pp. 127–28.

45 M. L. E. Moreau de Saint-Méry, *Description topographique, physique, civile, politique, et historique de la partie Française de L'Île Saint-Domingue* (Philadelphia: 1797–1798), vol. 1, pp. 44–45.

46 See, for example, Moreau de Saint-Méry, *Dance*, trans. Lily and Baird Hastings (Brooklyn: 1975 [Philadelphia 1796]), pp. 66–73; Fernando Ortiz, *Los instrumentos de la música afrocubana* (Havana: 1952–55), vol. 4, p. 196; *La africanía de la música folklórica de Cuba* (Havana: 1950), p. 2; Janheinz Jahn, *Muntu: Las culturas neoafricanas*, trans. Jasmin Reuter (Mexico: Fondo de Cultura Económica, 1978 [German ed., 1958]), pp. 118–19.

47 Fernando Ortiz, *La música afrocubana* (*La africanía de la música folklórica de Cuba*) (Madrid: Júcar, 1974), pp. 166–67. In the last few decades special methods have been developed to annotate African percussion, but this, far from negating what Ortiz had said, reinforces him in that it is the music of the West that has had to adapt itself to the African and neo-African elements of the Caribbean.

48 Ibid., pp. 167–69.

49 E. Duvergier de Hauranne, "Cuba y las Antillas," *Santiago* 26–27 (1977):299.

50 Alejo Carpentier, "La ciudad de las columnas," *Tientos y diferencias* (Havana: Ediciones Unión, 1966), pp. 55–56.

51 Léopold Sédar Senghor, "L'esprit de la civilisation ou les lois de la culture négro-africaine," *Présence Africaine* 8–10 (1956). Quotation taken from Jahn, *Muntu*, p. 277. There is an English edition, *Muntu: An Outline of the New African Culture*, trans. Marjorie Grene (New York: Grove Press, 1961).

52 Ibid., p. 229.

2   *Bartolomé de Las Casas: between fiction and the inferno*

1 *Historia de las Indias escrita por Fray Bartolomé de Las Casas Obispo de Chiapa*, 5 vols. (Madrid: 1875–76). The editing of the book was undertaken by the Marqués de Fuensanta and José Sancho Rayón, and it was published with a commentary by George Ticknor. Las Casas began writing the manuscript in 1527; the events related go up to the year 1520.

2 Ibid., vol. 1, p. x.

3 This has not been emphasized sufficiently. Bear in mind that in 1520 the Indies were essentially what we now call the Caribbean. Remember that Tenochtitlán fell definitively into Cortés's hands in August of 1521.

4 Antonio Benítez-Rojo, "Sugar/Power/Literature: Toward a Reinterpretation of Cubanness," trans. Jorge Hernández, *Cuban Studies 16*, ed. Enrico M. Santí and Carmelo Mesa-Lago (Pittsburgh: University of Pittsburgh Press, 1986), pp. 9–31.

5 Actually Saco was then preparing *Historia de la Trata* (History of the Slave Trade). Later the project would include two distinct works: *Historia de la esclavitud desde los tiempos más remotos hasta nuestros días*, 3 vols. (Paris: 1875–77), and then *Historia de la esclavitud de*

la raza Africana en el Nuevo Mundo y en especial de los países americo-hispanos (Barcelona: 1879), of which only one volume would be published.

6   See, for more details, the preliminary study by Lewis Hanke, "Bartolomé de Las Casas, historiador," *Historia de las Indias*, ed. Agustín Miyares Carlo (Mexico: Fondo de Cultura Económica, 1965), pp. xlii–xliii.

7   Ibid., p. xxxix.

8   Judgment of the prosecutor of the Consejo de las Indias in 1748. Quotation taken from Hanke, "Bartolomé de Las Casas, historiador," p. xl.

9   Royal order of confiscation. Ibid., p. xli.

10   Gonzalo Fernández de Oviedo y Valdés, *Historia general y natural de las indias*, 4 vols. (Madrid: 1851). The work was published with an introduction by José Amador de los Ríos, a member of the Academy of History.

11   Antonio de Herrera y Tordesillas, *Décadas o Historia general de los hechos de los castellanos en las islas y Tierra Firme del mar Océano*, 4 vols. (Madrid: 1601).

12   Hanke, "Bartolomé de Las Casas, historiador," p. xlii.

13   The scholars who have worked most on this kind of text are José Juan Arrom and Enrique Pupo-Walker. A tentative bibliography of their respective works would include: José Juan Arrom, "Becerrillo: Comentarios a un pasaje narrativo del Padre Las Casas," *Homenaje a Luis Alberto Sánchez* (Lima: Universidad de San Marcos, 1968), pp. 41–44; "Hombre y mundo en el Inca Garcilaso," *Certidumbre de América* (Madrid: Gredos, 1971), pp. 26–35; "Precursores coloniales del cuento hispanoamericano," *El cuento hispanoameri-cano y la crítica*, ed. Enrique Pupo-Walker (Madrid: Castalia, 1973), pp. 24–36; "Prosa nevelística del siglo XVII: Un 'caso ejemplar' del Perú virreinal," *Prosa hispanoamericana virreinal*, ed. Raquel Chang-Rodríguez (Barcelona: Hispamérica, 1978), pp. 77–100; and Enrique Pupo-Walker, "Sobre la configuración narrativa de los *Comentarios reales*," *Revista Hispánica Moderna* 39 (1976–77): 123–35; "La reconstrucción imaginativa del pasado en *El carnero* de Juan Rodríguez Freyle," *Nueva Revista de Filología Hispánica* 27 (1978): 346–58; "Sobre las mutaciones creativas de la historia en un texto del Inca Garcilaso," *Homenaje a Luis Leal*, ed. Donald W. Bleznick and J. O. Valencia (Madrid: Insula, 1978), pp. 145–61; "Sobre el discurso narrativo y sus referentes en los *Comentarios reales* del Inca Garcilaso," *Prosa hispanoamericana virreinal*, pp. 21–42; "La ficción intercalada: Su rele-vancia y funciónes en el curso de la historia," in his *Historia, creación, y profecía en los textos del Inca Garcilaso de la Vega* (Madrid: Porrúa, 1982), pp. 149–93.

14   See the books of Hayden White, *Metahistory: The Historical Imagination in Nineteenth Century Europe* (Baltimore: Johns Hopkins University Press, 1973) and *Tropics of Dis-course: Essays in Cultural Criticism* (Baltimore: Johns Hopkins University Press, 1978). See also Paul Veyne, *Comment on écrit l'histoire* (Paris: Seuil, 1971).

15   See "La ficción intercalada: Su relevancia y funciones en el curso de la historia." This text, in all respects, should be considered the first in-depth study of the "intercalated fictions" in the chronicles.

16   Ibid., p. 154.

17   The quotations that I shall take from this work refer to the third volume of the edition published by the Fondo de Cultura Económica (see note 6). The page numbers will appear in parentheses.

18   See, in his *Historia*, chapter 6 of book 3, where he speaks of the smallpox epidemic, and

chapter 1 of book 15, where he refers extensively to the plague of ants.

19 See the essay of Roberto González-Echevarría entitled "Humanismo, Retórica, y las Crónicas de la Conquista," in his *Isla a su vuelo fugitivo* (Madrid: Porrúa, 1983), pp. 9–25.

20 This refers of course to his famous essay "Das Unheimliche"—translated into English as "The 'Uncanny,'" and into Spanish as "Lo Insólito"—published in 1919 in *Imago*.

21 *Historia General y natural de las Indias*, p. 77. I am citing from the well-known edition of the Biblioteca de Autores Españoles (Madrid: Ediciones Atlas, 1959). Henceforth the page numbers will appear in parentheses.

22 I take this information from four sources. The first two are the histories of Las Casas and Oviedo, respectively; the others are *Contrapunteo cubano del tabaco y el azúcar*, by Fernando Ortiz, and *From Columbus to Castro*, by Eric Williams.

23 I hope that the reader will excuse me for not offering a description of the uncanny's effect on us. Freud himself, in trying to do so, fails miserably; the same occurs with other authors who have studied the uncanny, for example, Tzvetan Todorov in his *Introduction à la littérature fantastique* (Paris: Seuil, 1970)/*The Fantastic*, trans. Richard Howard (Ithaca: Cornell University Press, 1975). For one thing, in my opinion, the experience of the uncanny does not seem to be entirely objective, but variable from one person to another and, above all, from one culture to another. Another reason not to try to define it here.

24 In Oviedo's time the plantain was so new that he described it thinking that in fact he was dealing with a different fruit, native to the Canaries: "In truth they are not called plantains (nor are they such); but the fact is that, according to what I have heard from many people, the strain of plant was brought from the island of Gran Canaria." Later on Oviedo thinks it necessary to explain how the plantain is eaten, explaining that one must peel it first.

25 Concerning *fufú*, Fernando Ortiz says: "An African dish, still very popular in Cuba, made with yams and boiled, mashed plantains . . . the word *fufú* is widespread in Africa. *Fufú* is what a kind of food made with flour is called . . . Yucca flower is called *nfufu* in the Congo; in Angola, *faba*; in Ashanti, *fufú* ('a dish of the Negroes, prepared with yams or plantains, which after being boiled are mashed in a mortar, and with whose dough they make a kind of dumpling that they put in the soup'); in Accra, *fufú* ('favorite food of the natives, composed of yams, cassava, and mashed plantains'); in Dahomey, *fufú* ('indigenous dish based on maize, fish, and palm oil'). *Fufú* is the word used in the interior of Sierra Leone to indicate a dough made of yams. As you can see, the word extends far beyond the bantu region. All of these words, as Westermann maintains, are derived from *fufú*, 'white,' the color of flour or dough of yucca, plantain, etc." (*Nuevo catauro de cubanismos* [Havana: Editorial de Ciencias Sociales, 1974], p. 260).

26 I do not mean in any way to suggest by this that Las Casas was a precursor of the poststructuralist method. His deconstruction is involuntary and casuistic; it is produced on reflecting deeply (a rereading) upon the socioeconomic context from which African slavery emerged and in questioning its presumed Christian and institutional legality. As for the rest, including his defense of the Indian, Las Casas's thought falls inside Aristotelian discourse, except in certain areas of a mercantilist nature which can be explained by the fact that his activity as historian, politician, and polemicist is parallel to the new practices of the era's incipient capitalism.

27 The note appears between brackets in Miyares Carlo's edition.

28 Corominas gives it as an ancient form of *sublimado,* from vulgar alchemical Latin. Nebrija registers it in 1495. It seems to be an alteration of the mozarab *solimad,* from which it passed on to the Arabic (*sulaimani*) and also to the Catalan: the verb *soblimar,* which means "to scorch."

29 I refer to his famous essay "La pharmacie de Platon," *La dissémination* (Paris: Seuil, 1972).

30 See his important essay "Que' est-ce qu'un auteur?" [What Is an Author?], *Textual Strategies: Perspectives in Post-Structuralist Criticism,* trans. and ed. Josué V. Harari (Ithaca: Cornell University Press, 1979), pp. 141–60.

31 After Saco, the next great Cuban figure to identify himself with Las Casas is Fernando Ortiz, who, of course, identified also with Saco. See his book *José Antonio Saco y sus ideas cubanas* (Havana: El Universo, 1929).

32 I can't help remembering the text of *Cien años de soledad,* where García Márquez introduces the principal elements of Las Casas's narrative: the *solimán* of Melquíades, the banana plantation, and above all, the plague of ants that take over the Buendías' ancestral house and devour the family's last scion, in whom the forbidden act of incest has been realized. Remember also that the killing of the rebellious workers on the plantation is forgotten—repressed by Macondo's collective preconscious—and that their absence becomes present only in the memory of José Arcadio Segundo, which is hallucinatory, literary as it were. See Antonio Benítez-Rojo, "Presencia del texto lascasiano en la obra de García Márquez," in *Selected Proceedings of the 35th Annual Mountain Interstate Foreign Languages Conference,* ed. Ramón Fernández-Rubio (Greenville, S.C.: Furman University, 1987), pp. 37–44.

3 Nicolás Guillén: sugar mill and poetry

1 The work consists of a title page, a prologue by Laplante and Marquier, an introduction by Justo G. Cantero, a text descriptive of the mills, twenty-eight color plates, and eight black and white floor plans of the mills. See "Bibliografía azucarera," in *El ingenio,* vol. 3, p. 189. The twenty-eight plates include: sixteen views of sugar mills, ten views of boiler rooms, a panoramic view of the mills in the Magdalena valley, and a view of the sugar storehouses of Regla. Many of these pictures were engraved in wood and appeared in international publications such as *El Museo Universal, Le Monde Illustré,* and *Harper's New Monthly.* In 1981 three of them appeared on Cuban postage stamps, and in 1982 *Cubazúcar* reproduced a selection of twelve pictures. In the United States there are complete copies of *Los ingenios* in the Philadelphia Free Library and the Library of Congress. See Emilio C. Cueto, "A Short Guide to Old Cuban Prints," *Cuban Studies* 14, no. 1 (1984): 35.

Leví Marrero, as an off-print of volume 10 of his work in progress *Cuba: Economía y sociedad,* has edited and annotated a selection of Laplante's plates, using color slides taken by the Sección de Bellas Artes of the Biblioteca Nacional in Madrid. See Leví Marrero, ed., *Los ingenios de Cuba* (Barcelona: Gráficas M. Pareja, 1984). The most recent international exposition of Laplante's lithographs that I know of was put on at the Casón del Buen Retiro of the Museo del Prado in Madrid in March-April 1983. The lithographs were shown as part of a show entitled "Pintura española y cubana y litografías y grabados cubanos del siglo XIX (Colección del Museo Nacional de La Habana)." See this exposition's catalog, edited by the Dirección General de Bellas Artes y Archivos (Madrid: RAYCAR, 1983).

2   *El ingenio*, vol. 3, pp. 189–90.

3   Marrero, *Los ingenios de Cuba*, p. i.

4   Ibid., p. xviii.

5   Agustín Acosta, *La zafra* (Havana: Minerva, 1926). The numbers of the pages quoted will appear in parenthesis.

6   In this way sugar can be read as *vida* (life), and the absence of sugar as *muerte* (death).

7   The independence of Cuba (May 20, 1902) remained in question because of an amendment to the constitution. This amendment, introduced in the Constitutional Assembly in 1901 at the request of the United States, conceded that country the right to intervene in Cuban affairs. The Platt Amendment took its name from Senator Orville Platt, who drew up the projected law that Congress brought to President McKinley. It ceased to exist in 1934.

8   Jorge I. Domínguez, *Cuba: Order and Revolution* (Cambridge, Mass.: Harvard University Press, 1978), pp. 19–24.

9   The anti-imperialist theme in Cuban literature begins effectively with the dramatic piece *Tembladera* (1917) by José Antonio Ramos. In narrative fiction it begins, properly speaking, with *La conjura de la ciénaga* (1923), by Luis Felipe Rodríguez. Note that both genres precede poetry in the handling of the sugar/imperialism theme.

10   I take this quotation and the following one from José Antonio Portuondo, *El contenido social de la literatura cubana* (Mexico: El Colegio de México, 1944), p. 64.

11   Ramiro Guerra y Sánchez, *Azúcar y población en las Antillas* (Havana: Cultural, S.A., 1927)/*Sugar and Society in the Caribbean* (New Haven: Yale University Press, 1964).

12   See the comparison of Acosta with Guillén made by Nancy Morejón in her prologue to *Recopilación de textos sobre Nicolás Guillén* (Havana: Casa de las Américas, 1974), pp. 18–20.

13   Rebecca J. Scott, *Slave Emancipation in Cuba* (Princeton: Princeton University Press, 1985). It should be pointed out that when the lack of manpower became acute there was recourse to the importation of field hands from the other Antillean countries, principally Haiti and Jamaica. These also were Negro workers, and their wages were even lower than those of the Cuban Negroes.

14   I am quoting from the edition, in two volumes, of Angel Augier, *Nicolás Guillén: Obra Poética, 1920–1972* (Havana: Editorial de Arte y Literatura, 1974). The page numbers will appear in parentheses.

15   Gilles Deleuze and Félix Guattari, *L'Anti-Oedipe* (Paris: Minuit, 1972)/*Anti-Oedipus: Capitalism and Schizophrenia*, trans. Robert Hurley, Mark Seem, Helen R. Lane (Minneapolis: University of Minnesota Press, 1983).

16   Concerning the baroque character of *Motivos de son* and the revolutionary connotation implicit in Guillén's desire to assume his own racial Otherness, see Roberto González-Echevarría, "Guillén as Baroque: Meaning in *Motivos de son*," in *Nicolás Guillén: A Special Issue*, ed. Vera M. Kutzinski, *Callaloo* 31 (1987): 302–17.

17   Concerning the influence of Spengler on Guillén's thought at this time, see Roberto González-Echevarría, *Alejo Carpentier: The Pilgrim at Home* (Ithaca: Cornell University

Press, 1977), p. 52. On the influence of Spengler and Ortiz, see Aníbal González Pérez, "Ballad of the Two Poets: Nicolás Guillén and Luis Palés Matos," *Callaloo* special issue, pp. 285–301. These differences can be summed up in the following manner: on Spengler's part, his proposition was that African cultures were in an ascending cycle, unlike the period of decline into which the West had entered; as for Ortiz, he was revaluating, anthropologically, the Negro as an indispensable component of the Cuban nation. Nonetheless Guillén's poetic discourse in these years ostentatiously exhibited the European side of his double genealogy, though giving it a "Cuban color," that is, within his idea of *mestizaje*. See, for example, Gustavo Pérez Firmat, "Nicolás Guillén between the Son and the Sonnet," ibid., pp. 318–28.

18 In intercalating the couplets of "la charanga de Juan el barbero" throughout the poem, Guillén pursues the direction, already explored by Acosta, of giving certain areas of the text a popular spin in order to break the discourse's experimental technique. But what turns out to be insufficient in Acosta turns out to be a successful realization in Guillén. Guillén follows Acosta in his inexplicable recriminations against those whom the Plantation enslaves, and in the tone of bitterness and complaint found in most of the lines. The expedient of using North American stock market quotations as poetic materials also comes from Acosta.

19 As a book, *West Indies, Ltd.* is rather uneven. Its best poem, in my judgment, is "Sensemayá," one of Guillén's most notable texts with regard to the Afro-Cuban tenor of his poetry. For a brilliant analysis of this cryptic poem, see Vera M. Kutzinski, *Against the American Grain* (Baltimore: Johns Hopkins University Press, 1987), pp. 136–46. See also her excellent translation and edition of *The Daily Daily* (Berkeley: University of California Press, 1989).

20 Guillén entered the ranks of the Communist Party in the city of Valencia, in Spain, on the occasion of his attendance at the Second International Congress of Writers for the Defense of Culture, 1937.

21 Mintz, "The Caribbean as a Socio-Cultural Area," pp. 922 ff. On the theme of sugar and power, see also Mintz, *Sweetness and Power* (New York: Viking Penguin, 1985).

22 Other than Guillén, the only poet who has achieved this distinction is Agustín Acosta. This conjunction expresses very well the way that sugar and nation are synonymous in Cuba.

23 Michel Foucault, *Surveiller et punir* (Paris: Gallimard, 1975)/*Discipline and Punish*, trans. Alan Sheridan (New York: Vintage Books, 1979).

24 On the impact of the so-called revolutionary offensive on Cuban letters, see Antonio Benítez-Rojo, "*Narrativa de la Revolución Cubana*, de Seymour Menton," *Vuelta* III (1886): 42–45.

25 Kutzinski, *Against the American Grain*, pp. 164–201.

26 Jorge Luis Borges, *Otras Inquisiciones* (Buenos Aires: Emecé Editores, 1960).

27 Michel Foucault, *Les Mots et les choses* (Paris: Gallimard, 1966)/*The Order of Things: An Archeology of the Human Sciences* (New York: Vintage Books, 1973). See especially the preface.

28 A good example of the ideological partiality with which Martí's thought is interpreted inside Cuba is provided by the responses given by Cintio Vitier and Luis Toledo Sande to the texts published outside the island by Arcadio Díaz Quiñones and Enrico Mario

Santí. See the following texts: Arcadio Díaz Quiñones, *Cintio Vitier: La memoria integra-dora* (San Juan: Editorial Sin Nombre, 1987); Cintio Vitier, "Carta abierta a Arcadio Díaz Quiñones," and Arcadio Díaz Quiñones, "Comentarios a una carta de Cintio Vitier" both in *Claridad*, Dec. 4–10, 1987, pp. 17–20; Enrico Mario Santí, "José Martí and the Cuban Revolution," in *José Martí and the Cuban Revolution Retraced* (Los Angeles: UCLA Latin American Center Publications, University of Southern California, Los Angeles, 1986), pp. 13–23; Luis Toledo Sande, "De vuelta y vuelta," *Casa de las Américas* 163 (1987): 113–18.

29   Nicolás Guillén, *Sol de Domingo* (Havana: Ediciones Unión, 1982). Page numbers will appear in parentheses.

30   Reinaldo Arenas, *El central* (Barcelona: Seix Barral, 1981), p. 91. Concerning the icono-clastic and decentralizing nature of this poem, see Pedro Barreda, "Vestirse al desnudo, borrando escribirse: *El central* de Reinaldo Arenas," *Boletín de la Academia Puertorriqueña de la Lengua Española* 12, no. 2 (1984): 25–37.

4   *Fernando Ortiz: the Caribbean and postmodernity*

1   François Ewald and Jean-Jacques Brochier, "Une vie pour l'histoire," *Magazine Littéraire* 212 (1984): 22.

2   Jean-François Lyotard, *La condition postmoderne; rapport sur le savoir* (Paris: Minuit, 1979). Quotations from the English translation, *The Postmodern Condition: A Report on Knowl-edge*, trans. Geof Bennington and Brian Massumi (Minneapolis: Minnesota University Press, 1984), pp. xxiii–xxiv.

3   Ibid.

4   Moreno Fraginals, *El ingenio*, vol. 3, p. 246.

5   Fernando Ortiz, *Contrapunteo cubano del tabaco y el azúcar* (Havana: Jesús Montero, 1940). My quotations come from the Biblioteca Ayacucho edition, Caracas, 1978.

6   Roland Barthes, *Le degré zéro de l'écriture* (Paris: Seuil, 1953)/*Writing Degree Zero*, trans. Annette Lavers and Colin Smith (New York: Hill and Wang, 1977).

7   Ortiz writes: "Pelea que uvo Don Carnal con Doña Quaresma." Nevertheless, I refer the reader to Corominas's edition (Madrid: Editorial Gredos, 1967), p. 423.

8   Mavis C. Campbell, "African Religions and Resistance in the Caribbean under Slavery," paper presented at the XLIV Congress of Americanists, University of Manchester, 1982. Much of the information that I offer concerning the meaning of Afro-Caribbean beliefs within the slave rebellions I owe to the reading of this important paper.

9   Edward Long, *The History of Jamaica* (Manchester: Frank Cass and Co., 1970), p. 452.

10   C. L. R. James, *The Black Jacobins* (New York: Hill and Wang, 1965), pp. 20–22. Alejo Carpentier narrates this episode suggestively in *El reino de este mundo*.

11   James, *The Black Jacobins*, p. 86; Robert I. Rotberg, "Vodoun and the Politics of Haiti," in *The African Diaspora*, ed. L. Kinson and Robert I. Rotberg (Cambridge: Harvard University Press, 1976), pp. 353–54.

12   Rotberg, "Vodoun and the Politics of Haiti," pp. 354–55.

13   George E. Simpson, "The Belief System of Haitian Vodoun," *American Anthropologist* 47, no. 1 (1945): 36–37.

14   Campbell, "African Religions and Resistance in the Caribbean under Slavery."

15 Ibid.

16 Ibid.

17 William Luis and Julia Cuervo Hewitt, "Santos y santería: Conversación con Arcadio, santero de Guanabacoa," *Afro-Hispanic Review* 6, no. 1 (January 1987): 10.

18 Lyotard, *The Postmodern Condition*, p. 7.

19 Ibid., pp. 21–23.

20 For example, Ortiz says: "Tender care of tobacco and confident abandon with sugar; the work of a few and the task of many; immigration of whites and dealing in Negroes; freedom and slavery; artisanship and peonage; hands and arms; men and machines; finesse and roughness. In its cultivation: tobacco brings the farm and sugar creates the latifundio . . . In commerce: for our tobacco the whole world is a market, and for our sugar a single market in the world . . . Cubanness and foreignness. Sovereignty and colonization. Haughty crown and humble sack" (p. 14).

21 It should be pointed out that the contrapuntal form does not just organize the text of the "Contrapunteo," but also that of the complementary chapters, which intercalate the themes of tobacco and sugar in a dialogic format.

22 Although Ortiz uses the word *synthesis* with some frequency in his works, including the *Contrapunteo*, this word does not carry the Hegelian meaning. Gustavo Pérez Firmat has noticed this also. In the first chapter of his *The Cuban Condition: Translation and Identity in Modern Cuban Literature* (Cambridge: Cambridge University Press, 1989) he makes the following observation: "Although at one point Ortiz states that transculturation names the "synthesis" of cultures, the word properly designates the ferment and turmoil that *precedes* [his italics] synthesis" (p. 23).

23 It is curious that for Ortiz tobacco and sugar should turn out to be "masculine" and "feminine" respectively. In accord with this division, following his own words, capitalism and industrial power would be feminine. Not so art and traditional knowledge, which would be masculine. Of course, if Ortiz were alive and could read my commentary on his *Contrapunteo*, perhaps he would find it strange that, to me, tobacco and sugar should be opposite what they are to him. In reality, I don't think that the issue has much importance, since "masculine" and "feminine" are, perhaps, masks behind which the same mysterious entity, the Other, is concealed.

5 Carpentier and Harris: explorers of El Dorado

1 Alejo Carpentier, "Problemática de la actual novela latinoamericana," in *Tientos y diferencias* (Mexico: Universidad Nacional Autónoma, 1964). I quote from the Cuban edition (Havana: Unión, 1966). The page numbers cited will appear in parentheses.

2 Information that Carpentier provided in writing to the critic Roberto González-Echevarría. See *Alejo Carpentier: The Pilgrim at Home*, p. 173.

3 See the text of the writer Guillermo Meneses, published in *El Nacional*, Caracas, September 12, 1948, p. 4. González-Echevarría, in his cited work, reproduces a fragment in English (p. 170). I take the following lines from there: "He [Carpentier] brought back curare, arrows . . . Like Buffalo Bill he bartered powder and trinkets for arrows and quiver. He was able to look at the signs of the plumed serpent in the petroglyphs of the Amazon Territory. For three long days he was detained on a desert island, waiting

for the repair of a serious breakdown in the sloop in which he traveled. He ate tapioca and drank chicha among the Maquiritares. He was the personal friend of an Araguato [howler monkey] and agreed to write to a perfectly multicolored and brilliant family of macaws."

4 Lyotard, *The Postmodern Condition*, p. xxiv.

5 Roland Barthes, *L'Empire des Signes* (Geneva: Albert Skira, 1970). Quotation is from English translation, *Empire of Signs*, trans. Richard Howard (New York: Hill and Wang, 1982), p. 3.

6 I refer, of course, to *El arpa y la sombra* (1979).

7 Richard Schomburgk, *Travels in British Guiana, 1840–1844* (Georgetown: 1922).

8 González-Echevarría, *Alejo Carpentier: The Pilgrim at Home*, p. 177.

9 Robert Schomburgk, *A Description of British Guiana* (New York: Kelley, 1970).

10 Alexander von Humboldt, *Voyage aux régions équinoctiales du Noveau Continent, fait en 1799–1804* (Paris: 1807–39).

11 Alejo Carpentier, *Letra y solfa*, ed. Alexis Márquez Rodríguez (Buenos Aires: Nemont, 1976), vol. 1, p. 109.

12 Ibid., pp. 120–21.

13 Wilson Harris, *Palace of the Peacock* (London: Faber and Faber, 1960). Quotations will carry page numbers in parentheses.

14 The presence of Richard Schomburgk in *Los pasos perdidos* is perhaps most notable. González-Echevarría, whose commentaries on this novel are the most complete that I know of, demonstrates that Carpentier used Schomburgk's descriptions in elaborating certain passages of his text. See *Alejo Carpentier: The Pilgrim at Home* pp. 178–80.

15 For an excellent analysis of *Palace of the Peacock* and of much of Harris's work, the reader should consult Michael Gilkes, *Wilson Harris and the Caribbean Novel* (Hong Kong: Longman, 1975). My opinions about Harris's novel owe much to Gilkes's commentaries.

16 Cited by Gilkes, ibid., p. 44.

17 Ibid., p. 36. In a parallel fashion, the protagonist of *Los pasos perdidos*, as he goes further into the jungle, passes through a series of initiatory "tests." See especially the fragments numbered XX and XXI in chapter 4.

18 Wilson Harris, "Art and Criticism," in his *Tradition, the Writer, and Society* (London: New Beacon [1967] 1973), p. 10.

19 "'My left eye has an incurable infection,' I declared. 'My right eye—which is actually sound—goes blind in my dream.' I felt foolishly distressed. 'Nothing kills your sight,' I added with musing envy. 'And your vision becomes,' I hastened to complete my story, 'your vision becomes the only remaining window on the world for me'" (*Palace of the Peacock*, p. 18).

20 I refer to the double protagonist of "El Camino de Santiago," *Guerra del tiempo* (Mexico: Cía. General de Ediciones, 1958)/"The High Road of Saint James," *War of Time*, trans. Frances Partridge (New York: Knopf, 1970).

21 Europe, in Carpentier, acts as a metaphor of the Father. Its presence is irreplaceable, especially in cultural terms. See Antonio Benítez-Rojo's "La presencia de Francia en Carpentier," *Linden Lane Magazine* 4, no. 1 (1985): 22–23.

22 The text cited corresponds to the fragment numbered XXXIX in chapter 6. Quotation is

from English translation, *The Lost Steps*, trans. Harriet de Onís (New York: Knopf, 1978), pp. 276–77.

23 "Donne looked at her as at a larger and equally senseless creature whom he governed and ruled like a fowl" (*Palace of the Peacock*, p. 15).

24 *Palace of the Peacock*, p. 152.

25 Harris's style is one of the most poetic that one can find in the Caribbean novel. It constitutes, within what has come to be called "neo-baroque," a metaphorical extreme, as opposed to the metonymic value of Carpentier's language.

26 I use the name Caribana for the first time, to designate the Amazonian hinterland from which the great voyage of the Caribs to the Antilles began. The term already appears in Mercator's projections, and it speaks quite early of the impossibility of fixing clearly the geographical limits of the Caribbean basin. In any case, we would have to conclude that the Roraima upland, between Guyana, Venezuela, and Brazil, can be taken as one of the Caribbean's genealogical sources. Within its limits one finds the Cathedral of the Forms of *Los pasos perdidos* and the great waterfall of *Palace of the Peacock*. All of this provides sufficient argument for the thesis that the search for El Dorado is fundamentally a Caribbean and not a South American phenomenon.

27 In stating this opinion, I can't help remembering Borges. I'm thinking especially of his brilliant story "Tlön, Uqbar, Orbis Tertius."

6 Los pañamanes, *or the memory of the skin*

1 Victor Strafford Reid, "Identidad cultural del Caribe," *Casa de las Américas* 118 (1980) : 48.

2 Coming from St. Vincent. A large proportion of them were transported by the English colonial authorities to Belize.

3 Especially from Surinam. Like the "black Caribs," they constitute an ethnic group formed by the miscegenation of Africans and Indoamericans. Their history goes back to the great slave rebellions of the end of the eighteenth century, in which thousands of Negroes went into the jungle to carve out a life of freedom.

4 As we know, certain indigenous peoples who inhabited the present territories of the United States and Canada got involved in various colonial wars, as well as the Revolutionary War of 1776. I do not deny their participation as scouts and irregular troops, just their presence in the high political and military spheres that conducted the nation's wars.

5 Fanny Buitrago, *Los pañamanes* (Barcelona: Plaza y Janés, 1979). Numbers of quoted pages appear in parentheses.

6 Arthur Percival Newton, *The Colonising Activities of the English Puritans* (New Haven: Yale University Press, 1914).

7 The *Tinieblos* are: Terranova González, Epaminodas Jay Long, Pinky Robinson (sons of Prudence Pomare), Nicholas Barnard Lever (son of Maule Lever), and Gregorio Saldaña (orphan, grandson of Lorenza Vallejo).

8 See René Girard, *Violence and the Sacred*.

7   Viaje a la semilla, *or the text as spectacle*

1   Guillermo Cabrera Infante, *Tres tristes tigres* (Barcelona: Seix Barral, 1967). Quotation is from English translation, *Three Trapped Tigers*, trans. Donald Gardner and Suzanne Jill Levine (New York: Harper and Row, 1971), p. 3.

2   Pedro Mir, *Cuando amaban las tierras comuneras* (Mexico: Siglo XXI, 1978), p. 13.

3   Luis Rafael Sánchez, *La guaracha del Macho Camacho* (Buenos Aires: Ediciones de la Flor, 1976). Quotation is from English translation, *Macho Camacho's Beat*, trans. Gregory Rabassa (New York: Random House, 1980), p. 3.

4   Gabriel García Márquez, *Cien años de soledad* (Buenos Aires: Sudamericana, 1967). Quotation is from English translation, *One Hundred Years of Solitude*, trans. Gregory Rabassa (New York: Avon, 1971), p. 11.

5   Alejo Carpentier, *Viaje a la semilla* (Havana: Ucar, García, y Cía., 1944). Quotations are from English translation, "Journey Back to the Source," in *War of Time*, trans. Francis Partridge (New York: Knopf, 1970). Cited pages appear in parentheses.

6   See César Leante's conversation with Carpentier, "Confesiones sencillas de un escritor barroco," *Cuba* 24 (1964):33. Concerning the presence of music in Carpentier's work, see Helmy F. Giacoman, "La relación músico-literaria entre la Tercera Sinfonía 'Eroica' de Beethoven y la novela 'El Acoso' de Alejo Carpentier," *Cuadernos Americanos* 158, no. 3 (1968):113–29; Emil Volek, "Análisis del sistema de estructuras musicales e interpretación de 'El Acoso,' de Alejo Carpentier," *Philologica Pragensia* 12 (1969):1–24; Karen Taylor, "La creación musical en *Los pasos perdidos*," *Nueva Revista de Filología Hispánica* 26 (1977):141–53; Leonardo Acosta, *Música y épica en la novelas de Alejo Carpentier* (Havana: Letras Cubanas, 1981); Hortensia R. Morell, "Contextos musicales en 'Concierto Barroco,'" *Revista Iberoamericana* 123–24 (1983):335–50; Antonio Benítez-Rojo, "'Semejante a la noche'" de Alejo Carpentier y el 'Canon por tonos' de J. S. Bach," *Eco* (1983):645–67; "'El Camino de Santiago' de Alejo Carpentier y el 'Canon perpetuus' de Juan Sebastián Bach," *Revista Iberoamericana* 123–24 (1983):293–322; "Presencia de las formas de la música en 'Los fugitivos,' de Alejo Carpentier," in *The Latin American Short Story: Essays on the 25th Anniversary of Seymour Menton's* El cuento hispanoamericano (Riverside: University of California at Riverside, 1989), pp. 17–26; Argelia Fernández Carracedo, "El 'contrapunto' en *El arpa y la sombra*, de Alejo Carpentier," *Escritura* 12, no. 23–24 (1987):3–18.

7   There can be no doubt that Carpentier knew the structures of baroque canons, including the recurrent canon of *Viaje a la semilla*. For example: "In the epoch of the enigma canons, of the recurring canons, of open-ended contrapuntal games, to transform any theme into a rich sound structure was considered a proof of mastery—of one's knowing one's trade" (*Tientos y diferencias*, p. 46).

8   The "Trípili-Trápala" serves to situate the action of *Viaje a la semilla* in the first half of the nineteenth century. The moment in which the marqués plays it on the piano corresponds to the decade 1810–1820. See Carpentier, *La música en Cuba*. Partridge translates the last phrase, erroneously, as "under the peeling beams."

9   Claude Lévi-Strauss, *The Naked Man*, trans. John and Doreen Weightman (London: Jonathan Cape, 1981), p. 647.

10 Claude Lévi-Strauss, *Myth and Meaning* (New York: Schocken Books, 1979), pp. 44–54.

11 Jean Piaget, *Structuralism* (New York: Harper and Row, 1971), p. 78.

12   Concerning the avatars, attributes, and the cult of Elegua in Cuba, see Lydia Cabrera, *El monte* (Miami: New House, 1975), pp. 70–112.

13   The Haitian cult of Papa Legba and Maître-Carrefour is described in Alfred Metraux, *Voodoo in Haiti* (New York: Schocken Books, 1972).

14   Alejo Carpentier, "Histoire de lunes," *Cahiers du Sud* 157 (1933):747–59. Translated into English and profusely annotated by José Piedra, as "Tales of Moons," in a special issue edited by Roberto González-Echevarría of the *Latin American Literary Review* 16 (1980): 63–86.

15   Alejo Carpentier, "Los fugitivos," *El Nacional*, August 4, 1946, p. 9.

16   Alejo Carpentier, *El arpa y la sombra* (Havana: Letras Cubanas, 1979). Quotations are from the English translation, *The Harp and the Shadow*, trans. Thomas and Carol Christensen (San Francisco: Mercury House, 1990), p. 122.

17   Ibid., p. 125.

18   Ibid., p. 7.

19   In *El acoso*, the house is described as follows: "The fugitive came to the corner where the House of the Negotiation, without walls, was reduced to pillars still stuck into a marble floor strewn with stones, beams, stucco fallen from the ceiling. The grills and the lions with rings in their mouths had already been carried off. A string of wheelbarrows, heading upward, crossed the great salon, to flow into a service room, where various planks stuck out above a pile of shapeless debris. Next to the Andalusian figured gate, the garden's Pomona reclined with plinth and base, amidst the grass speckled with bits of plaster from the molding" (*El acoso* [Havana: Letras Cubanas, 1980 (1956)], pp. 195–96).

20   Alejo Carpentier, *¡Ecue-Yamba-O! Historia Afro-Cubana* (Madrid: Editorial España, 1933).

21   Concerning the influence of Spengler on Carpentier, see González-Echevarría, *Alejo Carpentier: The Pilgrim at Home*, pp. 55–57.

22   Alejo Carpentier, "Lo real maravilloso de América," *El Nacional*, April 8, 1948, p. 8.

23   *The Harp and the Shadow*, p. 125.

8 Niño Avilés, *or history's libido*

1   I quote from the edition of Editorial Universitaria, San Juan, 1979. Page numbers will appear in parentheses.

2   Edgardo Rodríguez Juliá, *La noche oscura del Niño Avilés* (Río Piedras: Ediciones Huracán, 1984). Page numbers will appear in parentheses.

3   Aníbal González, "Una alegoría de la cultura puertorriqueña: *La noche oscura del Niño Avilés*, de Edgardo Rodríguez Juliá," *Revista Iberoamericana* 135–36 (1986): 587.

4   For example, in that which refers to the character of the Puerto Ricans of the epoch. The novel says: "The creoles of this island are very happy and playful, there is no trace of surliness in them, they are hospitable to strangers and generous to neighbors . . . For the natives of this island, sustenance is no great worry or occupation, as I have seen them take breakfast and lunch from the many fruit trees that abound there . . . There are no people more given to celebration or more lazy than the creoles of San Juan Bautista. I swear that this sin of laziness is very fertile in loosening . . . the tedium . . . Also the idle are very inclined to gambling and to quick anger . . . We ought not forget that idleness

equally causes a general contempt for life . . . And it is no surprise that . . . as soon as they lose firmness of bone, agility in dancing, and skill in gambling, life becomes a nullity to these men whose youth and maturity are so boisterous" (pp. 307–8).

Abbad y Lasierra says: "The heat of the climate makes them indolent and unkempt; the country's fertility, which makes it easy for them to feed themselves, makes them even-handed and hospitable to strangers . . . They have the plantain grove beside their houses; they pick a green bunch when they have grown big; they cook these over a fire . . . The most appreciable entertainments for these islanders are dances; they have them for no greater reason than to pass the time and rarely is there none in one house or another . . . They are passionate for sedentary gambling diversions; cockfighting is very common . . . The same organic delicacy that makes them timid makes them look with contempt upon all dangers and even death itself" (pp. 182–88).

5   J. L. Vivas Maldonado, *Historia de Puerto Rico* (New York: Las Américas Publishing Co., 1974), p. 167.

6   Edgardo Rodríguez Juliá, *Campeche o los diablos de la melancolía* (San Juan: Instituto de Cultura Puertorriqueña, 1986), pp. 117–23.

7   Fernando Ortiz, *Historia de une pelea cubana contra los demonios* (Havana: Universidad Central de Las Villas, 1959).

8   Called *Crónica de Nueva Venecia*.

9   González, "Una alegoría de la cultura puertorriqueña," pp. 586–87.

10   The pan-Caribbean strength of *La noche oscura del Niño Avilés* comes from the fact that in Puerto Rico, it seems, there was no runaway slave settlement of any importance. Thus the novel becomes an echo of a generalized Caribbean phenomenon although the latter never occurred in Puerto Rico. See Guillermo A. Baralt, *Esclavos rebeldes: Conspiraciones y sublevaciones de esclavos en Puerto Rico, 1795–1873* (Río Piedras: Ediciones Huracán, 1985).

11   Pedro Mir, *Tres leyendas de colores* (Santo Domingo: Editora Taller, 1978), pp. 119–60.

12   Orlando Patterson, "Slavery and Slave Revolts: A Sociohistorical Analysis of the First Maroon War, 1665–1740," in *Maroon Societies: Rebel Slave Communities in the Americas*, ed. Richard Price (Baltimore: Johns Hopkins University Press, 1979), pp. 246–92.

13   Richard Price, "Introduction: Maroons and Their Communities," ibid., p. 1.

14   J. H. Parry and P. M. Sherlock, *A Short History of the West Indies* (London: Macmillan, 1965), p. 14.

15   José Luciano Franco, *La presencia negra en el Nuevo Mundo* (Havana: Casa de las Américas, 1968), p. 92.

16   Francisco Pérez de la Riva, "La habitación rural en Cuba," *Antropología* 26 (1952):20.

17   José Luciano Franco, *Las minas de Santiago del Prado y la rebelión de los Cobreros, 1530–1800* (Havana: Editorial de Ciencias Sociales, 1975), pp. 117–21. Franco took this description from the Archivo Nacional, *Real Consulado y Junta de Fomento*. File 141, No. 6,935.

18   The most recent—and rigorous—works that I know of are Mavis C. Campbell's *The Maroons of Jamaica, 1655–1796: A History of Resistance, Collaboration, and Betrayal* (Granby, Mass.: Bergin and Garvey, 1988), and *Nova Scotia and the Fighting Maroons: A Documentary History* (Williamsburg: Department of Anthropology, College of William and Mary, 1990).

19   The history of the maroons is very far from being over, especially in their political and

sociocultural impact. At present, maroon settlements persist in Jamaica and, principally, in Surinam.

20 Ogé was director of a group called *Colons Américains*, linked to the famous and influential *Société des Amis des Noirs*, in Paris, to which Mirabeau, Pétion, Necker, Sièyes, and Lafayette belonged (Knight, *The Caribbean*, p. 151).

21 Miguel Barnet, *Biografía de un Cimarrón* (Havana: Instituto de Etnología y Folklore, 1966)/*The Autobiography of a Runaway Slave*, trans. Jocasta Inness (New York: Pantheon Books, 1968).

22 "The word *mambí* seems to derive from the African word *m'bí,* a Congolese expression that alludes to the 'cruel, savage, harmful' as well as the powerful and divine: *Nsa-mbí:* 'god' " (Nicomedes Santa Cruz, "El negro en Iberoamérica," *Cuadernos Hispanoamericanos* 451–52 (1988):34.

23 Pedro Deschamps Chapeaux, "Cimarrones urbanos," *Revista de la Biblioteca Nacional José Martí* 2 (1969):145–64.

24 I am referring to the notion of *rhizome* put into play by Gilles Deleuze and Félix Guattari. The rhizome state can be understood starting from the rhizome of the vegetable world. It is a botanical anomaly if compared to a tree. It is subterranean, but it is not a root. It sends out multiplications in all directions. It is a labyrinth in process. It can be understood also as a burrow, or as the system of tunnels in an anthill. It is a world of connections and of trips without limits or propositions. In a rhizome one is always in the middle, between the Self and the Other. But, above all, it should be seen as a nonsystematic system of lines of flight and alliance that propagate themselves ad infinitum. See "Rhizome," *Deleuze and Guattari on the Line,* trans. John Johnson (New York: Semiotext(e), Columbia University, 1983), pp. 1–65.

25 González, "Una alegoría de la cultura puertorriqueña. . . ," p. 583.

26 See White, *Metahistory.*

27 John Esquemeling, *The Buccaneers of America* (London: George Routledge and Sons, n.d. [Amsterdam: 1678]).

28 Ibid., p. 40.

29 Ibid., pp. 243–44.

30 I am not referring here to the unconscious in a general sense, since the latter is not "one," but to its "other" side, recently investigated and called *crypt*. Starting from Freud, Nicholas Abraham and Maria Torok have demonstrated that the desire for a situation of intolerable pleasure, both for its excessive intensity and its unlimited duration, is buried in a kind of annex or "false" construction of the unconscious (crypt). The Thing buried in the crypt does not reveal itself in the conventional metaphors that tell the psychoanalyst about what is happening in the subconscious, but rather through a "cryptic" language that is just recently beginning to be explored. In any case, the Thing in the crypt can be understood as something dead and alive at the same time, a "dead-alive"—Derrida says—since it appears beyond evolution and remission. That which without a doubt turns out to be curious is that this desire for infinite pleasure is detected in fear, or other preventive states, that the very same unconscious generates as a defense mechanism. Thus it can be said that what is most feared refers cryptically to what is most desired. I think that an analogous relationship occurs, reciprocally, between history and the novel,

where I see a mutual desire *encrypted* by an encounter that is never effected. Such a kind of subliminal relationship of coexistence could be extended within certain limits to the poetic and the theoretical, as I insinuated in the chapter devoted to Guillén. Naturally, we're dealing here with intuitions that one would have to demonstrate. Concerning the crypt, see Nicholas Abraham and Maria Torok, *The Wolf Man's Magic Word: A Cryptonomy*, trans. Nicholas Rand, with an introduction by Jacques Derrida, "*Fors*: The English Words of Nicholas Abraham and Maria Torok," trans. Barbara Johnson (Minneapolis: Minnesota University Press, 1986 [Paris: Aubier Flammarion, 1976]). Concerning the application of this recent concept to the social sciences (Marx) and to post-modernist literary theory (Derrida), I recommend the reading of *Re-Marx* by Andrew Parker, soon to be published by the University of Wisconsin Press.

Acknowledgment is made to the following for permission to reprint portions of this book, originally published in slightly different form:

New England Review/Bread Loaf Quarterly, "The Repeating Island," trans. James Maraniss, ed. Sydney Lea, vol. 7, no. 4 (1985):430–52.

Callaloo, "Nicolás Guillén and Sugar," trans. Vera M. Kutzinski, ed. Charles H. Rowell, guest ed. Vera M. Kutzinski, vol. 10, no. 2 (1987):329–51.

University of Pittsburgh Press, "Fernando Ortiz and Cubanness: A Postmodern Perspective," trans. Jaime Martínez-Tolentino, *Cuban Studies 18*, ed. Carmelo Mesa-Lago, pp. 125–32. Copyright © 1988 University of Pittsburgh Press.

Acknowledgment is made for permission to quote from the following:

Thomas Gage's Travels in the New World, ed. J. Eric S. Thompson. New Edition copyright © 1958, 1986 by the University of Oklahoma Press.

The Postmodern Condition: A Report on Knowledge, by Jean-François Lyotard, trans. Geof Bennington and Brian Massumi. Copyright © 1984 by University of Minnesota Press.

The Daily Daily, by Nicolás Guillén, trans./ed. Vera M. Kutzinski, "Warnings, Messages, Announcing." Copyright © NYP The Regents of the University of California.

The Lost Steps, by Alejo Carpentier, trans. Harriet de Onís. Copyright © 1978 by Random House, Inc., Alfred Knopf, Inc.

Three Trapped Tigers, by Guillermo Cabrera Infante, trans. Donald Gardner and Suzanne Jill Levine. Copyright © 1971 by Harper and Row, Inc.

Empire of Signs, by Roland Barthes, trans. Richard Howard. Translation copyright © 1982 by Farrar, Straus & Giroux, Inc. Reprinted by permission of Hill and Wang, a division of Farrar, Straus & Giroux, Inc.

The Buccaneers of America, by John Esquemeling. Reprinted by permission of Corner House.

Macho Camacho's Beat, by Luis Rafael Sánchez, trans. Gregory Rabassa. Copyright © by Random House, Inc., Alfred Knopf, Inc.

"Is There a Caribbean Consciousness?" by Frank Moya Pons, *Américas*, vol. 31, no. 8, p. 33, by permission of *Américas*, a bimonthly magazine published by the General Secretariat of the Organization of American States in English and Spanish.

The Caribbean: The Genesis of a Fragmented Nationalism, by Franklin W. Knight. Copyright © 1978 by Oxford University Press.

The Harp and the Shadow, by Alejo Carpentier, trans. Thomas and Carol Christensen. Copyright © 1990 by Mercury House.

War of Time, by Alejo Carpentier, trans. Frances Partridge. Copyright © 1970 by Alfred A. Knopf, Inc. Reprinted by permission of Harold Matson Co.

Antonio Benítez-Rojo, Professor of Romance
Languages at Amherst College, has held visiting
positions at Pittsburgh, Irvine, Emory, Yale, and
Harvard. He is the author of numerous works of
fiction and criticism including, most recently, *Sea of
Lentils* and *The Magic Dog and Other Stories*.
James Maraniss, Professor of Romance Languages at
Amherst College, is author of *On Calderón* and
translator of Benítez-Rojo's *Sea of Lentils*.

Library of Congress Cataloging-in-Publication Data
Benítez Rojo, Antonio, 1931–
The repeating island : the Caribbean and the
postmodern perspective / Antonio Benítez-Rojo;
translated by James Maraniss.
—(Post-contemporary interventions)
Translated from Spanish.
Includes bibliographical references and index.
ISBN 0-8223-1225-5.—ISBN 0-8223-1221-2 (pbk.:
alk. paper)
1. Caribbean literature—History and criticism. 2.
Caribbean Area—Civilization. 3. Chaos (Theology)
in literature. I. Title.
II. Series.
PN849.C3B46 1992
809'.89729—dc20   91-36098CIP